Marlowe, History, and Sexuality

Two Nude Shepherds Seated against a Tree.
By Francesco Parmigianino. Photographer: Elke Walford.
With permission of Hamburger Kunsthalle, Hamburg

Marlowe, History, and Sexuality

New Critical Essays on Christopher Marlowe

Paul Whitfield White
Editor

AMS Press, Inc.

Library of Congress Cataloging-in-Publication Data

Marlowe, history, and sexuality: new critical essays on
  Christopher Marlowe / edited by Paul Whitfield
  White.
       p.   cm. – (AMS studies in the Renaissance, no. 35)
       Includes bibliographical references and index.
       ISBN 0-404-62335-2
       1. Marlowe, Christopher, 1564-1593 – Criticism and
       interpretation. 2. Homosexuality and literature –
       England – History – 16th century. 3. Intelligence
       service – Great Britain – History – 16th century.
       4. Literature and history – England – History – 16th
       century. 5. England – Civilization – 16th century.
       6. Renaissance – England. 7. Sex in literature.
       I. White, Paul Whitfield. II. Series.
PR2674.M27   1998
822'.3 – dc21   97-24447
                                                                      CIP

All AMS Books are printed on acid-free paper that meets the guidelines
for performance and durability of the Committee on Production
Guidelines for Book Longevity of the Council on Library Resources.

AMS Press, Inc.
56 East 13th Street
New York, NY 10003-4686 U.S.A.

MANUFACTURED IN THE UNITED STATES OF AMERICA

Contents

Notes on Contributors

RICK BOWERS is Associate Professor of English at the University of Alberta. Besides *John Lowin and "Conclusions Upon Dances"* (1988), he has published articles on Shakespeare, Dekker, and Webster. A book-length manuscript on Marlowe's drama is in process.

GEORGIA E. BROWN is Fellow and Director of Studies in English at Queens's College, Cambridge University. She has written articles on Marlowe, Spenser, and Elizabeth I, and the present essay forms part of a book-in-progress on fictions of authorship in the 1590s.

MARK THORNTON BURNETT teaches in the School of English at the Queen's University of Belfast. He is the coeditor of *New Essays on* Hamlet (1994) and of *Shakespeare and Ireland: History, Politics, Culture* (1997) and the author of *Masters and Servants in English Renaissance Drama and Culture: Authority and Obedience* (1997). His articles have appeared in such journals as *Criticism*, *English Literary Renaissance*, *Shakespeare Survey*, and *The Yearbook of English Studies*. Currently, he is editing *The Complete Plays of Christopher Marlowe* for Everyman.

THOMAS CARTELLI is Chair of the English Department and Humanities Division at Muhlenberg College. He is the author of *Marlowe, Shakespeare, and the Economy of Theatrical Experience* (1991) and is in the final stages of a book on postcolonial appropriations of Shakespeare.

PATRICK CHENEY is Associate Professor of English and Comparative Literature at Pennsylvania State University. He is the author of *Spenser's Famous Flight: A Renaissance Idea of a Literary Career* (1993) and of *Marlowe's Counterfeit Profession: Ovid, Spencer, Counter-Nationhood* (1997). He is also an editor of *Comparative Literature Studies*.

SARA MUNSON DEATS currently is Distinguished Professor and Chair of the English Department at the University of South Florida. She is President of the Marlowe Society of America, has published over two dozen articles and reviews on Marlowe, Shakespeare, and Renaissance drama, and has a book forthcoming from University of Delaware Press entitled *Sex, Gender, and Desire in the Plays of*

Christopher Marlowe. She is also codirector of the Center of Applied Humanitites at USF and coeditor of a series of books relating literature to social issues.

MARIO DIGANGI is Assistant Professor of English at Indiana University, Bloomington. He is the author of *The Homoerotics of Early Modern Drama* (1997) and of articles on Renaissance culture and lesbian/gay studies.

IAN FREDERICK MOULTON is Assistant Professor of English at Arizona State University West. His work has appeared in *Shakespeare Quarterly*, *English Literary Renaissance,* and the *Huntington Library Quarterly*. He is currently at work on a book entitled *Before Pornography: Erotic Writing, Nationalism, and Effeminacy in Early Modern England*.

CHARLES NICHOLL is the author of *The Reckoning: The Murder of Christopher Marlowe* (1992), winner of the James Tait Black Memorial Prize for Biography and the Crime Writers Association "Gold Dagger" for Non-fiction. His other publications include a study of Elizabethan alchemy, *The Chemical Theatre*, and a biography of the pamphleteer, Thomas Nashe, *A Cup of News*. He has also written travel books and a wide range of journalism. His latest book, a reconstruction of Sir Walter Ralegh's South American Expedition of 1595, will be published shortly.

ERIC RASMUSSEN, Associate Professor of English at the University of Nevada, Reno, is coeditor (with David Bevington) of *Doctor Faustus* in the Revels Play series (1993) and the edition of Marlowe in the Oxford Drama Library (1995), and author of *A Textual Companion to 'Doctor Faustus'* in the Revels Plays Companion Library (1994). He is currently coediting *Hamlet* for the New Variorum Shakespeare and *3 Henry VI* for the Arden Shakespeare.

DAVID RIGGS is Professor of English at Stanford University. He is the author of *Shakespeare's Heroical Histories:* Henry VI *and its Literary Tradition* and *Ben Jonson: A Life*, as well as articles on literary theory in the Renaissance.

ALAN SHEPARD is Associate Professor of English at Texas Christian University, where he teaches courses in early modern literature and culture and in contemporary drama. He has completed *Marlowe's Soldiers: Rhetorics of Masculinity in the Age of the Armada*.

LISA S. STARKS is Assistant Professor of Literature at Texas A&M University at Commerce. She has published on feminism, pedagogy, popular culture, women's literature, and Renaissance drama, including an article (coauthored with Sara Deats) on Marlowe's *Jew of Malta* in the Fall 1992 issue of *Theatre Journal*. Currently, she is guest editing a special issue of the journal *Post Script: Essays in Film and the Humanities* on Shakespeare and film.

JUDITH WEIL teaches at the University of Manitoba. She is the author of *Christopher Marlowe: Merlin's Prophet* (1977) and coeditor (with Herbert Weil) of the New Cambridge *King Henry IV, Part One* (1997). She is currently at work on a book about service and dependency in Shakespeare's poems and plays.

PAUL WHITFIELD WHITE is Associate Professor of English at Purdue University. He is author of *Theatre and Reformation: Protestantism, Patronage, and Playing in Tudor England* (1993) and various articles on late Medieval and early modern English drama. He is currently coediting a collection of essays on theatrical patronage in Shakespeare's England.

Introduction:
Marlowe, History, and Sexuality

Paul Whitfield White *~bud 98*

Two days after he was fatally stabbed in a Deptford rooming house on 30 May 1593, Christopher Marlowe was buried at the expense of the state in a nearby parish churchyard. The grave itself was unmarked, and there is no evidence that anyone other than the presiding minister, and possibly a few friends, were in attendance.[1] As if to perpetuate the near-anonymity of his own funeral, Marlowe left posterity virtually no personal papers to speak of. What remain are seven plays, two original poems, and a small collection of poetic translations of Ovid and Lucan.[2]

And yet Marlowe has emerged over the centuries to become one of the most celebrated figures of the Elizabethan age. That interest, both scholarly and popular, shows no sign of waning this decade. In 1993, two international conferences were held to honor the quatercentenary of Marlowe's death, and two separate Marlowe societies remain active on both sides of the Atlantic. At the annual Modern Language Association of America Convention, papers on Marlowe usually outnumber those for any other early modern English playwright, save William Shakespeare. In addition to the continuing flow of scholarly books and articles since 1993, at least four historical novels, not to mention several original plays, have been published or produced in which Marlowe appears as a major character.[3]

So why all this attention? The time-honored answer is that Marlowe was a great man of letters whose few surviving plays and poems — *Doctor Faustus, Tamburlaine, Hero and Leander* to name the frequently anthologized — embody in unsurpassed blank verse the rebellious, free-thinking spirit of the Elizabethan age. That spirit Marlowe championed in his personal life as a practicing spy, professed atheist, occasional felon, and notorious homosexual lover; or so we are led to believe from the remarkably consistent, if somewhat sensationalized, portrayal of Marlowe in English literary history and popular fiction, almost as if by design a fitting contrast to the perceived orthodoxy and quiet conformity of Shakespeare. In the postmodern climate of the last two decades, interest in Marlowe has intensified on account of his preoccupation with issues which past critics ignored, marginalized, or considered taboo: sexual

xi

desire, particularly homoerotic and transgressive, gender relations, colonialism, and alien mentalities and cultures. Beginning in the 1980s, politically oriented critics began focussing in fresh, new ways on Marlowe's relentless critique of state power and class conflict. Plays such as *Edward II* and *Dido, Queen of Carthage*, relatively neglected in the past, now are perceived to explore the complex interaction among politics, social class, and sexual desire in ways not treated by Shakespeare and other contemporaries. No less significantly, Marlowe engages centrally with current debates over the notion of autonomous authorship (not to mention autonomous selfhood) in the early modern period and the reliability of historical inquiry to reconstruct the past, particularly that of major literary figures. Recent historical fiction involving Marlowe has pursued these matters as seriously as conventional scholarship. To a novelist such as Anthony Burgess (*A Dead Man in Deptford*), for example, Marlowe illustrates the extent to which the totalized personal identities of literary celebrities, as they come down to us, are fictional constructs designed to meet the needs and demands of readers, if not the academy itself, a point that David Riggs and other participants in this anthology affirm. Yet if postmodern theory has markedly influenced the state of recent Marlovian scholarship, more traditional approaches continue to thrive.

This collection of essays attempts to capture the range and intensity of interest in Marlowe during the 1990s. All fourteen originated as papers presented at meetings sponsored by the Marlowe Society of America, either at one of the two annual sessions at the MLA since 1990 or at the third International Conference held at Cambridge in 1993. Designed for students new to Marlowe as well as more experienced scholars, the volume offers original commentary on Marlowe's life and most of his writings, including all seven plays, his major poetic achievement *Hero and Leander*, and the Elegies translated from Ovid. If the selections together represent a range of critical approaches, they also share an interest in situating both Marlowe and his writings within the England of the 1580s and 1590s; hence, the priority given to "History" in the volume's title. I have added "Sexuality" as well because a recurring theme throughout this collection is that Marlowe was as interested in the body natural as he was in the body politic (to paraphrase Mark Thornton Burnett below), boldly breaking with the traditions of mid-Elizabethan poetry and drama to explore sex and gender-related issues. The essays are ordered topically, beginning with those centering on Marlowe's intellectual life and his career. Next come studies addressing the relationship of the poems and plays to political, economic, and social conditions of England in the 1580s and 1590s. The final group of essays focuses centrally on the representation of gender and sexuality in the writings. An extensive bibliography following the essays and notes should aid those currently engaged in new research of Marlowe and Elizabethan culture.

Perhaps no poet/playwright of the Elizabethan age is more deeply implicated in his work than Marlowe; certainly this assumption has been an historical constant of Marlovian scholarship from the beginning and continues today despite theoretical assaults on the notion of autonomous authorship and the questions of collaboration surrounding the plays.[4] The first two essays here, by Charles Nicholl and David Riggs, demonstrate the continuing vitality and value of biographical approaches to Marlowe by examining different aspects of the interplay between Marlowe's life, his writings, and Elizabethan culture. In "'Faithful Dealing': Marlowe and the Elizabethan Intelligence Service," Nicholl observes how mutually supportive Marlowe's careers in the theatre and in spying were for one another. Marlowe used his literary status to gain *entree* into the circles surrounding his patron, Lord Strange, for espionage purposes. Conversely, the cultivated elusiveness of Marlowe's plays, where spectacle and apparent orthodoxy are undermined by irony and disaffection, was appropriate to — and to some extent professionalized in — his work as a spy. Nicholl suggests that as an *agent provocateur* counterfeiting money and infiltrating Catholic conspiracies surrounding Lord Strange on the Continent, "Marlowe seems to be living out the kind of tawdry, convoluted fictions which he put on stage in plays like *The Jew of Malta*, first performed at the Rose Theatre, by Lord Strange's company, in February 1592, just a couple of weeks after his ignominious return from Flushing."

According to Nicholl, the spy world within which Marlowe lived most of his adult life engendered a mentalité of non-commitment and religious detachment from both the Protestantism of the Crown and the Catholicism of its enemy. In "Marlowe's Quarrel with God," David Riggs complements this by showing that such "atheism" was shaped not only by state intelligence but also by the other institutions which taught individuals "how not to believe"— the church, grammar school, university, and the playhouses. Riggs suggests that while the figure of "Marlowe-the-atheist" is largely a nineteenth-century invention, "a romantic individualist who freely organized his own life and inscribed his beliefs in his writings," a subjectivity of religious unbelief was made possible in early modern England as a result of the changes ushered in by the Protestant Reformation. The full extent of Marlowe's heterodoxy will never be known, since "All the evidence about his (un)beliefs lies at one remove from his own voice," yet from the Spring of 1593 onwards the author of *Tamburlaine* and the subject of the Baines Note filled the role of the atheist needed by authorities to reaffirm religious and political orthodoxy and passed down by them to posterity.

Marlowe, as historical subject, continues to be examined in the next three essays, but they specifically focus on Marlowe's place within the changing and burgeoning literary culture of the late 1580s and 1590s. Iconoclastic and innovative, Marlowe is shown to defy the old rules about writing poetry and even about what constitutes a literary career. In "'Thondring Words of Threate': Marlowe, Spenser, and Renaissance Ideas of a Literary Career," Patrick Cheney argues that — his productiveness as a professional playwright notwithstanding — Marlowe self-consciously conceived of himself as a poet who "forged a place for himself out of and within the Elizabethan literary system." According to Cheney, Marlowe uses his Scythian hero Tamburlaine to critique Spenser's idea of a literary career and to satirize the pretensions of the "Brytanne Orpheus" to be a great poet, and, by implication, substituting himself as the age's new poet championing pleasure over didacticism as the main end of poetry. The essay gives us a clear sense of the rivalry between poets as Elizabethan verse approached its zenith.

In "Breaking the Canon: Marlowe's Challenge to the Literary Status Quo in *Hero and Leander*," Georgia Brown provides another fascinating glimpse into the literary world of the late 1580s and 1590s. Given the criticisms leveled against literature by moralists such as Stephen Gosson, Marlowe's self-consciously frivolous re-reading of classical myth in his epyllion *Hero and Leander* was an act of defiant self-assertion. Through such shameless re-interpretations of the classics, Marlowe makes his independence from inherited forms and values the basis of his authority and turns originality into a central rather than a peripheral concern. Marlowe's *Hero and Leander* contributed to the formation of an Elizabethan avant-garde as other writers, such as George Chapman, John Marston, and John Weever, used the epyllion to create fictions of their own youth and newness and to redefine the nature of authorship in self-conscious imitation of Marlowe's poem.

Like Brown's essay, Ian Moulton's discussion of the *Elegies*, translated from Ovid, demonstrates that it is in the poetry, as well as in the theatrical milieu, that the counter-voices of culture are acted out. Moulton situates the ten Elegies within the context of the Elizabethan practice of censorship, exploring the reasons for their suppression by the Bishops' Order of 1 June 1599, in a book which also included Sir John Davies' *Epigrams*. Challenging the standard view that the book was banned mainly because Davies' epigrams violated the prohibition against satires, Moulton proposes that Marlowe's elegies were also deemed subversive, for they critique the notion of monogamous love, explore the potentially troubling issues of sexual power and masculine gender identity, and celebrate effeminacy and the pleasures of subjection at a time of acute anxiety over virility among the male ruling class of England.

Since the publication of Stephen Greenblatt's *Renaissance Self-Fashioning* in 1980, Marlowe has been at the center of the subversion/containment debate which sees the radical heterodoxy of his dramatic heroes as either genuinely subversive of orthodox political and religious ideology or as ultimately legitimating the established order they attack. In the 1990s, critics have observed the limitations of political readings which buy into this binary opposition, suggesting that a play, for example, can be *both* subversive and supportive of the state, depending on the composition of a given audience and the circumstances under which it is produced.[5] This heightened awareness of potentially pluralistic responses to the plays is evident in the next few essays addressing political concerns.

In *"Edward II* and Elizabethan Politics," Mark Thornton Burnett turns our attention to the one play by Marlowe which, more than any other, has been seen to allegorize power politics and court culture in late Elizabethan England. Burnett resists a critical approach that finds stable analogues and correspondences between the action and characters of *Edward II* and events and political personages at Elizabeth's court. Instead, he says, the play is sufficiently diffuse in its operations to invite multiple (and sometimes contradictory) topical readings; at the same time, Marlowe's tragedy voices contemporary anxieties about the decline of Elizabeth, the danger of noble upstarts, civil strife, and the state of the body natural/politic.

No less sophisticated in its analysis of Marlowe's encoding of late Elizabethan political conflicts and issues is Alan Shepard's "'Thou art no soldier; Thou art a merchant': The *Mentalité* of War in Malta." This essay reads *The Jew of Malta* as an exploration of the conflicted attitude toward war in London in the 1580s and 1590s: while the play traffics in the anxiety and vulnerability of an island-nation still reeling from the Armada, it also critiques the discourse of hawkish militarism that was then infecting London and propagated in pro-war publications, several related to the play here for the first time. Structurally it does so by displacing the Islamic threat posed by Selim-Calymath, focusing our attention instead upon the internecine struggle between knights charged with Malta's defense and Barabas, whose peacefully ecumenical business habits would seem at first to compromise the knights' legendary thirst for war.

Like Burnett and Shepard, Rick Bowers, in "*The Massacre at Paris*: Marlowe's Messy Consensus Narrative," shows that while Marlovian drama potently dramatizes the political ideologies and practices of its own day, the plays can scarcely be categorized in simple terms as supportive or subversive of the state. Drawing on anthropological assumptions, Bowers argues that *The Massacre* is a "consensus narrative" ("a culturally determined story around which the truths, morals, and self-identifying features of a society resolve"), which separates it from comparable Protestant propagandist accounts of the sectarian violence occurring in Paris on St. Bartholomew's Day, 1572.

Judith Weil extends the collection's concern with historical issues and conditions in "'Full Possession': Service and Slavery in *Doctor Faustus*." This refreshingly original analysis of Marlowe's most discussed play locates the depiction of Faustus' demon possession and "dependency" on Mephistopheles within the larger Renaissance discourses of slavery and servitude, showing indeed that this central predatory relationship involving the play's major characters is mirrored in the low comedy domestic scenes involving Wagner and Robin. In both instances, those who serve the servants of others try to possess them for their own ends and are in turn possessed. The B-text of the play accentuates the dynamics of these predatory relationships, making more explicit concerns with servility already latent in the A-text. Weil concludes that Marlowe challenges us to recognize the agencies of dependent characters who make plays and stories happen, a recognition impossible if we sharply separate "high" and "low" elements of plots and cultures.

Weil's discussion casts further light on the problematic relationship between the "serious" and "comic" scenes in all early editions of *Doctor Faustus*, arguing that they were both part of the original design, and she sides with those textual critics who see the B-text as a development rather than an earlier version of the A-text. Eric Rasmussen addresses another problem that has vexed textual critics of the play, the provenance of the 1616 B-text. Challenging long-established opinions of W. W. Greg and Fredson Bowers, Rasmussen argues that the printed B-text originated as a playbook used by a prompter who during rehearsals and performances in the London theaters was responsible for getting actors on stage. Drawing on the peculiar placement of stage-directions and other evidence within the B-text and within similar play texts by Shakespeare, Massinger, and others, Rasmussen shares the opinion of other recent textual critics that the transmission of manuscripts from composition to censorship to printing was an exceedingly complicated and messy business, concluding that the version of the B-text released to the printer in 1616 was probably "an interleaved manuscript in a number of different hands, with various layers of addition, revision, playhouse annotation, and censorship."

No topic has captured the interest of Marlovian criticism in recent years more than sexuality.[6] Issues relating to sexual identity and practice are raised in many of the essays noted above, but in those which conclude this collection they are central. All four draw on materialist and constructionist models of sexuality which regard gender formation and sexual behavior as contingent on social conditions and therefore subject to change. Consequently, the essayists are sensitive to the problem — and avoid the danger — of imposing modern patterns of gender and sexual practice on the early modern subject, while they maintain Marlowe's distinction as a dramatist in exploring and perhaps even normalizing sexual relations and behaviors regarded as transgressive at the time. In "The Subversion of Gender Hierarchies in *Dido, Queene of Carthage*," Sara Munson Deats discovers in *Dido* a number of "fissures" in the deceptively smooth ideological surface of the narrative that Marlowe inherited from Virgil, a discourse that disrupts sexual differences. Thus, Jupiter's behavior towards Ganymede subverts both gender and status expectations, and the old patriarch's sexual preference here violates socially sanctioned sex/gender patterns. Moreover, Venus surprisingly elevates duty over love; Dido inverts traditional gender roles by both wooing and bribing her lover; her sister Ann is no less aggressive in pursuing love; and the Nurse's attempted seduction of Cupid parodies the transgressions of both Dido and Anna. As Brown and Moulton say about *Hero and Leander* and the Elegies, respectively, desire runs rampant and unabated in *Dido*, challenging conventional categories of sex, gender, and desire.

In her essay on *1 Tamburlaine*, Lisa Starks begins by acknowledging that the terms "sadism" and "masochism" — and "sadomasochism"— emerged in nineteenth-century psychological discourses as sexual "perversions" or preferences in modern subjects, and consequently can be misleading when applied to the early modern period. Yet *1 Tamburlaine* invests in fantasies of dominance and submission, cruelty, fetishization, and eroticism which Marlowe himself inherited from Western literary tradition and which would be received and transformed in the erotic novels of Sade at the end of the eighteenth century and those of Sacher-Masoch at the close of the nineteenth. Thus, Starks finds the modern discourses of sadomasochism useful in exploring such matters as Zenocrate's masochistic submission to her captor and Tamburlaine's sadistic killing of the Virgins. In terms of spectatorship, however, *1 Tamburlaine* taps into primarily masochistic fantasies and desires inherent in the pleasures of looking and viewing a play, as contemporary Elizabethan responses to the play suggest.

With respect to Marlowe's own sexual identity, the question is no longer *was* Marlowe homosexual, but rather what constituted homosexuality, if that term is applicable at all, in early modern England. In the early 1980s, Alan Bray's highly influential *Homosexuality in Renaissance England* warned of the dangers of imposing modern conceptions of homosexuality on early modern subjects and suggested that during this time sex between members of the same gender constituted one of various forms of "sexual excess." Yet Bray's thesis that "homosexuality" modernly conceived did not properly exist in early modern England remains the subject of scholarly and political controversy, as Mario DiGangi explains in "Marlowe, Queer Studies, and Renaissance Homoeroticism." Responding to developments in the history and theory of sexuality subsequent to Bray's seminal study, DiGangi argues that a historical approach to pre-modern sexuality must acknowledge that homoerotic relations in Renaissance England could be socially orderly as well as socially disorderly or sodomitical. His study suggests that the dominance of sodomy as a critical paradigm in Renaissance studies depends upon certain problematic, and anachronistic, assumptions about homosexuality. Finally, it puts these theoretical and political arguments into practice through a reading of Marlowe that resists interpreting a figure such as Edward II, and by extension King James I of England, as a sodomite.

In "*Queer Edward II*: Postmodern Sexualities and the Early Modern Subject," Thomas Cartelli concludes the book with a comparative analysis of Marlowe's *Edward II* and Derek Jarman's film adaptation of 1991. Complementing DiGangi's arguments, and similarly engaging with current queer theory, Cartelli suggests that Marlowe's play shows signs of a positive homosexual subjectivity, "implicitly normalizing the avowedly exceptional acts of the homosexual subject" in contrast to other constructions of King Edward and Gaveston in early modern histories by such writers as Michael Drayton and Elizabeth Cary, which Cartelli examines in some detail.

This anthology, I hope, reaffirms the importance of Marlowe to the study of Elizabethan culture, literature, and theater. The wide range of topics and issues that center around Marlowe's life and writings — espionage, rebellion, political power, religion, and sexuality — will ensure his appeal to scholars, fiction writers, and theater audiences well into the twenty-first century.

Needless to say, a critical anthology is a collaborative effort, and I would like to express my gratitude to all the participants who have faithfully and patiently awaited its coming to fruition. I also want to thank all of those who originally submitted essays for consideration in this volume, many of which were outstanding but could not be included because of restrictions imposed on the length and scope of essay collections. There are many others to whom I'm indebted for assistance and encouragement. I am especially grateful to Constance Brown Kuriyama, the former president of the Marlowe Society of America, along with the other members of the MSA executive committee, for asking me to undertake this project. The current president of the Society, Sara Munson Deats, has been a major source of encouragement and support throughout the process of completing the manuscript. I called on many scholars to provide imput on the selection of essays. For giving freely of their time and expertise, I am very grateful to Emily Bartels, Mark Thornton Burnett, Dympna Callaghan, Maurice Charney, Viviana Comensoli, David Fuller, William Ingram, Constance Brown Kuriyama, Thomas Pettitt, Eric Rasmussen, Charles Ross, Jyotsna Singh, and Judith Weil. I am no less indebted to John Hopper, the editor-in-chief at AMS Press, who assisted me in the final selection of essays and suggested many improvements. Several graduate students were indispensible in helping prepare this text for publication: Deborah Wallack, Christine McDermott, and Andrew J. Kunka. Andrew's absolutely essential copy-editing and desk-top publishing skills, honed while laboring for *Modern Fiction Studies* here at Purdue, were made available to me, thanks to a faculty incentive grant from the School of Liberal Arts.

Notes

1.   For contemporary references to Marlowe around the time of his death, see Millar MacLure, *Marlowe: The Critical Heritage 1588-1896* (London, 1979), and Charles Nicholl, *The Reckoning*, 19-20. The publisher Edward Blount's dedicatory note to Thomas Walsingham in his 1598 edition of *Hero and Leander* suggests that both he and Walsingham may have attended the funeral; see Nicholl, 19.

2.   In addition to the plays and poems, Marlowe is credited with two Latin pieces, a dedicatory epistle to Mary, Countess of Pembroke, and an epitaph to a Kentish gentleman, Sir Roger Manwood. Despite attempts by A. D. Wraight and others to expand Marlowe's canon, no other extant works have been shown convincingly to be his compositions. See *The Complete Works of Christopher Marlowe*, ed. Fredson Bowers, 2 vols. (Cambridge, 1973); see also Wraight, *Christopher Marlowe and Edward Alleyn* (Chichester, 1993).

3.   The novels are Liam Maguire, *Icarus Flying: The Tragical Story of
      Christopher Marlowe* (Morden, Surrey, 1993); Roger Chapman,
      Christopferus or Tom Kyd's Revenge (London, 1993); Lisa Goldstein,
      Strange Devices of the Sun and Moon (New York, 1993); and Judith
      Cook, *The Slicing Edge of Death* (London, 1993). Anthony Burgess' *A
      Dead Man in Deptford*, first published in London, 1987, was reprinted in
      1993 (London). Marlowe also figures prominently in Stephanie Cowell's
      novel, *Nicholas Cooke: Actor, Soldier, Physician, Priest* (New York,
      1993). A short story based on Marlowe's death is "A Sad and Bloody
      Hour," by Joe Gores, in *A Mammoth Book of Historical Whodunnits*, ed.
      Mike Ashley (London, 1993): 243-258. The most successful of the plays
      is Peter Whelan's *The School of Night* (London, 1993), produced at
      Stratford-on-Avon in 1992 and at the Barbican in 1993. Frank Ardolino
      reviews Chapman's novel, and Bruce Brandt reviews the rest of the above-
      cited novels and drama in *The Marlowe Society of America Book
      Reviews*, 14.2 (1994): 2-6. Recent scholarly books include Emily Bartels,
      Spectacles of Strangeness (Philadelphia, 1993); Thomas Healy,
      Christopher Marlowe (Plymouth, England, 1994); Thomas McAlindon,
      Doctor Faustus: Divine in Show (New York, 1994); Charles Nicholl, *The
      Reckoning* (London, 1992); Matthew Proser, *Gift of Fire: Aggression and
      the Plays of Christopher Marlowe* (New York, 1995); Eric Rasmussen, *A
      Textual Companion to 'Doctor Faustus'* (Manchester, 1994); Vivien
      Thomas and William Tydeman, *Christopher Marlowe: The Major Sources*
      (New York, 1994); A. D. Wraight, *Christopher Marlowe and Edward
      Alleyn* (Chichester, 1993); William Zunder, *Elizabethan Marlowe* (Hull,
      1994); Darryll Grantley and Peter Roberts (eds.), *Christopher Marlowe
      and English Renaissance Culture* (New York, 1996); Emily Bartels, ed.
      Critical Essays on Chirstopher Marlowe (New York, 1997). Add to these
      the on-going re-editing of Marlowe's plays and poems by Oxford
      University Press and the Revels Plays series.

4.   I take my cue here from Stephen Greenblatt, who observes, "In his
      turbulent life and, more important, in his writing, Marlowe is deeply
      implicated in his heroes, though he is far more intelligent and self-aware
      than any of them," (*Renaissance Self-Fashioning* [Chicago, 1980], 220).
      The paradox of much New Historicist analysis of Marlowe is that while
      maintaining a constructionist model of his identity shaped by and
      embedded in contemporary culture, there remains a tendency, as in earlier
      criticism, to couch his radicalism and "otherness" in terms which suggest
      an autonomous, individualized selfhood. The authorship question
      concerning Marlowe is raised by Emily Bartels in *Spectacles of
      Strangeness*, xvi-xvii. For a broader discussion of individualized
      authorship and collaboration in the theatrical community, see Stephen
      Orgel, "What is a Text?" in *Staging the Renaissance*, ed. David Scott
      Kastan and Peter Stallybrass (New York, 1991), 83-87.

5. Theodore Leinwand argues that both sides of the subversion/containment debate tend to emphasize a binarism of conflicting oppositional forces, whereas historical change is often effected through negotiation, compromise, and settlement, with no victory necessarily for one side. See his "Negotiation and New Historicism," *PLMA* 105 (1990): 477-90. I share James Shapiro's questioning of "whether the terms and categories of thought that dominate current historicist and materialist discourse (e.g., 'opposition,' 'containment,' 'subversion,' 'resistance') are simply too inflexible, or themselves too ideologically bound (however 'retheorized') to admit the possibility that the changes that may occur in individuals or societies through the mediation of theater can be quite random, subject to all kinds of unexpected and unpredictable changes. Theater . . . can be 'subversive,' but it is usually so in ways that are unforeseen by author, censor, or functionalist historicist." "'Tragedies naturally performed': Kyd's Representation of Violence in *The Spanish Tragedy* (c. 1587)," in *Staging the Renaissance*, 99-113: 101. As Alan Sinfield reflects, "the complexities of the [Elizabethan] power structure make it possible to envisage the literary text not necessarily as subversive, but as a site of contest." See his "Power and Ideology: An Outline Theory and Sidney's *Arcadia*," *English Literary History* 52 (1985): 259-79.

6. For a useful though provocative appraisal of the current state of criticism dealing with sexuality and gender in Marlowe, see chapter 4 of Jonathan Goldberg's *Sodometries: Renaissance Texts, Modern Sexualities* (Stanford, 1992), 105-44.

"Faithful Dealing": Marlowe and the Elizabethan Intelligence Service

Charles Nicholl

I

There is something very elusive about Christopher Marlowe. It is not just a matter of gaps and uncertainties in his biography: these he shares with all Elizabethan writers. With Marlowe it seems to go deeper. The elusiveness is intrinsic to him and is part of the fascination he exerts on all who study him: "That like I best that flies beyond my reach."[1]

His reputation was certainly ambiguous. During his brief life, Marlowe was both revered and reviled. "Wit sent from heaven, but vices sent from hell," was how one contemporary summed him up: a simplistic reaction, perhaps, but a typical one.[2] His "wit" — in the Elizabethan sense of mental brilliance, rather than just humor — survives in half a dozen plays and some rather beautiful poetry. His "vices" were (or, anyway, were said to be) atheism, blasphemy, and homosexuality, all of them considered vices at that time, indeed all of them considered *crimes* at that time: dangerous positions to take, dangerous tastes to have. He was also charged, variously, as a dabbler in magic, a smoker of tobacco, a forger of counterfeit coins, a brawler in the streets. Whatever the truth of these allegations, Marlowe comes down to us a disturber of the peace, a phrase which seems as pertinent to his writings as it is to his police record. His plays are indeed disturbing, and offer no peace — no easy solutions — to those who watch or read them.

When he died in 1593, at the age of twenty-nine, reactions were similarly divided. His friends and fellow-writers mourned the death of a unique poet, "Marley the Muses' darling" whose "raptures were all air and fire."[3] But many others — particularly the Puritans, who loathed him and all he stood for — saw his violent and sordid end as a manifest sign of God's judgment on him and his scandalous lifestyle. "See what a hook the Lord put in the nostrils of this barking dog."[4] So wrote one Puritan divine, applauding

1

Marlowe's death: a gentleman named Thomas Beard, in fact, who later became Oliver Cromwell's schoolteacher — an interesting continuity.

So: "heavenly wit" or "hellish vices"; the darling of the Muses or a blasphemous barking dog. These are difficult statements to reconcile: opposite superlatives. What is the truth behind them?

In one sense these strident superlatives blur the truth. They, as much as the long passage of history, make it hard to answer the question: what was this young man really like? But in another sense, I think, they contain a truth about Marlowe, which is precisely his ambiguity, his elusiveness at the center of this periphery of extreme reaction. Not knowing what Marlowe was "really like" is the biographer's problem four hundred years later, but perhaps it was also a problem for those who actually encountered him, dealt with him, and *thought* they knew him.

This certainly is the feeling I get from his portrait, painted in 1585, when he was a Bachelor of Arts at Corpus Christi College in Cambridge, and rediscovered there in 1953, during renovation work on the Master's Lodge, where it had probably originally hung. (I am assuming for the moment that it is Marlowe: there are very good grounds for believing it is, but no final proof.)[5]

It shows a striking young man: twenty-one years old, self-assured, a bit flashy. He stands with his arms folded, right over left. The stance is confident, self-completing. It requires no props. It serves also to show off the rows of bossed golden buttons sewn down the sleeves of his doublet, fourteen on each arm. The doublet is superb: close-fitting, winged at the shoulders, with big padded sleeves tapering to a narrow wrist. The material, black or deep brown, has the look of velvet. The zigzag pattern is made of small slashes in the material, showing the glossy, peach-colored lining underneath — a "flame-colored taffeta," perhaps, like a tart's petticoat. The doublet is so good he can offset it with casualness. He wears no ruff, no fussy ornamental pickadils, just a shirt of the fine linen called "cobweb lawn," the collar falling over the top of the doublet, an inch of cuff at the wrists. His brown hair is long, brushed up and back. A stray curl catches on his collar.

All this, you might say, is a kind of statement. It is what he has made of himself, for this moment: a certain way of standing, a particular jacket, a hairstyle. The statement is one of prestige, of courtliness. It shows him as a young man with money to spend — not just the doublet, which even second-hand would have cost him thirty shillings or more; not just the rows of golden buttons like so many counterfeit coins; but the very fact of the portrait. It was not everyone who could afford the services of a good "limner." The portrait itself is a luxury.

Other parts of the statement are harder to read. The lips especially are a problem. You cannot say if he is smiling: if he is, it is not a warm smile, not a smile of complicity. He looks back out at the artist, at the world, with a quizzical gaze. The smile seems ready to mock us. We have been taken in so easily: it is only a portrait, a game he is playing.

I have looked long and hard at this portrait, and after a while my gaze has traveled down from the sardonic face and the snazzy doublet to consider something I cannot see: his left hand. It is concealed, perhaps under the right sleeve, more probably in it, in the pocket they had often had in those big padded sleeves. I find myself wondering: what has he got in there? A purse? A dagger? Some close-printed text in *octavo*?

After all these years almost everything is hidden, but even if we could stand there in front of him, on a day in 1585, we still might not know what he was hiding from us.

This sense of a statement whose meaning you cannot quite grasp, this sense of theatricality, this sense of something hidden: to me these are the keynotes of Christopher Marlowe. They are certainly a keynote of his plays, which are full of passion and violence and spectacle, and full also of rather orthodox opinions, yet which contain beneath that surface, beneath their overt statements, another atmosphere entirely: cool, sardonic, disaffected. T. S. Eliot, who did much to rehabilitate Marlowe's literary reputation early in this century, described the dominant mode of his plays as not so much tragedy, as a kind of "serious, even savage farce."[6] Here too is that duplicity of reaction which Marlowe invites: his drama as serious farce.

These general impressions on the theme of Marlowe's ambiguity lead to what I consider the most fascinating aspect of Marlowe's career, the one I have investigated in my book *The Reckoning,* and the one I wish to sketch out here — his career in the Elizabethan intelligence service: his work as a spy.

Let me briefly put this in context. I am using "spy" as a catch-all term — they would more likely have used the word "intelligencer," or "espial," or "projector" — and I am using it in the context of a society rife with secret politics, with intrigue and suspicion and surveillance. To say that Marlowe was a spy is to say that he was one of hundreds of men employed, on a largely freelance basis, by the government — primarily by the great Elizabethan spy-master Sir Francis Walsingham, and after his death in 1590, by such figures as Sir Robert Cecil, Sir Thomas Heneage, and the Earl of Essex.

Protestant England was not only at war with Catholic Spain and her allies, but also at war with an "enemy within" in England —

Popish plotters, Jesuit missionaries, underground priests, and many other, more harmless Catholics who got caught up with them and often went with them to the gallows. To counter this threat, Walsingham ran a huge, Securitate-style network of spooks and informers, dedicated to the penetration and exposure of Catholic groupings at home and abroad.

It was, to begin with, a largely private affair, financed out of his own purse, but as international tension increased, the Queen was persuaded to invest regular sums of public money in it. This, it is generally said, makes Walsingham's organization the first "official" secret service in English history. The earliest subvention on record was in the summer of 1582, when a warrant under the Privy Seal granted him £750 per annum in quarterly installments. In 1585, with the outbreak of war in the Netherlands, the payments rose to about £2000 a year (about $1.5 million in modern terms), and continued at that level through the years of crisis.[7] It is at this stage of increased funding and activity that Marlowe enters the lower ranks of the intelligence world.

The beginnings of Marlowe's dealings with the Elizabethan secret service take us back to his days at Cambridge in the mid-1580s, back to the time of the Corpus Christi portrait: that young man who seems to promise so much, yet also hides so much.

On 29 June 1587, the Privy Council met at St. James' Palace in Westminster. Their business that day included the drafting of a sharply-worded communiqué to the authorities of Cambridge University. It concerned a student named Christopher Morley, who was due to receive his Master of Arts degree the following month, but was being "defamed" by certain people who wished to block his candidature.

The letter itself is no longer extant, but there is a full summary of it in the Council minutes:

> Whereas it was reported that Christopher Morley was determined to have gone beyond the seas to Reames and there to remain, their Lordships thought good to certify that he had no such intent, but that in all his actions he had behaved himself orderly and discretely, whereby he had done Her Majesty good service, & deserved to be rewarded for his faithful dealing. Their Lordships' request was that the rumor thereof should be allayed by all possible means, and that he should be furthered in the degree he was to take this next Commencement, because it was not Her Majesty's pleasure that anyone employed, as he had been, in matters touching the benefit of his country, should be defamed by those that are ignorant in th'affairs he went about.[8]

Morley was, without any doubt, Christopher Marlowe of Corpus Christi College. The same spelling of his name is found in other documents, including the coroner's inquest on his death, and though there was another Christopher Morley at Cambridge, he did not take his M.A. in this year.[9] This is definitely Marlowe, and this certificate of good behavior drawn up on a summer morning in 1587 is the earliest record of his involvement in confidential government work. He has been employed, says the Council, "in matters touching the benefit of his country." He has "done her Majesty good service." He deserves to be rewarded, not defamed, for his "faithful dealing."

The chief rumor against Marlowe, which the Council expressly refutes, was that he "was determined to have gone beyond the seas to Reames and there to remain." "Reames" is Rheims, in Northern France, and in the 1580s going to Rheims meant one thing and one thing only. It meant turning your back on Queen and Country, and enlisting in the Catholic struggle against the established church and government of England. It meant, in a word, defection. Rheims was the home of the English College, one of the two chief Catholic seminaries for young Englishmen. (The other was at Rome, and a third would shortly be founded at Valladolid.) It was a rallying-point for English exiles, a center for anti-government propaganda, and a training center for missionaries returning to convert the country back to the Old Faith.

So the accusation against Marlowe in 1587 is a serious one: that he is a malcontent young Catholic and that he plans to defect to the Catholic cause. The government's unequivocal answer is that he had "no such intent" and that those who have broadcast these rumors are "ignorant in th'affairs he went about."

So here, once again, are two very different reactions to Marlowe, two quite opposing statements about his behavior at Cambridge. According to one he is a potential traitor; according to the other he is a faithful servant of the Queen. In this case the key to these opposites is not so hard to find. They are really different *layers* of behavior. On the surface Marlowe appears to be a Catholic sympathizer, but this is only a pose. In reality he is the government's man, working in some way against the Catholics. This is the only realistic interpretation of the Council's wording.

This document is, in effect, a Privy Council warrant or "warranty," an official exoneration of Marlowe from charges of treachery because he is really, as the spy-novels put it, "one of ours." The full text of a similar warrant survives, issued by the Council in 1590, on behalf of an "espial" named John Edge, who planned to infiltrate Spanish groups in the Netherlands by posing as a Catholic.[10] It is described as Edge's "certificate of allowance." Should he "incur some danger or reproof" for his actions, the Council promises to "acquit him," and "preserve his credit against such as might maliciously, or ignorantly and for lack of knowledge of his intent to do such good service to her Majesty, condemn or reprove him." This is not, however, an unqualified promise. He will be protected by the Council if, and only if, he has provided "something worthy of knowledge," or performed some "action laudable and profitable for Her Majesty." Results were required before the government gave its protection.

This document is very close in its wording to the Council's certificate for Marlowe, and broadly confirms the circumstance which required it. Marlowe has been posing as a renegade Catholic; he has suffered "reproof" from people ignorant of his true role as a government agent; and the Council has intervened to "preserve his credit." We can take it a bit further and say that he must have been quite a useful agent. The Council is prepared to stand by him, and judging from the Edge document, they would only do this if they felt he was worth it. The rumors against him are in themselves an index of his effectiveness. His Catholic pose — his cover — was good enough to take in the Cambridge authorities, who intended to withhold his degree as a result.

The Council's countermand — that the idle talk against Marlowe should be "allayed by all possible means," and that he should be "furthered in the degree he was to take" — proved effective, and he duly received his degree, and left Cambridge a Master of Arts.

II

What, then, was Marlowe up to at Cambridge? What is this "good service" he has done for the government? What part has he played in Walsingham's secret war against the Catholics?

Cambridge University has a long tradition of intellectual dissent, and for many young intellectuals in the 1580s it was Catholicism which provided a focus for their disaffection: a clandestine cause. They were drawn to it more out of restlessness than religious conviction: it had that forbidden, atmospheric aura. I think it quite likely (though not essential) that Marlowe tended that way himself. He certainly deplored the ascendancy of the Puritan faction in the university, as did his fellow student Thomas Nashe, whose covert Catholic leanings I have examined elsewhere.[11]

In this sense, the rumors against Marlowe at Cambridge may not have been as "idle" as the Council pretended. He quite possibly was — at some stage, at least — what he was rumored to be: a loud young malcontent with fashionable papist sympathies. This would certainly figure in terms of Elizabethan spy-craft, for the turning of Catholics, through pressure or promises, was one of the government's standard policies. All of the chief anti-Catholic agents used by Walsingham were themselves Catholics before they became spies. Perhaps this is the case with Marlowe too. It is a favorite maxim of those in the deception business that the truth is the best cover of all.

In some ways this pull towards Catholicism in the 1580s is similar to the flirtations with Communism at Cambridge in the 1920s and '30s. It was a gesture of anti-orthodoxy, of going over to the enemy. At its outer reaches — Burgess, Philby, Blunt, etc. — lay a career of treason, but for most it was just a *dilettante* game. There are many differences — not least that Catholicism was nostalgic rather than new, reactionary rather than radical — and, anyway, these broad parallels can be misleading. Let us just say that this Elizabethan spy-story begins, as that later one did, at Cambridge, in those old rooms whose walls are, even in high summer, chill to the touch.

We can pinpoint a little more clearly the kind of targets an anti-Catholic spy might have had at Cambridge in these years. The government kept tabs on Catholics of all sorts — in the "interests of national security," as we now put it, and especially so after England's formal entry into war with Spain in 1585 — but their chief concern was not with the peaceable majority of recusants (i.e., those who remained openly loyal to Catholicism but took no part in pro-Spanish conspiracy). They were concerned with the secret militants, the potential enemies of the State. At Cambridge this meant the young men who went to Rheims to train as missionaries, and even more, it meant those who encouraged and helped them to do so.

As early as 1581, during Marlowe's first year at university, the Rheims seminary had established a secret recruitment network at the university. This was one of the achievements of the first Jesuit mission to England, spearheaded by Edmund Campion and Robert Persons. In September 1581, reporting to the General of the Jesuits at Rome, Father Persons says: "At Cambridge I have at length insinuated a certain priest into the very university, under the guise of a scholar or a gentleman commoner, and have procured him help not far from the town. Within a few months he has sent over to Rheims seven very fit youths."[12] It was this area of covert recruitment and conversion that most worried the authorities. Among the scores of "fit youths" that went from Cambridge to Rheims there is one name that catches the eye: John Ballard.

Ordained at Rheims in the early 1580s, he returned to England under the alias of "Captain Fortescue" and became the prime-mover of the famous Babington Plot, whose aim was to assassinate Queen Elizabeth and place Mary Stuart on the throne as a Catholic Queen of England. Ballard and the other plotters were arrested in 1586 and executed: the route from Cambridge to Rheims led him, and many others, to the gallows.[13]

The exposure of the Babington plot brought home to the government just how dangerous these cells of Catholic extremism at Cambridge could be. Thus, for the spymaster Walsingham, they become important targets for surveillance and infiltration, and judging from the Council's certificate, issued in the summer of 1587, Marlowe was among the "espials" entrusted with this task. He is moving among these potential defectors to Rheims, he appears to be one of them — in a part of his heart he perhaps *is* one of them. But he is also working against them, for the "benefit of his country," and perhaps more particularly, for those financial rewards which the Council says he has "deserved."

The government described Marlowe's service as "faithful dealing," but in the performance of it there must have been much deception, much unfaithful dealing towards people he consorted with day by day at Cambridge, people whose disaffections he in some measure shared. We do not know what kind of pressure he was under, or how deeply he damaged those on whom he informed, but in our estimation of Marlowe we have to take on board these elements of falsehood and coldness, that hidden left hand behind the velvet sleeve.

III

A recently discovered letter opens up another episode in the secret political career of Christopher Marlowe.[14] It was written by Sir Robert Sidney, the younger brother of the late Sir Philip Sidney. He was governor of the port of Vlissingen, or Flushing, in the Netherlands, which was then an English possession, a "cautionary town" handed over by the Dutch in return for English military assistance against the Spanish invaders.

Sidney's letter is dated 26 January 1592. It was written, from Flushing, to Lord Burghley, who was, broadly speaking, his boss back in England. It concerns the activities of a young man whom he describes as a "scholar" named Christofer Marley, and who is without any doubt Christopher Marlowe, found once more in variant spelling and in shady circumstances.

In January 1592, we learn, Marlowe was lodged in a "chamber" in Flushing. There he was arrested on a charge of coining, or counterfeiting money. According to the charge he had "induced" a goldsmith named Gilbert to forge the coins. A Dutch shilling had already been "uttered," or issued, and other false coins had also been manufactured. Marlowe and Gilbert were duly deported back to England to be interrogated by Lord Burghley. Sidney's letter went with them, explaining what he knew about the case. It was delivered to Burghley, together with the two prisoners, by Sidney's ensign or "ancient," David Lloyd.[15]

One interesting revelation in the letter is that Marlowe's "chamber-fellow" in Flushing, the man who actually informed on him, was the spy Richard Baines, who a year later was to provide the authorities with a detailed list of Marlowe's alleged heresies and blasphemies — the notorious "Baines Note." Knowledge of this earlier encounter between Baines and Marlowe has added fresh perspectives to that crucial and sinister "Note."

On this occasion in Flushing, according to Baines, Marlowe "had intent to go to the enemy." He was intending, in other words, to defect to the Catholic forces fighting the English in the Netherlands, or perhaps more particularly to the group of English Catholic exiles, based in Brussels, who were busily plotting — as so many had before them — the overthrow and assassination of Queen Elizabeth.

Once again, the charges against Marlowe are extremely serious. Coining was itself a capital offense, under the heading of "petty treason," and his alleged "intent to go to the enemy" made it doubly treasonable. It is therefore significant, I think, that Marlowe escapes any serious punishment for this crime. He was certainly free by May of 1592, for in that month we happen to know he was tangling with the constables of Shoreditch and was bound over to keep the peace towards them.[16] If he suffered any punishment for his efforts as a coiner, it can have been no more than a couple of months' imprisonment.

Far more likely, I believe, is that he suffered no punishment at all, because he was once again working for the government, and quite possibly for Lord Burghley himself (or, more precisely, for Burghley's son, Sir Robert Cecil, who was the specialist in undercover operations in this post-Walsingham era). I see this as the true context of the Flushing episode: that Marlowe's efforts as a coiner were not done with criminal intent, but as a means of infiltrating those groups of Catholic exiles in Brussels. His purseful of forged money would, in itself, be a way into those groups, whose grand revolutionary plans were chronically starved of cash. Marlowe is found, once more, working undercover: one of scores of young

Englishmen flitting around the frontlines of the Low Countries, playing the meddlesome game of the government "projector."

I relate this, in turn, to Marlowe's connection with Ferdinando Stanley, Lord Strange. In the Sidney letter, Marlowe is quoted as saying he is "very well-known to my Lord Strange," and we know from other sources that Strange was a patron of Marlowe's in the early 1590s and that his theater company — Lord Strange's Men — gave the world premières of some of Marlowe's plays.

Lord Strange was the son and heir of the Earl of Derby. Though not himself a Catholic, he came from an ancient and profoundly Catholic family, and he was blood-related to the Queen through both his father and his mother. This made him an ideal figurehead for Catholic plotters: a Catholic pretender to the throne — albeit a reluctant one, and by no means the only one in these years after the elimination of Mary Stuart for that role. There is plenty of evidence of the Catholic hopes heaped upon Strange's shoulders, and of the government's vigilant surveillance of him and his retinue of followers, as a result. Chief among these pro-Strange plotters was his cousin, Sir William Stanley, who had defected to the Spanish cause in 1587, and whose headquarters was now in Brussels. It was this Stanley circle in Brussels, I believe, that Marlowe was intending to infiltrate when he was arrested in Flushing.

This is an interesting crossover between Marlowe's career as a writer and his career as a spy. It is as a writer that he finds a place in the circles around Lord Strange, but once he has that *entrée* he is of use to the government — as an intriguer, an *agent provocateur,* an infiltrator into those conspiracies that surrounded the unfortunate Strange.

There is another crossover, of course, in the sheer theatricality of espionage. I have called this episode "the comedy of the Dutch Shilling" — a touch of serious farce, perhaps. In episodes like this, Marlowe seems to be living out the kind of tawdry, convoluted fictions which he put onstage in plays like *The Jew of Malta*, first performed at the Rose theater, by Lord Strange's company, in February 1592, just a couple of weeks after his ignominious return from Flushing.

IV

These are the fragmentary documents of Marlowe's career as an undercover agent against the Catholics. They record his alibis, his pretenses. He is a wild young Catholic bound for Rheims; he is a seditious coiner intending to defect to the Spanish cause; and yet really he is neither of these things. These appearances of commitment to the enemy are only to cover — or, as they put it, to "color" — his role as a spy or projector against them. This does not mean that I think he was committed to the other side — to the English government, to Protestantism, to conformity. The keynote of this world is precisely non-commitment: to belong to both sides, and to neither.

These documents, in turn, raise questions about other, controversial aspects of Marlowe's career. Those terrific blasphemies and heresies reported by the spy Baines and others — how genuine were they? Were they too, like his militant Catholic sympathies, only a pose, an elaborate provocation? And then there is the last and most puzzling document of Marlowe's career — the coroner's inquest on his death. Was he really stabbed during a trifling quarrel over a "sum of pence," as the coroner reports, or is there another, more complex story beneath the surface of the bruited "tavern brawl"?

We will probably never know for certain, but I think these are questions worth asking. Marlowe leaves us with questions rather than statements, just as he would have wished — leaves us in that terrain of ambiguity in which he himself lived, both as a writer and as a spy, and in which he perhaps found a kind of perilous freedom amid the enforcements and conventions of the day.

Notes

1. *The Massacre at Paris*, in *Christopher Marlowe: The Complete Plays*, ed. J. B. Steane (1969; Harmondsworth, 1988), 542 (I.ii.42).
2. Folger MS V a 355, f. 7. This epitaph on Marlowe occurs in the anonymous *Progress to Parnassus*, one of a trio of plays performed at St. John's College, Cambridge, c. 1599-1601. See J. B. Leishman, ed., *The Three Parnassus Plays* (London, 1949).
3. George Peele, *The Honour of the Garter* (1593); Michael Drayton, *Epistles of Poets and Poetry* (1635). Other early obituarists of Marlowe include Thomas Edwards in *Narcissus* (1595); Thomas Nashe in *Christ's Tears* (2nd ed, 1594) and *Lenten Stuff* (1599); George Chapman in *Hero and Leander* (1598); and William Shakespeare in *As You Like It* (c. 1599).
4. Thomas Beard, *The Theatre of God's Judgements* (1597), 147-48.
5. On the portrait, see Noel Purdon, "Quod me Nutrit," *Cambridge Review* (1967); A. D. Wraight, *In Search of Christopher Marlowe* (London, 1965), 63-71.
6. T. S. Eliot, *The Sacred Wood* (London, 1920), 92.

7. Conyers Read, *Mr Secretary Walsingham and the Policy of Queen Elizabeth*, 3 vols. (Oxford, 1925), 2: 370-71. Payments to Walsingham are recorded in the Signet Book, payments by him in the Declared Accounts of the Treasurer of the Chamber, both in the Public Record Office, London. See also accounts drawn up by Francis Lake, 1585-89 (PRO, State Papers 12/240, No 49).
8. PRO, Privy Council Register (Eliz) 6, f 381b.
9. On the other Christopher Morley, see John and J. A. Venn, *Alumni Cantabrigienses* (Cambridge, 1922-27), 3: 231; John Bakeless, *The Tragicall History of Christopher Marlowe*, 2 vols. (Cambridge, MA, 1942), 1: 78-81. He commenced M.A. at Trinity College in 1586. He appears to be related to the musician Thomas Morley, and may have been the author of MS poems signed Infortunatus Ch. M., sometimes attributed to Marlowe: see Sakunta Chaudhiri, "Marlowe, Madrigals & a New Elizabethan Poet," *Review of English Studies* 39 (1989).
10. Edge's warrant is transcribed in John Strype, *Annals of the Reformation* (Oxford, 1824), Vol. IV, No. 30. The original, dated 9 October 1590, was in the hand of Lord Burghley, and was signed by "several of the Lords" of the Privy Council. Edge later received £25 "for his charges and pains" (PRO E351/542, f 155). The importance of such documents is stressed by Walsingham's secretary, Robert Beale: "For dealing with such as the laws of the realm esteemeth traitors . . . see first you have a good warrant to deal in those causes" ("Instructions for a Principal Secretary," MS 1592, in Conyers Read, vol. 1, Appendix).
11. Charles Nicholl, *A Cup of News: The Life of Thomas Nashe* (London, 1984), 158-60, 225-29, 253-55.
12. *Letters and Memorials of Father Robert Persons*, ed. Leo Hicks (Catholic Record Society, 1942); E. L. Taunton, *History of the Jesuits in England* (London, 1925), 88.
13. Ballard was arrested at the lodgings of Robert Poley, who had infiltrated the conspiracy on behalf of Walsingham (CSP Scotland, Vol. 8, 588, 602). Poley was later one of the three men present at the stabbing of Marlowe in Deptford in 1593. Another who was present, Nicholas Skeres, had also been employed against Babington in 1586 (ibid., 583-84). I examine these connections in detail in *The Reckoning* (London, 1992), 115 ff. It is plausible, but not proven, that Marlowe knew both Poley and Skeres in this *milieu* of anti-Catholic espionage in the mid-1580s.
14. PRO, State Papers 84/44, f 60; R. B. Wernham, "Christopher Marlowe at Flushing in 1592," *English Historical Review* 91 (1976): 344-45.
15. On 3 March 1592, Lloyd received £13 6s 8d under Burghley's warrant, "for bringing of letters from Sir Robert Sidney, importing her Majesty's special service, together with three prisoners committed to his charge" (PRO, E351/542, f 169 verso). The third prisoner was a man named Evan Fludd.

16. Middlesex County Records, Session Roll 309, No. 13, "Christopher Marle his Recognizance," 9 May 1592; Mark Eccles, *Christopher Marlowe in London* (Cambridge, MA, 1934), 104-09.

Marlowe's Quarrel with God

David Riggs

The scandal of Marlowe's life lay in his appearing to be an atheist and a good poet at the same time. As such, he put pressure on Strabo's time-honored claim that "it is impossible for one to become a good poet unless he has previously become a good man." Could a bad man write first-rate plays? The Cambridge undergraduates who wrote *The Pilgrimage to Parnassus,* a play produced just nine years after Marlowe's death, saw him as a figure who embodied contradictory values:

> Marlowe was happy in his buskined muse,
> Alas unhappy in his life and end.
> Pitty it is that wit so ill should dwell,
> Wit lent from heaven, but vices sent from hell.

The undergraduates are the only contemporaries to ask about the relationship between Marlowe's life and art; they conclude that he is an enigma, a pitiable conjuncture of vice and wit. The contradiction remained manageable so long as Marlowe had the status of a minor figure. Once he became a valuable item of cultural property, however, the problem of his moral character had to be confronted. At the close of the eighteenth century, when Thomas Warton informed readers of his *History of English Poetry* that Marlowe deserved to be ranked among "the most distinguished tragic poets of his age" (qtd. in MacLure 57-58), the antiquary Thomas Ritson immediately objected on moral grounds. "I have a great respect for Marlow as an ingenious poet," he countered, "but I have a much higher regard for truth and justice."[1]

A footnote in Warton's *History* had led Ritson to the Harleian manuscripts, where he found a "Note" containing Marlowe's "damnable Judgment of Religion, and scorn of Gods word" written by the Elizabethan informer Richard Baines. The Note indicated that Marlowe was not only a proselytizing atheist, but also a counterfeiter and a consumer of "boys & tobacco" (qtd. in MacLure 36). By publishing Baines' Note, "the strongest (if not the

15

whole) proof that now remains of his diabolical tenets and
debauched morals," Ritson intended to disable any further claims
on Marlowe's behalf. Hitherto, his admirers had endeavored "to
rescue his character; either by boldly denying, or artfully
extenuating the crimes alleged against him"[2]; henceforth, no one
could deny that he was guilty as charged. This was wishful thinking
on Ritson's part. Nevertheless, he had set the agenda for two
centuries of criticism and scholarship: could a bad man become a
major author?

I

The answer to this question had to be no. But since Marlowe
ineluctably wore the appearance of a debauched libertine, a
hardened sinner if ever there was one, the task of rescuing him for
ethical humanism assumed paramount importance in the rapidly
expanding Marlowe industry. The first line of defense was, and
remains, denial. Although Marlowe's nineteenth-century editors
printed selected passages from the "Baines libel," as it came to be
known, they expurgated its most lurid blasphemies. Lest anyone be
misled by the extracts that did appear, Marlowe's early biographers
mounted a full-scale attack on Baines' credibility. Edmund Malone
discovered that a man named Richard Baines had been hanged in
1594, just a year after the Note was written, and assumed (wrongly)
that the felon and the informant were the same person. Upon this
hint, James Broughton, who compiled the earliest collection of
Marlowe's life-records, concluded that Baines was "some pitiful
culprit who strove to avert punishment from himself by becoming
the accuser of others." Every contemporary of Marlowe's who
alluded to his atheism received similar treatment. The testimony of
Thomas Beard and William Vaughan, the two divines who
independently confirmed the gist of Baines' report, was disallowed
on the grounds of their presumed anti-theatrical prejudice:
"Everyone knows that the Puritans grossly vilified all those who in
any way encouraged the theater," Broughton argued, "It was not
probable that Marlowe . . . who had severely ridiculed their manners
and attire [!] would escape their malicious aspersions." Marlowe's
editor A. H. Bullen dismissed Robert Greene's allegations in the
Groatsworth of Wit as the "crazy death bed wail of a weak and
malignant spirit." His biographer John Ingram stigmatized
Marlowe's chamber-fellow Thomas Kyd, another accuser, as a man
"of whom nothing kind has ever been recorded," a mean-spirited
mercenary who turned his pen "to any hack work, however
derogatory, in order to gain sustenance."[3]

The second line of defense was displacement. While Victorian scholars denied that Marlowe had been an atheist in the first place, Victorian critics constructed a romantic Marlowe whose blasphemies signified an impulse that was acceptable to modern readers — free thought, anti-philistinism, the quest for transcendence. Edward Dowden and A. C. Bradley redefined him as a prototype of the modern poet who lived for his art, suffered for his excesses, and died young. His immorality, like that of Byron and Shelley, took on a redemptive meaning; his atheism was not an anti-religious act but was rather a manifestation of the artist's unrelenting search for truth. Yet Marlowe could not attain classic status merely on the basis of his intellectual daring; mainstream Victorian educators expected great authors to affirm the enduring power of traditional moral values. The requisite proof of Marlowe's probity came in the form of *Doctor Faustus*. Prior to the mid-nineteenth century, his advocates found little to admire in the play, apart from a few individual speeches. By the 1880s it had become one of the greatest plays in the English language.[4] Marlowe's masterpiece not only had the satisfying contours of a moral tale, but it also gave a conservative twist to the reports about his atheism. In recounting the story of an educated unbeliever who sold his soul to the devil, the author achieved a mature perspective on his own excursion into free thought. As an intellectual, he identified with his protagonist; as a Christian, he repudiated him. The precise balance of his sympathies remained an open question and thus supplied an infinite quantity of grist for the mills of interpretation. Like every great poet, Marlowe was ambivalent.

This intrepid seeker after truth enabled the playwright's twentieth-century biographers to invent a Marlowe who had indeed uttered the blasphemies transcribed by Baines and others, yet had not attacked God directly. Tucker Brooke characterized the assertions that previous scholars found too corrosive to repeat in public as "shrewd critical observations" on "the philosophy of religion." The thrust of the Baines Note, according to F. S. Boas, was an "attack on the verbal inspiration of the Bible, on what is now known as 'fundamentalism.'" Likewise, John Bakeless did not see why "liberal Christians of our own day" should be shocked by the assertion that "Christ was a bastard and his mother dishonest."[5] Marlowe had merely anticipated the Higher Criticism of Scripture that was endemic in post-Victorian Christianity.

The blasphemer completed his pilgrimage to Parnassus in the pages of Paul Kocher's *Study of His Thought, Learning, and Character*, published in 1946. Kocher demonstrated that the Baines Note contains a well thought-out exposition of anti-Christian teachings in the tradition of Celsus, Porphyry, and Lucretius. He further showed that Marlowe consistently stages these doctrines in his plays. But Kocher believed that "there is an unquenchable desire in the human spirit to reach God," and so shrank from the full implications of his own findings. Instead, he argued that Marlowe was an intuitive deist who retained a strong residual attachment to Christianity (thus, there were "moments when the ingrained creed sought to take possession of him again, moments when he almost felt that his life had failed of its highest consummation") and spent his life "groping his way back towards reconciliation with God." Despite his wealth of learning, Kocher's thesis strained credulity to the breaking point. Reviewing his book for *The Nation*, William Empson remarked that the thrust of Marlowe's quarrel with God is unmistakable, and "a critic who muffles it up, from whatever kindly intention, cannot be saying anything important about him." At the same time, by stressing the centrality of the Note, Kocher provoked opposition from unreconstructed skeptics like the *TLS* reviewer who reiterated that Baines and Kyd could never be trusted in any event.[6]

At present the Victorian and modern Marlowe is an exhausted paradigm, the relic of an era that expected the great tragedians to uphold a high moral standard. Nevertheless, the old construct continues to do the residual work of foreclosing inquiry into the relationship between Marlowe and Elizabethan culture. Thus the Marxist Simon Shepherd, who describes his own position as anti-patriarchal, begins his recent book on the playwright by dismissing Marlowe-the-atheist as a "mythical figure." Shepherd's disdain for his subject's biography typifies the asymmetry of Marlowe studies at the present time. During the past two decades, critics such as Shepherd, Jonathan Dollimore, Alan Sinfield, Stephen Greenblatt, Jonathan Goldberg, Leah Marcus, Jonathan Crewe, Michael Keefer, and Emily Bartels have interpreted Marlowe's work in ways that enable us to conceive of it as an important site of resistance,[7] but Marlowe's life records, and especially the very materials that would test and extend such interpretations, have remained out of bounds.

The mythical atheist was a nineteenth-century author, a romantic individualist who freely organized his own life and inscribed his beliefs in his writings. The Elizabethan Marlowe cannot fill this role for the simple reason that he has left no first person utterances behind for our perusal (the sole exception is a fawning Latin dedication to the Countess of Pembroke published six months before his death). All of the evidence about his (un)beliefs lies at one remove from his own voice. It consists of reported speech transcribed by informants, observations by hostile witnesses, and passages culled from his plays. His name does not appear on the title-page of any of his works attributed to him until after his death in 1593. The skeptical critique of this evidence rightly insists that Marlowe-the-atheist has no known abode apart from these documents: he is an irretrievably textual being, the protagonist in a series of overlapping narratives that commences about six months before his death and persists on into its immediate aftermath. But where does one go from there? The pseudo-skeptical hypothesis that Marlowe's accusers were out to destroy the reputation of an innocent man is even less plausible than the theory it sets out to refute: for this line of argument presumes access to the motives and sensibilities not only of Marlowe, but also of every Elizabethan who testified against him.

Seven of Marlowe's contemporaries allude in writing to his blasphemies; the number increases to eleven if we include writers who refer to him by pseudonyms. This dossier is unprecedented in its intricacy and scope, its points of contact with literature and politics, and its murderous outcome. Elizabethan atheism, in Stephen Greenblatt's apt phrase, was always "the thought of another." Marlowe was the other. Within the annals of early modern unbelief, he marks the point at which the so-called "close" atheist is haled out of the closet, thrust into the gaze of private and public scrutiny, and brutally called to account for his alleged transgressions. The sixteenth-century divine Thomas Beard correctly identified Marlowe as the first modern Englishman who challenged comparison with the great blasphemers of antiquity: "not inferior to any of the former in Atheisme & impiety, and equall to all in manner of punishment."[8]

The right question is not "Was he or wasn't he?" but rather "Why Marlowe?" Why was he chosen by history to fill this role? The answers to this question cannot lie in his conscious choices, about which there is nothing to know; they lie in the history of the role itself as it evolved over time and bore upon his peculiar circumstances. Although this essay will proceed in chronological order and follow the course of Marlowe's personal history, it is not about an individual subject; instead, it describes the social and discursive framework within which a figure like Marlowe could be produced. My narrative will focus on the institutions — church, grammar school, university, the state intelligence apparatus, and the playhouses — that taught individuals how not to believe.

This itinerary leads back, in turn, to the question left dangling by the Cambridge undergraduates: why do the twin motifs of "wit lent from heaven" and "vices sent from hell" figure so prominently in the Marlowe archive? What does his story reveal about the relationship between literary achievement and moral truancy? This connection originated within the educational system itself, where the rise of atheism was inextricably linked with the spread of literacy, the imitation of Greek and Latin writers, and the skeptical thrust of sixteenth-century dialectic. English atheists became articulate with the advent of Protestant humanism. It was the unintended consequence of an educational program designed to yoke literacy to belief, and eloquence to religion. While this project possessed enormous marketing power, the grand synthesis between learning and piety proved elusive in practice. The contradictions between self-empowerment through letters and self-abnegation before God could be managed and displaced, but never resolved.[9] This crisis within Christian humanism created a conceptual space to which real subjects were called, and within which Marlowe's life and art become legible.

II

Unbelievers first appeared on the cultural landscape of early modern England in the mid-1500s, when Sir John Cheke coined the word *"Atheists"* to describe people who do not "care whether there be a God or no, or whether . . . he will recompense good Men with good things, and bad Men with what is Evil." Since Cheke assumed that every rational creature has an innate knowledge of God, it did not occur to him that atheism could ever pose a threat to revealed religion; he saw it as a curiosity, a strange example of the depths to which depravity could sink. But the specter of godlessness rapidly grew to alarming proportions. In a sermon delivered in 1549, Bishop Latimer warned King Edward VI of a report "that ther be greate manie in Englande that say there is no soule, that thincke it is not eternal, but like a doges soul, that thinke there is neither heaven nor hell." Four years later, Archbishop Cranmer drafted the first statute that distinguishes blasphemy from the older crime of heresy. At the end of the 1560s, Cheke's pupil Roger Ascham complained that the word "atheist . . . is no more unknown now to plain Englishmen, than the person was unknown sometime in England." In 1572, George Carleton informed Lord Burghley that "The realm is divided into three parties, the Papists, the Atheists, and the Protestants." By the 1580s, observers on all sides — mainstream Protestants, Puritans, Catholics, and Separatists — agreed that, in Bishop Cooper's words, "the School of *Epicure*, and the Atheists, is mightily increased in these daies." The libertine Thomas Nashe warned that "there is no sect now in England so scattered as Atheism." Bacon too reckoned that there was "no heresy which strives with more zeal to spread and sow and multiply itself than atheism." Richard Hooker warned readers of *The Laws of Ecclesiastical Polity* that atheists had arisen in fulfillment of St.

Peter's prophecy that mockers would flourish in the last days of the world, and urged the imposition of the death penalty to "restrain the furie of this wicked broode." In the early seventeenth century, the Spanish ambassador Gondomar estimated the number of English atheists at 900,000, or a fourth of the adult population.[10]

Who were these people? Where did they come from? English atheism became conceptually possible under the auspices of the Protestant Reformation. The same institutional apparatus simultaneously produced believers and nay-sayers. This historic transformation commenced in the 1530s, when the Protestant reformers' faith in Bible reading, the widespread availability of cheap printed texts, and King Henry VIII's desire to impose a standard creed on all of his subjects, created the impetus for the first program of universal education in English.[11] The reformers' initial presumption that the vast majority of the English people *did not know* the core doctrines of the Christian Church was born out by their own fieldwork. During Bishop Hooper's visitation of Gloucester in 1551, for example, the examiners questioned 311 parish priests about their knowledge of the Ten Commandments, the Apostle's Creed and the Lord's Prayer in English. Of those questioned 171 could not repeat the Ten Commandments, 10 could not say the Lord's Prayer and 27 did not know its author. In seizing the opportunity to educate his illiterate subjects, the King took over the pastoral office of providing religious instruction. Henry and his Christian humanist advisers proceeded on the mistaken assumption that words imprint ideas on the impressionable minds of new readers. Although *The ABC and Catechism* was meant to instill belief, this foundational text could just as easily provide an occasion for disbelief. People who have been told what to think ("I believe in one God the father almighty") have the alternative, which did not exist before, of denying what they are required to affirm. Writing shortly after the accession of Elizabeth, the humanist Goddred Gylby traces the origins of atheism back to a primal scene of failed assimilation: "men are now a days here in England glutted as it were with godes word," he wrote, "and therefore almost ready to vomit up againe that which thei have received . . . some turning to curious arts, & som contemning al artes & sciences, some Epicures, som Atheistes."[12]

The turn to atheism began with the Arian heresy and other forms of anti-credal thought described in John Proctor's *The Fall of the Late Arian* (1549) and Bishop Roger Hutchinson's *The Image of God* (1550). The late Arian had conducted a rigorously literal reading of the New Testament before being burned at the stake in 1549. Taking the Protestant quest for a precise understanding of Scripture to its logical conclusion, he found that the Bible continuously refers to the unity of God (but never to the Trinity) and to the humanity of Christ. By insisting on Christ's mortality, the Arian heresy disabled the machinery of divine justice evoked in the creed, where the Son "descended into hell . . . [and] ascended into heaven . . . From thence he shall come to judge the quick and the dead." If Christ was mortal, everyone is mortal, and no one is subject to eternal punishment. In his widely read *Decades* (1577), the theologian Henry Bullinger hotly chastises these "shamelesse, and ungodly wretches, who have in their mouth, that no man ever returned from death or from belowe, who by his return proved that soules remane alive, when the body is dead." Bullinger accuses the Arians of feigned ignorance: "But malicioulsy they lye," he continues, "disembling that they knowe not that, which certeinely they know. For who knoweth not that Christ . . . was raised againe from dead?"[13] When Bullinger says that the Arians "know" Christ was raised from the dead he means that they have read this in the creed; but of course knowing a text also involves the capacity to interrogate and refute it.

The fall of the late Arian is a seminal instance of how atheism was produced in early modern England. The Arians did not deny the existence of God; they disputed God's capacity to intervene in their lives via the Son and the Holy Ghost. Modern historians of religion have likened them to their Enlightenment counterparts, the deists and unitarians. But this analogy assumes that God remains changeless across the ages, and ignores the ways in which He is reconstructed within history. Early English unbelief contested a "reformed" God who used the fear of punishment to discipline unruly subjects. A century later, deism and unitarianism contrived to preserve the idea of a benevolent God in a universe from which His menacing Biblical forbear had largely been dislodged. The former was an act of resistance; the latter, of accommodation. The late Arian does not argue that God is comprehensible in the book of nature; he argues that God is incomprehensible. The word deism did come into the language during the sixteenth century, but it *meant* godlessness until well into the seventeenth. Within the world of post-Reformation Christianity, belief in God was inextricably linked to the fear of God; a deity who did not enforce his commandments — a God without sanctions — might as well not exist. "Atheism and theomachy rebels and mutinies against the power of God," Bacon explains, "not trusting to his word, which reveals his will, because it does not believe in his power." Hence, anyone who rejected the immortality of the soul, the existence of heaven and hell (especially the latter), and the operations of Providence qualified as an atheist.[14]

The most familiar synonyms for the new coinage were "epicure" and "libertine." Just as atheism literally means "without

God," these terms implied a condition of freedom (however illusory) from the disciplinary regime of divine law. The concept encompassed both practical atheism, "whereby men deny God in their deeds, lives, & conversations" and speculative atheism "when a man doth avouch, hold, and maintain that there is no God at all." Hypocrites — also known as "close" or "inward" atheists — kept their impiety in the closet; "open" or "outward" atheists flaunted God in public. In its most restrictive (and nearly modern) sense, the word denoted individuals who openly denied the existence of God. Although early modern writers stretched this broad-bottomed concept to include notional states of godlessness, they compensated for its elasticity by arguing that there is a logical progression from practical to speculative, and from close to open, atheism. Distinctions between these various styles of unbelief remained fluid and permeable; hence, attempts to locate specific individuals at any given point along the spectrum (was Raleigh a skeptic *or* an atheist?) are bound to miss their mark.[15]

Since hardly anyone was accused of public blasphemy — Marlowe is the great exception — it is fair to ask if contemporary allegations about the extent of Elizabethan atheism had any basis in reality. Were contemporary observers describing actual subjects? Or were they projecting an internal crisis of belief onto an imaginary horde of sensationalized unbelievers? From an empirical standpoint, neither hypothesis leads anywhere; the closet remains closed. From a theoretical perspective, both hypotheses converge in one explanatory axiom: atheism enabled Elizabethan subjects to conceive of organized resistance to divine authority. As Ascham was the first to notice, the "word" and the "person" had a symbiotic relationship to one another. Even when the divines who wrote against atheism were voicing their own anxieties, they created positions for real people to fill.

The critical moment in the genesis of atheism occurs when the subject of divine law discovers that he is going to be punished for following his natural inclinations. By insisting that the vast majority of the human race is predestined to sin and damnation and can do nothing about it, Calvin put extraordinary pressure on this moment. "Why then belike we must sin / And so consequently die," in Doctor Faustus' well-known syllogism: "Ay, we must die, an everlasting death. / What doctrine call you this?" Since the only God the reprobate could ever know was a God of wrath, they had every incentive, as Calvin puts it, "to rob him of his justice and Providence, shutting him up as an idler in heaven." In his explication of Psalm 14.1 "The fool hath said in his heart, there is no God," Calvin equates the godless fool with the unregenerate sinners of Romans 3: everyone who stands convicted "under the law" — that is, everyone who knows the law and remains unvisited by the Holy Spirit, everyone who does not belong to the elect — counts as a practical atheist. The same gloss appears in the Geneva Bible and became a commonplace in Protestant theology. Theodore Beza, for example, describes the atheist in Psalm 14 as "*a most sorowful description of the natural man.*" The natural man epitomized a basic contradiction in reformed Christianity. Divine justice exists in order to terrorize him into good behavior, yet he has ample inducement not to believe in the very law that transforms him into a God-fearing citizen.[16]

The subject's duties under divine law were spelled out in Romans 13:1, the cornerstone of Protestant political theory: "Let every soul be subject unto the higher powers," Paul writes, "For there is no power but of God, and the powers that be are ordained of God." Luther invoked this text to prove that secular Princes, "the powers that be," were subject neither to the papacy, nor to the popular will, but were authorized by divine right. Calvin cited the same passage to argue that the dread of divine punishment is the ultimate basis of civil society. The problem with Romans 13:1 is that Paul legitimates all superior power by referring it back to God. As secular princes claimed the God-given right to impose a state religion of their own choosing (an interpretation that turns the original sense of Romans 13:1 upside down), their position became indistinguishable from the Machiavellian doctrine that religion is an instrument of state power. In his oft-cited remarks about the origins of speculative atheism in England, Ascham blames an influx of returned travellers, "epicures in living, atheists in doctrine," who "counte as Fables, the holie misteries of Christian religion. They make Christ and his Gospell, onlie serve Civill pollicie." But these "Italianate Englishmen" returned to a country where the national religion had changed four times between 1547 and 1558. They simply took the Tudor mandate of uniformity-in-religion enforced by princely rule to its logical destination. On the grassroots level, even the humblest parishioner could well ask "is not religion a policy to keep people in obedience?"[17]

Within the Elizabethan establishment, hypocrisy, or "close" atheism, offered the only viable way of resolving these contradictions. As commentators frequently remarked, the Psalmist stipulates that unbelief occurs in private, where the fool speaks in his heart. By staying in the closet, the "close" atheist avoided giving scandal to God and corrupting public morals; by remaining silent, the fool tacitly conceded that his ideas were foolish. "It is not said; *the Foole hath thought in his Hearte*," Bacon notes: "he rather saith it by rote to himselfe, as that he would have, then that he can thoroughly believe it." With breathtaking candor, no less an authority than Archbishop Whitgift declared the Church of England to be "full of hypocrites, papists, atheists, and other wicked persons," a state of affairs that he claimed was perfectly normal in the post-apostolic era. But Elizabethan atheism was a progressive phenomenon, and during the late 1580s and early 1590s, this compromise position came under enormous strains. Resurgent Puritan militants like John Bate, John Udall, and William Penry, together with the Separatists Henry Barrow and Robert Browne, demanded that atheists and hypocrites be rooted out of their sinecures in the church, the universities, and the government. At the same time, conservatives and moderates like Cooper, Hooker, and Bacon sensed that close atheists were on the verge, or in the process, of agitating in public. The enduring symbol of this moral panic was Christopher Marlowe.[18]

III

Like everyone who prepared for a career in the ministry, schools, or universities, Marlowe was trained to function as a close atheist within the Church. Alexander Nowell's *Catechism of First Instruction and Learning of Christian Religion* (1573) taught Elizabethan schoolboys that most of them were predestined to sin and therefore could not experience the ecstatic "renning of the spirit" that assured the fortunate few of their place among the elect. But the *Catechism* further assured them that it was perfectly acceptable to pretend otherwise: "Many by hypocrisie and counterfaiting of godlinesse do joyne them selves to this fellowship, which are nothing lesse than true members of the Chirch." The *Catechism* did require reprobate scholars to retain a "generall" or "dead" faith in the God who had consigned them to everlasting torment; at the same time, however, the all-embracing criterion of conformity made it exceedingly easy to carry on as a hypocrite within the establishment. Bacon contended that "the great *Atheists*, indeed, are *Hypocrites*: which are ever Handling Holy Things, but without Feeling; so as they must needs be cauterized in the End."[19]

During his six years at Cambridge, Marlowe learned the intellectual foundations of speculative atheism. The disputations that comprised the core of the B.A. course exposed inconsistencies within the Bible and subjected individual texts to contradictory interpretations. "[T]he whole Scriptures," complained Henry Barrow, "must in these their schooles and disputations, be unsufferably corrupted, abused, wrested, perverted" by the disputers, who "must handle, divide, utter and discusse, according to their vaine affected arts of logick and rhetorick." The M. A. course offered extensive training in natural philosophy (astrology, cosmology, medicine) and introduced Marlowe to the ancient sources for modern atheism: Aristotle's *de Anima*, Pliny, Lucretius, and Lucian. This curriculum was supposed to produce a Protestant ministry fortified by a deep understanding of God's word and works; but since belief, "the gift of God," could not be learned, the system could just as easily produce a sophisticated unbeliever like Doctor Faustus. John Case, a Fellow of New College, Oxford from 1572 to 1600, encountered swarms of these "scorpions and locusts" during his time at the university.[20]

From a professional standpoint it did not matter whether or not these students believed in God: so long as there was no record of any impropriety, closet atheists were free to seek employment within the conformist establishment. But in Marlowe's case there was impropriety. Shortly before he was to receive his M.A., in the summer of 1587, the Cambridge authorities were informed that he intended to join the English seminary at Rheims. When the university transmitted this report to the Privy Council, the Council replied that Marlowe "had no such intent, but that in all his actions he had behaved himself orderly and discreetly, whereby he had done her majesty good service and deserved to be rewarded for his faithful dealing." By commissioning Marlowe to spy on dissident Catholics, the government scripted him into two roles — loyal servant and subversive other — that were diametrically opposed to one another. The Privy Council's letter to Cambridge smoothes over this double insertion by equating the real Marlowe with the loyal subject ("he had no such intent"), indicating that the seditious Marlowe was merely playing a part. But such distinctions did not hold up in practice. Sir Francis Walsingham, the head of Elizabeth's spy system, routinely recruited informants by "turning" individuals who were already involved with the Catholic underground; here the spy's loyalty to the state was suspect from the start. Moreover, even the most zealous spy could be persuaded to do business with his victims — it was all in a day's work. The Privy Council valued Marlowe because of his contacts in the recusant community, and because of his willingness to betray it. These were equally reasons not to trust him. The original informant could have been right.[21]

Sequestered in a no man's land that was both Protestant and Catholic, double agents personified the godless creed of "politic religion." In describing his own evolution from seminarian to spy, Marlowe's accuser Richard Baines recalled that he "began to deride what was seen as important to our religion . . . a sure road to heresy, infidelity, and atheism." When Baines himself recruited English seminarians at Rheims in 1582, he did not appeal to their residual sense of patriotism. Instead, he tried to persuade them that religion consisted of fictions imposed on gullible believers; that "the mystical ceremonies of dreadful sacrifice . . were no more than pretty gestures, performing which even a Turk would look holy"; that "there was no fire by which souls may be tortured but it was the worm of conscience"; that he "could teach a more useful method of prayer — reciting the twenty four letters of the alphabet."[22]

In the meantime, Marlowe began to write scripts for the London acting companies. In 1576 the actors had erected the first purpose-built theater since Roman times and begun offering commercial entertainment to metropolitan audiences on a daily basis. During the decade that followed, the militant wing of the Puritan faction initiated a strident debate about the cultural significance of these facts. Taking their case to the public in sermons and pamphlets, John Northbrooke, John Field, Philip Stubbes, Stephen Gosson, Anthony Munday and William Rankins characterized the playhouse as a site of anti-Christian rites and performances. Field accused the actors of raising "flagges of defiance against God." Reminding his readers that plays were "invented by the devil, practicsed by the heathen gentiles and didicat to their false idols, Goddes and Goddesses," Stubbes argued that modern theaters "renue the remembrance of heathen idolatrie": "if you will learne to contemne God and all his lawes, to care neither for heaven nor hel . . . you need goe to no other school." The fact that the actors performed plays based on Scripture only made matters worse, according to Munday, since "the reverend word of God & histories of the Bible, set forth on the stage by these blasphemous players, are so corrupted with their gestures of scurrilitie, and so interlaced with uncleane, and whorish speeches, that it is not possible to drawe anie profite out of the doctrine of their spiritual moralities." When Northbrookc's Youth reminds Age that "many times they play histories out of the Scriptures," Age replies: "Assuredly that is very evill so to doe, to mingle scurrilitie with Divinitie, that is, to eate meate with unwashed hands."[23]

Like other Elizabethan allegations about the spread of godlessness, these claims can neither be proved nor disproved. Very few of the many plays written for the public stage during this decade are extant; and in any case, the charges mainly refer to performance practice and spectatorial license. The closet remains closed. Nevertheless, the antitheatrical critics put the compromise position of "close" atheism under a new kind of strain: for the thrust of the Puritan case against the theater was precisely that it took place in public, on the sabbath, and so gave scandal to God. Since God is not mocked, these performances were bound to bring divine retribution, not only on players and playgoers, but on the city and nation as well. The collapse of the galleries at Paris Garden on

Sunday, 13 January 1583, a misfortune that claimed the lives of at least seven spectators, confirmed this hypothesis in spectacular fashion. Field, Stubbes, and Rankins demanded that performances come to a halt before God struck again. "For as the majestie of God is impatient of any aspiring mind to be partaker of his deitie," Rankins warned, "so dooth hee with a sharpe whippe scourge those blasphemers, that attribute anie dignitie belonging to heaven his head, or the earth his footstoole to any other but himselfe."[24]

Tamburlaine the Great, which the Lord Admiral's Men performed in the year Rankins' pamphlet appeared, is the first extant play to challenge the antitheatrical critics on their own ground. Tamburlaine's famous paean to the "aspiring mind," at once defines his stance and recapitulates two of the seminal Renaissance texts on atheism. The first half of his oration echoes and reaffirms Ovid's account of creation in Book I of the *Metamorphoses*, where "Nature" fashions humanity out of the four elements. Just as the elements are "Warring in our breasts for regiment," Ovid's Nature teaches the strong to displace the weak, the son, Jove, "To thrust his doting father from the Chaire." What the orthodox moralist stigmatizes as evil, the play implies, embodies the violence and desire that constructed the social order in the first place. The second half of Tamburlaine's speech echoes and repudiates Calvin's account of the soul in *The Institutes of the Christian Religion*. Replying to natural philosophers who would "destroy the immortality of the soul and deprive God of his rights," Calvin emphasizes the soul's innate desire for celestial knowledge. He praises the "manifold nimbleness" with which it "surveyeyth heaven and earth," "measure[s] the skie," and "gather[s] the number of the starres . . . with what swiftness or sloweness they go their courses." The soul ascends the heavens because it wishes "to clime up even to God and to eternall felicity," for man's own "felicitie . . . is that he be joined with God, and therefore it is the chief action of the soule to aspire thereunto." In Tamburlaine's revision of this much-traveled itinerary, "Our soules" proceed along the same course, comprehending "the wondrous architecture of the world / And measuring every wandring planet's course"; but Tamburlaine's journey ultimately leads not to God, but to "That perfect bliss and sole felicity, / The sweet fruition of an earthly crowne."[25]

In subordinating religion to force, Tamburlaine exposes the central contradiction in the Protestant theory of the state. Although Romans 13:1 prohibits rebellion ("Let every soul be subject unto the higher powers"), the relentlessness of Paul's logic compels him to enfranchise a successful usurper ("for the powers that be are ordained of God"). The stereotypical figure of the "scourge of

God" is an attempt to resolve this contradiction by reducing the usurper to a doomed and unthinking instrument of God's justice. But Tamburlaine invokes the orthodox doctrine of obedience in a sophisticated defense of his own right to disobey. Since he is termed "The scourge of God and terror to the world," he concludes that "I must apply myself to fit those terms / . . . / And plague such peasants as resist in me / The power of heaven's eternal majesty."[26] Marlowe's hero is God's double agent, licensed by divine authority to wreak havoc in his name. From a theological standpoint, such agents can never act autonomously, for they are constrained by predestination, bondage of the will, and innate belief enforced by the fear of punishment. On the stage — as Tamburlaine and Kyd's Hieronimo both discover — the role liberates the scourge from the very God who enfranchises him.

Tamburlaine's attack on God reaches a crescendo shortly before the end of Part Two, when he burns the Koran and defies its author: "Now Mahomet, if thou have any power / Come down and work a miracle." Since Tamburlaine dies two scenes later, pious commentators have inferred that God does, finally, give him his comeuppance. But atheists were supposed to die horrific deaths — railing, convulsing, frantic at the prospect of divine correction; such performances offered irrefutable proof that the wicked did indeed possess an innate fear of God, however involuntary. But Tamburlaine dies at peace with himself, in serene assurance that his sons "Shall retain my spirit though I die / And live in all your seeds immortally" (V.iii.173-74).

Although *Tamburlaine* became the most widely imitated play in the Elizabethan repertory, its success left Marlowe in a vulnerable position. Shortly after *Tamburlaine*'s debut, Robert Greene publicly taxed "mad and scoffing poets, that have propheticall spirits as bold as Merlin's [Marlowe's] race," for "daring God out of heaven with that atheist Tamburlaine" and for wantonly uttering "such impious instances of intollerable poetry."[27] Although Greene makes these allegations in a spirit of affable raillery, they do indicate the nature of Marlowe's predicament. He had now come under adverse scrutiny twice in the same year — first for sedition, then for public impiety.

IV

During the last eighteen months of his life, Marlowe was subjected to a devastating series of accusations. In January of 1592, Richard Baines, now his chamber-fellow at Flushing, accused him of counterfeiting and of intending "to goe to the Ennemy" — Spain

— "or to Rome." Marlowe responded by leveling the same accusations at Baines. The terms under which the two men were released remain unclear, but the government continued to receive intelligence reports about Marlowe. When an anonymous rhymester subsequently nailed a seditious libel based on *Tamburlaine* to the door of the Dutch Church in London, the Privy Council launched a full-scale investigation. The most spectacular charges involved the crime of blasphemy. In the course of ransacking the belongings of Thomas Kyd, another ex-roommate, the authorities found a handwritten transcript of "vile heretical conceits denying the divinity of Jesus Christ" copied from *The Fall of the Late Arian*. Although sections of the manuscript are written in the italic hand that Kyd — a scrivener — would have used, he told Lord Keeper Puckering that it belonged to Marlowe, and had been "shuffled" with his papers by mistake. In the meantime, the London gang-leader Richard Chomeley informed one of the Council's spies "that one Marlowe is able to showe more sounde reasons for Atheisme then any devine in Englande is able to prove devinitie & that Marloe told him he had read the Atheist lecture to Sir Walter Raleigh and others" (undated spy's report, 1592-93).[28]

Was Marlowe now a *bona fide* atheist? Was he being falsely accused? Or was he attempting to entrap others who were suspected of that crime — Raleigh, for example, whom Father Parsons had recently accused of heading a "school of atheism"? Within the fluid, opportunistic world of the double agent, it is hard to imagine what sort of evidence could categorically exclude any of these alternatives. As a spy, Marlowe served the state by voicing what the crown regarded as treason and heresy; the state retained the capacity to determine whether he counted as a loyal servant or subversive other. In this instance, the Council ordered a professional informer named Thomas Drury to procure testimony from Marlowe's former chamber fellow and enemy twin Richard Baines. Bear in mind that Baines had already concocted, used, and confessed to his own version of the atheist lecture, which was published on the continent in 1583 and again in 1588, that someone in the government had questioned Baines about Marlowe when the two of them were sent back from Flushing, and that Drury was in regular communication both with Baines, who "did use to resort" unto him, and with the Council, whom he supplied with intelligence. In other words, the Council knew all along what Baines could tell them about Marlowe. The fact that Kyd's allegations about Marlowe's atheism are similar to those in Baines' Note lends credence to Baines' story; but Kyd's testimony was extracted under torture, and the men who obtained it were in communication with both him and Drury at approximately the same time. The authorities did not merely seek the Baines Note; they produced it.[29]

Baines' report on Marlowe's "damnable Judgment of Religion, and scorn of God's word" contains the first written exposition of atheism in early modern Europe. The informant cites some eighteen separate theses. Taken in sequence, these proceed from a literalistic critique of the Bible to the claim that religion consists of persuasive fictions to the conclusion that Marlowe can "write a new religion" based on "a more Excellent and Admirable method" than either Catholicism or Protestantism. Baines offers Marlowe's interpretations of John 13:23 and Romans 13:1 as illustrations of this excellent new method. Marlowe's gloss on the passage from John preserves the literal sense of the text ("Nowe there was one of his disciples [i.e. John], which leaned on his bosom, which Jesus loved") but glosses it according to a logic of carnal desire: "St. John the Evangelist was bedfellow to Christ and leaned always in his bosom . . . he used him as the sinners of Sodoma." This reading entails a new precept: "That all they that love not boys and tobacco are fools." The precept brings Marlowe's new religion into conflict with the law. Where the letter of Romans 13:1 requires obedience, the ungodly interpreter appeals to the internalized voice of the spirit, arguing that "Paul was a timerous fellow in bidding men to be subject to magistrates against his conscience." Although Marlowe's conclusions are outrageous, his premises are orthodox: he takes the Protestant stress on the prerogatives of the inspired lay interpreter to its natural destination. Luther had foreseen this outcome when he wrote that "The ungodly out of the gospel do seek only a carnal freedom, and become worse thereby, therefore not the Gospel but the Law belongeth unto them." Marlowe's new religion uses the gospel to overturn the law. Marlowe "doth not only hould [these opinions] himself," Baines concluded, "but almost into every Company he Cometh he perswades men to Atheism, willing them not to be afeard of bugbeares and hobgoblins, and utterly scorning both god and his ministers." Kyd corroborated these allegations: "[I]t was his custome," he wrote, "in table talk or otherwise to jest at the devine scriptures gybe at praiers, & strive in argument to frustrate & confute what hath byn spoke or wrytt by prophets & such holie men."[30]

Baines' Note defines the moment when blasphemy unites with sodomy, steps out of the closet, and coalesces around an actual figure of opposition. Open atheism cannot be the thought of an anonymous other; it requires a real subject. By the Spring of 1593, Marlowe was ready to fill this role. He had been taken with a counterfeit shilling in Flushing; Robert Greene had publicly accused him of saying "(like the fool in his heart) There is no God"; the

Dutch Church libeler had used *Tamburlaine* as the model for a genuine popular uprising; the government had assembled a dossier of spy's reports, culminating in the Note itself. Although the full extent of Marlowe's atheism only becomes legible within the state security apparatus, its appearance there signals a genuine crisis in sixteenth-century Protestantism. By making fear the ultimate guarantor of belief, Calvin's God had staked his prestige on the impossibility of an open atheism that went unpunished. The handful of ancient blasphemers who had dared God out of heaven (Caligula, Diagoras, Dionysius) were the exceptions that proved the rule: for, as Calvin put it, no one "ever trembled with greater distress at any instance of divine wrath" than they. Rankins explains why:

> [T]he mighty Jehova inkindled his wrath and sent wormes to devoure the guts of this Arius. . . . And Dionisius Aropagita, for blaspheming the name of God, suddainly sanck into the earth. . . unhappy wife of Job, that willed him to curse God and die, with her children, and all the rest of her substance, was suddainly wasted and consumed. . . .[31]

Tamburlaine, and now Marlowe, put this axiom into play.

Blasphemers trembled because death could come either at the hands of the law or of God Himself, intervening through agents raised up by Him for that purpose. This overdetermined punitive apparatus meant that Marlowe was subject to the combined forces of state power, casual violence, and divine wrath. All three factors came into play at the end of his life. The killing occurred under the aegis of state power, was subsequently represented as an act of causal violence in which Marlowe struck the first blow, and thus became an apt occasion for divine intervention. Indeed, during the months leading up to Marlowe's death, Robert Greene publicly predicted that God would soon strike down the "famous gracer of tragedians." Four years later the Puritan minister Thomas Beard re-articulated this version of Marlowe's demise in his popular book *The Theater of God's Judgements*. The story appealed to Beard because of its transparent exemplary force. Marlowe had "denied God and his sonne Christ . . . But see what hooke the Lord put in the nosthrils of this barking dogge." Three years later the conformist minister William Vaughan reiterated this providential narrative in *The Golden Grove*: "one Christopher Marlow by profession a play-maker . . . about 7. yeeres a-goe wrote a booke against the Trinitie: but see the effects of Gods justice . . . ." The divines rejoiced in Marlowe's killing for the same reason that Field, Stubbes, and Rankins revelled in the collapse of the Bear House at

Paris Garden. These occurrences demonstrated that their Lord and Master was, as Greene put it, "a God that can punish enemies."[32]

This last version does justice neither to Marlowe nor to God, who need not be held responsible for the lethal acts that continue to be done in His name. Baines' atheist lecturer still offers the most vivid image of Marlowe's predicament. The lecturer knows too much for his own good. Like Baines, he has taken in the atheist critique of mainstream religion; unlike Baines, who had been paid off with a church living at Waltham,[33] he does not enjoy the option of conformity and hypocrisy. He can incorporate his forbidden knowledge into a strategy of self-presentation, as Marlowe does in *Tamburlaine*, but this is a dangerous game. When Tamburlaine entered the real world of oppositional politics, he took Marlowe with him. The atheist lecturer continues to play despite the risk. He recognizes that his dissidence has been produced within a Protestant theocracy, but he does not accept the corollary that his rebellion is doomed or ineffectual. Like Marlowe — and here the two figures converge at last — he is silenced at the moment when he becomes visible as a figure of opposition. The leading question, then, is how to undo that silencing? This essay makes a start in that direction.

Notes

1. Strabo, *Geography*, ed. and trans. H. L. Jones (London, 1917), 1: 63. Qtd. in Millar MacLure, ed. *Marlowe: the Critical Heritage*, (London, 1979), 46. Hereafter cited as MacLure.
2. MacLure, 36 (the Baines Note) and 66 (Ritson).
3. *The Gentleman's Magazine*, January-June 1830, 125, 123; A. H. Bullen, ed., *The Works of Christopher Marlowe* (New York, 1885), lviii; John Ingram, *Christopher Marlowe and his Associates* (London, 1904), 232-33.
4. Thomas Dabbs, *Reforming Marlowe* (Lewisburg, PA, 1991), 93-100, 105-07, 88-91.
5. C. F. Tucker Brooke, *The Life of Marlowe* (London, 1930), 62; F. S. Boas, *Christopher Marlowe* (Oxford, 1940), 258; John Bakeless, *The Tragicall History of Christopher Marlowe* (Cambridge, MA, 1942), 111.
6. Paul Kocher, *Christopher Marlowe* (Chapel Hill, 1946), 334, 332; William Empson, "Two Proper Crimes," *The Nation* 163 (1946), 444-45; Review of Kocher, *Times Literary Supplement* 19 July 1947, 364.
7. Simon Shepherd, *Marlowe and the Politics of Elizabethan Theater* (Brighton, 1986), xii. See Jonathan Dollimore, *Radical Tragedy* (Chicago, 1984); Alan Sinfield, *Literature in Protestant England 1560-1660* (London, 1983) and *Faultlines* (Berkeley, 1992); Stephen Greenblatt, *Renaissance Self-Fashioning* (Chicago, 1980); Jonathan Goldberg,

"Sodomy and Society: the Case of Christopher Marlowe," *Southwest Review* 69 (1984), 371-78 and *Sodometries* (Stanford, 1992); Leah Marcus, "Textual Indeterminacy and Ideological Difference: The Case of *Dr. Faustus,*" *Renaissance Drama* 20 (1989), 1-29; Jonathan Crewe, "The Theater of the Idols: Marlowe, Rankins, and Theatrical Images," *Theater Journal* 34 (1984), 321-33; Michael Keefer, "History and the Canon: The Case of *Dr. Faustus,*" *University of Toronto Quarterly*, 56 (1987), 498-522; Marlowe, *Dr. Faustus: a 1604-Version Edition*, ed. Michael Keefer (Peterborough, 1991); Emily Bartels, *Spectacles of Strangeness* (Philadelphia, 1993).

8. For contemporary accounts that refer to Marlowe by name see "Remembraunces of words and matters against Richard Cholmeley" by an unnamed spy, Harleian MS 6848, fol. 190, reprinted in A. D. Wraight, *In Search of Christopher Marlowe* (New York, 1965), 354; the Baines Note in MacLure, 36-38; Kyd's letters to Sir Thomas Puckering in MacLure, 32-35; Thomas Beard, *The Theater of God's Judgements* (1597) in MacLure, 41-42; Francis Meres, *Palladis Tamia* (1598) in MacLure, 45-46; and William Vaughan, *The Golden Grove (*1600) in MacLure 47. Henry Oxinden's manuscript notations in the Prideaux copy of the 1629 edition of *Hero and Leander* and in Oxinden's commonplace books are reprinted and discussed in Mark Eccles, "Marlowe in Kentish Tradition," *Notes and Queries* 13, 20, and 27 July 1935. For allusions that evidently refer to Marlowe but do not cite him by name see Robert Greene, *Perimedes the Blacksmith* (1588) in MacLure, 28-29; Greene's *Groatsworth of Wit Bought With a Million of Repentance* (1593) in MacLure, 30; Thomas Nashe, *The Unfortunate Traveller* (1593) in *The Works of Thomas Nashe*, ed. R. B. McKerrow and F. P. Wilson, 5 vols. (Oxford, 1958), 2: 264; and Lynette and Eveline Feasy, "Nashe's *The Unfortunate Traveller*: Some Marlovian Echoes," *English* 7 (1948): 38; and William Rankins, *Seven Satires* (1598) in MacLure, 42-43. Stephen Greenblatt, "Invisible Bullets," *Shakespeare's "Rough Magic,*" ed. Peter Erickson and Coppelia Kahn, (Newark, DE, 1985) 279-80.

9. See Anthony Grafton and Lisa Jardine, *From Humanism to the Humanities: Education and the Liberal Arts in Fifteenth- and Sixteenth-Century Europe* (Cambridge, MA, 1986).

10. John Strype, *The Life of the Learned Sir John Cheke* (1705), 251; *The Second [to Seventh] Sermon of Master Hugh Latimer*, sig. B4r; Edward Cardwell, ed., *The Reformation of Ecclesiastical Laws as Attempted in the Reigns of King Henry VIII, King Edward VI and Queen Elizabeth* (Oxford, 1850), 28-29; qtd. in Leonard W. Levy, *Treason Against God: A History of the Offence of Blasphemy* (New York, 1981), 186-87; Roger Ascham, *The Schoolmaster,* ed. Lawrence V. Ryan (Ithaca, 1968), 71; *Calendar of State Papers, Domestic, Addenda, 1566-1579*, 439; T[homas] C[ooper], *An Admonition to the People of England* (1589), 125; Thomas Nashe, *Christ's Tears Over Jerusalem* in *Works*, ed. McKerrow, 2: 121-

22; "Of Atheism" from the *Meditationes Sacrae* (1597) in *The Works of Francis Bacon*, ed. James Spedding, Robert Ellis, and Douglas Heath, 7 vols. (London, 1859), 7: 251; Richard Hooker, *Laws of Ecclesiastical Polity*, Vol. 2, ed. George Edelen (Cambridge, MA, 1977), Book 5, ch. 2.2, 24; Martin Havran, *The Catholics in Caroline England* (Stanford, 1962), 83. Gondomar's tally distinguishes between recusants, Catholics attending Protestant worship, Puritans, mainstream Protestants, and atheists. For modern accounts of unbelief in this period see, George Buckley, *Atheism in the English Renaissance* (Chicago, 1932); Don Cameron Allen, *Doubt's Boundless Sea* (Baltimore, 1964); William Elton, *King Lear and the Gods* (San Marino, 1966); G. E. Aylmer, "Unbelief in the Seventeenth Century" in *Puritans and Revolutionaries*, ed. Donald Pennington and Keith Thomas (Oxford, 1978), 22-46; Patrick Collinson, *The Religion of Protestants* (Oxford, 1982), 189-241; David Wooton, "The Fear of God in Early Modern Political Theory," Canadian Historical Association, *Historical Papers* 18 (1983), 56-79; Michael Hunter, "The Problem of 'Atheism' in Early Modern England," Royal Historical Society, *Transactions* 35 (1985), 135-57; Michael Hunter and David Wooton, eds. *Atheism from the Reformation to the Enlightenment*, (New York, 1992). Many of the primary sources cited herein are referred to in these books and articles.

11. T. W. Baldwin, *William Shakspere's Petty School* (Urbana, 1943), 9-108; Jonathan Goldberg, *Writing Matter* (Stanford, 1990), 31-40. For evidence about increased literacy rates during this period, see David Cressy, *Literacy and the Social Order* (Cambridge, 1980), 160-63.

12. Rosemary O'Day, *The English Clergy* (Leicester, 1979), 27; Cicero, *An Epistle or Letter of Exhortation*, trans. G. Gylby (1561), sig. A2.

13. Henry Bullinger, *Fifty Godly and Learned Sermons. Divided into Five Decades* (London, 1577), 763. For accounts of early anti credal dissidents, see also John Woolton, *A Treatise of the Immortality of the Soul* (1576); and George Williams, *Radical Reformation* (Philadelphia, 1962), 778-90.

14. Bacon, "Of Heresies," from *Meditationes Sacrae* (1597) in *Works*, 7: 253. See Wooton, "The Fear of God in Early Modern Political Theory." For the sixteenth-century definition of "deism," see Hunter, "The Problem of 'Atheism,'" 156.

15. See Hunter, "The Problem of 'Atheism'" especially 139, 142, 143, 153; William Perkins, *A Treatise of Man's Imaginations* (1607), 526-27.

16. Christopher Marlowe, *Dr. Faustus*, ed. Michael Keefer, I.i.45-47; John Calvin, *Institutes of the Christian Religion*, trans. John Allen. 2 vols. (Philadelphia, 1936), 1: 59; *The Psalms of David and Others with J. Calvin's Commentaries*, trans. Arthur Golding (1571), sig. F3v; Theodore Beza, *The Psalms of David Truly Opened and Explained* (1580), sig. B5v; Wooton, "The Fear of God."

17. Shankar Raman notes the latent contradiction in Romans 13:1 in "Desire and Violence in Renaissance England: Christopher Marlowe's *Edward II*."

Deutsche Vierteljahrsschrift, forthcoming. Ascham, *The Schoolmaster*, 70-71; Gervase Babington, *A Very Fruitful Exposition of the Commandments by Questions and Answers* (1583; 1590), sig. A1 a-b.

18. Bacon, "Of Atheism," in *Essayes or Counsels, Civil and Morall*, ed. Michael Kiernan (Cambridge, MA, 1985), 51; *The Works of John Whitgift*, ed. J. Ayre (Cambridge, 1851-3), 3: 176; for Whitgift's idea of the visible church, see Peter Lake, *Anglicans and Puritans?* (London, 1988), 35 and 28-37. For Puritan and Separatist attacks on the "antichristian" Church of England, see John Udall, *The State of the Church of England* (1588), John Bate, *The Portraiture of Hypocrisy* (1589), and Henry Barrow, *A Brief Discovery of the False Church* (1590) in *The Writings of Henry Barrow*, ed. Leland Carlson (London, 1962).

19. *Catechism*, 49 ("renning of the spirit"), 23 ("dead" faith), and 47 (hypocrisy); Bacon, "Of Atheism" in *Essayes*, 53.

20. Henry Barrow, *A Brief Discovery*, 345. For a similar critique see *The Writings of Robert Harrison and Robert Browne*, ed. Leland Carlson and Albert Peel (London, 1953), 173-93; John Case, *Ancilla Philosophiae* (Oxford, 1599), sig. A-Av, as cited in Allen, *Doubt's Boundless Sea.*

21. For the Privy Council's letter, see Wraight, *In Search of Marlowe*, 88; Goldberg, "Sodomy and Society," 373; Charles Nicholl, *The Reckoning: The Murder of Christopher Marlowe* (London, 1992), 94-168; John Michael Archer, *Sovereignty and Intelligence: Spying and Court Culture in the English Renaissance* (Stanford, 1993), 67-93 and passim.

22. *Concertatio Ecclesiae Catholicae in Anglia adversus Calvinopapistus et Puritanos*, ed. John Gibbons and John Fenn (Trier, 1588), 240. Translation supplied by Roy Kendall in "Richard Baines and Christopher Marlowe's Milieu," *English Literary Renaissance* 24 (1994): 507-52.

23. John Field, *A Godly Exhortation by Occasion of the Late Judgement of God, Shewed at Paris Garden* (1583), sig. B5v; Philip Stubbes, *The Anatomy of Abuses* (1583), sig. L6r; Anthony Munday qtd. in E. K. Chambers, *The Elizabethan Stage*, 4 vols. (Oxford, 1923), 4: 211; John Northbrooke, *A Treatise Wherein Dicing, Dancing, Vain Plays . . . are Reproved* (1577), 65.

24. William Rankins, *A Mirror of Monsters* (1587), sig. G1v. Compare Stubbes, *Anatomy*, sig. P4r-v; Field, *A Godly Exhortation*, passim.

25. *Tamburlaine the Great*, ed. J. S. Cunningham (Manchester, 1981), *Part One*, II.vii.1329. All citations to *Tamburlaine* in my text are from this edition. Anthony Brian Taylor, "Notes on Marlowe and Golding," *Notes and Queries* 34 (1987), 192-93; Taylor, "Tamburlaine's Doctrine of Strife and John Calvin," *English Language Notes* 27 (1989), 30-31. See also Crewe, "The Theater of the Idols."

26. *Tamburlaine, Part Two*, IV.i.155-58. Lynette and Eveline Feasey, "Marlowe and the Homilies," *Notes and Queries*, 195 (1950), 7-10.

27. Qtd. in MacLure, 29-30.

28. R. B. Wernham, "Christopher Marlowe in Flushing in 1592," *English Historical Review* 91 (1976), 344-45; Arthur Freeman, "Marlowe, Kyd, and the Dutch Church Libel," *English Literary Renaissance* 3 (1973), 44-52; for Kyd's letters see Wraight, 238-39, 314-15; for the unnamed spy's report on Chomeley, see Wraight, 354-55; Baines' Note is in MacLure, 36-38.

29. For Drury, Baines, and Puckering see E. S. Sprott, "Drury and Marlowe," *Times Literary Supplement* 2 August 1974; and Roy Kendall, "Richard Baines and Christopher Marlowe's Milieu."

30. Goldberg, "Sodomy and Society"; *Selections from the Table Talk of Martin Luther*, trans. Captain Henry Bell (1892), qtd. in Christopher Hill, *The World Turned Upside Down* (New York, 1972), 125-26. For Kyd, see Wraight, 316; for Baines, see MacLure, 36-38.

31. Wooton, "The Fear of God"; Bacon, "Of Atheism"; Calvin, *Institutes,* 1: 55-56, 61; Rankins, *A Mirror of Monsters*, sig. G1r-v.

32. MacLure, 30, 41-42, 47, 30.

33. Constance Kuriyama, "Marlowe, Shakespeare, and the Nature of Biographical Evidence," *University of Hartford Studies in Literature* 20 (1988), 9.

"Thondring Words of Threate" Marlowe, Spenser, and Renaissance Ideas of a Literary Career

Patrick Cheney

The phrase "thondring words of threate" does not come from Marlowe, *Tamburlaine,* or Marlowe's dramatic experiments in tragedy; it comes from Spenser, *The Shepheardes Calender,* and Spenser's poetic representation of tragedy in his pastoral. I would like to situate the Marlovian tragedy of *Tamburlaine* within Spenser's *October* eclogue because we find there an important but neglected origin of Marlowe's project: Spenser's mapping of Renaissance ideas of a literary career.[1]

Ever since 1793, when George Steevens noted the similarity between Tamburlaine's crown in *2 Tamburlaine* (IV.iii.116-24) and Arthur's helmet in *Faerie Queene* I (vii.32), critics have suspected an interchange between the two poets. Almost exclusively, however, they have identified shared passages, argued over which poet imitated which, and generalized about similarities and differences in their styles, temperaments, or ideologies. From the crowning Baldwin/Watkins debate in the 1940s, we now believe that Marlowe imitated Spenser; from the Roma Gill article in the 1990 *Spenser Encyclopedia,* we appear to agree that Marlowe imitated Spenser in 21 of the 22 documented borrowings; and from Stephen Greenblatt's short but brilliant analysis in *Renaissance Self-Fashioning,* we acknowledge that "Spenser and Marlowe are . . . mighty opposites, poised in antagonism."[2]

Greenblatt's analysis characterizes both the value and the limitation of past criticism. Beginning with the two poets' different modes of constructing identity, he remarks: "If Spenser sees human identity as conferred by loving service to legitimate authority, to the yoked power of God and the state, Marlowe sees identity established at those moments in which order . . . is violated" (222). Moving to the poets' translation of identity into types of heroes, Greenblatt observes: "If Spenser's heroes strive for balance and control, Marlowe's strive to shatter the restraints upon their desires" (222).

39

And specifying his argument with one famous example, Greenblatt compares Spenser's representation of Arthur's helmet with Marlowe's representation of Tamburlaine's crown: "What is sung by Spenser in praise of Arthur is sung by Tamburlaine in praise of himself. . . . Marlowe's scene is self-consciously emblematic, as if it were a theatrical improvisation in the Spenserean manner, but now with the hero's place taken by a character who, in his sadistic excess, most closely resembles Orgoglio" (224).

Greenblatt's analysis inspires further investigation. What, for instance, do we make of Marlowe's maneuver through which Tamburlaine sings what Spenser himself has sung? What would motivate Marlowe to stage an "improvisation" of "the Spenserean manner"? And why would the dramatist rewrite Prince Arthur as the sadistically excessive Scythian shepherd? Given the might of the opposition between the two poets, why have *we* not scrutinized that opposition in more detail? Remarkably, we have not discovered a lens that can bring the two contemporaries into significant alignment.

One reason may be that only recently have critics like Greenblatt and Richard Helgerson made available a powerful lens for viewing rivals within a literary system. Accommodating to the Elizabethan literary system Greenblatt's principle that "Self-fashioning is achieved in relation to something perceived as alien" and that this "threatening Other . . . must be . . . attacked and destroyed" (9), Helgerson argues that Spenser fashions his identity as "laureate" poet out of the practices of, and ultimately at the expense of, the Elizabethan "amateurs" — a class of poets, Helgerson says in passing, that includes Marlowe.[3] What Helgerson does not say is that an amateur like Marlowe, who also becomes a "professional" or money-earning dramatist like Shakespeare, fashions his identity out of a laureate like Spenser. In fact, what is engaging about Marlowe in this context is the dynamic equation he creates between laureate, amateur, and professional classes of poets.

Thus I propose to view the mighty opposition through the one lens critics neglect: the career-oriented. By career-oriented, I mean a lens oriented to the Renaissance idea of a literary career, and in particular the "commonplace of Renaissance criticism — the [Virgilian] progression from pastoral to epic."[4] The careeric lens, I wish to argue, is precisely the lens through which we can bring the mighty opposition into significant alignment.

I

Marlowe himself constructs a careeric lens when he opens the Prologue to *1 Tamburlaine*:

> From jigging veins of rhyming mother-wits,
> And such conceits as clownage keeps in pay,
> We'll lead you to the stately tent of War,
> Where you shall hear the Scythian Tamburlaine
> Threat'ning the world with high astounding terms
> And scourging kingdoms with his conquering sword.
>
> (*1 Tamb* Prologue 1-6)

Most critics observe that Marlowe here is expressing "his contempt for the popular theatre of the day" and "his preference for a serious and elevated theme."[5] A few critics; however, do acknowledge that Marlowe is also imitating Spenser's projected Virgilian turn from pastoral to epic in the *October* eclogue:

> Abandon then the base and viler clowne,
> Lyft up thy selfe out of the lowly dust:
> And sing of bloody Mars, of wars, of giusts,
> Turne thee to those, that weld the awful crowne,
> To doubted Knights, whose woundlesse armour rusts,
> And helmes unbruzed wexen dayly browne.[6]
>
> (*October* 37-42)

In both passages, writers advertise their progression from a lower to a higher genre. Both represent this progression through identical images: clownage to war. Both identify similar paradigms to trace the progression: Marlowe represents comedic pastoral as a low-cost and subservient jig, with epic as a martial theater of state; Spenser represents pastoral as a low-based heap of dust from which the young poet must arise, with epic as a military display of royal awe and courtly courage. And both situate the poet's career within the patronage system: Marlowe, cynically ("keeps in pay"; see Leech 42); Spenser, hopefully ("Turne thee to those").

The differences between the two passages, however, are also striking. For instance, Spenser weds the "crowne" of the sovereign with the "helmes" of her "knights" as a synecdoche for epic — a wedding that Marlowe may rewrite when he appropriates Prince Arthur's martial helmet through Tamburlaine's plundered crown. Similarly, Marlowe changes Spenser's self-reflexive, lyrical, "sing[ing]" poet to his own, equally self-reflexive, dramatic, listening audience ("you shall hear"). Finally, in the last two lines Marlowe redraws an important equation between language and action, poetry and empire, when he conjoins "high astounding terms / And . . . conquering sword."[7]

By recalling the analyses of Greenblatt and Helgerson, we can speculate that in his Prologue Marlowe is fashioning his amateur identity as an Elizabethan professional dramatist out of Spenser's laureate art. In *his* inaugural work, Marlowe presents himself as a serious rival to the "new Poete" (E. K., *Dedicatory Epistle to SC* 19) — England's Virgil, the heir of Chaucer, and the direct descendent of Orpheus.[8] What Marlowe proposes is a non-Virgilian career model that moves from amatory poetry, represented by his translation of Ovid's *Amores* and by *The Passionate Shepherd to His Love*, to the higher genres of tragedy and epic, represented by his seven plays and by his two experiments in "epic": the "minor epic" *Hero and Leander* and the translation of Book I of Lucan's *Pharsalia*.[9] I aim to show that Marlowe finds his warrant for this "Ovidian" model of a literary career in Spenser himself. For, as Spenser says in a historically important yet neglected line in his passage on tragedy in relation to epic from his pastoral eclogue, "Bacchus fruite is frend to Phoebus wise" (*October* 106). As early as 1579, nearly a decade before the advent of great Elizabethan tragedy, in a Panic poem projecting the epic career of the Renaissance poet, Spenser is encouraging his colleagues to reconcile Panic and Apollonian verse with Dionysian drama. Marlowe, for one, appears to have taken Spenser's encouragement seriously — but, as we will see, precisely to counter the intentions of the New Poet.

This thesis explains many features of *Tamburlaine 1* and *2,* but it also compels us to observe Marlowe here forging a place for himself out of and within the Elizabethan literary system. The four features that I wish to emphasize highlight the "high astounding terms" through which Marlowe situates himself in this system. Strikingly, the terms are of action, ambition, metamorphosis, and power. They are naturally the main terms by which Spenser advertises himself in *The Shepheardes Calender* and the 1590 *Faerie Queene*. What characterizes the imitation is precisely what Greenblatt observes in only one example: Marlowe transfers to Tamburlaine the terms Spenser selects for himself.

First, whereas Spenser presents himself turning from pastoral to epic, Marlowe presents Tamburlaine as a shepherd usurping the title of a king. Second, whereas Spenser confidently advertises himself as the poet of *translatio imperii,* Marlowe shows Tamburlaine brutally migrating his empire from east to west. Third, whereas Spenser introduces himself as the new Protestant poet of wedded love,

Marlowe depicts his king's wooing of and marriage to the Egyptian princess Zenocrate as an "offensive rape" (*1 Tamb* III.ii.6).[10] And fourth, whereas Spenser vaunts the telos of his verse to be an intimate relation between poetic and martial fame and Christian glory, Marlowe presents Tamburlaine exploding this relation. The sweet fruition of an earthly crown. Marlowe's appropriation of Spenser's self-reflexive terms and actions permits us to characterize the interchange between the two poets as "metadiscursive" — as discourse about discourse.[11] I want to suggest that in its most comprehensive form, the intertextual discourse between the mighty opposites *is* career-oriented. This is quite precisely the case, since the documented borrowings permit me to show Marlowe imitating Spenser in the four discursive domains that I see the New Poet fusing in his idea of a literary career: artistic, political, erotic, and theological. Read from this perspective, the *Tamburlaine* plays, which often hint at Tamburlaine's poetic powers, function as Marlowe's critically charged, metadiscursive project — his public and dramatic attempt to "overgo" Spenser as England's new national poet. As Zenocrate inscribes Tamburlaine's powerful sense of metadiscursive competition, "His talk [is] much sweeter than the Muses' song" (*1 Tamb* III.ii.50); or as Tamburlaine himself appropriates Spenser's Orphic terms, "my words are oracles" (*1 Tamb* III.iii.102). I want to recall that a treasured commonplace of Marlowe criticism — "Tamburlaine is a poet" — has a special historical context. The seventeen borrowings from Spenser in the two plays insist that much of what we say about Tamburlaine we see as Marlowe's competitive rewriting of Spenser.[12]

II

I mean "Marlowe's competitive rewriting of Spenser" quite literally. Critics have not pursued the significance of Greenblatt's observation that what Spenser assigns to himself Marlowe assigns to Tamburlaine. For the most part, they have kept to the other side of the coin; they have pursued the significance of Marlowe's assigning to Tamburlaine the speeches he does. In relating author to protagonist, critics divide into two major camps.

The first, which we might term the "romantic," draws an equation between Marlowe and Tamburlaine, as represented by G. K. Hunter: "The creative daring of *Tamburlaine's* author, his clear intention to defy theatrical orthodoxy, mirrors exactly the creative daring of his hero."[13] This impulse emerges from Marlowe's contemporary antagonists, for in 1588 Robert Greene criticizes Marlowe for "daring God out of heaven with that Atheist

Tamburlan," while in 1593 Gabriel Harvey criticizes the dramatist for his "tamburlaine contempt."[14] If we agree that Marlowe establishes an equation between himself and his protagonist, we can, from the perspective of the present argument, read his two-part play as an advertisement for himself as the shepherd who becomes a king, the rival to the New Poet, who was just then advertising himself in similarly "high astounding terms."

The second camp of critics, the "ironic," denies an equation between Marlowe and Tamburlaine, as represented by Roy W. Battenhouse: "Certainly, . . . there is no very good reason for identifying Marlowe with his stage-character Tamburlaine."[15] If we agree that Marlowe distances himself from Tamburlaine, we can, from the perspective of the present argument, assume that Marlowe is criticizing the shepherd who becomes a king.

While Battenhouse's "ironic" reading has the limitations that most critics now assign to it, I want to suggest that we need to pause a little more over his argument than recent critics have done. In particular, I want to follow his lead in order to link Marlowe's detachment from Tamburlaine with Marlowe's imitation of Spenser. I do so to reverse and then revise his formulation. Specifically, I want to align the division between the two camps of critics with a strategy identified by Greenblatt, in which Marlowe's genius resides in his power to construct a single narrative having both an orthodox and an unorthodox significance: Marlowe condemns Tamburlaine as an anti-Christian villain who succumbs to Christian authority; simultaneously, Marlowe exults in Tamburlaine as an anti-Christian hero who challenges Christian authority.[16] I then want to superimpose Marlowe's dramatic strategy in representing Tamburlaine — what Charles Nicholl calls "these ambidextrous responses" (170) — onto the topic of Marlowe's imitation of Spenser.

Who is the shepherd who becomes a king?

Literally, he is "Tamburlaine."

In Marlowe's evocation of Tamburlaine as an anti-Christian hero who challenges the orthodoxy, the Scythian Shepherd inscribes Christopher Marlowe, a serious rival in the Virgilian program to England's New Poet. But in Marlowe's evocation of Tamburlaine as an anti-Christian villain who succumbs to Christian authority, he inscribes Edmund Spenser, the "masqued" pretender to Christian authority. The *Tamburlaine* plays are simultaneously an advertisement for Marlowe as England's new poet and a critique of Spenser as the old poet.

Marlowe's strategy is to restate the Virgilian progression within a "tragical discourse" (Robert Jones, "To the Gentlemen Readers"), and his professional goal is to deauthorize the medium of published verse in order to construct a new zone of authority for the (disreputable) Elizabethan stage.

It is Marlowe's new zoning project — his rival poetics — that I wish to throw into high relief.

What renders this project unique in the history of poetic rivalry, so far as I can tell, is Marlowe's brilliant strategy of relying on one dramatic figure — Tamburlaine — to represent "the figure of the rival poet" — both the writerly self and the artistic Other: both himself and Spenser. Greenblatt appears on the verge of discovering this strategy when analyzing Marlowe's "borrowing" of Spenser's Arthurian plume: "even as we are struck by the radical difference, we are haunted by the vertiginous possibility of an underlying sameness. What if Arthur and Tamburlaine are not separate and opposed? What if they are two faces of the same thing, embodiments of the identical power?" (224).

Two faces of the same thing . . . What if? Greenblatt is not the first to propose a haunting similarity between the mighty opposites. Our very first comparison — by Leigh Hunt in 1844 — is eloquent on the vertiginous possibility of an underlying sameness: Marlowe's "imagination, like Spenser's, haunted those purely poetic regions of ancient fabling and modern rapture, of beautiful forms and passionate expressions, which they were the first to render the common property of inspiration, and whence their language drew 'empyreal air.' Marlowe and Spenser are the first of our poets who perceived the beauty of words" (*Imagination and Fancy*, qtd. in MacLure 91). My guess is that Spenser would be horrified. He worked hard to dissociate his art from the kind Marlowe popularized, but it is striking that some of his original readers — Lord Burleigh, for instance — mistook the one for the other (*Faerie Queene* IV.Pr.1). If I am right, however, Marlowe does succeed in the *Tamburlaine* plays in challenging Spenser's authority precisely by representing their "underlying sameness."

III

Marlowe's metadiscursive inscription of his hero as a rewriting of Spenser is clear in the first or artistic domain: his documented imitation of the Proem to Book I of the 1590 *Faerie Queene*. To open his Proem, Spenser announces his typological fulfillment of his *October* advertisement (quoted earlier):

> Lo I the man, whose Muse whilome did maske,
> As time her taught, in lowly Shepheards weeds,
> Am now enforst a far unfitter taske,

For trumpets sterne to chaunge mine Oaten reeds. (1)

In this passage, Spenser identifies himself as the author of *The Shepheardes Calender* and announces his generic turn from Virgilian pastoral to Virgilian epic.

Repeatedly, Marlowe reminds us that his hero is a shepherd who becomes a king. We first encounter the idea on the title page to the 1590 edition: "Tamburlaine the Great. Who, from a Scythian Shephearde by his rare and woonderfull Conquests, became a most puissant and mightye Monarque." We encounter the idea again in Robert Jones' *Dedicatory Epistle:* "I have here published in print for your sakes the two tragical discourses of the Scythian shepherd Tamburlaine, that became so great a conqueror and so mighty a monarch" (111). Both prefatory advertisements alert us to the central feature of Marlowe's ensuing narrative.

Thus, in his first appearance, Tamburlaine inscribes his identity in Spenserian terms to his future wife: "I am a lord, for so my deeds shall prove, / And yet a shepherd by my parentage" (*1 Tamb* I.ii.34-35). Consequently, in his first act Tamburlaine exchanges attire with Spenserian precedent: "Lie here, ye weeds that I disdain to wear! / This complete armour and this curtle-axe / Are adjuncts more beseeming Tamburlaine" (41-43). As critics observe, in exchanging shepherd's "weeds" for a warrior king's "armour," the oaten reed for the "curtle-axe," Marlowe is imitating Spenser's career "chaunge" from pastoral to epic. Applying the dramatic strategy of *ambidexterity* identified by Nicholl, we can say that Marlowe is, on the one hand, boldly advertising his own generic progression ("Lie here, ye weeds"), and, on the other, criticizing Spenser for arrogance in advertising his ("disdain to wear").

In *1 Tamburlaine,* as critics also note, the Scythian Shepherd targets Spenser again in order to justify his own self-metamorphosis and quest for fame: "Jove sometimes masked in a shepherd's weed, / And by those steps that he hath scaled the heavens, / May we become immortal like the gods" (I.ii.198-200). The lines brilliantly reproduce the very process of competitive imitation that Marlowe is enacting. Not simply does Tamburlaine become immortal by imitating Jove the masking shepherd, but Marlowe achieves fame by imitating the masking shepherd Spenser. A great reckoning in a little room.[17]

Marlowe's metadiscursive inscription of his hero as a rewriting of Spenser is also clear in the second or political domain: his imitation of Spenser's program of *translatio imperii*.[18] Not merely is Marlowe's hero a shepherd who becomes a king, but repeatedly he is "the monarch of the East" (*1 Tamb* I.i.43, I.ii.185, *2 Tamb* III.ii.22; see *1 Tamb* II.vii.62) who brutally moves his empire westward. In *1 Tamburlaine,* for instance, the king proclaims, "Those walled garrisons will I subdue, / And write myself great lord of Africa: / So from the East unto the furthest West, / Shall Tamburlaine extend his puissant arm" (III.iii.244-47). In the past, critics have glossed this passage — and the similar one in *2 Tamburlaine* ("Stretching your conquering arms from east to west" [I.iii.97]) — by turning to Spenser's description of the Church of England in *Faerie Queene* I, where the sovereign "scepters" of Una's ancestors "stretcht from East to Westeme shore" (I.i.5; see Bakeless 1: 207). But Spenser's line is a religious and political version of the translation of empire that he personalizes in *October* and that I shall argue is the most direct source especially of the second *Tamburlaine* passage, as the nearly identical phrasing implies. Continuing his description of the "awful crown" of epic (already quoted), Spenser writes: "There may thy Muse display her fluttryng wing, / And stretch her selfe at large from East to West" (43-44). Spenser's self-reflexive advertisement for *translatio imperii* helps explain Marlowe's otherwise peculiar notion that Tamburlaine *writes* empire through kingly action. I will return to the avian image of the Muse's imperial wing shortly.

That Marlowe's paradigm for *translatio imperii* — "east to west" — has specifically Spenserian evocations is clear from another example: a speech of Tamburlaine's from which I have quoted twice before, in which Tamburlaine presents himself as a shepherd who becomes a king and then dramatizes his change by donning the attire of a warrior, adding that he will "Measur[e] . . . the limits of his empery / By east and west as Phoebus doth his course" (*1 Tamb* I.ii.39-40). By having Tamburlaine inscribe the arc of his "empery" from "east to west" within this Spenserian matrix, Marlowe can both advertise himself as the new poet of empire and criticize Spenser as the false poet of empire.

As the above episode anticipates, Marlowe's metadiscursive inscription of his hero as a rewriting of Spenser is clear in the third or erotic domain: his imitation of Spenser's Protestant representation of erotic desire.[19] In addition to Tamburlaine's turn from shepherd to king and his translation of empire from east to west, Marlowe's hero woos Zenocrate as an act of male mastery — a critique of Spenser's falsely imitated Ariostan claims to sympathy for the female sex (*Faerie Queene* I.iii.1-2) and his equally hypocritical Chaucerian assertions about the mutuality between the sexes (*Faerie Queene* III.i.25).

Tamburlaine's soliloquy in *1 Tamburlaine,* in which he debates whether to abide by his humanist-based code of manly reason or to listen to his new romantic-based code of feminine passion, seems deeply indebted to Spenser. "Ah fair Zenocrate, divine Zenocrate," he begins, "Where Beauty, mother to the Muses, sits / And comments volumes with her ivory pen" (V.i.135, 144-45):

> What is beauty, saith my sufferings, then?
> If all the pens that ever poets held
> Had fed the feeling of their masters' thoughts
> And every sweetness that inspired their hearts,
> Their *minds* and muses on *admired* themes;
> If all the heavenly quintessence they still
> From their *immortal* flowers of poesy,
> Wherein as in a *mirror* we perceive
> The *highest* reaches of a human wit —
>
> . . . .
>
> But how unseemly is it for my sex,
> My discipline of arms and chivalry,
>
> . . .
>
> To harbour thoughts effeminate and faint!
> (*1 Tamb* V.i.160-77; emphasis added)

The "mirror" image here, I suggest, may echo a passage in *October* in which Piers explains to Cuddie about the Neoplatonic power of Colin Clout's love: "for love does teach him climbe so *hie,* / And lyftes him up out of the loathsome myre: / Such *immortall mirrhor,* as he doth *admire,* / Would rayse ones *mynd* above the starry skie" (91-96; emphasis added).[20] Whereas Piers imagines the male's mental admiration of the female's immortally beautiful mirror as the vehicle for Neoplatonic inspiration and transcendence, Tamburlaine problematizes the process, fearing its effeminizing violation of his martial code. The lines with which Tamburlaine's soliloquy concludes ("The most obscure passage in the text of the play" [Harper, ed., 77]) appear to imitate Spenser's passage on his turn from pastoral to epic, as William Baldwin's analysis suggests, but the language is more widely Spenserian, as is the basic thought, which the play is at pains to explode: that "love and honour . . . can never be incompatible, since love of beauty provides the inspiration necessary to the heroism of the warrior" (Harper, ed., 77).

Tamburlaine concludes his soliloquy by talking of how he feels

> the lovely warmth of shepherds' flames
> And march [or mask] in cottages of strewed weeds
> Shall give the world to note, for all my birth,
> That virtue solely is the sum of glory
> And fashions men with true nobility.[21]
> (*1 Tamb* V.i.186-90)

Assimilating claims for the virtue of eros to the career model of shepherd and king, Marlowe relies on key words from Spenser's epic: "virtue," "fashions," and "true nobility." For, in *The Letter to Ralegh*, Spenser states that the "generall end . . . of all the booke is to *fashion* a gentleman or *noble* person in *vertuous* and gentle discipline" (3: 485). Marlowe echoes the word *discipline* earlier in the soliloquy when Tamburlaine refers to "My discipline of arms and chivalry," a euphonious parody of Una's "discipline of faith and veritie" (I.vi.31). In *Tamburlaine,* Marlowe presents his protagonist as the lover and husband of Zenocrate first to criticize Spenser's advertisement of himself as the national poet of love and marriage, and second to map out thereby the domain of homoeroticism lying latent in the play (see, e.g., Kuriyama). For Marlowe, love of female beauty inspires masculine violence, both sexual and social, as Tamburlaine's initial "lawless rapine from a silly maid" reveals (*1 Tamb* I.ii.10), and as his final response to Zenocrate's death confirms: "This cursed town will I consume with fire / Because this place bereft me of my love" (*2 Tamb* II.iv.137-38).

Tamburlaine's soliloquy also introduces us to our last "high astounding term" through which Marlowe relies on metadiscourse to rewrite Spenser: "glory." The idea of fame and glory runs powerfully throughout the *Tamburlaine* plays — to the extent that the idea dominates the text like perhaps no other. Cosroe calls Tamburlaine "the man of fame, / The man that in the forehead of his fortune / Bears figures of renown and miracle" (*1 Tamb* II.i.2-4), and Tamburlaine himself claims that his goal is to "spread . . . [his] fame through hell and up to heaven" (V.i.468).[22]

In *October,* as the already quoted image of the winged imperial Muse indicates, Spenser relies on an avian image of fame to represent his Virgilian career model: "For Colin fittes such famous flight to scanne" (88; see *Spenser's Famous Flight* 14-18, 3-37). In *Tamburlaine,* Marlowe often represents fame as winged (e.g., *1 Tamb* I.ii.202-06, II.iii.55-59, III.iii.156-60). But his clearest response to Spenser's "famous flight" occurs when Theridamus tells Olympia of Tamburlaine's project:

> And eagle's wings joined to her feathered breast,
> Fame hovereth, sounding of her golden trump,
> That to the adverse poles of that straight line
> Which measureth the glorious frame of heaven,
> The name of mighty Tamburlaine is spread.
> (*2 Tamb* III.iv.62-66)

Here Marlowe reduces the famous flight to the perfect bliss and sole felicity of an earthly crown. In Marlowe's project, earthly fame is irreconcilable with Christian glory.

In this career context, not simply Greenblatt's generalized context of heroic and artistic "identity," must we read Tamburlaine's appropriation of Arthur's helmet — Marlowe's master-trope for a tragedy of violent infamy. Spenser had represented Arthur's "haughtie helmet" (I.vii.31) as topped by a "loftie crest" with a "bunch of haires discolourd diversly," which "shake" and "daunce for jollity" (32),

> Like to an Almond tree ymounted hye,
> On top of greene Selinis all alone,
> With blossomes brave bedecked daintily;
> Whose tender locks do tremble every one
> At every little breath, that under heaven is blowne.
>
> (*Faerie Queene* I.vii.32)

In the "Almond tree," Spenser alludes to Numbers 17:5-8, in which Aaron's rod blossoms and bears ripe almonds, revealing him to be ordained by God for glory, while in "greene Selinis" Spenser alludes to Virgil's *Palmosa Selinus* in the *Aeneid* (III.705), signifying the town of the victor's palm — a representation, that is, for military victory and its reward, the palm or fame.[23] While "ymounted hye" and "all alone" both suggest pride and individuality, "jollity," "daunce," "tender," and "tremble" all suggest a playful humility — a paradigm of virtue that Spenser calls in *Epithalamion* "proud humility" (306). Spenser locates the Christian almond tree on "top" of the classical hill — a fusing of classical and Christian, as well as an accurate model of the hierarchical relation between the two (Christian on top, classical on bottom). By fusing Scripture with Virgil, Spenser can use his "greene Selinis" simile as a trope for the cohesion between Arthur's military fame and his Christian glory.

By contrast, Marlowe describes Tamburlaine's crown this way:

> And in my helm a triple *plume* shall spring,
> Spangled with diamonds dancing in the air,
> To *note* me emperor of the threefold world:
> Like to an almond tree ymounted high
> Upon the lofty and celestial mount
> Of *ever-green* Selinus, quaintly decked
> With blooms more white than Herycina's brows,
> Whose tender blossoms tremble every one

> At every little breath that thorough heaven is blown.
> (*2 Tamb* IV.iii.116-24; emphasis added)

This is close to "plagiarism"; but, as critics note, Marlowe is "imitating" in the Renaissance sense: borrowing and transforming. Greenblatt writes: "Lines that for Spenser belong to the supreme figure of civility, the chief upholder of the Order of Maidenhead, the worshipful servant of Gloriana, for Marlowe belong to the fantasy life of the Scythian Scourge of God" (224).

To this, I would add Marlovian metadiscourse ("note me"), signaled by four of Marlowe's additions. First, he adds the word "ever" to Spenser's simple "green" to create the phrase "evergreen," perhaps to clarify the *laurel* greening of Selinus — a trope for the poet's art. Second, Marlowe inserts the line comparing the blossoms on the almond tree to "Herycina's brows" (the brows of Venus); this is a crucial move because it overwrites Spenser's fusion of Virgil and Scripture with an Ovidian-based trope that eroticizes the entire simile (*Amores* II.x.11, III.ix.45, *Ars amatoria* II.420, *Met* V.363; see Baldwin 158-62; and Cunningham, ed. 296). Third, Marlowe replaces Spenser's orthodox troping of the hierarchical Christian cosmos "*under* heaven" with the nonhierarchical troping "*thorough* heaven," further deconstructing Spenser's Christian ideology. Finally, Marlowe clarifies the avian base of the crown image, "plume" (as opposed to Spenser's non-avian "crest" and "haires"). Tamburlaine's "triple plume" has more than the obvious military significance. The plume is a bird's feather — a quill, the poet's actual writing implement. Thus Tamburlaine's "plume" functions as a metonym for the equation between words and action, "high astounding terms" and "conquering sword."

In *Edward II*, Marlowe unpacks the metadiscursive significance of the military plume in a speech by Mortimer, who interrogates Edward darkly: "When wert thou in the field with banner spread? / But once! And then *thy soldiers marched like players, / . . .*; and thyself, . . . / Nodding and shaking of thy spangled *crest*, / Where women's favours hung like labels down" (II.ii.181-86; emphasis added). The metadiscursive significance of the plume emerges even more powerfully when we recall, as Hamlet does, that tragic actors wore, not simply the buskins on their feet, but a "forest of feathers" on their head.[24] Thus inscribed, Tamburlaine invents his return flight to his origin — not Spenser's New Jerusalem (*Faerie Queene* I.x.61), but Samarcanda, an eastern House of Pride, as Marlowe's documented borrowing here reveals (*2 Tamb* IV.iii.107 and *Faerie Queene* I.iv.4); not by the wings of Christian glory, but, as another documented borrowing reveals, on the martial chariot of Lucifera —

"drawn with princely eagles" (127 and *Faerie Queene* I.iv.17). Tamburlaine's motive? To "Be famous" (110).

The metadiscourse ordering the plume here throws into high relief the comment by Paul Alpers, who singles out the Selinus stanza as "one of the most admired in *The Faerie Queene*" and suggests, "following Eliot's acute observation. . . , that 'Marlowe's mighty line' owes as much to the additive, formulaic verse of *The Faerie Queene* as to any earlier blank verse" ("Style," *The Spenser Encyclopedia* 675). Alpers anticipates a salient point. In Tamburlaine's plume, Marlowe mimetically inscripts his Spenserian origin. But the dramatist rewrites that origin: *tragically, materially, vertically* — on the stage, on earth, in time: in a forest of feathers. This is Marlowe's famous flight.

IV

I would like to conclude, then, by recalling the passage in *October* from which my title comes and in which I believe Marlowe formally finds the genesis of his tragic art. Indeed, if Marlowe's plays are about a shepherd who becomes a king, we can expect the imitative system in *Tamburlaine 1* and *2* to derive from both *The Shepheardes Calender* and *The Faerie Queene*. In *Spenser's Famous Flight,* I argue that the bulk of *October* shows Spenser revising the Virgilian career model of pastoral and epic with a four-genre model: Virgilian pastoral, Virgilian epic, Petrarchan love lyric, and the Augustinian-based hymn (7). I further suggest that at least one of Spenser's major disciples, Michael Drayton, follows Spenser in shaping his literary career around this model (40-41). At the end of the eclogue, I also observe, Spenser appears to introduce an alternate and even separate model, which another disciple, Samuel Daniel, follows (43-45). In this model, the poet moves from Ovidian verse to tragedy and epic, as the shepherd Cuddie explains to Piers:

> For lordly love is such a Tyranne fell:
> That where he rules, all power he doth expell.
> . . .
> Who ever casts to compasse weightye prise,
> And thinks to throwe out thondring words of threate:
> Let powre in lavish cups and thriftie bitts of meate,
> For Bacchus fruite is frend to Phoebus wise.
>
> . . .
> Thou kenst not Percie howe the ryme should rage.
> O if my temples were distain'd with wine,
> And girt in girlonds of wild Yvie twine,

> How I could reare the Muse on stately stage,
> And teache her tread aloft in bus-kin fine,
> With queint Bellona in her equipage.[25]
>
> (*October* 98-114)

Is Marlowe in essence not born here, and with him Elizabethan tragedy? That brilliant analyst of the Elizabethan literary scene, Joseph Hall, implies as much when he echoes Spenser's phrasing to describe Marlowe in *Virgidemiae*: Marlowe "vaunts his voyce" in "thundring threats" (I.iii; qtd. in MacLure 41). Richard Levin believes that Marlowe is the Rival Poet of Shakespeare's *Sonnets*, and now Maurice Charney, James Shapiro, and Thomas Cartelli have brought the two dramatists into significant alignment.[26] But we must not forget that in the Elizabethan literary system Marlowe initially found his artistic genesis, not in the plays of a fellow professional, but in the nondramatic works of the "Brytanne Orpheus" (R.S., *Commendatory Verse* to the 1590 *Faerie Queene* 4:4).

In *Tamburlaine,* Marlowe drinks the Bacchic fruit, girts his head with the ever-green garland of wild Selinus, and rears the muse on stately stage. But unlike the gentle Daniel, he does not teach the muse to tread aloft in buskin *fine*, with Bellona *queint* in her equipage. Instead, he relies on alcohol to stage a metadiscursive poetics of violent infamy that powerfully contests the art of England's New Poet. What Marlowe contests *is* the famous flight, with its elitist artistic progression through the (aristocratic) Virgilian genres, its tyrannical political program of *translatio imperii,* its hypocritical Protestant doctrine of wedded love, and its huge claim to link poetic and martial fame with Christian glory. As Clarke Hulse says, Marlowe qualifies as "an inspired poet" (96) in the Platonic tradition indebted to Orpheus, but "Marlowe's inspiration appears to be of a dark kind; he is one of those whom Cicero feared would be made dangerous by their eloquence. One may wonder, in fact, if Marlowe is not Plato's first kind of madman, whose fury arises not from divinity, but from alcohol, lechery, or mental disturbance" (100).

In Tamburlaine's "Threat'ning the world with high astounding terms," Marlowe throws back to Spenser his "thondring words of threate." But in the process Marlowe teaches Elizabethan culture, including his great dramatic successor, the plumed swan of Avon, what Spenser had failed to teach, when he chose not to publish his now oblivious *Nine Comedies* or take the fiery Cuddie's advice to let the buskin walk on the Elizabethan stage, choosing instead to follow "the olde famous Poete Chaucer" (E. K., *Dedicatory Epistle* to *SC* 1-2) in relocating dramatic tragedy within the lyric genre of the complaint (*Spenser's Famous Flight* 258, n. 18): just how, when staging the stately tent of war, the Ovidian dramatist could make Bacchus a friend to Phoebus.

Thou kenst not, Spenser, how the rhyme should rage.[27]

Notes

1. All quotations from Spenser come from *The Poetical Works of Edmund Spenser,* eds. J. C. Smith and Ernest de Selincourt, 3 vols. (Oxford, 1909-10). I modernize the archaic i-j and u-v, as well as other obsolete typographical conventions such as the italicizing of names and places. All quotations from Marlowe's *Tamburlaine* come from *Tamburlaine the Great,* ed. J. S. Cunningham (Manchester, 1981). All quotations from other Marlowe plays come from *The Plays of Christopher Marlowe,* ed. Roma Gill (London, 1971). All quotations from Marlowe's nondramatic poetry come from *The Complete Poems and Translations,* ed. Stephen Orgel (Harmondsworth, 1971).

2. In *The Plays of William Shakespeare* (London, 1793), Steevens expressed surprise at finding Spenser's 1590 simile in Marlowe's 1587-88 play; but Todd, in *The Works of Edmund Spenser* (London, 1805), explained that Marlowe had access to Spenser's manuscript and was thus the "plagiarist" (qtd. in *The Works of Edmund Spenser: A Variorum Edition,* ed. Edwin Greenlaw, et al., 11 vols. [Baltimore, 1932-57] 1: 252-53). Until 1942, critics agreed with Todd, including Georg Schoeneich, *Der Litterarische Einfluss Spensers auf Marlowe* (Halle, 1907); and Charles Crawford, "Edmund Spenser, 'Locrine,' and 'Selimus,'" *Notes and Queries* 7 (1901), 61-63, 101-03, 142-44, 203-05, 261-63, 324-25, 384-86. Then T. W. Baldwin argued that Spenser was the plagiarist ("The Genesis of Some Passages Which Spenser Borrowed from Marlowe," *English Literary History* 9 [1942],157-87). But W. B. C. Watkins rejected Baldwin's argument ("The Plagiarist: Spenser or Marlowe?" *English Literary History* 11 [1944], 249-65). For readers today, Gill states the consensus, which agrees with Todd and Watkins ("Marlowe, Christopher," *The Spenser Encyclopedia* [Toronto, 1990], 453-54; my tabulation of 22 borrowings comes from Gill's citations). See Douglas Bush, "Marlowe and Spenser," *Times Literary Supplement* (1 January 1938), 12; John D. Jump, "Spenser and Marlowe," *Notes and Queries* 209 (1964), 261-62; A. B. Taylor, "Britomart and the Mermaids: A Note on Marlowe and Spenser," *Notes and Queries* 216 (1971), 224-25; David Wright Coe, "Arthur and Tamburlaine's Cosmological Dispute: A Clash of Realities in the Works of Spenser and Marlowe" (diss. U of Texas at Austin, 1980); and Patrick Cheney, "Love and Magic in *Doctor Faustus:* Marlowe's Indictment of Spenserian Idealism," *Mosaic* 17.4 (1984), 93-

109. Greenblatt's short analysis in *Renaissance Self-Fashioning: From More to Shakespeare* (Chicago, 1980), 222-24, has attracted surprisingly little response.

3.   Richard Helgerson, *Self-Crowned Laureates: Spenser, Jonson, Milton and the Literary System* (Berkeley, 1983), 21-54. On Marlowe, see 36. As yet, no one has investigated Marlowe's "idea of a literary career." This state contrasts with that in Spenser studies: see, e.g., David L. Miller, "Spenser's Vocation, Spenser's Career," *English Literary History* 50 (1983), 197-231; Joseph Loewenstein, "Echo's Ring: Orpheus and Spenser's Career," *English Literary Renaissance* 16 (1986), 287-302; Richard Rambuss, *Spenser's Secret Career* (Cambridge, 1993); and my *Spenser's Famous Flight: A Renaissance Idea of a Literary Career* (Toronto, 1993).

4.   William Stanford Webb, "Vergil in Spenser's Epic Theory," in *Critical Essays on Spenser from "ELH"* (Baltimore, 1970), 8. Orig. pub. *English Literary History* 4 (1937), 62-84.

5.   J. W. Harper in his notes to *Tamburlaine* (London, 1971), 7. Similarly, in his gloss on "jigging," Cunningham finds Marlowe referring only to conventions of the Elizabethan stage (113). On "the kinds of drama" to which Marlowe refers, see Clifford Leech, *Christopher Marlowe: Poet for the Stage*, ed. Anne Lancashire (New York, 1986), 42-67.

6.   See John Bakeless, *The Tragicall History of Christopher Marlowe,* 2 vols. (1942; Hamden, CT, 1964), 1: 208. Kimberly Benston does refer to the Virgilian origins of Marlowe's Prologue, but he neglects the Spenserian origin ("Beauty's Just Applause: Dramatic Form and the Tamburlanian Sublime," *Christopher Marlowe,* ed. Harold Bloom [New York, 1986], 215).

7.   On word and sword, see David H. Thurn, "Sights of Power in *Tamburlaine*," *English Literary Renaissance* 19 (1989), 6-7 and n. 7. Harry Levin does gloss Marlowe's "threatening" with a Gascoigne phrase from *The Steele Glas:* "In rhymeless verse, which thundereth mighty threates" (qtd. in *The Overreacher: A Study of Christopher Marlowe* [Cambridge, MA, 1952], 11).

8.   On this Spenserian genealogy, see Thomas H. Cain, "Spenser and the Renaissance Orpheus," *University of Toronto Quarterly* 41 (1971), 24-47. Critics do place Marlowe in the Orphic tradition (Clark Hulse, *Metamorphic Verse: The Elizabethan Minor Epic* [Princeton, 1981], 96-102), but without reference to Spenser. Henry Petowe sees Marlowe as continuing the Orpheus tradition: "Marlowe must frame to Orpheus' melody / Hymns all divine to make heaven harmony" (*The Second Part of "Hero and Leander"* 87-88 [in Orgel, ed. *The Complete Poems,* 95]). I return to this topic later.

9.   In a forthcoming book, *Marlowe's Counterfeit Profession: Ovid, Spenser, Counter-Nationhood,* I argue that in *Ovid's Elegies* Marlowe translates a generic pattern of amatory poetry, tragedy, and epic in order to advertise an

"Ovidian" career model and that his experiments in tragedy and epic begin to fulfill the advertisement. H. Levin anticipates this argument: Tamburlaine's "ascent from 'Scythian Shephearde' to 'mighty Monarque' . . . suggests the course that Marlowe was taking, leaving the pastoral fields of Ovidian lyricism and proceeding in the direction pointed by Lucan's epic imperialism" (32). Hulse calls the Ovidian narrative poem a "minor epic" (16-34), and he emphasizes its role as "the proving ground for . . . epic" (12).

10. On "rape" here, see Alan Shepard, "Endless Sacks: Soldiers' Desire in *Tamburlaine*," *Renaissance Quarterly* 46 (1993), 749.

11. On metadiscourse, I follow Harry Berger, Jr., *Revisionary Play: Studies in the Spenserian Dynamics* (Berkeley, 1988), 462-73. Richard A. Martin helps me understand Marlowe's corresponding project in *Tamburlaine*, which manipulates "the conventions of romance" to "tragedy" ("Marlowe's *Tamburlaine* and the Language of Romance," *PMLA* 93 [1978], 248). See also Marjorie Garber, "Marlovian Vision/Shakespearean Revision," *Research Opportunities in Renaissance Drama* 22 (1979), 3-9; and Greenblatt, who repeatedly draws attention to Marlowe's self-reflexive theatricality (e.g., 201).

12. The quotation on Tamburlaine as a poet comes from A. D. Hope, "*Tamburlaine*: The Argument of Arms," in Bloom 53; orig. pub. in *The Cave and the Spring: Essays on Poetry* (Chicago, 1970).

13. G. K. Hunter, "The Beginnings of Elizabethan Drama," *Renaissance Drama* 17 (1986), 46. Thurn helps explain how Marlowe could identify with a tragic protagonist who ultimately succumbs to death (4-6). Both Richard Levin ("The Contemporary Perception of Marlowe's *Tamburlaine*," *Medieval and Renaissance Drama in England* 1 [1984], 51-70), and Peter Berek, ("*Tamburlaine*'s Weak Sons: Imitation as Interpretation Before 1593," *Renaissance Drama* 13 [1982], 55-82), emphasize that contemporary references and allusions to *Tamburlaine* reveal that Marlowe did not condemn his hero.

14. Greene, *Perimedes the Blacksmith,* qtd. in *Marlowe: The Critical Heritage,* ed. Millar MacLure (London, 1979), 29; Harvey, *A New Letter of Notable Contents,* qtd. in MacLure, 40. R. Levin notes that Greene and Harvey "equate . . . Marlowe with the playwright's protagonist" (65). In *The Reckoning: The Murder of Christopher Marlowe* (London, 1992), Charles Nicholl denies that Harvey targets Marlowe (60-64); but Harvey's criticism of Marlowe as Tamburlaine is part of the historical record. For instance, Harvey refers to "Marlowes bravados" and calls atheism "no Religion, but precise Marlowisme" (qtd. in Hale Moore, "Gabriel Harvey's References to Marlowe," *Studies in Philology* 23 [1926], 341). For two astute analyses of Marlowe's identification with Tamburlaine, see Constance B. Kuriyama, *Hammer or Anvil: Psychological Patterns in Christopher Marlowe's Plays* (New Brunswick, 1980), 1-52; and Matthew

N. Proser, "*Tamburlaine* and the Art of Destruction," *University of Hartford Studies in Literature* 20 (1988), 37-51.

15. Roy Battenhouse, *Marlowe's Tamburlaine: A Study in Renaissance Moral Philosophy*, 2nd ed. (Nashville, 1964), 239. See R. Levin's overview of the "ironic" critics (especially 51 and 66-67, n. 1); they include Douglas Cole, *Suffering and Evil in the Plays of Christopher Marlowe* (Princeton, 1962), 86-120; John P. Cutts, *The Left Hand of God: A Critical Interpretation of the Plays of Christopher Marlowe* (Haddonfield, NJ, 1973), 29-107; W. L. Godshalk, *The Marlovian World Picture* (The Hague, 1974),102-68; and Charles G. Masinton, *Christopher Marlowe's Tragic Vision: A Study in Damnation* (Athens, OH, 1972), 14-55. See Berek, who finds Marlowe "irretrievably ambivalent about his hero's defiant self-creation" (56).

16. Greenblatt writes: "All the signals of the tragic are produced, but the play stubbornly, radically, refuses to become a tragedy" (202). See also Nicholl 170; Johannes H. Birringer, "Marlowe's Violent Stage: 'Mirrors' of Honor in *Tamburlaine*," *English Literary History* 51 (1984), 231-32; and Alan Sinfield, "Tragedy, God, and Writing: Hamlet, Faustus, Tamburlaine," in *Faultlines: Cultural Materialism and the Politics of Dissident Reading* (Berkeley, 1992), 240.

17. We should not simply universalize a passage like this, as David Daiches does in finding "symbols for the undefinable ambitions of the unfettered human imagination" ("Language and Action in Marlowe's *Tamburlaine*," in Bloom 85; orig. pub. in *More Literary Essays* [Chicago, 1968]).

18. On *translatio imperii* in the Renaissance, see William Kerrigan and Gordon Braden, *The Idea of the Renaissance* (Baltimore, 1989), 5-7; and David Quint, "Epic and Empire," *Comparative Literature* 41 (1989), 4-8. On *translatio imperii* and fame, see Elizabeth J. Bellamy, *Translations of Power: Narcissus and the Unconscious in Epic History* (Ithaca, 1992),190-91. On Marlowe's critique of empire and imperialism in *Tamburlaine*, see Stephen X. Mead, "Marlowe's *Tamburlaine* and the Idea of Empire," *Works and Days* 7 (1989), 91-103; Roger Sales, *Christopher Marlowe* (New York, 1991), 56-59; and especially Emily C. Bartels, *Spectacles of Strangeness: Imperialism, Alienation, and Marlowe* (Philadelphia, 1993), 53-81.

19. On marriage in sixteenth-century England, see Heather Dubrow, *A Happier Eden: The Politics of Marriage in the Stuart Epithalamium* (Ithaca, 1990), 1-41, especially 13-14.

20. On the Neoplatonic "mirrhor" (from Plato, *Phaedrus* 255d), see Robert Ellrodt, *Neoplatonism in the Poetry of Spenser* (Geneva, 1960), 32-34. On "immortal mirrhor" as a troping of Elizabeth, see Thomas H. Cain, *The Yale Edition of the Shorter Poems of Edmund Spenser*, ed. William A. Oram, et al. (New Haven, 1989),167-69. On Neoplatonism in Tamburlaine's soliloquy, see Michael J. B. Allen, "Tamburlaine and

Plato: A Colon, A Crux," *Research Opportunities in Renaissance Drama* 23 (1980), 21-31.

21. On Baldwin's emendation of "march" in line 187 to "mask," see 175-76. See also Cunningham, ed., 202.

22. I know of no extended discussion of fame and glory in Marlowe. But see Mark Thornton Burnett on a related term: "Tamburlaine and the Renaissance Concept of Honour," *Studia Neophilologica* 59 (1987), 201-06. On honor and fame in the Renaissance, see *Spenser's Famous Flight* 256, n. 11; for histories of fame, see 248, n. 6; and on poetic fame and Christian glory in Spenser, see 248-49, n. 7.

23. See Spencer, *The Faerie Queene*, ed. A. C. Hamilton (London, 1977), 103.

24. *Hamlet* 3.2.275, in *The Riverside Shakespeare*, ed. G. Blakemore Evans, et al. (Boston, 1974). I'm grateful to Professor Robert R. Edwards for reminding me of the *plume* as a poet's *quill* (personal communication).

25. In *Edmund Spenser's Poetry*, 3rd ed. (New York, 1993), Hugh Maclean and Anne Lake Prescott gloss the first line of this passage — "For lordly love is such a Tyranne fell" — as an "Ovidian conceit" (528, n. 9).

26. Richard Levin, "Another Possible Clue to the Identity of the Rival Poet," *Shakespeare Quarterly* 36 (1985), 213-14; Maurice Charney, "Jessica's Turquoise Ring and Abigail's Poisoned Porridge: Shakespeare and Marlowe as Rivals and Imitators," *Renaissance Drama* 10 (1979), 33-44, and talks at the MLA Convention in New York, 1992, and the Third International Conference on Marlowe in Cambridge, England, 1993; James Shapiro, *Rival Playwrights: Marlowe, Jonson, Shakespeare* (New York, 1991); and Thomas Cartelli, *Marlowe, Shakespeare, and the Economy of Theatrical Experience* (Philadelphia, 1991).

27. For encouragement with this essay, I would like to thank Constance Kuriyama, David Riggs, and Paul Whitfield White. For an astute reading of an earlier version, I especially want to thank Professor Riggs.

Breaking the Canon:
Marlowe's Challenge to the Literary Status Quo in *Hero and Leander*

Georgia E. Brown

Why did Marlowe write *Hero and Leander*? Most critics have attempted to answer this question by approaching the poem as an essay on love. William Keach, for example, maintains that Marlowe's poem is about "the risks, limitations and disappointments of romantic love."[1] Marlowe's intentions are ultimately unrecoverable, but one way of approaching the question is to consider Marlowe's poem in its generic context. *Hero and Leander* is part of the epyllion craze that swept England in the 1590s, and Marlowe's choice of genre defines his interpretation of authorship and his attitudes towards literature. Although love has its attractions, in this essay I will focus on the role *Hero and Leander* played in the literary culture of the 1590s.[2] Marlowe's poem, I will argue, is really about poetry, youth, and shame, and it is only partially about love and the relationship within the sexes, or between the sexes. No doubt Marlowe capitalizes on the scandalous appeal of his erotic tale, but he also uses his erotic material to redefine the role of author and reader and to explore the nature of literary morality. This study explores some of the ways *Hero and Leander* capitalizes on its marginal status and exploits its own guilty errors in order to promote a shamelessly self-indulgent authorial voice, one which came to be associated with a late-Elizabethan literary *avant-garde*.

Most critics who deal with the phenomenon of the 1590s do so by implication, and the primary focus of their study remains the "great" authors and "major" genres which have been awarded a place in the canon by the standards of traditional criticism.[3] As a result, the role played by genre in redefining attitudes towards literature and in mediating the opposing forces of tradition and change has largely been ignored. The particular nature of the 1590s requires a generic approach which acknowledges the range of activity in a particular form, the work of neglected writers as well as canonical figures. Moreover, the 1590s marks the growth of the idea of a literary community, as writers, readers, and Stationers came to see themselves as members of an interdependent community with its own rules, its own personnel, and its own history. Even the best critics of the 1590s, such as Joel Fineman, emphasize individuality at the expense of the interplay between individuality and convention. While acknowledging the dangers of a generic approach, its tendency to highlight conventionality and uniformity at the expense of individuality, I will explore some of the advantages the epyllion offered Marlowe and how he used it to respond to a particular historical and cultural situation. Moreover, the poem raises questions about the relationship of the periphery to the center in the culture of the 1590s and I will show how in Marlowe's hands a brief, disjunctive form like the epyllion contributes to the radical reappraisal of literature in the decade.

The epyllion, which literally means small epic, is a brief narrative poem which is ostensibly about love. It derives its material from Ovid, usually from the *Metamorphoses*, but also from the *Amores*, *Heroides* and *Tristia*, and it treats its subject matter in a particular way. Thus the epyllia are witty, erotic and sophisticated poems which place great emphasis on style and invention. Apart from such technical flourish, the genre is also characterized by extreme self-consciousness as the epyllion writers raid each other, copy each other, and continue each other's work in an ostentatious way, thereby establishing themselves as a group of poets who are instantly fashionable and instantly recognizable, just as George Chapman and Henry Petowe attempted to annex some of Marlowe's charisma by completing *Hero and Leander*.[4] The epyllion was developed in answer to the criticisms which had been leveled against poetry in the 1570s and 1580s. These had attacked poetry on two fronts: the moralists attacked the philosophical basis of literature and its pernicious, immoral effects on writers and readers, while those who were literature's friends often felt compelled to attack the poor quality of what was being produced. Gradually, through the pages of controversy and debate, a literary programme was discovered in response to criticism, and ways of improving the status and quality of English literature were defined.[5] To a certain extent, the critics of literature set the agenda for the 1590s, and they were partly responsible for the twin focus on literary morality and literary technique which became a characteristic feature of the epyllion. Thus when Thomas Lodge inaugurated the new form, with the publication of *Scillaes Metamorphosis* in 1589, he also inaugurated a new standard of poetic achievement. However, the epyllion genre did not become popular until 1593 with the appearance of Shakespeare's *Venus and Adonis* and Marlowe's *Hero and Leander*.[6] These two poems made the epyllion particularly fashionable for young writers, but this was a short-lived phenomenon, and by about 1600 the epyllion had started to give way to other more fashionable forms, particularly satire. The genesis of the genre in the pages of debate may help to explain its relatively short life-span, as the literary agenda changed during the 1590s, partly because of the impact of the epyllion, and new issues and new problems came to the fore which rendered the epyllion redundant. Such issues needed different generic approaches, and the epyllion, which had been born in the Inns of Court, was replaced by the newer Inns of Court fashion for satire.[7]

Once of the most striking characteristics of the literary culture of the 1590s is the centrality of marginal forms. Indeed, the innovations which characterize literary activity in the period often took place in these marginal forms, and the most characteristic genres of the decade — for example, the epyllion, the epithalamium, the sonnet sequence and the complaint — all explore threshold states and points of coming into being. They preserve and re-enact the experience of transformation, whether this involves change from youth to maturity, from solitude to society, from private to public, or from one genre to another. *Hero and Leander* is one such marginal form, a brief epic which brings itself to a premature close. Yet its importance to the literary culture of the 1590s lies in its very marginality. In fact, Marlowe's poem capitalizes on its own short-comings. Ostensibly, it sets out to tell the story of the love affair between Hero and Leander, but it wanders into florid descriptions, extended analogies, and narrative digressions, the most famous being the story of Mercury and the country maid, all of which challenge the readers' narrative expectations. It even ends abruptly with the phrase "*Desunt nonnulla,*" "some things are lacking." Such narrative and tonal surprises serve to assert authorial control over the text, turning *Hero and Leander* into a confident assertion of the narrator's virtuoso poetic skills.[8] Moreover, the poem is a polymorphic text full of other forms, such as blazon, pastoral, and satire, which threaten to engulf the narrative at moments such as the elaborate description of Leander's beauties (51-90) or the digression of Mercury and the country maid (385-484).

Thus *Hero and Leander* expands what we might expect to be marginal narrative and generic elements, and in its promotion of the periphery to the center, it proclaims its association with Ovid's *Metamorphoses* with their own structural elaboration of peripheral narrative material. In the 1590s, the *Metamorphoses* came to epitomize literary creativity through its association with the metamorphic power of wit, and writers acknowledged a parallel between the principle of transformation and literary imagination.[9] Thus while the epyllion, like the pastoral, is presented as the inaugural gesture in a writer's career, the epyllion substitutes the Ovidian model for Virgilian *gravitas*. The Virgilian career pattern complements the Humanist conception of literature which emphasizes allegory and didacticism and always points to values that are outside the fictional boundary of the text. In opposition to this seriousness, the epyllion writers open their careers with erotic gallimaufries which move between forms for aesthetic reasons and parody the need for consistent morality. Witty, erotic, metamorphic Ovid is set up as a challenge to Virgil. A very different career is being mapped out by the epyllion, and it is one whose structure stands in opposition to the respected Virgilian archetype.[10]

The stylistic elements of *Hero and Leander* constitute a witty defense of authorial status, asserting authorial whim as the origin and end of the text. Not only do its polished eroticism and witty metamorphoses set new standards of poetic achievement, but Marlowe also adapts his classical and specifically Ovidian models to engage with contemporary debates about the nature and value of poetry. In short, *Hero and Leander* defends the creative power of the individual and defines a specific space for literature which is free from the strictures of morality. As Henry Petowe points out in the preface to his continuation of *Hero and Leander* (1598), his poem is "the first fruits of an unripe wit, done at certain vacant hours"; thus it is presented as a digressive and dilatory activity which highlights the relationship between literature and leisure, as well as the relationship between the epyllion and youthfulness.[11] Similarly, Marlowe's *Hero and Leander* is presented as a locus of private recreative activity for both writer and reader, as well as its protagonists, as it defines an area of activity which is beyond the limits and conditions of normal experience. From one perspective, the love affair between Hero and Leander is nothing more than a holiday romance, as they meet during the festival of Adonis, a time of celebration which is set off from normal business:

> (For his sake whom their goddesse held so deare,
> Rose-cheekt *Adonis*) kept a solemne feast,
> Thither resorted many a wandring guest,
> To meet their loves; such as had none at all,
> Came lovers home, from this great festivall.
>   (91-96)

Apart from the production and consumption of tales, the leisure activity that figures most prominently in Marlowe's poem is sex. *Hero and Leander* is about sexual activity which has been forbidden or marginalized. Lovely Hero is "Venus' nun" and has vowed herself to chastity in the service of the goddess of love, yet she falls in love with Leander, perhaps not surprisingly given the nature of

Venus. The descriptions of Hero and Leander are interwoven with references to violent, forbidden, or perverted sexuality. The description of "*Venus* glasse" (142), the pavement in Venus' temple, invokes the context of transgressive sexuality:

> There might you see the gods in sundrie shapes,
> Committing headdie ryots, incest, rapes:
>
> (143-44)

The whole text indulges in erotic fantasy, most famously in the description of Leander's encounter with Neptune, where the homoerotic overtones allude to another form of forbidden and marginalized love:

> The god put *Helles* bracelet on his arme,
> And swore the sea should never doe him harme.
> He clapt his plumpe cheekes, with his tresses playd,
> And smiling wantonly, his love bewrayd.
> He watcht his armes, and as they opend wide,
> At every stroke, betwixt them would he slide,
> And steale a kisse, and then run out and daunce,
> And as he turnd, cast many a lustfull glaunce,
> And threw him gawdie toies to please his eie,
> And dive into the water, and there prie
> Upon his brest, his thighs, and everie lim,
> And up againe, and close beside him swim.
> And talke of love: *Leander* made replie,
> You are deceav'd, I am no woman I,
> Thereat smilde *Neptune*, and then told a tale,
> How that a sheapheard sitting in a vale,
> Playd with a boy so faire and kind,
> As for his love, both earth and heaven pyn'd;
>
> (663-80)[12]

Through his indulgence in peripheral sexualities and the unexpected roles he ascribes the sexes, Marlowe promotes what is marginal and even what is transgressive. Given the criticisms that had been leveled against poetry and poets by moralists such as Stephen Gosson in *The Schoole of Abuse* (1579), Marlowe's self-consciously frivolous re-reading of classical myth was an act of defiant self-assertion. Marlowe uses such subject matter to define his own radicalism, his own newness, and his own independence from the literary status quo. In other words, he asserts his prodigality and originality — the very things that Gosson had decried in his attack on wits as "unthrifty schollers that despise ye good rules of their ancient masters, and run to the shop of their owne devises defacing olde stampes, forging newe Printes, and coyning strange preceptes."[13] *Hero and Leander* obviously constitutes a type of writing that stands in opposition to received ideas. It is a transgressive form, one which breaks down the standards of the status quo, and this includes the accepted standards of male and female behavior. In particular, Marlowe's epyllion challenges the Petrarchan model of the relationship between the sexes, of the silent, passive female object of desire who is pursued by the dominant male, and it does so by acknowledging the erotic equality of the sexes. Thus both Hero and Leander are unworldly and inexperienced in the ways of love, and, far from being passive, Hero overcomes her initial reluctance and embraces Leander's propositions with enthusiasm. Moreover, both figures are presented as the objects of erotic desire, and descriptions of their beauties assume an androgynous quality:

> . . . I could tell ye,
> How smooth his brest was, & how white his bellie,
> And whose immortall fingars did imprint,
> That heavenly path, with many a curious dint,
> That runs along his backe, but my rude pen,
> Can hardly blazon foorth the loves of men.
> Much lesse of powerfull gods . . . .
>
> (65-71)

Marlowe replaces the traditional blazon of feminine beauty with an unconventional blazon of masculine beauty and the narrator goes on to praise Leander's "orient cheekes and lippes" (73) — the very elements that would be praised in a conventional Petrarchan blazon of the female object. Marlowe exploits desire not only to undermine the dominant literary mode of Petrarchanism but also to question the nature and even the possibility of literary morality.[14]

The poem establishes a parallel between reading, writing, and cupidinous desire, because the production and consumption of tales frequently have as their goal the satisfaction of selfish desire, even sexual desire. When, for example, Neptune tries to seduce Leander, his strategy includes telling the tale of the shepherd and the boy:

> Thereat smilde *Neptune*, and then told a tale,
> How that a sheapheard sitting in a vale,
> Playd with a boy so faire and kind,
> As for his love, both earth and heaven pyn'd;
>
> (677-80)

But if, as one suspects, the very production of Neptune's tale both satisfies and arouses Neptune's own desires, as he pictures the shepherd playing with his beautiful boy, in an instance of masturbatory fiction-making, then reading is also presented as seeking its own satisfactions. Before Leander swims the Hellespont, Marlowe compares him to a book that is easy to read:

> Therefore even as an Index to a booke,
> So to his mind was yoong *Leanders* looke.
>   (613-14)

The content of this particular book is love and passion. The digressions and the abrupt conclusion to *Hero and Leander* make the readers self-conscious about their narrative desires, about their desire to know more, but in the context of *Hero and Leander*, the knowing characters are those, like Neptune, who are aware of their sexuality, and, in Marlowe's poem, the desire to find out what happens is the desire to find out about the sexual adventures of Hero and Leander. Narrative desire is exposed as the desire for carnal knowledge. In particular, Marlowe challenges the concept of chaste literature by suggesting parallels between female sexuality and the behaviour of male authors. As *Hero and Leander* ironizes feminine coyness, it reveals the self-interest which motivates all action. In fact, the narrator exploits and exposes such coyness in himself, most notably in the digression of Mercury and the country maid, where he attacks the country maid's coyness:

> And knowing *Hermes* courted her, was glad
> That she such lovelinesse and beautie had
> As could provoke his liking, yet was mute,
> And neither would denie, nor graunt his sute.
> Still vowd he love, she wanting no excuse
> To feed him with delaies, as women use:
> Or thirsting after immortalitie,
> All women are ambitious naturallie,
> Impos'd upon her lover such a taske,
> As he ought not performe, nor yet she aske.
>   (421-30)

Women, we are told, are coy only to encourage, but the country maid is not the only person handing out delays at this point in the narrative, because the narrator is also coy: he is also guilty of delay for precisely the same reasons, as he tries to whet the readers' appetites by making them wait. His brand of masculine coyness sorts nicely with his own ambitions and his desire to uncover his power to manipulate the audience. Again the text draws a parallel between writing and cupidinous desire which challenges traditional conceptions of literary function, conceptions that limit literature to the moral and didactic.

The frank eroticism of *Hero and Leander* can be related to other texts of the 1590s which insist on their sexuality and insinuate a connection between the frank treatment of sexual matter and literary innovation, such as Sir John Harington's preface to his translation of *Orlando Furioso*, published in 1591. Both Harington and Marlowe question the possibility of morality and the nature of the moralists by drawing parallels between reading, writing, and cupidinous desire. As Harington explains, what he calls "self-pleasing" motivates both writer and reader, and, like Marlowe, he defends himself against charges of immorality by shamelessly capitalizing on what is marginal and transgressive, by bringing his shame to the fore. Even Lucrece, Harington claims, that most chaste and honorable of Roman matrons, is motivated by erotic self-interest and reads purely for pleasure, only remembering to blush when someone is looking![15] Literary invention thus becomes a source of erotic satisfaction for the inventor and the reader, and narcissism and lust are substituted for morality. In both *Orlando Furioso* and *Hero and Leander*, error becomes the principle that connects the diverse elements of the poem following the model of Ovid's meandering *Metamorphoses*. Yet Ovid's text is associated with error in moral as well as structural ways, as it arouses feelings of guiltiness and shame because of its erotic content.

In his reply to Stephen Gosson's *Schoole of Abuse* in *Defence of Poetry Musick and Stage Plays*, probably written in 1579, Thomas Lodge defends literature by defending Ovid, the very epitome of literariness: "who liketh not of the promptnes of *Ovid*? who not unworthely cold bost of himself thus *Quicquid conabar dicere versus erat* [everything I tried to say was verse]? who then doothe not wonder at poetry?"[16] Thus through the Ovidian model literariness comes to be associated with guiltiness and even with wantonness, but it is precisely this sense of guilt which is explored and exposed in *Hero and Leander* where what is taboo inspires creation. The kind of literature represented by Marlowe's text is by its very nature errant, as it turns away from sober civic or spiritual business towards self-indulgent recreative activity and uses wit to promote desire. For the authors of the 1590s, who sought to defend writing against restrictive criticism, Ovid became an important model which valorized authorial individuality, flexibility, and technical skill. Ovid's compendious epic suggested ways in which competing values could be brought together to challenge existing conceptions of literature, and his luxuriant wantonness challenged the simplicity of conventional moral judgments based on the denial of sensual experience by insinuating a connection between poetic creativity and sexual desire which made literary morality a chimerical goal and eventually freed literature from didacticism. Yet, neither Ariosto, Harington, nor the metamorphic wits of the 1590s attempt to conceal their errors: instead they capitalize upon them because, in the context of the 1590s, error is the concomitant of individuality as writers affirm their newness through their *deviations* from established models and traditions. To be different, to be original, to deviate from the expected is, by definition, deviant and shameful.

All these guilty errors, errors which are both structural and moral, might be expected to arouse a few blushes, and indeed they do. *Hero and Leander* is full of incidents of exposure, of embarrassment and blushing, but although blushing is often interpreted as a sign of modesty, in *Hero and Leander* it is a sign of foreknowledge, even in the most naive of characters, and it is associated with sin, shame, and the anxieties of exposure. Perhaps the most striking example comes at the end of the poem, where Hero's blush is compared to day-break in a complex of shame and exposure:

> Thus neere the bed she blushing stood upright,
> And from her countenance behold ye might,
> A kind of twilight breake, which through the hcare,
> As from an orient cloud, glymse here and there.
> And round about the chamber this false morne,
> Brought foorth the day before the day was borne.
>
> (801-06)[17]

In this case, Marlowe literally turns shame into poetry, and rather than deny literature's association with negativity and triviality, he makes this association the basis of his self-defense. In fact, Marlowe's obsession with incidents of shame suggests that the invocation of shame is enabling, and, as Michel Foucault has argued, the invocation of repressive laws and taboos may play a tactical role in the transformation into discourse.[18] The exploitation of shame in *Hero and Leander* makes the boundary between shame and shamelessness hard to distinguish. Shamelessness is a defense against shame, a form of narcissistic self-display which asserts the individual's power to rise above criticism. Thus the shamelessness of *Hero and Leander* is another strategy of authorial self-assertion, a paradoxical way of turning the negative potential of literature into something that is liberating and enabling, whilst still remaining within the conventions of literary criticism, which dismissed such licence as errant and shameful.

Arthur Kinney and Richard Helgerson are responsible for focusing our attention on the theme of shame in Elizabethan culture, but my study of *Hero and Leander* suggests that the complex of shame should not only be seen in the context of Christian Humanism, as they argue.[19] While some authors reinvoked the comforting scheme of rebellion, guilt, and repentance in the 1590s, thereby assuming an authorial identity supported by the governing ethos of their age, others developed forms of authorship defined by their opposition to the status quo and the principles of humanist morality. Shame in Marlowe's epyllion is associated with the anxieties of exposure and may figure authorial anxieties about publication in all its senses. Hero's physical exposure before Leander is a reworking of the myth of Diana and Actaeon, and Marlowe's poem is full of scenes of illicit viewing, and guilty visual pleasures:

> His hands he cast upon her like a snare,
> She overcome with shame and sallow feare,
> Like chast *Diana*, when *Acteon* spyde her,
> Being sodainly betraide, dyv'd downe to hide her.
>
> (743-46)

The matrix of exposure and cupidinous desire characterizes the production of the text, as the reader voluntarily or involuntarily participates in the role of voyeur. The voyeur represents a similar sort of threat to his/her Diana as the public does to the author of a printed text, as both threaten the autonomy of the individual with passive objectification, and the myth of Diana and Actaeon raises the problems of personal purity, violation, and pollution, the very problems that are raised by publication. Yet, as I have argued, the theme of shame is bound up with late Elizabethan understanding of literariness, partly because of the influence of Ovid and partly as a consequence of humanist attacks on the merely literary. Shame is a form of *anagnorisis*, or recognition, and it marks a shift from ignorance to knowledge, from innocence to self-consciousness, often expressed through sudden blushing — a physical sign of inner metamorphosis. *Anagnorisis* delivers a shock to readers, and through its suddenness, it expresses a kinship with the themes of wonder, wandering, and error that are of central importance to the epyllion. *Hero and Leander* works in perverse and apparently haphazard ways as its narrative takes surprising turns, but like *anagnorisis* it offers forms of knowledge and experience which are inaccessible to other kinds of writing and grounds the claims that literature is a special and useful activity in its own right. As Terence Cave points out, *anagnorisis* operates in a very different way from rational cognition. It works "surreptitiously . . . and often perversely, seizing on precisely those details that from a rational point of view seem trivial."[20] A paradoxical structure comes into play as Marlowe shamelessly derives value from the shameful, just as he shamelessly based his authority on the very prodigality that had marginalized and trivialized literary activity. By acknowledging the shamefulness of self-exposure and the shamefulness of his individuality, Marlowe finds a way to speak in specifically literary ways.

Hero and Leander exemplifies the way Marlowe cultivates an association with activities on the margins of physical, mental, or cultural experience. Rather than edify his readers, Marlowe sets out to enthrall and fascinate them with behaviour that both attracts and repels them. Paradoxically, he exploits marginal and transgressive activities to define his authority and his translation of the pornographic *Amores*, and his dramatic interest in homosexuality and black magic, all contribute to the image of the artist as the purveyor of spiritual dangers.[21] The association with black magic, for example, serves much the same purpose as the invocation of "divine *Musaeus*" (52) and the mystical powers of this proto-poet at the start of *Hero and Leander*. It is a way of glamorizing and dignifying authorship by laying claim to special powers which enable Marlowe to redefine the status of literature. Thus while *Hero and Leander* asserts its author as the origin and end of the text, it frees literature from didacticism and turns its triviality and its potential for shame into the grounds of its discourse, defining a space for literary activity which is no longer dependent on external values, but works to fulfill its own aesthetic. In its oblique and self-consciously marginal ways, *Hero and Leander* contributes to the professionalization of letters.

The most striking articulation of professional concerns comes at the moment when the poem is at its most digressive, which again insinuates a connection between literariness and the errant. Marlowe's interest in the state of poetry receives direct expression, or rather indirect expression in *Hero and Leander*, in the digression of Mercury and the country maid. Ostensibly, this story explains why the destinies are hostile to love, but, at the end of the digression, Marlowe's text digresses once again to explain why poets and scholars are poor. The text undertakes a witty defense of its narrator's status, but does so by relating its defence to the digressive and dilatory experience of love. *Hero and Leander* defends "the *Muses* sonnes" (476) from the scorn of society and attacks the evil economy which has perverted the proper relationship between merit and reward. In the corrupt society which provides the context for *Hero and Leander*, worthless "*Midas* Brood" (475) is honored above poets and scholars, while ignorance and stupidity reap higher rewards than marginalized learning. This confusion of values is caused by the Fates, who hate Mercury, the patron of learning, and do everything in their power to upset him:

> Yet as a punishment they added this,
> That he and *Povertie* should alwaies kis.
> And to this day is everie scholler poore,
> Grosse gold, from them runs headlong to the boore.
> Likewise the angrie sisters thus deluded,
> To venge themselves on *Hermes*, have concluded
> That *Midas* brood shall sit in Honors chaire,
> To which the Muses sonnes are only heire:
>
> (469-76)

Marlowe speaks on behalf of poetry, and while this is an act of self-promotion, it is simultaneously an act of professional self-defense. *Hero and Leander* speaks on behalf of a community which it helped construct, as the text gives matter for his successors, in the form of images to be reworked or stories to be completed, that bind these writers together as a self-consciously literary community. Among many things, *Hero and Leander* is a social statement, one which derives its meaning from its relationship to a community of writers and readers. Even its dedication, which was supplied by Edward Blount, records the process of socialization, as it turns the private nature of Sir Thomas Walsingham's patronage of Marlowe into public knowledge, thereby locating the epyllion within a specific readership and within a specific economy of exchange. Compared to the drama, the epyllion offered Marlowe a very different mode of address, one which appealed to a sophisticated coterie audience and could offer access to more exclusive social circles.[22] The production of literature is presented as a collaborative process which involves the active participation of an elite group of readers who share the writer's motives and aspirations. *Hero and Leander* does not merely commemorate this literary community, it also creates it as the proper production, and reception of the text guarantees entry into this elite. Moreover, it is indulgence in emotion that corroborates the claims to be a literate, cultivated elite, as the narrator wryly observes when Leander shows pity for Neptune: "And who have hard hearts, and obdurat minds, / But vicious, harebraind, and illit'rat hinds?" (701-02) Thus Marlowe's poem argues for a new kind of literary community, one in which the exchange of intellectual wares will confer both status and financial rewards on writers. It argues for the socialization of literature and highlights the benefits of a proper community of exchange, but in order to achieve this community, the epyllion must also develop its own justifications for publication and exposure. Leander's arguments against chastity carry witty implications for the real business of publication as he tries to get Hero to enter the economy of sexual exchange. He attacks the idea that integrity is maintained through privacy and solitude:

> One is no number, mayds are nothing then,
> Without the sweet societie of men.
>
> (255-56)

Thus Marlowe insinuates the possibility that objects only acquire value when they enter the market-place, with the result that honor and merit are not intrinsic attributes but are conferred by the processes of exchange. Thus chastity, and other forms of retirement, in Leander's slyly seductive speech, actually preclude honor and fame. As Leander goes on to point out to Hero:

> Base boullion for the stampes sake we allow,
> Even so for mens impression do we you.
>
> (265-66)

Hero and Leander is a self-consciously modern poem that enables Marlowe to subvert traditional concepts of value and proportion by magnifying and promoting what are usually considered to be marginal structural and thematic elements. It is concerned to prove the value and dignity of poetry and to reform the practice and reception of literature, not in the terms laid down by orthodox humanist morality, but in the terms of the developing aesthetic and literary morality of the 1590s. This morality finds value in the trivial and marginal and makes its apparent weaknesses the basis of its claim to importance. Thus the poem is an agent for change, a way of taking up positions on the frontiers of the thinkable, but its frivolities and witticisms are not incompatible with its serious corrective aims. Histories of the 1590s identify important changes in attitudes towards literature in that decade. They talk about a new sense of the dignity of authorship and the start of the professionalization of letters. It is my contention that these developments took place primarily in marginal and non-canonical texts like *Hero and Leander*. Through his shameless reinterpretations of the classics, Marlowe made his independence from inherited values the basis of his authority and turned originality into a central rather than a peripheral concern. Inevitably, our definitions of centre and margin, major and minor, canonical and non-canonical, are challenged by Marlowe's transformation of Ovidian texts into the minor epic. The radicalization of these classic texts complicates our understanding of canonicity in the late Elizabethan period and may even open new perspectives on our own definitions of the canon.

Notes

1.   William Keach, *Elizabethan Erotic Narratives* (Hassocks, 1977), 87.
2.   Examples of epyllia from the 1590s are reproduced in Elizabeth Story Donno, ed., *Elizabethan Minor Epics* (London, 1963), and Nigel Alexander, ed., *Elizabethan Narrative Verse*, The Stratford-Upon-Avon Library 3 (Cambridge, MA, 1968).
3.   Such critics include Stephen J. Greenblatt, *Renaissance Self-Fashioning: From More to Shakespeare* (Chicago, 1980), 157-221, and Joel Fineman, *Shakespeare's Perjured Eye: The Invention of Poetic Subjectivity in the Sonnets* (Berkeley, 1986). By contrast, Jeffrey Knapp is less restricted by conventional hierarchies and opens his study of early modern colonial discourse, *An Empire Nowhere: England, America, and Literature from* Utopia *to* The Tempest, The New Historicism: Studies in Cultural Poetics 16 (Berkeley, 1992) with a brief review of traditional explanations of the English literary Renaissance: the Reformation, the rediscovery of the classics, the rise of nationalism and individualism, and the discovery of America (1-4). He argues that England's conception of its own powerful immateriality appealed to poets who also located value in "apparent deficiency" (5).
4.   Walter Allen, "The Non-existent Classical Epyllion," *Studies in Philology* 55 (1958), 515-18, questions whether the epyllion existed as a classical genre. However, the density of cross references and the incestuousness of the Elizabethan epyllion suggest that Elizabethan writers saw such poems, and wanted them to be seen, as a distinct genre. As Rosalie Colie has pointed out, generic systems have social importance for writers and offer "a ready code of communication both among professionals and to their audiences"; *The Resources of Kind: Genre-Theory in the Renaissance*, ed. Barbara K. Lewalski (Berkeley, 1973), 8. In the case of the epyllion, genre becomes a badge of modernity, the mark of an Elizabethan avant-garde.
5.   Elizabeth Story Donno discusses the inter-relationships between attack and defense in "The Epyllion," *English Poetry and Prose 1540-1674*, ed. Christopher Ricks (London, 1970), 82-98. Russell Fraser, *The War Against Poetry* (Princeton, 1970) analyzes contemporary attacks on literature.
6.   Marlowe was killed at Deptford on 30 May 1593. The allusions to *Hero and Leander* in other epyllia, such as Thomas Edwards' *Cephalus and*

Procris (1595) 2: 71-78, prove that Marlowe's poem was known before the publication of the earliest extant edition in 1598, and must have been circulating in manuscript form at least. (*Cephalus and Procris* is reproduced in Donno, ed., *Elizabethan Minor Epics*.)

7.   Lodge dedicated *Scillaes Metamorphosis* to his educated, leisured, and youthful contemporaries at the Inns of Court and Chancery. The dedication of the epyllion to someone associated with the author's youth became a characteristic of the genre. Eroticism and satire are closely linked in the 1590s. Compare the structure of the volume that included both Marlowe's translation of the *Amores* and Sir John Davies' satirical *Epigramms* which was banned in June 1599 (see Ian Moulton's essay below).

8.   All quotations are from *Hero and Leander By Christopher Marlowe: A Facsimile of the First Edition*, 1598, ed. Louis L. Martz, The Folger Facsimiles (New York, 1972). I normalize the use of u, v, and s throughout. The first edition did not divide the poem into sestiads, nor did it include summaries of the action. These first appeared in the second edition of 1598, which included Chapman's continuation, and they serve to fix and limit the meaning of the poem.

9.   Elizabethan interpretations of Ovid are analyzed by Gerald Snare, "Chapman's Ovid," *Studies in Philology* 75 (1978), 430-50.

10. Marlowe defines himself in ways that are similar to those used by Catullus, Calvus, and Cinna. These so-called "New Poets" (the term is Cicero's) appropriated the decadence and technical flourish of the Alexandrian School to define their difference from the Roman literary status quo. Richard Carew, "The Excellencie of the English Tongue" (1595-96?), identifies Shakespeare and Marlowe with Catullus: "Will you reade Virgill? take the *Earl of Surrey: Catullus? Shakespeare*, and *Marlowes* fragment . . . ." See *Elizabethan Critical Essays*, G. Gregory Smith, ed., 2 vols. (1904; Oxford, 1950), 2: 293. However, the Elizabethans were unaware that Musaeus was a member of the Alexandrian School. Gordon Braden, *The Classics and English Renaissance Poetry: Three Case Studies* (New Haven, 1978), 55-153, discusses Elizabethan interpretations of Musaeus.

11. Petowe's and Chapman's continuations of *Hero and Leander* are reproduced in *Christopher Marlowe: The Complete Poems and Translations*, ed. Stephen Orgel (1971; Harmondsworth, 1979). The phrasing of the preface imitates the dedication of Shakespeare's *Venus and Adonis* and Petowe's gracefully self-deprecating irony highlights the association of the epyllion with youth and recreation.

12. Gregory W. Bredbeck, *Sodomy and Interpretation: Marlowe to Milton* (Ithaca, 1991), 87-139, argues that Marlowe's homoeroticism undermines the naturalness of heteroerotic desire. While I agree that *Hero and Leander* is a radical poem, I focus on the way Marlowe uses peripheral sexuality to promote a particular image of an urbane authorship and readership.

13. Stephen Gosson, *The Schoole of Abuse 1579: and A Short Apologie of The Schoole of Abuse 1579*, ed. Edward Arber, English Reprints 3 (London, 1868), 28. I normalize the use of u and v.

14. In contrast, Philippa Berry, *Of Chastity and Power: Elizabethan Literature and the Unmarried Queen* (London, 1989), 137-38, argues that the genre of the epyllion subjects female desire to "viciously satiric treatment" which censures female fantasies of sexual dominance. I argue the epyllion also satirizes male desire, and its primary target is not women but the hypocrisy of literary morality and the limitations of Petrarchanism. Moreover, the epyllion includes women in its elite circle of readers. For example, Chapman's continuation of *Hero and Leander* is dedicated to Lady Walsingham.

15. See Sir John Harington's preface to *Orlando Furioso* in *Elizabethan Critical Essays*, G. Gregory Smith, ed., 2 vols. (1904; Oxford, 1950), 2: 218 and 209-10, respectively.

16. *The Complete Works of Thomas Lodge*, 4 vols. (1883; New York, 1963), 1: 11. I normalize the use of u and v. Arthur Kinney, *Markets of Bawdrie: The Dramatic Criticism of Stephen Gosson* (Salzburg, 1974), 17, dates Lodge's Reply to 1579.

17. Levinus Lemnius, *The Touchstone of Complexions*, trans. Thomas Newton (London, 1581) argues that "Bloud and vital Spyrite are in their ,chiefest Pryme and most abound in lusty and flourishing yeares" (M2v). Moreover, blood makes people "pursue the inticementes of all sensual lustes and unbrydled affection," (N5v) so that they lead what Lemnius calls "a Minstrelles life" (N5v) and "wholy addicte themselves to inglorious excesse, unseasonable watching, and immoderat lust of carnal venerie" (N5v). I normalize the use of u and v.

18. Michel Foucault, *Power/Knowledge: Selected Interviews and Other Writings 1972-1977*, ed. Colin Gordon (Hassocks, 1980), 55-62. For Foucault, power is a form of control by stimulation and thus contains its counter-voices, but I argue Marlowe's invocation of taboo in *Hero and Leander* undermines the literary status quo.

19. Arthur F. Kinney, *Humanist Poetics: Thought, Rhetoric, and Fiction in Sixteenth-Century England* (Amherst, 1986), esp. 295-362 and Richard Helgerson, *The Elizabethan Prodigals* (Berkeley, 1976), passim.

20. Terence Cave, *Recognitions: A Study in Poetics* (Oxford, 1988), 3. On 1-4 and 55-83, Cave identifies *anagnorisis* as the very essence of fiction and emphasizes its associations with scandal and *peripeteia*.

21. Jonathan Goldberg, "Sodomy and Society: The Case of Christopher Marlowe," *Staging the Renaissance: Reinterpretations of Elizabethan and Jacobean Drama*, ed. David Scott Kastan and Peter Stallybrass (London, 1991), 75-82, discusses the ways sodomy was embedded in other discourses of subversion. For Goldberg, it is the theatrical milieu where the counter-voices of culture are acted out, but Marlowe's epyllion suggests they are also expressed in lyric.

22. M. C. Bradbrook argues in "Beasts and Gods: Greene's *Groats-Worth of Witte* and the Social Purpose of *Venus and Adonis*," *Shakespeare Survey* 15 (1962), 62-72 that Shakespeare's epyllion also makes "a claim to social dignity for its author" (70).

"Printed Abroad and Uncastrated": Marlowe's *Elegies* with Davies' *Epigrams*

Ian Frederick Moulton

In 1596, in an order of High Commission, John Whitgift, Archbishop of Canterbury, declared his intention to regulate personally

> divers copies [of] books or pamphletts [which] have been latelie printed and putt to sale, some conteyning matter of Ribaldrie, some of superstition and some of flat heresie. By means whereof the simpler and least advised sorts of her majesties subjects are either allured to wantonness, corrupted in doctrine or in danger to be seduced from that dutifull obedience which they owe unto her highness.[1]

Three years later, on 1 June 1599, Whitgift and Richard Bancroft, Bishop of London, issued the proclamation known as the Bishops' Order, an order which represents one of the most overt efforts of the Elizabethan authorities to control the burgeoning London book trade.[2] It specifies that both histories and plays must henceforth be licensed by the State, bans satires and epigrams altogether, and lists some dozen volumes which are to be called in and destroyed, most of which are collections of satiric verse.[3] On the fourth of June a book burning was held at the Stationers' Hall. One of the books thrown on the pyre that day was a slim volume containing 48 epigrams by Sir John Davies, and ten of Ovid's Elegies from the *Amores*, translated by Christopher Marlowe.

The Bishops' Order has generally been understood as an effort to control political discourse in England, and thus it has been argued that the offensive portion of the Marlowe/Davies volume was Davies' Epigrams — which fell, after all, under the general ban on epigrams and satires.[4] And yet, as Whitgift's linkage of wantonness, corrupt doctrine, and social disobedience in the 1596 order makes clear, works thought of as ribald or licentious were not differentiated from politically subversive or heretical works, but were included in a

77

broad range of material which could seduce the innocent. As recent studies of the concept of sodomy in early modern Europe have indicated, it is not easy to separate erotic disorder in the period from other disorderly acts;[5] erotic writing was clearly seen as having political consequences. Just as Gaveston in *Edward II* is attacked more for his political over-reaching than for his sexual relations with Edward (1.4.401-19), sodomy in early modern England was not seen as a specifically sexual crime, but rather as a part of a continuum of "unnatural" actions which also included witchcraft, treason, and heresy.[6]

Given an understanding of corruption which does not draw strong distinctions between a "private" realm of the erotic and a "public" political realm, I believe that Marlowe's translations of Ovid may well have been perceived as socially disorderly. For while Marlowe's *Elegies* are — generically speaking — erotic lyrics rather than overtly political satires, they raise potentially troubling issues of sexual power and masculine gender identity. The *Amores'* decision to reject the "Muse upreared . . . of Armes" in favor of the "numbers soft" of love (Elegy 1.1.5, 22) had been strongly criticized in Augustan Rome, and was also perceived as threatening to patriarchal social structures in Elizabethan England. Throughout the 1590s the continuing war with Spain and concerns about Elizabeth's age and infertility exacerbated an often-articulated anxiety about virility among the male ruling class of England, whose fear of effeminization seems to have been part of a larger European trend.[7] And perhaps to a greater extent than Ovid's originals, Marlowe's translations celebrate effeminacy and argue for the pleasures of subjection. It is better, the volume suggests, to be a captive of pleasure than a conqueror of men.[8]

To understand the potentially offensive nature of Marlowe's Ovid, one must turn to the larger debate over the moral status of erotic poetry in Elizabethan England. Erotic writing in early modern England was often linked to the notion of effeminacy — that is, to the various processes by which a man could show himself womanly, thus losing his claim to the powers and prerogatives granted him as a male by the established hierarchy of gender. To modern ways of thinking which divide sexual activity and identity into the homo and the heterosexual, the notion of effeminacy in early modern England seems both complex and, in fundamental ways, contradictory. A man could become effeminate by spending too much time with women, and acting too much like women in speech, dress, and deportment.[9] But a man could also be considered effeminate if he took the passive (i.e., feminine) role in intercourse with men. In many ways, the concept of effeminacy put early modern men in a double bind: sexual relations between men and women were conceived of as a "natural" site for the demonstration of masculine mastery, and the assumption that a man should naturally take the active role in sexual encounters was fundamental to early modern constructions of masculinity. And yet, to take erotic possession of a woman was to weaken oneself as a man, spiritually through a moral surrender to effeminate pleasure and physically through the spending of valuable seed. To escape such weakening, men could leave the company of women for that of men — literally or metaphorically abandoning a "thrice-driven bed of down" for "the flinty and steel couch of war" (*Othello* 1.3.233-34). But the exclusively homosocial company of men was no guarantee against effeminacy, for to be a passive or subordinate partner in a sexual relationship with another man was also conceived of as "womanly."

In the late sixteenth century, moralistic pamphlets by Stephen Gosson, Philip Stubbes, and others explicitly connect lascivious poetry, effeminacy, and military weakness.[10] In Stephen Gosson's *Schoole of Abuse* (1579, reprinted 1579, 1587), poets are attacked with the same register of terms employed against women in contemporary anti-feminist tracts and sermons. Indeed, for Gosson, poetry *itself* is effeminizing, unless its content is explicitly martial or devotional:

> The right use of auncient Poetrie was too have the notable exploytes of woorthy Capitaines, the holesome councels of good fathers, and vertuous lives of predecessors set downe in numbers, and songe to the Instruments at solemne feastes, that the sound of the one might draw the hearers from kissing the cupp too often.
>
> (sig. A7)

Contemporary poets, however, follow an ethic and aesthetic more suited to camp-followers than to the camp: like prostitutes adorning their bodies with jewels, poets use "good sentences . . . as ornamentes to beautifye their woorkes, and sete theyre trumperie to sale without suspect." "No marveyle," Gosson concludes, that "Plato shut [poets] out of his Schoole, and banished them quite from his common wealth, as effeminate writers, unprofitable members, and bitter enemies to virtue" (sig. A2-3).

Like prostitutes, effeminate poets are dangerous because of their capacity to (as Whitgift put it) allure the innocent to wantonness. In *The Anatomie of Abuses* (1583, reprinted 1583, 1585, 1595), Philip Stubbes saw a similar threat in the proliferation of ballad makers:

> Who be more bawdie than they? Who uncleaner than they, who more licentious and loose minded: who more incontinent than

they? And briefly, who more inclyned to all kind of insolencie
and lewdness than they: wherefore, if you wold have your sone
softe, womanish, uncleane, smooth mouthed, affected to bawdrie,
scurrilitie, filthie rimes and unsemely talking; briefly if you
would have him, as it were transnatured into a woman or worse,
and inclyned to all kind of whordome and abhomination, set him
to dauncing school, and to learn musicke, and then you shall not
faile in your purpose.

(Sig. O5)

While Stubbes is concerned here primarily with the corrupting
effects of singing and dancing, the rhetoric of effeminacy addressed
itself to all poetic forms, from street verse and ballads to vernacular
translations of classical texts and aristocratic coterie verse such as
Nashe's "Choice of Valentines." Wendy Wall has demonstrated
that even genres we think of as "high," such as Petrarchan sonnets,
could be seen as potentially disruptive of traditional gender
categories (265).

The specter of effeminate weakness not only threatened to
undermine the basis of domestic mastery of a husband over his wife
and children; it also had the potential to destabilize national
structures of mastery by putting in question the authority of
England's male, aristocratic ruling class. Individual effeminacy had
dire national consequences; if the prime of English manhood were
effeminized, how could they defend the country against its foreign
enemies? Gosson in particular is obsessed with what he perceives as
a decline in the "olde discipline of Englande" (sig. B8), and his
fears were shared by scholarly courtiers such as Roger Ascham and
Gabriel Harvey.[11] While Harvey praises Petrarch (as Gosson would
certainly not have done) he too fears that lewd effeminizing poetry
will weaken English manhood: "The date of idle vanities is
expired," Harvey announces; England needs "Spartan
invincibility," not the "bawdye . . . songes of Priapus."[12]

Harvey's enthusiasm for Petrarch's love poetry indicates that the
critique of erotic writing was not univocal; poems that for one
reader were the eloquent voice of "pure Love it selfe" could easily
be taken by another for "filthy rymes in the nastiest kind."[13] The
status of poetry in late sixteenth century England was, of course, the
subject of much debate. The discourses which figured poetry as
effeminizing were not monolithic, and they were countered both by
defenses of poetry such as Sidney's, which argued that coterie verse
was a useful and virtuous attribute of the humanist soldier and
courtier,[14] and more broadly by the various discourses which
attempted to gender the emergent figure of the author as a "man in
print."[15] While few writers openly or profoundly questioned the

patriarchal hierarchy of gender in early modern England, the moralistic stance exemplified by Gosson and Stubbes was widely contested within literary culture. Some poems from the 1590s, chief among them Marlowe's Ovidian narrative *Hero and Leander*, openly celebrate a playful disruption of gender categories. If Gosson, Stubbes, and others were horrified at the effeminate weakness of English manhood, others clearly found it a source of play, of humor, of delight.

By promulgating the Bishops' Order, the established Church attempted a forceful intervention into these debates. But, despite the book burning at the Stationers' Hall, in the long run the Bishops' Order was largely ineffective, as can be illustrated by the subsequent fate of the Marlowe/Davies volume. Not only do copies of two different editions of the volume still exist from the 1590s, but by the early seventeenth century a new edition appeared, this time including not just ten Elegies, but Marlowe's complete translation of the *Amores*. My interest here, however, is with the editions which appeared in the 1590s. Like the later editions, the 1590s texts were published surreptitiously, and purport to have been printed at Middleburgh in the Low Countries; their compiler is unknown; it is almost certain, however, that neither Marlowe nor Davies had any hand in the publication of their poems.[16] It is generally held that the translations of Ovid are a product of Marlowe's youth at Cambridge. Why, if Marlowe had translated all the elegies, were only ten chosen for publication in the 1590s? Was it a simple matter of availability, or is there a discernible principle of inclusion?

It has been argued that the elegies chosen were simply those which are most licentious,[17] but the simplicity of this scheme has been refuted by the inclusion of Elegy 1.15, which deals not with sexual frolics but with the immortality of poetry. Fredson Bowers and others who have done bibliographic work on Marlowe's *Elegies* have detected "no discernible order" (151) in the organization of the volume, beyond the choice to open the volume with the first elegy of Book I, which serves as an introduction both to Ovid's complete collection and the selection in the 1590s translation. And yet, while there is no obvious logical principle of inclusion, the poems of the 1590s volume do combine to form a rough narrative.

Almost any selection of random texts, of course, will yield a narrative if one is sought there. But the narrative which can be discerned in the possibly random selection of Marlowe's elegies published in the 1590s is a narrative of effeminacy and masculine sexual failure which finds numerous parallels in other texts of the same period and has strong resonances in late sixteenth century European culture as a whole. After the first elegy, in which the speaker promises to write of nothing but love, comes elegy 1.3, in which the narrator devotes himself to his beloved alone, and 1.5, in which he has intercourse with her on a lazy afternoon. The next two texts included, Elegies 3.13 and 1.15, deal with the discourses of love — in the first, the speaker admonishes his beloved not to speak of her infidelities, and in the second he praises the immortality of his own poetic arts. In contrast to the imputed immortality of poetry, the next poem, Elegy 1.13, deals with the transience of time: it is a plea, like Donne's "The Sun Rising," that time might stand still for the lovers.

Thus, despite its seemingly random and jumbled selection of Ovid's poems, the collection nonetheless has a clear beginning, in which a monogamous relationship is constructed: first the speaker devotes himself to speaking of love, then to a particular woman, at which point the relationship is consummated. This construction of monogamy is undermined in the seventh and eighth poems of the collection: in Elegy 2.4 the speaker meditates on his potential desire for all women, and in Elegy 2.10 he finds himself in the dilemma of loving two at once. The ninth poem in the collection is the infamous Elegy 3.6, on the speaker's impotence, and the volume concludes with the second of the *Amores*, Elegy 1.2, in which the speaker represents himself as a bound captive before love's triumphal chariot.

If one accepts the narrative I have constructed, the 1590s selection of Elegies represents the male speaker's decision to devote himself to sexual love for a woman as a fall into impotence and powerlessness, a loss of manly strength, and even of identity. The speaker of Marlowe's elegies begins by rejecting virile martial pursuits for effeminate, sexual ones, and ends by being symbolically castrated: "I lately caught will have a new made wound, / And captive like be manacled and bound" (1.2.29-30). His protestations of monogamy and fidelity in the earlier poems ("If men have faith, Ile live with thee for ever" [1.3.16]) prove impossible to fulfill:

> I cannot rule myself, but where love please,
> Am driven like a ship upon rough seas.
> No one face likes me best, all faces move.
>   (2.4.7-9)

Desire once pursued leads not to fulfillment or satiety within a monogamous relationship, but rather to a proliferation of desire and loss of control: "pleasure addes fuell to [the speaker's] lustful fire" (2.10.25).

> Oft have I spent the night in wantonesse,
> And in the morne beene lively nere the lesse.

He's happy who loves mutuall skirmish slayes,
And to the Gods for that death Ovid prayes.
Let souldiours chase their enemies amaine,
And with their blood eternall honour gaine.
. . .
But when I dye, would I might droupe with doing.
                                            (2.10.27-32, 35)

The "death" of orgasm is here contrasted with the honorable, manly death of a soldier in a very different moral register than that of *The Schole of Abuse*. But the pleasurable loss of identity in climactic physical ecstasy is paralleled in the next poem by the loss of gender identity which comes with the speaker's impotence. Having lost his sexual potency, Marlowe's speaker is no longer fully a man:

Like a dull Cipher, or rude block I lay,
Or shade, or body was I who can say?
. . .
Neither was I man nor lived I then.
                                            (3.6.15-16, 60)

Most troubling of all to the patriarchal hierarchy of gender which seeks to found itself on quantifiable sexual difference is that the speaker's weakness is embodied in the very organ which should guarantee his superior status: his penis.[18] He has lost rational control of his body, and faced with his inability to control his desires, the speaker renounces further use of his recalcitrant member:

like one dead it lay,
Drouping more then a rose puld yester-day.
Now when he should not jette, he boults upright,
And craves his taske, and seekes to be at fight.
Lie downe with shame, and see thou stirre no more,
Seeing thou wouldst deceive me as before.
                                            (3.6.65-70)

The speaker's masculine member has changed to a vaginal rose.
    Like Tamburlaine's son Calyphas, who prefers "a naked lady in a net of gold" to the swords and cannons of the battlefield (*1 Tamburlaine* 4.1.66-67), in the final poem the speaker of Marlowe's *Elegies* succumbs to "martial justice" (*2 Tamburlaine* 4.2.21) and is made a captive. He, like the "effeminate brat" Calyphas (*2 Tamburlaine* 4.2.87), has forfeited his masculine

identity and the social prerogatives it carries, and has been reduced to the subordinate position of a woman or a child.[19]

But the elegies are much more ambivalent than *Tamburlaine* in their attitude towards subjection. As a group, they celebrate the surrender to erotic pleasure at least as much as they warn of its dangers. Despite his sexual failure in Elegy 3.6, the speaker never renounces his pursuit of pleasure, and in Elegy 1.2 he gives himself willingly to the bondage of love:

> Loe I confesse, I am thy captive I,
> And hold my conquered hands for thee to tie.
>
> (1.2.19-20)

Marlowe's *Elegies* may thus be interpreted as advocating seriously what his *Hero and Leander* advocates laughingly: that the blurring and shifting of gender boundaries is desirable, and that the loss of traditional masculine gender identity is a price worth paying for sensual delight.

I believe that the refusal of the *Elegies* to denounce the effeminate subjection and loss of masculine identity which they describe in such detail may have played a major role in their being banned under the Bishops' Order. Although many poems of the 1590s could be read as advocating a surrender to Love, Marlowe's *Elegies* go further: they link effeminacy to precisely the form of sexual activity that early modern culture was moving to validate above all others. In a period in which there seems to have been an increasing effort to regulate sexuality in the form of heterosexual, monogamous marriage,[20] the 1590s selection of Marlowe's elegies argues that, even when employed in monogamous devotion to a woman, the "numbers soft" of love will lead to promiscuity and a loss of rational control — a loss which, as its figuration as military defeat suggests, has consequences which go beyond those of personal sexuality.

While Protestant pamphleteers and others were actively promoting companionate marriage as an ideal in the period,[21] there was a certain amount of resistance to the concept. Francis Bacon, for example, in his 1625 essay "On Marriage and the Single Life" demonstrates a marked ambivalence towards marriage. Though he does not disapprove of marriage as such, he argues that "certainly, the best workes, and of greatest Merit for the Publike have proceeded from the unmarried, or Childlesse Men."[22] Bacon contends that "unmarried Men are best Friends; best Masters; best Servants," though he adds that marriage often makes men better subjects, and that while generals should not marry, common soldiers may fight better if they are defending their wives and children.

Bacon thus associates marriage with subjection and subordination, and suggests that, ideally, the male members of the ruling class should not marry. He ends by quoting the commonplace that, when asked at what age a man should marry, a sage replied "A young Man not yet, an Elder Man not at all." That Bacon's ideal goes against one of the fundamental principles of a patriarchal society — the need to marry and procreate in order to produce legitimate male heirs — points to the theoretical contradictions inherent in the notion of a society in which males are considered superior, but can only reproduce their perfections through sexual union with "inferior" women.[23] Both *The Fifteen Joyes of Marriage* (an anonymous translation [c. 1507] of an anti-feminist French poem by Antoine de la Sale) and a recent translation of Ercole Tasso's "booke against woemen" or *Of Marriage and Wiving* were singled out for burning by the Bishops' Order, in all likelihood because they were seen as subversive in their opposition to marriage as a social institution.[24]

While like these banned anti-feminist texts, the 1590s arrangement of Marlowe's *Elegies* associates sexual passion for women with subjugation, and like the anti-theatrical pamphlets it links erotic poetry with effeminization and loss of control, its moral vision is far removed from that of anti-feminist writers or moralistic pamphleteers; the *Elegies* do not function as a cautionary tale. They celebrate desire as much as they warn of its dangers, and coupled as they are with the subversive wit of Davies' epigrams, their own subversiveness appears in heightened relief. For although epigrams as a genre can be seen to have a conservative, regulatory function mocking vice and folly in order to encourage conformity to a "rational" and "natural" social order — Davies' epigrams, like much satire in the 1590s, were seen by the Bishops and others concerned with policing public morals as provoking the vices they condemned. And although Davies attacks various corruptions of the body politic, his epigrams are often equally concerned with the body natural, its habits and desires. For example, Epigram 33, "In Francum," meditates on a mixture of punishment and pleasure not unlike that enjoyed by Marlowe's speaker tied to Love's chariot — a structure of pleasure which would later come to be called sado-masochism (as Lisa Starks' shows in chapter 13 below):

> When Francus comes to solace with his whoore
> He sends for rods and strips himself stark naked:
> For his lust sleepes, and will not rise before,
> By whipping of the wench it be awaked.
> I envie him not, but wish I had the powre,
> To make my selfe his wench but one halfe houre.

There is an intriguing ambiguity here, turning on the phrase "whipping of the wench," which can be read as describing either the beating of the whore by Francus or the beating of Francus by the whore. The dynamics of sexual power in the poem are thus uncertain, and the uncertainty is compounded by the (presumably male) narrator's wish to make himself the wench — and thus either to beat (or be beaten by) Francus. In this instance at least, rather than solidifying social norms of gender identity and behavior, Davies' epigrams — like Marlowe's *Elegies* — call them into question.

Clearly Marlowe's *Elegies* were not alone in their focus on issues of male sexual dysfunction and the uncertainty of masculine gender identity. But though other poems of the 1590s which addressed similar concerns — like Thomas Nashe's "Choice of Valentines" — were harshly criticized for their obscenity, they were not named in the Bishops' Order of 1599.[25] This is because, like much bawdy verse and satire which has survived from early modern England, they were not published, but circulated instead in manuscript commonplace books kept primarily by the young men of the Universities and the Inns of Court.[26] The demand for English translations of the *Amores* can be judged by the appearance in some commonplace books of abysmally bad translations of some of the more explicit poems. Marlowe's translations have often been criticized for their clumsiness, and certainly, in terms of poetic sophistication they lag far behind their Latin originals. But compared with some of the other translations of the more popular elegies circulating in manuscript, they are paragons of elegance. Compare, for example, Marlowe's lines from Elegy 1.5:

> What armes and shoulders did I touch and see,
> How apt her breasts were to be pressed by me.

to the same lines transmuted by one Robert Mills:

> Oh whatt fayre shoulders what wel framde armes was I fingering
> Oh w[i]th how easy an hand her milke whyte papps was I pressinge.
>   (Bodleian Rawl MS poet 85, f. 81-81v)

Marlowe's translations of Ovid seem to have been disseminated primarily through the public space of the printed book market rather than through elite coterie circles. While many copies of Davies' Epigrams are found in manuscript, manuscript copies of Marlowe's *Elegies* are extremely rare.

Although the *Amores* were readily available to anyone who could read Latin, their appearance in print in English could easily be a cause for concern to those, like Archbishop Whitgift, who were worried about what "the simpler and least advised sorts of her majesties subjects" were reading. Accompanying a widespread eagerness to translate canonical classical texts into the vernacular was a corresponding anxiety that such translations cheapened the material they made available. And in the case of erotic writing like the *Amores*, the need to keep such texts from circulating beyond an educated male elite was especially strongly felt. What if women read them? What if servants did? The 1590s volume is very thin and small; it could easily have been concealed on one's person — perhaps it was carried about in codpieces in the manner of similarly diminutive volumes of ballads or Petrarchan sonnets, to be produced at an opportune moment to serenade one's beloved. Master Matthew in Jonson's *Every Man In His Humour* carries *Hero and Leander* — among other things — in his hose for just such a purpose (5.5.19-20). Paradoxically, while the *Elegies* selected for the 1590s volume tell a tale of ritual castration and loss of masculine identity, in the years following its suppression by the Bishops' Order, the possession of the volume itself came to be seen as a testament to sexual power: marginalia found on the title page of the Marlowe/Davies volume now in the British Library (C 34 a 28) announces proudly that its unexpurgated contents are "Printed abroad, and uncastrated."[27]

Notes

1. Qtd. in Sheila Lambert, "State Control of the Press in Theory and Practice: The Role of the Stationers' Company before 1640," *Censorship and the Control of Print in England and France 1600-1910*, ed. Robin Myers and Michael Harris (Winchester, 1992), 1-32, 15. She cites 20 March 1595/6 Liber A fo 67v.

2. The most extensive treatment of the Bishops' Order and its social and literary implications is Lynda Boose's article "The 1599 Bishop's Ban, Elizabethan Pornography, and the Sexualization of the Jacobean Stage," *Enclosure Acts: Sexuality, Property, and Culture in Early Modern England*, ed. Richard Burt and Robert Archer (Ithaca, 1994), 185-200, which effectively refutes the notion that the 1599 ban was simply a ban on satire.

3. The text of the Privy Council order is reproduced in Edward Arber, ed., *A Transcript of the Registers of the Company of Stationers of London*, 5 vols. (London, 1875-77), 3: 677-78, and in Boose, 188-89.

4. See Roma Gill's introduction to *The Complete Works of Christopher Marlowe Volume I: Translations* (Oxford, 1987), 7.

5. See Alan Bray, *Homosexuality in Renaissance England* (London, 1982), 14-16; Jonathan Goldberg, *Sodometries: Renaissance Texts, Modern Sexualities* (Stanford, 1992), 19, 120-24.

6. See Greg W. Bredbeck, *Sodomy and Interpretation: Marlowe to Milton* (Ithaca, 1991), 5. Bruce R. Smith, in *Homosexual Desire in Shakespeare's England* (Chicago, 1991), 41-53, notes that the sodomy laws of Henry VIII (25 Henry VIII c. 6) mark a shift in the status of certain forms of sodomy; whereas buggery, for example, was previously considered a crime against religion (heresy), it comes to be treated as a political offense. Smith remarks that in Elizabethan England sodomy laws were seldom enforced, and then mostly for the rape of male children.

7. While in articles such as *"A Midsummer Night's Dream* and the Shaping Fantasies of Elizabethan Culture: Gender, Power, Form," *Rewriting the Renaissance*, ed. Margaret Ferguson, et al. (Chicago, 1986), 65-87, Louis Montrose has tended to relate fear of effeminization among the English aristocracy to their anxieties about serving under a virgin Queen, such fears were prevalent outside both the aristocracy and England. See Patricia Parker, "Gender Ideology, Gender Change: The Case of Marie Germain," *Critical Inquiry* 19 (1993), 337-64, and Pierre Darmon, *Trial by Impotence: Virility and Marriage in Pre-Revolutionary France*, trans. Paul Keegan (London, 1985), on the "richly documented . . . preoccupation with impotence" in France between 1580 and 1595. In *Making Sex: Body and Gender from the Greeks to Freud* (Cambridge, MA, 1990), 125-32, Thomas Laqueur relates aristocratic male fear of effeminization to a court environment where "political and social success depended not only on might and cunning [perceived as masculine], but on the gentler skills of courtesy, dress, conversation [perceived as feminine]." He cites Hoby's translation of Castiglione's *Courtier*. See Norbert Elias, *The Civilizing Process* (1978, 1982), trans. Edmund Jephcott (Cambridge MA, 1994), esp. 258-70, on the general process of "courtization" of the warrior classes in the fifteenth and sixteenth centuries.

8. Of course in his other writings Marlowe did not consistently privilege subjection over conquest. *Tamburlaine* is in fact a powerful statement of the opposite view, that it is better for a man to triumph in battle than to surrender to languorous pleasure.

9. See Valerie Traub, *Desire and Anxiety: Circulations of Sexuality in Shakespearean Drama* (New York, 1992), 132-34.

10. See Gabriel Harvey, *Pierces Supererogation* (London, 1593), STC 12903, sig. F4-G2; Philip Stubbes, *The Anatomy of Abuses* (London, 1583), STC 23376, sig. O5; and Stephen Gosson, *The Schoole of Abuse* (London, 1579), STC 12097, sig. A2-7v, B7. In "Nobody's Perfect: Or, Why Did the English Stage Take Boys for Men?" *South Atlantic Quarterly* 88 (1989), 7-29, Stephen Orgel argues that "the deepest fear in anti-theatrical tracts . . . is the fear of universal effeminization" (17).

11. For Ascham, whose attack on Italianate Englishmen in *The Scholemaster* (London, 1570), STC 832, was the first of many, the most dangerous effeminating and corrupting books have a foreign origin. But he, like Gosson, sees a need for martial "discipline and good ordering of [noble] yougthe" (sig. G1) and sees the primary source of their corruption as "mery bookes" (sig. I2v).

12. *Pierces Supererogation* sig. F4v-G2. Harvey is responding to both the state of war between England and Spain, and the circulation of "filthy rymes" (probably "Choice of Valentines") by Marlowe's friend Thomas Nashe.

13. Harvey (sig. F4-4v) applies the first phrase to the poems of Petrarch, the second to those of Nashe.

14 It is not by chance that Sidney's *Defense of Poetry* begins with an analogy between poetry and the masculine art of horsemanship.

15. See Wendy Wall, *The Imprint of Gender: Authorship and Publication in the English Renaissance* (Ithaca, 1993), for a detailed and nuanced discussion of the gendering of print culture in early modern England. She goes so far as to suggest that some male authors adopted women's voices in an attempt to overcome the stigma of effeminization by creating a gap between the fictional gender of the speaker and the gender of the author — thus distancing the feminine voice from the masculine writer (263-72). The phrase "man in print" is quoted by Wall (1) from the 1604 introduction to *Diaphantus* by Anthony Scoloker (STC 21853, sig. A2v).

16. There are two significantly different 1590s editions of the volume (STC 6350 and 6350.5), but both include the same ten translated elegies, in the same order. For bibliographic details on the publication of the *Elegies* see Fredson Bowers, "The Early Editions of Marlowe's *Ovid's Elegies*," *Studies in Bibliography* 25 (1972), 149-72, as well as Gill's introduction to the volume of Marlowe's translations.

17. For the history of this argument, see Gill, 7.

18. While the Galenic "one-sex" model of gender may well have been dominant in early modern England, the penis was nonetheless a potent sign of gender power. Even if male and female genitalia were seen as morphologically identical, whether these organs were internal or external was crucially important in establishing gender identity and the social position which followed from that identity.

19. See especially *2 Tamburlaine* 4.1-4 in which Calyphas "dishonor[s] manhood and [his] house" (4.1.32) by refusing to fight for his father. He prefers wine, women, and cardplaying to combat. Returning from battle, Tamburlaine kills Calyphas in disgust, and he orders that his "effeminate brat" be buried by Turkish concubines, so that not even a "common soldier shall defile / His manly fingers with so faint a boy" (4.2.87-90). See also *2 Tamburlaine* 1.4.20-34 in which Tamburlaine expresses his fear that his sons will love music and dancing and be "too dainty for the wars."

20. Stubbes (sig. H4v) advocates marriage as an alternative to "whoredom," echoing St. Paul's ambivalent formulation that "it is better to marry than to burn" (I Cor. 7.9). On the emergent ideal of companionate marriage in the seventeenth century, see Lawrence Stone, *The Family, Sex and Marriage in England 1500-1800*, 1977, abridged ed. (New York, 1979), 382-84, and Catherine Belsey, *The Subject of Tragedy: Identity and Difference in Renaissance Drama* (London, 1985), 138-39.

21. See, for example, Miles Coverdale's translation of Heinrich Bullinger's *The Christen State of Matrimonye* (Antwerp, 1541), STC 4045, and its revision (attributed to "Theodore Basille" [Thomas Becon]), *The Golden Boke of Christen Matrimonye* (London, 1542), STC 4047, as well as Robert Cleaver and John Dod's *A Godlie Form of Householde Government* (London, 1610), STC 5382.

22. Francis Bacon, *The Essayes or Counsels, Civill and Morall*, ed. Michael Kiernan (Oxford, 1985), 24-26.

23. See Phyllis Rackin, *Stages of History: Shakespeare's English Chronicles* (Ithaca, 1990), 158-61, on the dependence of patriarchal power on women in the patrilineal society of early modern England.

24. The futility of the Bishops' Order may be gauged by the appearance in 1603 of a prose translation of *The Fifteen Joyes of Marriage* (STC 15257.5), this time entitled *The Batchelar's Banquet* and falsely attributed to Thomas Dekker (STC 6476).

25. Harvey, sig. F4., attacked Nashe for having produced an "unprinted packet of bawdye, and filthy Rymes in the nastiest kind." In his satiric poem "Paper's Complaint," included in *The Scourge of Folly* (London, 1611), STC 6341, John Davies of Hereford claims that "good-mens hate" tore Nashe's poem "in pieces" because of its references to a "dampned Dildo" (sig. Q4v, lines 65-70).

26. On the proliferation of erotic and satirical verse in manuscript in the period, see Arthur Marotti, *Manuscript, Print, and the English Renaissance Lyric* (Ithaca, 1995), esp. chapter 2, "Sex, Politics, and the Manuscript System," 75-133.

27. This annotation probably dates from the eighteenth century.

Edward II and Elizabethan Politics

Mark Thornton Burnett

It has long been recognized that Marlowe's work has a metatheatrical dimension and that his plays contemplate the use of language, the fashioning of identity, the place of emblems and shows, the ends of writing, and the larger textual system in which communications take place.[1] Less immediately obvious, perhaps, is the political inflection of these considerations, the precise Elizabethan nuances that such issues involved. The present paper attempts to make up for some of these omissions in Marlovian criticism and to read *Edward II* in terms of a dialogue with civil unrest, an unruly noble faction, the security of the crown, and speculation about the direction that the monarchy might take: practices and processes that were, when the play was composed in 1591-92, specific products of its historical moment. It is not my intention to employ mimetic analogy as a methodology in determining the play's contradictory effects; rather, my interest is in tracing the various discourses which saturate Marlowe's text, in mapping the ideological terrain in which *Edward II* circulates.

I

Edward II abounds in emblematic devices, dramatic displays, and self-conscious demonstrations of theatrical mastery and exuberance. The signs of royalty are continually invoked (as in the images of lions, for example), either to stress Edward's hostile intentions or to illuminate the suggestion that his power has declined and been corrupted. The king will have Kent "display [his] ensigns in the field,"[2] but he is singularly ill-equipped for successful military operations. Triumphal processions for Edward have become excuses to publicize his infatuation for Gaveston; they are no longer the symbolic realizations of superiority or prowess.

Similarly, language as a means of disseminating and containing power has lost its efficacy. The first impression is that language has the potential to insist even further upon Edward's weakness and to stress his dependency: when Gaveston is banished, Edward exclaims "Rend not my heart with thy too-piercing words" (1.4.117), and,

91

towards the end, is plagued by Lightborn, who is devilishly inventive in his supervision of a range of punishments; as the assassin instructs: "amplify his grief with bitter words" (5.2.64). Ultimately, however, it is a phenomenon of general linguistic inadequacy that the play rehearses. Words do not command as they might and convey no more than a sense of semantic crisis. "Cease, brother, for I cannot brook these words" (1.1.159), cries Edward to Kent, later complaining that "Anger and wrathful fury stops my speech" (1.4.42). Shows and vocabularies, rhetoric and marches, both fail to register the sovereign's control over his world and subjects.

What these repeated anxieties support is an idea of uncertain identity and a crumbling hold on the self, and a shifting impression of the system over which Edward wields a waning authority. Given particular attention is the conviction that names do not reinforce rule or even fit, that the multiple mechanisms whereby power was instituted are in disrepair.[3] Edward lavishes titles upon Gaveston, but the new honors work against him and contribute to the discontent that brings about the favorite's downfall. The play stands, finally, as an ontological struggle between an overlooked aristocracy who subscribe their names to rid the kingdom of Gaveston and an ailing king who discovers that, although he bears "the name of king" (5.1.28), he cannot sway a discontented faction or prevent his fate. In the concluding stages, titles and nomenclature are wholly robbed of their mystical potency, Edward identifying himself only to realize that "at that name, / I feel a hell of grief" (5.5.88-89).

Of a piece with these reflections are acts and images of writing, which crystallize fears aired elsewhere that language is unreliable and that royal pronouncements can be manipulated.[4] Mortimer writes to have Edward executed — he later glories in being able to "seal . . . cancel, [and] do what [he] will" (5.4.49) — and, with an appropriate perspicacity, the king sees his "tragedy written in [Lightborn's] brows" (5.5.73). Much of the action of *Edward II* springs from assertions of the will through royal means — pageants, announcements, seals, and textual communications — but the play simultaneously questions the validity and consequences of these efforts, highlighting the monarch's disempowerment and the appropriation of instruments of authority by those who are theoretically the crown's closest servants and supporters.

II

What is not so often suggested is that these representations have political resonances and material importance.[5] One way of addressing *Edward II*'s concerns is to see them refracting questions about the perpetuation of the royal name and the future identity of the crown in a period of crisis. The stress on titles embodies an attempt to puzzle out the implications of the methods adopted by Elizabeth's frustrated nobility in their search for honors, while also reverberating with worries about reproduction, lineage, and descent. Lists of names in *Edward II* serve dramatic functions and, at the same time, have a fluctuating place in a wider political economy, recalling Elizabeth's failure to reward generously and possibly looking forward to James' radically contrasting and extravagant appointment procedures.

That there are points of contact between Edward and Elizabeth might be contested; I am not, however, arguing for easy correspondences. Instead, I am drawn to a theatrical realization of political and sexual contests, which only brings to mind the contradictory position of the Queen in Elizabethan culture. The frequent association of Edward with the sun and sunshine, for instance, echoes the iconographical presentation of Elizabeth and the Protestant associations which gathered about her, particularly in Reformation propaganda. The vacillations that mark Edward have a tangential relation to Elizabeth's waverings (either over the fate of Mary, Queen of Scots, or the succession) and uneven policies. But in Edward, many of the distinctive features of Elizabeth are inverted. Some accounts of the Spanish Armada hold that the Queen appeared as a general in armor at Tilbury in 1588 to address her troops, but Edward parades in battle with his soldiers "like players, / With garish robes, not armour . . . Bedaubed with gold" (2.2.182-84).[6] The presence of Elizabeth haunts *Edward II*, in such a way as to evoke apparent similitudes and to destabilize clear-cut resemblances.

If the cult of Elizabeth was one ideological pressure on the imaginative conception of *Edward II*, the drama can equally be seen to be responding to the dynamic of a contemporary crisis at court. The structure of *Edward II* centers around the competing claims of the king's will and the material demands of his noble followers. From the opening scene, Edward's struggle for dominion over a questioning support system is apparent, as his first words indicate: "Will you not grant me this?" (1.1.76). The assorted nobles quickly emerge as the cause of the king's dissatisfaction with his influence; Lancaster is condemned as "aspiring" (1.1.92), and the "Barons and earls" are distinguished by their "pride" (1.1.106).[7] What the noble faction requires — apart from the exile of fawning flatterers — is never specifically spelled out, but it is clear that a guiding principle in the drama is to examine the extent of the king's power and the nature of his policies in the context of fractious voices that clamor for attention and acknowledgment.

To what degree this competition for representation replicates the flux of patronage opportunities at the Elizabethan court is impossible accurately to determine. *Edward II* cannot be straightforwardly assessed in terms of its cultural reflexivity, and the play blurs as many political images as it precisely identifies. Nevertheless, some of the play's debates can be located in a wider discursive field, which sets off questions about the relationship between financial incentives and aristocratic resentment. Sir Robert Naunton remarked in 1641 that Elizabeth "ruled much by faction and parties, which she herself both made, upheld, and weakened, as her own great judgment advised," and it is a comment with a significant bearing on the ways in which Edward allows himself to be dominated by a select group of (mostly servile) advisors.[8] It is also useful to take account of the fact that, as Wallace MacCaffrey notes, Elizabeth "stinted her grants of hereditary honor to a bare minimum, and the size of the peerage remained constant at some fifty odd families . . . On balance, the total peerage was no larger in 1603 than in 1558."[9] About the treasury of her favor Elizabeth exercised a pronounced husbandry; fixed annual fees to courtiers were not increased to keep pace with a rise in prices; and cash gifts were only occasionally distributed.[10] Of course, the chief characteristic of Marlowe's monarch is his reckless mode of expenditure rather than his prudent nursing of limited resources, although this serves to strengthen the overlap between the play and its political contexts. It is as if Edward works as a negative instance of a more prudent Queen, pointing up the dangers of irresponsibility but also alerting audiences to the rivalries generated when noble services went unrewarded.

Parallels between Edward's circumstances and Elizabeth's threatened ascendancy did not escape contemporary commentators. Most instructive, I think, is to read *Edward II* through the lenses of the numerous tracts on the succession, published in the 1580s and 1590s, that swamped the literary marketplace. A key issue in these accounts is the problem of a dissatisfied and disgruntled noble faction. In Peter Wentworth's *A pithie exhortation*, in existence in draft as early as 1587, it is argued that clarifying the succession will bind the Queen to her subjects, unlike Edward II who was "deposed by his Nobilitie and commons, as one . . . not worthie to be a king."[11] Robert Parsons made an identical comparison in *A conference about the next succession* (1594): "diuers . . . knights of the Parlament were sent vnto [Edward II] . . . depriued him, and [chose] . . . his sonne in his place."[12] Such potentially dangerous parallels between Edward and Elizabeth had a common aim: in certain circumstances it was justified, the tracts claimed, for subjects in a misused and misgoverned kingdom to take responsibility for the future of the state. Marlowe's play is implicated in these discussions. In the drama, Mortimer and Lancaster in particular criticize Edward's lavish expenditure, his neglect of his servants, and his refusal to grant to his loyal followers political preferment. A scenario such as this must have held a certain relevance to those acquainted with the jockeying for power at the Elizabethan court, since the Queen's parsimonious denial of advancement to the members of her entourage nursed grievances and fueled speculation about deposition: released from prison in 1600, the Earl of Essex immediately set about attempting to recover royal approval. His efforts were ill-fated. Denied the renewal of his sweet-wines monopoly and excluded from the Accession day tilt, he rebelled in 1602 with catastrophic consequences.[13] The stated aim of the revolt — that Essex wished to liberate the Queen from the influence of "evil councillors" and, like the nobles in Marlowe's play, to rid the country of lowly born and cowardly disposed antagonists — could do nothing to halt his execution.[14]

One immediate manifestation of a mismanaged kingdom without a successor was civil unrest. No outright riot colors the presentation of noble factions in *Edward II*, but the play is no less concerned with the prospect of internal feuding, warfare, and related threats to the security of the social order. At one point in the play even Gaveston contemplates hatching a rebellion, while Mortimer, styling himself the people's favorite, plans to do the same. Civil "mutinies" (1.2.65), according to Isabella, are about to upset the realm. Again the succession tracts are enlightening in this respect. *An answer to the first part of a certaine conference* (1603) by Sir John Hayward maintains that the deposition of Edward II was a "violent furie . . . [the] occasions of wars . . . [and] disorders."[15] Play and tract join to discharge anxieties about a kingdom whose fate hangs in the balance.

The speed with which the central authorities decided upon Essex's execution is a charged indication of the fears aroused by a favorite, smarting from neglect, who could rally a powerful noble faction to his cause. The experience equally reflects the fragility of the bonds that linked the Queen to her subjects, and the ease with which an alienated aristocrat might have been able to topple a monarchy which had still not nominated its successor, although Essex does not seem to have had a coherent plan should his insurrection have proved successful. Many critics have noticed the images of beheading and execution that pepper *Edward II* with insistent regularity.[16] Mortimer vows to secure the "glozing head of [the] base minion" (1.1.132), Gaveston, but is rebuffed by an enraged Edward who rises to heights of anger when abused by the nobles — "in lakes of gore," he exclaims, "Your headless trunks, your bodies will I trail" (3.1.135-36) — and has his wish finally granted: the head of Mortimer adorns the play's last scene. Cumulatively, however, these reiterated ideas have a broader cultural referentiality at a time when the question of the next monarchical head was being vigorously debated, and distinguish themselves from similar imagistic patterns in the later drama of the Jacobean period. They form an alliance with fears about the relationship between Elizabeth's body physical and the body politic, and with the terrifying prospect of a sovereignless country. The parliamentary session of 1593 grappled with precisely this question, taking up suggestions first made in Wentworth's 1587 succession tract. "As therefore you are our head," Wentworth stated, addressing Elizabeth, "shew your self to have dutifull care and loue to your bodie, that if you may help it . . . you leaue it not headles, as a dead trunk."[17] Admittedly the body/state analogy was a common one, but in the late 1580s and early 1590s it took on a keen and revitalized appositeness, notably in *Edward II*, which repeatedly contemplates the situation of a state threatened by noble groupings agitating to take power into their own hands.

III

Marlowe's play, therefore, was only one recasting of the reign of Edward II in the period, and it belonged with a host of related interpretations of the misgoverned and misgoverning king which were forwarded in official circles and made available to a literate public. The implied connections between Elizabeth and Edward were not confined to the stage alone, and in the drama and in parliamentary pronouncements questions were asked about the dangers of noble factions and the likelihood of civil dissent.

Briefly, however, I wish to move away from Elizabeth and back towards the fortunes of her servants in an effort to determine related aspects of the material embeddedness of *Edward II* and to broach its treatment of issues of gender and class. By concentrating on the representation of social mobility in the play, a fresh appreciation of its political meanings, which applied to the Elizabethan as well as to the Jacobean courts, can be elaborated.

Inevitably social origins were of key importance for the contemporary courtier wishing to be promoted. What marked the Elizabethan court was the way in which merit and achievement could compensate for relatively humble familial connections. In an alternative system of promotion, many of Elizabeth's favorites would have been hampered by their lack of gentle credentials. According to a 1566 memorandum, Cecil condemned the Earl of

Leicester for his inability to "produce no more than two ancestors, namely his father and grandfather and these both of them enemies and traitors to their country," while Elizabeth herself was not averse to reminding her followers of their humble beginnings.[18] When in the Netherlands in 1586, Leicester accepted from the Estates General the titles of Governor and Captain General of Holland, Zeland, and the United and Confederate Provinces, and the Queen made her disapproval clear in a letter: "We little thought, that one whom we had raised out of the Dust, and prosecuted with such singular Favour above all others, would with so great Contempt have slighted and broken our Commands in a matter of so great Consequence, and so highly concerning us and our Honor."[19] Likewise, when Sir Christopher Hatton, a former favorite and son of a minor Northamptonshire squire, became Lord High Chancellor in 1587, his enemies were immediately ready to denigrate him as "a mere vegetable of the Court, that sprung up at night."[20] For a limited number of aspirants, honors were reaped at the Elizabethan court, but the acquisition of privilege was always dependent on the Queen's sometimes whimsical policies and could provoke, in addition, the resentment of courtiers passed over in the race to win advancement.[21]

I will not try to detail those aspects of Marlowe's work which reproduce collisions over the ways in which contemporary court appointments were secured and distributed. Few texts fall neatly into the category of a transparent biographical schema. *Edward II*, which underplays obvious historical allusions, is no exception to the rule. It also needs to be stated, however, that the rhythms of the play articulate some of the political uncertainties for which the Elizabethan court was noted. When Edward asks Baldock about his social qualifications — "where wast thou born? What is thine arms?" (2.2.241) — the scholar replies, "My name is Baldock, and my gentry / I fetched from Oxford, not from heraldry" (2.2.242-43), which self-consciously gestures towards the signs of gentility, towards the decline of an emphasis on blood in the sixteenth century and towards the growing interest in professional accomplishment as one route to preferment. Of the characters in *Edward II* who function to display attitudes towards blood most forcibly, Gaveston must stand as a prominent instance. Many accusations are leveled at Edward's favorite, but it is his origins that provoke the fiercest comment. He is "base and obscure" (1.1.100), a "peevish Frenchman" (1.2.7), "sly [and] inveigling" (1.2.57), a "peasant" (1.4.7), an "Ignoble vassal" (1.4.16), "hardly . . . a gentleman by birth" (1.4.29), a "lown" (1.4.82), a "night-grown mushroom" (1.4.284) and an "upstart" (1.4.422). As a foreigner or stranger in England (who is also marked by his predilection for

French and Italian expostulations), Gaveston constitutes an implicit threat to the Elizabethan class system. Of course, Gaveston does not clearly typify an Elizabethan courtier, and part of the effect of Marlowe's play is to hint at a range of possible significations. Nevertheless, he does work to introduce a range of contemporary preoccupations. In some ways, Gaveston, "Lord Marshall of the realm" (1.4.355), looks forward to that other earl marshall, the Earl of Essex, who saw himself as the natural leader of a community of honor in opposition to a "debased régime of upstarts," and even the king's favorite can claim that his "mounting thoughts" (2.2.77) set him over and above the lords, sitting "at home" eating their "tenants' beef" (2.2.75).[22] Similarly, while he encourages questions about contemporary promotion procedures, and even privileges a conservative reaction to a dramatic social rise (this is one of the areas in which Marlowe defends establishment positions rather than subjecting them to a critical treatment), Gaveston is also important as an index of anxieties about unwanted influences and, as more honors are heaped upon him, it seems as if the country is on the brink of an alien engulfment.

In *Edward II,* meanings are never discrete and often shade into each other to form unexpected combinations and suggested lines of argument. I have maintained that the meteoric ascent of a Baldock or a Gaveston works as a rhetorical construction of the contest for honors characteristic of the Elizabethan court, but this is not the only effect that it produces. The anxiety that a sovereign could fall prey to alien influences animates the succession tracts as well as the drama. The proposed marriage of Elizabeth and the Duke of Anjou precipitated a wave of publications hostile to the match, including John Stubbs' *The gaping gulf* (1579) in which it is stated that England is endangered by French domination, a frenzied reaction also taken up in Wentworth's 1587 exhortation; recollecting the disastrous marriage of Mary Tudor and Philip II, he holds that "the land . . . may easily become a praie to any of our forraine malitious enemies."[23] The possibility either of invasion or of a foreign prince dictating to an English monarch had a long history and in the 1590s reached new levels of xenophobic intensity.

At this point I intend to leave behind the situation of the Elizabethan court and to address, instead, James VI of Scotland, for it is with the latter that the political ramifications of *Edward II* become vitally apparent. Much has been made of the similarities between Edward II and Henri III, with his homosexual leanings and lovers or "mignons." In a number of French League pamphlets from the 1580s, explicit analogies are made between the Gascons, Gaveston and Epernon, who were, as Julia Briggs states, "both uniquely favored by the King, both lining their pockets at the expense of church and commonwealth, both protectors of heretics who threatened the well-being of the realm."[24] These pamphlets also parallel the fate of Henri III with Edward's depravities.[25] We might do well to consider James VI simultaneously, a monarch who impinges indirectly on Marlowe's play and on the predicaments it anatomizes. From an early stage, James' extravagances and proclivities were a cause for concern. "His Majesty," stated the Scottish chronicler, Moysie, "having conceived an inward affection to the Lord d'Aubigny [Esmé Stuart, the Duke of Lennox, upon whom James showered titles], entered into great familiarity and quiet purposes with him."[26] Fontenay, the French ambassador, said of the young James: "his love for favourites is indiscreet and wilful and takes no account of the wishes of his people."[27] Several favorites (namely Arran and Lennox) were (like Gaveston) maneuvered into exile or obscurity by Elizabeth's faction, but even on the eve of his succession James was still entertaining such men (Huntly being a prime example), and they came to be known as the king's "minions." In 1588 Lord Hume described Alexander Lindsay, the younger brother of the Earl of Crawford, as "the king's only minion and conceit . . . his nightly bed-fellow," while Francis Osborne in his memoirs of the reigns of Elizabeth and James stated of the king's "younger" favorites: "these went under the appellation of his . . . minions, who, like burning-glasses, were daily interposed between him and the subject."[28] If Elizabeth was one of the ideological determinants behind *Edward II*, then it would seem that James, and the titles he so liberally advanced, were no less important considerations in moulding the play's conceptual possibility.

Obviously the intersecting careers of James and Edward have an intriguing appeal.[29] Given the political insecurities which marked the close of Elizabeth's reign, the history of Edward II proved a suitable point of reference, but the king was also invoked as it became increasingly clear that James VI would ascend to the throne of England and as more information about the Scottish monarch became available. An early Jacobean satire declared that Robert Carr "was a great favorite: neither Pierce Gaveston nor the Spensers with Edward 2nd nor the Earle of Warwicke with Henry the 6 nor the Duke of Suffolk with Henry the eighth as this man was with King James," and the sentiments were echoed in a letter of 1621 in which Sir John Chamberlain reported Sir Henry Yelverton's objections to the king's favorites: "[Yelverton] indeavored too cast many aspersions upon the Lord of Buckingham and his regall authoritie (as he termed yt) and further comparing these times in some sort to those of Edward the second wherin the Spensers did so tirannise and domineer."[30] Now it would not be wise to claim more for Marlowe than is readily warranted, or to suggest that *Edward II* enjoys some uncannily prescient capacity; however, there are ways in which author and text were enmeshed in the political configuration of England in the 1590s, and when the issue of the succession is broached, these connections become abundantly evident.

In one of his 1593 depositions testifying to Marlowe's monstrous opinions, Thomas Kyd noted that "He wold p[er]swade w[th] men of quallitie to goe vnto the k of Scotts whether I heare *Royden* is gon and where if he had liud he told me when I sawe him last he meant to be."[31] Without falling into the snare of biographical fallacy, I would like to point towards some of the interpretive dilemmas which Kyd's cryptic remark raises. Always meticulous but sometimes over ingenious, Charles Nicholl reflects usefully on the incident to which the comment refers. On the trip to Scotland he states: "It has an overtone of sedition, and there is little doubt what that overtone is. It concerns the whole matter of the succession, the question that hung over all others in the political world at this time . . . . they [Marlowe and Roydon] are involved in this drift towards James, propagandising for it, persuading wealthy 'men of quality' to join the pro-Jacobean faction."[32] There would certainly appear to be an implication of James in *Edward II*: the word "minion," in its singular and plural forms, is used ten times, and occurs, incidentally, six times in *The Massacre at Paris*, a work whose concerns coincide with the historical chronicle in several respects. Usually Edward is condemned by the nobles for wanting to "frolic with his minion" (1.2.67) and for being "lovesick for his minion" (1.4.87), but even the king avails himself of the term when he remarks: "Were he a peasant, being my minion, / I'll make the proudest of you stoop to him" (1.4.30-31). This introduces again the vexed question of Marlowe's own ideological position, although, of course, a formulation about authorial intention would not be appropriate. The effect of the play, however, is to frustrate the expectation that Marlowe might be using the genre of the historical narrative either to curry favor with the monarch-elect or to pass criticism on court immoralities. *Edward II* is sufficiently diffuse in its operations to work in the same moment as a dramatic warning about the perils of royal office and as a tacit celebration of the expression of unorthodox sexualities.

I have been at pains in this account to stress the location of *Edward II* in larger debates and conflicts. The play is part of diverse interrelations, does not settle upon any one royal model or counterpart, amplifies echoes even as it suppresses them, and steers the action in unexpected directions. Not so much an image of James, Edward in Marlowe's play evokes a more complex set of meanings, touching upon the issue of the succession and

illuminating the relationship between a monarch and his closest
advisors. In addition, a related aspect of James is captured in
Gaveston, Edward's base-born minion. Of course, James was of
royal pedigree, but in 1591-92, he was an unknown quantity, and
was actually condemned as a "forraine pretender [who] . . . may
iustly be feared" in some contemporary treatises.[33] Even while still
in Scotland, James was renowned for the open character and French
flavor of his court, with its informal rituals and European offices
(such as the "Great Chamberlain"), one consequence of Esmé
Stuart's sojourn with Henri III.[34] Indeed, in 1592, James was
contemplating an English invasion.[35] *Edward II* is a particularly
slippery text, both encouraging what appear to be unambiguous
identifications and denying singular analogous interpretations.
Nevertheless, the anxieties that were aroused by James were not
neglected by Marlowe, only dramatically translated into an intricate
and elusive rehearsal of constructions of the monarch's weakness
and susceptibility, and into speculation about the possibility of the
adulteration of the English royal lineage.

I have been stressing a three-part approach to Marlowe's play.
The shows, emblems, and metadramatic features of *Edward II* have a
political import. They are imbricated in related structures of
meaning and are linked both to the perceived state of the realm in
the early 1590s and to Elizabeth and James, whose pressure on the
drama is felt in scenes in which nobles or favorites transgress the
boundaries that ideally kept them at one remove from their more
powerful princely overlords. As a whole, these considerations find
an outlet in ruminations upon the succession. Clearly Elizabeth's
reign did not share the same characteristics as Edward's ill-fated
government, but several comparisons suggest themselves. The play
opens with a succession — "'My father is deceased; come
Gaveston, / And share the kingdom with thy dearest friend'" (1.1.1-
2), Edward intones — while characters in later scenes pay
scrupulous attention to the legitimacy of Edward III's claims to the
throne; the Champion proclaims him the "true king" (5.4.74) in an
aggressive public declaration. In the first scene, Edward I's funeral
is still fresh in the memory; the play closes with the stage property
of Edward II's hearse and with Edward III's minority.

Although the drama neatly commemorates the commencement
of the new reign with a smooth lineal progression, Elizabeth's
position was not so stable. One of the objections to the proposed
Anjou match in the 1570s was that the kingdom would be left in the
hands "of an infant," and, as anxiety mounted in the 1590s,
scurrilous stories about the virgin Queen's illegitimacy circulated.[36]
Only recently the problems of a minority had been glimpsed: James
VI of Scotland assumed a majority in 1587 but was still in his

twenties in the early 1590s and, although married, had not yet produced an heir. In addition, as Curt Breight states, the "Elizabethan succession problem in the 1590s was growing especially acute." He adds: "the early succession play of the 1560s, *Gorboduc*, was reprinted in 1590; Peter Wentworth, parliamentarian agitator on this issue, was jailed for the first time in August, 1591, but went ahead and published a tract in 1593 which caused permanent imprisonment; and Father Robert Parsons published in 1594 a book on the succession which irritated the Elizabethan regime."[37] Once again Marlowe's play resists an obvious connection with contemporary anxieties, making its points through omission or dramatic inversion rather than through transparent analogy. The result is that *Edward II* underwrites the differences between one monarchical system whose future is guaranteed and another whose continuation is far from secure.

IV

The immediate contexts for the succession anxieties which *Edward II* negotiates are a series of related events and policies, all of which testify to the belief (justified to an extent) that England was potentially at the mercy of foreign insurgences.[38] It was clear by the early 1590s that Elizabeth was not likely to produce an heir, a fact that exacerbated already virulent anti-alien sentiments. The execution of Mary, Queen of Scots, in 1587 only partly took away from the foreign menace, as hard upon it was the launching of the Armada in 1588. The Catholic League in the Netherlands proved an additional headache, which was not relieved by Leicester's disastrous 1585-86 campaign. Worried by the possibility of a Spanish take-over in France (which had implications for England's security), Elizabeth sent aid to Henri IV in 1589, and was once again disappointed, this time by Willoughby, the leader of the allied force. Throughout the period Elizabeth was celebrated as a Protestant sovereign who would resist Catholic resistance. She was equally endangered at home. There were English Catholic conspiracies against her in 1583 and again in 1586, but their failure did not deter the Scottish Catholic earls from meeting to invade England in 1589. A further Scottish Catholic plot, the "Spanish Blanks," was quashed in 1592-93. And in the midst of other troubles James was pestering the Queen to be recognized as the lawful claimant to the English throne.

To pinpoint those moments where *Edward II* mimes the contours of Elizabethan foreign policy and attitudes towards traditional enemies is not my imperative. But I am struck by the ways in which the play figures the vulnerability of the kingdom: it constitutes a point of intervention in a discursive field of anxieties about borders and gains energy from the mood of conspiratorial intrigue that vexed contemporaries. In this sense, *Edward II* sparks off associations with fears directed against the French in the *Henry VI* plays, and with the more general conviction that papal forces in the 1590s were seeking to bring about England's destruction.[39] England in *Edward II* is a kingdom besieged. Hemmed in and threatened from within and without, the country is encroached upon by foes on all sides. The state of England is *Edward II*'s essential subject. The first assailant is Rome, and Edward responds in a violently Protestant, anti-clerical vein, declaring

> Proud Rome, that hatchest such imperial grooms,
> For these thy superstitious taper-lights,
> Wherewith thy antichristian churches blaze,
> I'll fire thy crazèd buildings and enforce
> The papal towers to kiss the lowly ground,
> With slaughtered priests make Tiber's channel swell,
> And banks raised higher with their sepulchres.
>
> (1.4.97-103)

An outburst not found in the historical source material, these lines chime with contemporary anti-Catholic popular feeling, and have a political edge: the Bond of Association was created to prevent a Catholic succession; William Camden in 1588 instructed the Queen to fear "the Papists at Home"; and Sir Christopher Hatton denounced in a 1589 parliamentary session "those vile wretches, those bloody priests and false traitors here in our bosoms."[40] A special commission was set up in 1591 to locate priests and their supporters.[41] At his trial, the Earl of Essex was accused of entertaining "Papists, Recusants, and Atheists for his . . . abettors."[42] Typically Marlowe complicates a neat assessment by granting to a failing monarch sentiments that would have won instant approval among contemporary public amphitheater audiences.

The condemnation of Rome is eventually conflated into perceptions of the threat of kingdoms closer to home: all of England's neighbors are realized as dangerous. Ireland is imagined as a haven for Edward's minions, but at the same time it is feared as a nursery for conspiracy; Mortimer states: "Know you not Gaveston hath a store of gold, / Which may in Ireland purchase him . . . friends?" (1.4.258-59). In Scotland is another warring party (Old Mortimer is captured there), while France is as antagonistic: "The King of France sets foot in Normandy" (2.2.9) states Mortimer, and it is from France that he and Isabella devise their counter-attack. Even the "haughty Dane" is not exempt, and Edward is berated for allowing him to command "the narrow seas" (2.2.167). In an arresting speech, which crystallizes the fear of encroachment and specifically refers to the O'Neills, who rebelled in Ireland against English rule in the 1560s and 1570s, Lancaster states:

> Thy garrisons are beaten out of France,
> And, lame and poor, lie groaning at the gates;
> The wild O'Neil, with swarms of Irish kerns,
> Lives uncontrolled within the English pale;
> Unto the walls of York the Scots made road
> And unresisted drave away rich spoils.
> (2.2.161-66)[43]

Finally these forces coalesce into local, domestic forms: Edward is betrayed by Rice ap Howell, a Welshman, and when Bristol allies with the rebel cause, the king's fate is sealed.

V

In its clear investment in the ways in which power is textualized, *Edward II* bristles with sixteenth-century political preoccupations. The play does not, however, fit into a strict analogical or allegorical framework, for at any moment a particular character or scene can introduce a range of (sometimes contradictory) meanings. For example, Edward II and Edward III suggest the various situations of James, and Gaveston functions as an instance of favoritism while also articulating the difficulties of unrequited noble associations. The Earl of Essex is suggested in noble objections to Edward's predilections as well as in Gaveston's own declarations.

The reign of Edward II occupied a charged place in the late 1580s and the early 1590s, but Marlowe does not extend his contribution to identifying particular groupings precisely. His method, in contrast, is to hint at diverse considerations — debates about the lawfulness of resistance, about mastery and servitude, about the deposition (or even murder) of the sovereign, about the neglect of the kingdom, and about the rewards of service. Many of these questions have an Elizabethan urgency, particularly when the play mediates the ambitions of the nobility, parliamentary prerogatives, the problem of a monarch surrounded by flatterers and an abhorrence of foreign rule. But topicality never gives way to open criticism or approval. Comparisons are generally played down, even though there is every indication that the anomalous part played by Elizabeth is a key component in the representation of Edward's mixed fortunes. At the same time the play casts glances ahead to Jamesian interests, contemplating succession, the division of the kingdom and new geographical arrangements. In 1993, the quatercentenary year, scholars enjoyed a Marlowe retrospective: it provided a salutary opportunity to reflect upon the contexts of his work and the future political configurations that his plays predict.

Notes

1. Debra Belt, "Anti-Theatricalism and Rhetoric in Marlowe's *Edward II*," *English Literary Renaissance* 21 (1991), 139; Stephen Greenblatt, *Renaissance Self-Fashioning: From More to Shakespeare* (Chicago, 1980), 203, 213.

2. *Edward II*, ed. Charles R. Forker (Manchester, 1994), 1.1.135. All other quotations from the play will refer to this edition.

3. On names in the play, see David H. Thurn, "Sovereignty, Disorder, and Fetishism in Marlowe's *Edward II*," *Renaissance Drama* 21 (1990), 126.

4. Marjorie Garber briefly comments on writing in *Edward II* in "'Here's Nothing Writ': Scribe, Script, and Circumspection in Marlowe's Plays," *Theatre Journal* 36 (1984), 319.

5. On the intersection of material and political elements in *Edward II*, see Alan Bray, "Homosexuality and the Signs of Male Friendship in Elizabethan England," *History Workshop* 29 (1990), 9. It will be clear that my account is indebted throughout to Marie Axton's *The Queen's Two Bodies: Drama and the Elizabethan Succession* (London, 1977), a book which does not, however, address Marlowe's play.

6. That Elizabeth actually appeared in armour at Tilbury to deliver her address is disputed by Susan Frye, "The Myth of Elizabeth at Tilbury," *Sixteenth Century Journal* 23 (1992), 95-114, who points to the lack of contemporary description of the event.

7. Here, as elsewhere, I am responding to John D. Cox's argument about the frustrations of preferment and the contemporary figuration of the Earl of Essex as an aspirant in *Shakespeare and the Dramaturgy of Power* (Princeton, 1989), 58, 71, 114.

8. Sir Robert Naunton, *Fragmenta Regalia* (1641), ed. Henry Morley (London, 1889), 103-04.

9. Wallace MacCaffrey, *Elizabeth I* (London, 1993), 364.

10. W. T. MacCaffrey, "Place and Patronage in Elizabethan Politics," *Elizabethan Government and Society: Essays Presented to Sir John Neale*, ed. S. T. Bindoff, J. Hurstfield, and C. H. Williams (London, 1961), 102, 104, 116.

11. Peter Wentworth, *A pithie exhortation to her majestie for establishing her*

successor (London, 1598; STC 25245), 35, 36, 79.

12. Robert Parsons, *A conference about the next succession to the crowne of Ingland* (London, 1594; STC 1939), 58.

13. Mark Thornton Burnett, "Giving and Receiving: *Love's Labour's Lost* and the Politics of Exchange," *English Literary Renaissance* 23 (1993), 300.

14. Mervyn James, *Society, Politics and Culture: Studies in Early Modern England* (Cambridge, 1986), 423; D. M. Loades, *Politics and the Nation 1540-1660: Obedience, Resistance and Public Order* (London, 1974), 311.

15. Sir John Hayward, *An answer to the first part of a certaine conference* (London, 1603; STC 12988), sig. K1r.

16. See Thurn, "Sovereignty," 122-24.

17. Wentworth, *A pithie exhortation*, 7.

18. MacCaffrey, *Elizabeth I*, 92.

19. William Camden, *The History of the Most Renowned and Victorious Princess Elizabeth Late Queen of England*, ed. Wallace T. MacCaffrey (Chicago, 1970), 214.

20. J. E. Neale, *Queen Elizabeth I* (Harmondsworth, 1967), 306.

21. In this connection, see Cox, *Shakespeare*, 71.

22. See James, *Society*, 423.

23. John Stubbs, *The discouerie of a gaping gulf* (London, 1579; STC 23400), passim; Wentworth, *A pithie exhortation*, 25.

24. Julia Briggs, "Marlowe's *Massacre at Paris*: A Reconsideration," *The Review of English Studies* 34 (1983), 264.

25. Briggs, "Marlowe's *Massacre*," 264-65.

26. David Harris Willson, *King James VI and I* (London, 1966), 36.

27. Willson, *James*, 53.

28. Maurice Lee, Jr., *John Maitland of Thirlestane and the Foundations of the Stewart Despotism in Scotland* (Princeton, 1959), 177; *Secret History of the Court of James I*, 2 vols. (Edinburgh, 1811), 1: 274.

29. Several critics have touched upon points of contact between James VI and *Edward II*: see John M. Berdan, "Marlowe's *Edward II*," *Philological Quarterly* 3 (1924), 197-207; Charles R. Forker, "Sexuality and Eroticism on the Renaissance Stage," *South Central Review* 7.4 (1990), 2, 18-19.

30. David Lindley, *The Trials of Frances Howard: Fact and Fiction at the Court of King James* (London and New York, 1993), 212-13; *The Letters of John Chamberlain*, ed. Norman Egbert McClure, 2 vols. (Philadelphia, 1939), 2: 369.

31. Arthur Freeman, *Thomas Kyd: Facts and Problems* (Oxford, 1967), 183.

32. Charles Nicholl, *The Reckoning: The Murder of Christopher Marlowe* (London, 1992), 260-61.

33. Parsons, *A conference*, 227.

34. Neil Cuddy, "The revival of the entourage: the Bedchamber of James I, 1603-1625" in David Starkey, D. A. L. Morgan, John Murphy, Pam Wright, Neil Cuddy, and Kevin Sharpe, *The English Court: From the*

Wars of the Roses to the Civil War (London, 1987),179-80. Gaveston is also granted the office of "Lord High Chamberlain" (1.1.153).

35. Willson, *James*, 111.
36. Stubbs, *The discouerie*, sig. D1r; Christopher Haigh, *Elizabeth I* (London, 1988), 161, 170.
37. Curt Breight, "Realpolitik and Elizabethan Ceremony: The Earl of Hertford's Entertainment of Elizabeth at Elvetham, 1591," *Renaissance Quarterly* 45 (1992), 37.
38. Haigh, *Elizabeth I*, 128, 130-31, 133, 137, 144, 161; Loades, *Politics*, 301; Eric S. Mallin, "Emulous Factions and the Collapse of Chivalry: *Troilus and Cressida*," *Representations* 29 (1990), 145; J. E. Neale, *Elizabeth I and her Parliaments*, 2 vols. (London, 1969), 2: 241; Willson, *James*, 101, 110.
39. Cox, *Shakespeare*, 83; Carol Z. Wiener, "The Beleaguered Isle: A Study of Elizabethan and Early Jacobean Anti-Catholicism," *Past and Present* 51 (1971), 56.
40. Camden, *The History*, 313; Loades, *Politics*, 287, 315.
41. Loades, *Politics*, 315.
42. James, *Society*, 418.
43. See John Warren, *Elizabeth I: Religion and Foreign Affairs* (London, 1993), 123-25.

"Thou art no soldier; Thou art a merchant": The *Mentalité* of War in Malta

Alan Shepard

Gold "is such a weapon of so much might"[1]

Christopher Marlowe's abbreviated career as a London playwright coincided with one of the most tense periods in England's national life, as it struggled to remain neutral in the continental wars of religion, to compete in the nascent efforts to colonize the new world, and to defend itself against aggressive enemies, especially Spain. In 1585 an ordinarily dovish Queen Elizabeth had dispatched troops commanded by the Earl of Leicester to aid fellow Protestants suffering under Spain's rule in the Low Countries, defending her provocative action by way of England's "lawful commerce and entercourse of friendship and marchandise" with its people, and waited for the rumored Spanish attack on England's shores.[2] After the Armada's defeat in 1588, the nation was kept in a state of high military readiness and public anxiety well beyond Marlowe's death in 1593. In the half-dozen years he worked in London, then, war fever ran very high. It makes sense that as a young playwright he would capitalize on it; the wild popularity of *Tamburlaine the Great* points to his strong commercial instincts. It also makes sense that all of his plays are to some degree engaged in the general talk of war, its philosophical and practical dimensions, then circulating in England. *Edward II, The Massacre at Paris*, even the B-text of *Doctor Faustus* offer a panorama of speculations about the nature of empire, particularly the circumstances or personalities that make an empire weak. One of Marlowe's answers is especially surprising. With varying degrees of precision his plays indict martial law — and especially its concomitant notion that a national defense is contingent upon a prescriptive code of masculinity — as putting a nation most at risk.

Marlowe's critique of martial law also leaves him at odds with the

109

more orthodox view put forward by veteran soldiers and gentlemen alike in the military treatises printed in London in the period. These treatises are seldom taken into account by readings of Marlowe's plays, even though they constitute another kind of military script available for public consumption at more or less the same time as his plays were being staged. The treatises supply an important context for reading a play like *The Jew of Malta*. While it clearly traffics in the jingoistic hostility toward Turks and Jews that is common in Elizabethan drama,[3] simultaneously, I propose, it critiques the affective consequences of militarism upon civic life.

I

Almost universally, such handbooks present England's defense as being contingent upon the beleaguered integrity of a brittle code of nationalized masculinity, far more than upon munitions or even military strategy. Moreover, many if not all of the handbooks take a pessimistic view of the present state of English manhood; as Barnabe Rich recapitulates some six years into James' reign, peace having been made with Spain and France, "*Peace* breedes Cowards, it effeminates our mindes, it pampers our wanton wils, and it runs headlong into all sorts of sinne . . . . The Souldiour, who in the time of warre savoreth of sweat, (the true testimony of exercise and labour) in the time of Peace, is all to bee spiced with perfumes (the witnes of effeminate and womanish nicite)."[4] Perversely, Rich champions the idea that peace is more injurious than war because, self-reflexively, a peaceful nation wounds itself.

On the one hand, the veterans' gloom and doom recapitulates the medieval idea that civilizations inevitably spiral toward decay. On the other hand, the veterans often propose that martial law could stop what was too commonly seen as England's disintegration by purging various infections in the commonweal. Under martial law, they hold, a chivalric episteme could be resurrected, and England could be made safe again from enemies both foreign and domestic. Ironically, as Maurice Keen reminds us, prognostications about the decline of chivalry, down to the familiar claims that its adherents are being emasculated by new customs, "are as old as chivalry itself"; but whereas medieval writers inveighed against "black knights"[5] who violated a set of chivalric ideals, sixteenth-century commentators who tried to police the exercise of English manhood were faced with an unprecedented shift toward the commercial organization of life.[6]

In the contemporary military treatises it is possible to see how the ground has shifted. No longer is the battle between honorable and miscreant knights, but between common soldiers and merchants, whom the soldiers — taking the high ground — paint as the gravest internal threat to a strong England. Examples of soldiers' efforts to revoke the role of merchants as arbiters of the direction in which England was headed include a pair of pamphlets by Geoffrey Gates and William Blandy, authors respectively of *The Defence of Militarie Profession* (1579) and *The Castle of Pollicye* (1581). Using a notary as his amanuensis, Gates presents himself as an "unlettered man" who defends the integrity of a life at arms by claiming that soldiers pursue a "profession" as specialized as any career in the law or the church.[7] Further, in times of military conflict, then England will "know the value of a soldier, & lick the dust off the feete of her men of prewesse: then would the lawer and the marcheant humble themselves to the warriers, & be glad to geve honour and salary to the martialist" (18). Gates' special antipathy for merchants becomes even more apparent when his pamphlet is read in tandem with his friend William Blandy's *The Castle*, in which Gates now plays the role of an eager but naïve pupil in a socratic dialogue that draws out Blandy's ostensible wisdom about war in contemporary life. If *The Castle*'s structure harkens back to medieval monastic dialogues between a master and novice, its apologia of common soldiers and invective against merchants are quintessentially modern. Dedicated to Philip Sidney, whose implied patronage supplies the cover of aristocratic privilege, *The Castle* moves in a few pages from ethereal, obligatory topics, such as the nobility of reason to mundane pronouncements about tactics.

The *Castle* comes alive when Gates asks Blandy to describe his vision of a "perfect commonwealth."[8] Answering what is in effect his own question, Blandy spins out a soldier's fantasy of paradise. Rather than consign the responsibility for making war to mercenaries, as does the archetype of a "perfect commonwealth" in the sixteenth century — More's *Utopia* — Blandy's own text enthusiastically embraces the profession of arms. In *Utopia* mercenaries are presented as merchants of death, whose ambiguous outsider status as hired killers is tied to their rapacious appetite for lucre, which is said to overwhelm all honor; even Barabas the Jew claims to have worked as a mercenary (2.3.190). In *The Castle*, by contrast, soldiers are positioned just below the king. There, by "skill and vertue in warlike practices," they help rule the "multitude" (27, 26). Blandy situates them near the apex of the hierarchy because of their central role in making a nation safe. Thus is Gates' argument (as described above) elaborated and embellished by Blandy: "Dame Nature [has bestowed upon soldiers] the clearnesse and shining glory of vertue and nobility: yet she hath imparted unto them a most sharp wit and ready capacity, great value and singuler providence" (27). The bloody material consequences of war are erased and the soldiers' aggression naturalized by an appeal to the lexicon of natural philosophy, which presupposes a sublunary interdependence of soldiers and Nature that is then belied by the phrase "singuler providence." It sounds as if Blandy aims to deify soldiers as demigods who in his commonwealth reside above the fray of ordinary life, and therefore beyond temptation to serve Mammon as merchants of death. Yet demigods require an evil force against which they are able to display their nobility. For Blandy, that evil force is merchants en masse. When Gates asks where merchants go in the pecking order, the question opens Blandy's valve. *The Castle* moves in its last pages to a withering attack on English merchants. As scapegoats their alleged behaviors are used to justify what Blandy hopes is a return to martial law and the renewal of a chivalric ethos. He charges them with reckless disregard for the physical and moral integrity of the nation. Sometimes they are like vampirish predators, sucking the blood of their aristocratic betters by selling them their own fantasies, as when Blandy says a merchant "harkeneth after the wants, phantasies, spending humors of gentlemen of his owne countrey . . . . [They] give theyr Countrye to often most unnaturally a deepe and deadlye wound" (28). This not-so-subtle appeal to gentlemen's anxieties about the diminishing of class privilege in an age increasingly commercial is followed by appeals to religious and gender prejudices. Some merchants are popish or effeminate or worse. Even speaking about them may be enough to compromise Blandy's standing among true men, or so he feigns in an outburst against Gates' demand that the status of merchants be stated more precisely:

> Will you that I write more then I have spoken? Would you
> me attempt the commendation of theyr state: If so, I shall
> hardly avoyd the suspition of feare, or flattery:
> acknowledging notwithstanding how unable a man I am to
> yelde to the good and vertuous Marchaunt the true guerdon
> of his due desert. Would you me instruct them in theyr kinde
> of life? Should my pen pinch or improve their daynty fare?
> Should I be so bolde, as to enter into theyr house-chappell,
> and mangle theyr to to much carved Imagery, nipp theyr soft
> & nice nightbeds? (28)

Blandy fears that if he were to give merchants even a modicum of respect, he might be contaminated by their soft habits of mind as well as by the material comforts they hawk as part of their new world order of peace for profit. And the Middle English noun "guerdon" reminds playgoers that in the new world of international trade — think of Barabas' trading range, from Malta to "*Florence, Venice, Antwerpe, London, Civill [Seville], Frankeford, Lubecke, Mosco, and where not*" — soldiers are reduced to vying with merchants for the accolades once almost exclusively available to knights, whose international exchanges had focused on pummeling enemies, as in the Crusades, and on bringing home booty gained by violence.[9] Yet outrageously, Blandy hints that merchants, not soldiers, are the destroyers: "theyr kinde of life," with its "to to much carved Imagery" and private chapels — he aims to tar merchants by suggesting they share the supposed desire of English Catholics to sabotage the nation from within.[10] This exchange between Gates and Blandy typifies the notion of many veterans-turned-writers that, to keep England safe from Spain or its lesser enemies, its soldiers must beat back the advancing merchants, whom the soldiers perceive as too greedy ever to be trusted to put the nation's defense before their own profit.

As we shall see, this charge is caricatured by Marlowe in the early scenes of *The Jew of Malta*, where Barabas' greed is but one reason he dismisses all obligation to defend Malta from the Turks. As he proclaims to his fellow Jews as they prepare to meet Ferneze in 1.1, "If any thing shall there concerne our state assure your selves I'le looke — *unto my selfe [Aside]*" (1.1.172-73). *The Jew of Malta* dissects civilian alienation from the state; it traces the affective damage to civilian life that follows the confiscation of property without due process, showing how that violence against property authorizes various kinds of emotional violation that express the loss of civility, trust, and respect for humanity that, as the play demonstrates, is part and parcel of a militarist ethos that is no longer working for Malta or England.

Marlowe presents a collision between ancient and contemporary models of empire, the one depending upon military plunder from, say, the Roman legion or the Hospitallers, the other requiring the suspension of the impulse to conquer in favor of voluntary commercial exchanges and international cooperation. *The Jew of Malta*, as a critique of the reactionary efforts of soldiers aiming to halt the transition, implicitly privileges commerce such as is taking place in the first scenes of the play. Marlowe's favorable treatment of commerce, if not of Barabas as its most successful representative, anticipates the response of Enlightenment philosophers, who theorize the spread of commerce as a civilizing phenomenon. *The Jew of Malta* glances toward a world of great merchants (not epic warlords) who are the engines of peaceful contact among nations. To sustain a successful business venture, a merchant must not only set aside prejudice, but also genuinely reciprocate with merchants from other nations; hostile commercial contact would eventually regress into war. War itself disrupts opportunities for commerce, even on a microeconomic plane, as is humorously made clear in the play. As the courtesan Bellamira complains in act 3, the Turkish warships anchored off the coast of Malta are keeping away clients, merchants from Padua and Venice: "Since this town was beseiged, my gain grows cold" (3.1.1). As Bellamira opens her body to any man who can pay, regardless of nationality or faith, Barabas likewise demonstrates an ecumenical pragmatism in his business affairs that sets aside the nationalist concerns of the state. Ignoring the incompatible mishmash of religious and political philosophies of nations, his argosies call at ports across the globe; he trades promiscuously, even with Persians, the sworn enemies of Malta, cultivating an ever-expanding network of relations that supercedes traditional boundaries. As when Barabas names the "Scatter'd Nation" of great Jews, those of Greece, Portugal, Bairseth and the like (1.1.121), it is suggested that wealth creates an identity independent of, sometimes contrary to, the state's interest; while the two are not necessarily incompatible, the prospect of commercially gained wealth and the ancient model of the state as a superstructure for raiding wars are clearly so. Marlowe implies what Enlightenment scholars would later say, that peaceful contact diminishes prejudice and violence among nations. Montesquieu's treatment of the idea is representative of the eighteenth-century belief that merchants are in effect humanitarians. In *The Spirit of Laws* he writes, "Commerce is a cure for the most destructive prejudices."[11]

Malta is a brilliant choice of setting for Marlowe's concerns. In the sixteenth century it was the second Mediterranean base of the Hospitallers (later, the Knights of Malta), one of three Roman Catholic orders of monk-soldiers organized in the twelfth century to crusade against the infidels. Over time their mission was reduced to patrolling the Mediterranean Sea, for which they got a number of islands as staging areas. They received control of Malta from Charles V in 1530, survived a long seige by 200 Turkish warships and 30,000 men in 1565, and surrendered it to none less than Napoleon in 1798. For more than two centuries the Knights protected Christian merchant ships and pirated Turkish and other Islamic ships in the region.[12] Consistent with Marlowe's effort to diminish respect for a military ethos, however, his knights of Malta have reduced themselves to an indolent if not cowardly existence. Military values have become so much firewood. Crusades for the greater glory of God have been replaced by the occasional sea battle, and that a fading memory, in which the booty is its own highest reward. Deliberately these are not English soldiers, so Marlowe could paint them in an exceedingly unfavorable light with near-immunity. As Emily Bartels comments, "the Knights stood as a threat to Elizabethan England because of their militant Catholicism and their control over Mediterranean commerce, and the play encourages its audiences' prejudices against them as it erases the one historical event (their success in freeing Europe from the Turks) which secured what was already very limited English support after the Reformation."[13]

Under all the grandstanding about religious and military honor is a universal appetite for gold, what the Basso names as "the wind that bloweth all the world" (3.5.3). Ironically, only the Turks consistently acknowledge this truth; everyone else speaks from both sides of their mouths. Yet only Barabas seems to revel in the gap between false and authentic speech, in the free play of language that is itself epistemologically unmoored. As the consummate outsider in Malta he takes up chameleonic self-fashioning not only to advance himself, but eventually as a way to collude with the hegemonic state apparatus while simultaneously undermining it, a goal necessarily shared by few of the island's other inhabitants. He prizes opportunities to practice his skill at extemporaneously shaping his identity to the moment: "We Jewes can fawne like Spaniels when we please; and when we grin we bite" (2.3.20-21). As something of an outsider it is in his interest to check the state's power. Yet as its most prominent merchant, it is also in his interest to keep the state viable as a commercial marketplace. And so through much of the play he pictures his adversarial relationship with Malta as a game, as an endless loop of what he sees as interdependent transactions.[14] This helps to explain, for example, his otherwise puzzling decision to resign the governorship of Malta in act 5. Though he has previously expressed a desire to see Ferneze whipped to death (5.1.68), he bargains away his new powers only a few lines into office. Giving it back, Barabas chats up his enemy, pretending nonchalance while throwing down a merchant's gauge, daring the governor to pay him back: "let me see what mony thou canst make" (5.2.94); the challenge imitates Ferneze's in act 1 as the Jew's estate is seized. The resignation from office is consistent with the Jew's idea that the more powerful man is one who makes kings, as he tells us· "Why, is not this a kingly kinde of trade to purchase Townes by treachery, and sell 'em by deceit?" (5.5.47-48).

However, as is clear in act 5, Barabas pushes the game too far, and the denouement traps spectators in a uncomfortable critique of the hypocrisy surrounding all the Knights' presumptive moral authority as monk-soldiers. While we may not feel pity as Barabas boils to death in a trap of his own design, we must ask why Ferneze and his fellow Hospitallers do not rescue him when he pleads for Christian mercy. Sacrificing him, they affirm solidarity with the fraternity of soldiers everywhere, even their arch-enemies the Turks. The merchant is sacrificed in symbolic recompense for the Turkish sailors whom he orders "massacred" even as they showed faith in the hospitality of a victors' banquet (5.5.107). Moreover, the knights' refusal to extend succor to the one figure who most passionately subscribes to the commercial paradigm clears the way to remake Malta as a sanctuary for the weakened traditions of chivalry, an island of the old school amidst irremediable social change. No one else there, least of all Barabas' fellow Jews Zaareth and Temainte, will stand in the way of its reincarnation as a port for warships, not for argosies with silk and spice and diamonds in their holds — the commercial seascape conjured up in the exchanges of Barabas and his factors in 1.1. The final moments of act 5 press the idea of a nostalgic return to a golden age of chivalry. Following the accepted battlefield treatment of noble prisoners, Ferneze spares Calymath's life (as *he* would not, were the tables turned), holding him for ransom. Proud of himself, Ferneze contrasts his own generosity to "a Jewes curtesie" (5.5.108); he imagines no merchant who would immolate a squadron of soldiers at a victory banquet is capable of respecting the protocol for the treatment of subdued nobles, even though that is exactly what Barabas has done in treating the imprisoned Ferneze with charity. Yet there is some earlier evidence that the tradition itself is waning: with no trace of regret, Admiral Martin del Bosco has reported "slaine" the captain of the sailors he sells as slaves in Malta (2.2.17).

Further, the term courtesy itself has been robbed of significant meaning over the course of the play. In 1.2, for instance, Calymath upbraids the basso who niggardly demands the instant payment of Malta's tribute — "What, *Callapine*, a little curtesie" (1.2.23), though Calymath himself has just twice said he "dare not dally" and "shall not tarry" waiting for the tribute to be paid (1.2.12, 16). In 2.3 Lodowick, negotiating for Abigail's hand, says that as a suitor he expects to be put through some ritual test so as to "deserve her" (2.3.68), yet speaks crudely of her with rival Don Mathias; Barabas likewise contributes to bankrupting chivalric courtship by directing Abigail to "make love" to Lodowick "with all the curtesie you can affoord; / Provided, that you keep your Maidenhead" (2.3.238, 225-26). Within both private and public arenas, from diplomacy to love, courtesy is being detached from any signified meaning; it is indiscriminately available to all, regardless of honor, nationality, religious faith, or economic status.

The disintegration of chivalry and its implied militarist ethos is most on display in the seizure episode in 2.2. The scene demonstrates that the knights' hostility toward Barabas, the greatest and most visible entrepeneur in Malta, expresses more than theological prejudice.[15] Their anti-Semitism, I suggest, is a red herring, for none of the principals acts in a way that would affirm religious belief as a guiding principle; beyond expedience, the seizure helps them compensate psychologically for their own failures. The Jews summoned to appear are forced to part with half their wealth on the grounds of "the common good" and their own "inherent sinne" and "monstrous sinne" of "covetousnesse" (1.2.98, 109, 124). But these Jews have long been allowed to do business and amass wealth in Malta, and in any case the Knights show little regard for the common good, far less than is expected of them. More to the point is that the Hospitallers, operating within a medieval economy fed by the spoils of war, have been profligate losers at their own game. As Ferneze explains, with the tribute ten years in arrears, the sum cannot now be raised "By reason of the warres, that robb'd our store; / and therefore are we to request your ayd" (1.2.48-49). In other words, the knights have failed to collect enough loot from pirated ships, presumably because of their "Tributary league" (2.2.23) with the Turks: they find themselves in a catch-22. Barabas seems deliberately to misinterpret the "request" as an invitation to become a soldier. "Alas, my Lord, we are no souldiers" (1.2.50), he replies, turning back on them their cherished image of themselves as superior to the civilians they protect. Taking the bait, the First Knight answers with sarcastic envy: "Tut, Jew, we know thou art no souldier; thou art a Merchant, and a monied man, and 'tis thy mony, *Barabas*, we seeke" (1.2.52-54). Pragmatically, the second knight explains it as the cost of doing business in a foreign land: "Have strangers leave with us to get their wealth? Then let them with us contribute" (1.2.60-61); we must remember, however, that Barabas is no more an outsider than the knights themselves; indeed, they are arguably colonialists in ways he is not, for as he points out elsewhere, merchants are less interested in "Principality" than in profit (1.1.135). Marlowe's audience might have known that in 1586 Queen Elizabeth had demanded of "merchant strangers" working in London almost £5,000 to help prepare for war with Spain, and otherwise relied upon some forced loans and confiscations in order to repay huge debts from wars earlier in the century with France and Scotland.[16] But the demands are not alike, for the knights of Malta as yet do not intend to fight off the Turks as England would soon fight Spain. In fact, their acquiescence ironizes Calymath's false flattery of them in 1.2 as he withdraws to await their payment with "Farewell great Governor, and brave Knights of *Malta*" (1.2.32). As is the feudal concept of courtesy, so that of bravery is being gutted in Malta.

Into the midst of the public and private crises occasioned by Calymath's return to Malta arrives Admiral Martin del Bosco. Like all great military officers in Marlowe's plays, del Bosco is a subtle rhetorician, and in a brief exchange in the Senate House manages to reform the knights into fire-breathing warriors who are again "at deadly enmity with Turkes" (2.2.33). He comes in fresh from burning and sinking a Turkish fleet. The battle had been joined after he refused to lower his topsails as a sign of respect.[17] So in Malta he is shocked to find fellow Catholics submissively in "league" with the infidels (2.2.23). The dialogue sparked by his arrival anatomizes the inflammatory rhetoric of war fever, as the

Admiral takes charge of Malta's defense. He scarcely need be invited into this catalyzing role, as he is by the First Knight, who is now inspired to fight, though earlier he had goaded Ferneze to submit to the Turks (1.2.157-59). Sounding remarkably akin to the Younger Mortimer wresting command of a beleagured England from Isabella, del Bosco insists that Malta "be rul'd by me" (2.2.39). His tactics are to raise their hopes of becoming a viable military unit again, then to shame them by telling a story of their Order's defeat in the battle of Rhodes (1513), the Hospitallers' first Mediterranean base, lost after a long Turkish siege. Historically, the Order had eventually surrendered Rhodes and negotiated safe passage for its surviving members. Del Bosco misrepresents the outcome, claiming they had fought to the death, so that "not a man surviv'd / To bring the hapless news to Christendom" (2.2.50-51). The defeat had been "Europe's shame" (2.2.31). Implied in del Bosco's narrative is the potential for that shame to be compounded now; he appeals not only to the knights' sense of duty, but to their fear of being emasculated in the eyes of a visibly successful warrior. Under this strain, Ferneze declaims as if he were playing Hercules at the Rose Theatre:

> So we will fight it out; come, let's away:
> Proud-daring Calymath, instead of gold,
> We'll send thee bullets wrapt in smoke and fire:
> Claim tribute where thou wilt, we are resolv'd,
> Honour is bought with blood and not with gold.
> (2.2.52-56)

In spite of del Bosco's tutelage, however, the knights are allowed to be seen as only belligerent, not brave, for they virtually disappear until act 5. No opportunity to recuperate their honor comes their way, as Marlowe shifts our attention to domestic matters, tracing militarism's impact upon the affective life of Malta's other inhabitants.

II

Marlowe is careful to suggest that the language of war has penetrated all of Maltese culture, as civilians construct images of themselves by imitating the knights of Malta at their peak; they do so, sometimes unwittingly, as a way of joining the hegemonic group, in this case, soldiers. As even del Bosco understands, the transmittal of war fever to the demoralized or the young depends upon simple acts of imitating those who worship arms, as the admiral advises the rejuvenated "warlike" Ferneze (2.2.45, 47). Barabas, for example, despite his occupation as a merchant adventurer, persists in representing himself as a soldier instead. After his goods are seized he borrows the vocabulary of war, specifically the vocabulary of the vanquished, to characterize his emotional state, asking his compatriot Jews for the

> liberty at least to mourne,
> That in a field amidst his enemies,
> Doth see his souldiers slaine, himselfe disarm'd,
> And knowes no meanes of his recoverie,
>
> (1.2.202-05)

and later speaking of his "former riches" as being "like a souldiers skarre, / That has no further comfort for his maime" (2.1.9-11). While some of this talk may simply be a machiavellian attempt to position himself inside the charmed circle of warriors, from whence revenge would be more accessible, there is too much material in the play suggesting that Barabas takes the confiscation as he does because — like del Bosco — he is still invested in a zero-sum vision of the world, in which a man can only win or lose. As Stephen Greenblatt observes his geneology, "Barabas is brought into being by the Christian society" (206).

Other than Barabas, martial law's impact is principally suffered upon Abigail and, to a lesser extent, Bellamira. The female bodies function as focal points in a symbolic economy; upon them the civilian men strive to replicate at least figuratively the absolutism that equates masculine strength with the lack of all human compassion, what Barabas says is the knights' ability to have their "unrelenting flinty hearts suppresse all pitty in [their] stony breasts" (1.2.141-42), an image repeated in his advice to Ithamore about how to succeed in Malta (2.3.171).

Throughout the play, Abigail and particularly the representation of her body are treated with grave disrespect. In a series of what might easily be considered figurative sexual assaults, her priest confessor, her suitors — including her "love," Don Mathias (2.3.237) — and her father fantasize about the pleasures of disfiguring, penetrating, and defiling her body. While their fantasies are regularly couched in the language of commerce — getting, selling, profiting, and so forth — I argue next that the transgressive treatment of her body critiques and usually condemns the men's martial fantasies of dominion, and that these fantasies have less to do with commercial than chivalric ideas about gender, though at first study the language might seem to confirm the early modern complaint that the triumph of a commercial mode over more ancient ways of organizing social life threatens to cheapen all human relationships.

To take the series of fantasies in ascending order of complexity, we begin with the moment of Abigail's death. Like Edward II she has taken sanctuary in a monastic house to escape a life saturated with violent, ambitious men who, as Michael Drayton says of Edward's foes, have "acted without Humane Pittie."[18] Admittedly Abigail's death is not nearly the spectacle Edward's is, and playgoers have less sympathy invested in her character. Yet it is appalling when her confessor Father Barnardine answers her very last words — "And witness that I dye a Christian" — with a crude, callow reply: "I, and a Virgin too, that grieves me most" (3.6.40-41).[19] Elizabethan jokes about corrupt Roman Catholic priests notwithstanding, Marlowe seems utterly serious to me at this moment, which records the contrast between Abigail's sincere spirituality and Barnardine's false ministry. In one line he manages not only to offend the doctrine of conventual abstinence by presenting her virginity as an occasion of grief, but more importantly, I think — because Marlowe shows more respect for a secular model of human dignity than for canonical expression — Barnardine visually penetrates Abigail in an act of symbolic necrophilia.

Like the good father, Abigail's suitors Don Mathias and Lodowick also take pleasure in imagining sexual intercourse with her, in which the prize of her virginity is again an integral part of their initial fantasies. Their interest in her body has two distinct movements in the play. In act 1 they are aligned as homosocial pals who from a distance glibly imagine the pleasure of sexual intercourse with Abigail; in acts 2 and 3, they become jealous rivals in an unwinnable, fatal competition orchestrated by Barabas. As the play proceeds, then, these gallants are transformed from cads into gentlemen at arms, which as Barabas draws out, makes them rather more than less vulnerable because their fantasies about chivalric honor overwhelm good sense. In act 1, united in their schoolboy banter, they seem invincible. They are economically advantaged and socially privileged, and Mathias in particular shows little compassion for Barabas and Abigail's new circumstances. It seems he might be speaking of himself as he tells Lodowick that Abigail is so

> matchlesse beautifull;
> As had you seene her 'twould have mov'd your heart,
> Tho countermin'd with walls of brasse, to love,
> Or at the least to pitty.

> (1.2.84-87)

Later in act 2, Lodowick will seem impervious to Barabas' effort to ensnare him with images of Abigail's "diamond," while Mathias lacks all discretion. He instantly deduces that Barabas' "sudden fall" (1.2.367) has "humbled" Abigail into holy orders; word is out, and it is perceived to shame them both. As if the seizure also authorizes Mathias to take charge of Abigail's virtual body, he rejects the convent for her as a kind of sexual and reproductive death. She is

> the sweetest flower in *Citherea*'s field,
> Cropt from the pleasures of the fruitfull earth,
> And strangely metamorphis'd Nun.
>
> (1.2.379-81)

His ribald puns tease out the physical pleasures of sexual intercourse, juxtaposed to the meager spiritual rewards of faith:

> Tut, she were fitter for a tale of love
> Then to be tired out with Orizons:
> And better would she farre become a bed
> Embraced in a friendly lovers armes,
> Then rise at midnight to a solemne mass.
>
> (1.2.369-73)

In his eyes Abigail is thus only a fantastical body, a vessel more fit for the phallus than for prayer, which he stands ready to penetrate with his "tale of love." Given this kind of talk it is somewhat difficult to comprehend that in act 3 the suitors kill one another in a duel they think designed to preserve honor — their own and Abigail's, for as they become gentlemen at arms, she necessarily becomes their chivalric inspiration. Sons of the aristocracy prove mindlessly vulnerable to the machinations of a merchant who resurrects an aristocratic rite as a weapon in his class war, while the status of Abigail's virtual body is again staged as a function of the fictions surrounding an ancient model of plunder.

The father-daughter relationship is affectively the most complex in the play. She is devoted to him; he is devoted to victory at all costs. A sign that Barabas customarily thinks of even his domestic life in the vocabulary of the militarism that dominates Malta is in his oath, said without perceptible irony, that he holds Abigail "as deare/ As *Agamemnon* did his *Iphigen*" (1.1.139-40). As an expression of paternal love, this offers cold comfort. It does, however, reveal a fascinating piece of his fantasy life in which he casts himself as a great Greek general.[20] As Patricia Joplin says about the sacrifice of Iphigenia in Euripides, however, "the unmaking of Homeric heroes is also the unmasking of the cultural fictions that veil the sacrificial violence at the basis of political domination."[21] Initially it is Abigail, not her father, who proposes a response to the seizure of their estate that dares to contest the veiled fictions of martial law. As a first response, she advocates mutilating herself in a public forum, "not for my selfe, but aged *Barabas*." She shall

> With fierce exclaimes run to the Senate-house,
> And in the Senate reprehend them all,
> And rent their hearts with tearing of my haire,
> Till they reduce the wrongs done to my father.
>
> (1.2.232-35)

But as Barabas knows, Malta has become a place where persuasive speech counts for little, even in the Senate; he teaches Abigail that "things past recovery / Are hardly cur'd with exclamations" (1.2.236-37). From this point father and daughter are never again so united as dissidents. For while she may be ready to injure herself in her father's cause, as a woman in a highly patriarchal world, she is unable to injure anyone else, even when she discovers that her father has plotted against her suitors' lives. That, she says, has "murdered me" (3.3.46), "yet never shall these lips bewray thy life" (3.3.77).

While Abigail's injury remains effectively inarticulated, Barabas' rage against his forced submission to the knights' absolute authority is eventually inscribed on Abigail's body. For men in the play, submitting is always shameful, as we are reminded by the force of del Bosco's allusion to the battle of Rhodes and Barabas' disgust with his fellow Jews (and himself) who "basely thus submit your selves" to Malta's soldiers (1.2.79). By abusing Abigail, Barabas seeks to erase his shame by projecting it onto her, and this process takes place entirely inside the convent that had served as their home before it was confiscated too. In a state run by a monastic order, the nunnery is inevitably part of the state apparatus, here a place where religious and military disciplines meet, a site in which the power of the capricious state is naturalized as religious piety. In the first attack on the convent, Abigail is a reluctant but cooperative accomplice. While Barabas feignedly condemns her supposed entry into the novitiate by calling her "thy fathers shame" (1.2.344), she colludes not only with his plan, but unwittingly with his effort to transfer his shame to her through incestuous expressions of desire for gold. Late at night, awaiting his return to the window where she will hand down the booty, she prays:

> gentle sleepe, where e're his bodie rests,
> Give charge to *Morpheus* that he may dreame
> A golden dreame, and of the sudden walke,
> Come and receive the Treasure I have found.
>
> (2.1.35-38)

She prays that he may experience a nocturnal wet dream so

powerful it would awaken him into a state of acquisitive satisfaction.
As if in answer, at midnight he returns to the window to hail her
success with sexually charged praise:

> Welcome the first beginner of my blisse:
> Oh *Abigal, Abigal*, that I had thee here too,
> Then my desires were fully satisfied,
> But I will practise thy enlargement thence:
> Oh girle, oh gold, oh beauty, oh my blisse!
> [s.d.] *Hugs his bags.*
>
> (2.1.50-54)

The paratactic ecstasy of the final line makes fatherhood, sex,
pleasure, and wealth grammatically contiguous, emotionally fused.
While his promise of Abigail's forthcoming "enlargement" has a
straightforward denotative meaning, in its context it also opens up
more than one bawdy connotation for a virginal nun — would it be
vaginal dilation? pregnancy? emancipation from the cloister? We
are teased by Marlovian ambiguity again as Abigail responds to his
speech, sending him away so as "to shun suspition" (2.1.57). In a
study of incest in early modern drama, Richard McCabe reminds us
that the topic "served as a powerful focus for scrutinising all forms
of allegedly 'natural' authority."[22] In the midnight exchange of
gold and parental affection through the windows of the convent,
indeed, the tableau of a lovers' rendezvous invites playgoers to
contemplate not only the potential dangers of absolute paternal
authority (where is Abigail's mother anyway?),[23] but also the
righteousness of Christian dogma that naturalizes violent conquests,
as in the capture of this real estate that has been gladly converted
into church property, as the inevitable and laudable victory of
Christs' soldiers. In Barabas' final engagement with Abigail, he
protests the entitlement expressed in the Church's use of his house.
Scheming to injure his daughter and her sisters, he sends alms in the
form of poisoned porridge, mocking the nuns who have displaced
him as being privileged and unwary consumers of charity, and in
effect taking back his house by making it over once more into an
erotic zone, but now also a site of mass murder.

Anthropologist Mary Douglas observes that "food is not likely
to be polluting at all unless the external boundaries of the social
system are under pressure . . . . [Then] we should expect the orifices
of the body to symbolise its specifically vulnerable points" in the
symbolic economy of that society.[24] To express such pressure on
stage, Marlowe frequently relies upon the motif of contaminated
food. Usually it signifies that tyrants achieve new heights of control
over a community by making the act of eating a shameful
expression of submission instead of a regenerative act of self-

mastery. Thus Tamburlaine tries to humiliate Bajazeth by forcing him to eat from the tip of a sword; Doctor Faustus mocks the Vatican by throwing around its gourmet food; Gurney reports having been almost overcome by the stench of the sewer as he threw meat to Edward II; and Barabas impregnates a pot of porridge with the "blood of *Hydra*, *Lerna*'s bane; the jouyce of Hebon, and *Cocitus* breath, and all the poysons of the stygian poole"; then speaking, it seems, of himself, he says, "and in this vomit your venome, and invenome her that like a fiend hath left her father thus" (3.4.100-05). Metonymically, Barabas replaces his daughter's mouth for her vagina.[25] Particularly powerful is his trope of evacuating his "venome" by vomiting it into the porridge and indirectly into his daughter's mouth: again he is transferring the rage bred in him by having been forced to yield not only his estate, but his dignity too. As late as act 5 he is continuing to decry the loss of his goods and land and vowing to help Calymath "slay" women and children and "fire the Churches [and] pull their houses downe," acts that signify a Tamburlainesque rage directed against the community that has betrayed him, but provoked solely by its soldiers' own aggression (5.1.64-65).

The play's second best merchant thrives amidst Barabas' distress because she collaborates with the state. Bellamira the courtesan regulates access to a female body to turn a profit, pursuing the capitalist game at its most physical. Neither enslaved to her procurer Pilia-borza nor exploited by Ithamore, Bellamira might appear to be in charge of her destiny. Yet she is nonetheless answerable to the Knights of Malta, in part by reifying their manichean vision of women, who may be only as pure as Abigail or as public as she. In this way, as Augustine observed, prostitutes are localized sites of disorder, mistresses of order: "Remove prostitutes from human affairs, and you will destroy everything with lust."[26] We see her collusion with authority in act 5. Once she learns that Ithamore and Barabas are responsible for setting up Lodowick and Mathias and strangling the friars, she hastens to report their deeds to Ferneze, even though doing so shall stop the flow of ducats to her purse: she acts not in her own, but in the state's best interest. Her interview with Ferneze captures Bellamira's ambiguous status in Malta and explains in part why she makes an effort to associate herself with what Ferneze duplicitously refers to as having the "law"; even before she is able to speak he tries to dismiss her, so she is forced to assert herself: "What e'er I am, yet Governor heare me speak" (5.1.40, 9).

If Bellamira is in abstract ways exploited by the systematic oppression of women in Malta, in a concrete way she also profits from it by manipulating Ithamore. Unlike her Venetian and Paduan clients who are free traders, Ithamore is still a prisoner of war, a galley slave who seeks to find in intimacy with Bellamira more than sexual gratification. So we might see their "relationship" as a metaphor of the mutual dependence of merchants and soldiers. The parody of Ithamore's petrarchan pursuit of the courtesan magnifies the deleterious effects of commerce and war both. Under the spell of a quean, Ithamore looks to a strong woman to have his war-torn identity repaired and restored, much as Aeneas does in *Dido, Queene of Carthage*. Ithamore seems to believe that physical intimacy offers an escape from a violent world in which he takes himself to be "not worthy to look upon her" (4.2.36). This is in fact his first response to Bellamira's letter, delivered by courier, stating her "interest" in him. Perhaps "she / sees more in me than I can find in my selfe," he marvels, "for she writes further, that she loves me ever since she saw me, and who would not requite such love?" (4.2.32-35). As Jacques Rossiaud explains of thirteenth-century Dijonnais who used prostitutes, "There were images of a golden age suspended at the deepest level of consciousness among the poor; there was a desire to return to the primitive community."[27]

In *The Jew*, likewise, money becomes the vehicle of a primitive golden age fantasy: Ithamore is metamorphosed from slave to gentleman, from soldier to petrarchan poet. When the lovers meet, Ithamore finds that he also loves her at first sight, as the tradition dictates, proclaiming hers "the sweetest face that ever I beheld" (3.1.26), and he revels in his lady's exalted gaze — her eye "twinckles like a Starre." "Come gentle *Ithimore*, lye in my lap," she coos, continuing the game, facetiously bestowing upon him the rank of gentleman. As with Ben Jonson's Dol-Common, the clever con in *The Alchemist*, Bellamira feeds herself by feeding a gull's fantasy of vaulting material and sexual limits.[28] But as is made clear by Ithamore's cavalier use of his master's ducats, he values 'love' above gold. When she demands payment for her affections, Ithamore is quick to respond: "I'le goe steale some mony from my Master to make / Me hansome" (4.2.49-50). We might conclude that underneath the comedy, Ithamore's entanglement with Bellamira exposes the insidious mental violence done by capitalism upon those who worship at its altar as a matter of survival: the disenfranchised poor, for example, like Ithamore, who discover in affluent Malta that poverty is degrading. Ithamore signals as much when he reflects upon how Pilia-borza appeared to him at the (unjust) public execution of friar Jacomo: Pilia-borza "gave me a letter from one / Madam *Bellamira*, saluting me in such sort as if he had meant to / make cleane my Boots with his lips" (4.2.29-31). Self-reflexively, Ithamore indulges in a comic but sado-masochistic fantasy of being served by another slave.

In responding to Bellamira, Ithamore hopes to create himself as someone other than a soldier or slave. Repeatedly his aim is spoofed. He is so lost in "imaginative aggrandizement"[29] that he mistakes her name as "sweet Allamira" (4.2.53), accessible to all. Pilia-Borza jokes that the slave would "make a rich Poet" (4.2.122). Indeed, Ithamore has just finished an aria to his beloved that is the quintessence of all that a prisoner-of-war-become-slave might hope to escape into: "we will leave this paltry land, / And sail from hence to *Greece, to lovely Greece,*" he promises himself as much as Bellamira (4.2.89-90). Casting himself as a pastoral Adonis who shall live in perpetual ecstasy in a classical paradise, Ithamore transports himself far from the bloody world of infanticide and sadistic torture that his master claims to solicit from him.

> I'le be thy Jason, thou my golden Fleece;
> Where painted Carpets o'er the meads are hurl'd,
> And Bacchus' vineyards over-spread the world:
> Where woods and forests go in goodly greene,
> I'll be Adonis, thou shalt be Loves Queene.
>   (4.2.86-92)

Suddenly Ithamore's violent impulses have been redeemed by the prospect of escape into a life of peace and pleasure, yet we cannot help but keep in mind that the diminishing of his violent mind has been induced by a mercantile relationship with a quean, and that his abandoning the ways of war is only a mirage, albeit a pleasingly comedic one.

While Ferneze and Bellamira carve the world into those who sell and those who fight, the play resists that dichotomy by showing how a mercantilist epistemology is indebted to the mental structures of warmaking, by showing how deeply the ideals of war lurk in the interstices of civilian life. And how differently this internecine struggle for hegemony is treated only a few years later by Ben Jonson and Francis Beaumont, for whom the decline of chivalric manhood and the apparent triumph of crass commercialism in what one Beaumont scholar calls the "postheroic age" becomes a source of deep if sometimes rueful comedy.[30] Their knights lack all substance. Sir Epicure Mammon, the effete gull at the center of *The Alchemist*, whose legacy is gutted by petty thieves masquerading as doctors of the mysteries of science, cannot defend himself against merchants of fantasy in the newly commercial world, just as William Blandy had feared. The apprentice Rafe in *The Knight of the Burning Pestle* laments "there are no such courteous and fair well-spoken knights in this age." And through a series of misadventures with princesses and giants he grandly and ironically aims to fill that lacuna, recasting English manhood "as true as steel."[31] As Rafe can only ape the chivalric code, not live it, Beaumont hints that in 1607, ancient chivalric manhood exists as no more than a pale fiction, beyond the ken of all but commercially minded playwrights.

Notes

1. Thomas Styward, *The Pathwaie to Martiall Discipline* (London, 1581), STC 23413, 3.
2. Elizabeth I, *Proclamations. A Declaration of the Causes Mooving the Queene of England to give aide to the Defence of the People afflicted and oppressed in the lowe Countries* (London, 1585), STC 9189, 19. N.I. Matar, "English Renaissance Soldiers in the Armies of Islam," *Explorations in Renaissance Culture* 21 (1995), cites a Bill passed in Parliament in November, 1575, forbidding Elizabeth's "'subjects from engaging in the service in the Low Countries, or of any other foreign prince or state as mariners or soldiers'" (81 [*Calendar of State Papers, Domestic* 1:506]). For an exhaustive study of merchants' status and role in sixteenth and seventeenth century England, see Robert Brenner, *Merchants and Revolution: Commercial Change, Political Conflict, and London's Overseas Traders, 1550-1653* (Princeton, 1993), especially chapter one and the postscript.
3. Matar, 81-94, makes a compelling argument that a number of early modern English plays present Muslims sympathetically, especially as the employers of out of work English soldiers in Islamic armies, so long as the English did not fight other Christians.
4. Barnabe Rich, *A Roome for a Gentleman* (London, 1609), STC 20985, sig. B1r-v.
5. Maurice Keen, *Chivalry* (New Haven, 1984), 233, 234.
6. While there are problems with calling what goes on in Malta "capitalism," other terms — mercantilism is one alternative — are not necessarily more accurate. Moreover, in *Worlds Apart: The Market and the Theater in Anglo-American Thought, 1550-1750* (Cambridge, 1986), 44, Jean-Christophe Agnew notes that some historians argue for "the presence of a protocapitalist market in England almost from the moment of the Conquest." He offers a short bibliography on the question (260 n. 90).
7. Geoffrey Gates, *The Defence of Militarie Profession* (London, 1579), STC 11683, 6. Subsequent citations are indicated parenthentically. In *Lords of all the World: Ideologies of Empire in Spain, Britain and France, c. 1500-1800* (New Haven, 1995), 183, Anthony Pagden observes that early modern nobles complained that merchants "lacked a noble idea of their profession," and therefore lacked the moral foundation to lead.
8. William Blandy, *The Castle, or picture of pollicy shewing forth . . . the duety, quality, profession of a perfect and absolute souldiar, the martiall feates, encounters, and skirmishes lately done by our English nation*, 1581 (New York, 1972), 26. Subsequent citations are indicated

128   MARLOWE, HISTORY, AND SEXUALITY

parenthetically.

9. Christopher Marlowe, *The Complete Works of Christopher Marlowe*, ed. Fredson Bowers. 2 vols., 2nd ed. (Cambridge, 1981), 1:4.1.71-72. All subsequent references are to this edition, and given parenthetically.

10. Blandy was removed from a fellowship at New College, Oxford, shortly after becoming B.A. in July 1566, for popery (DNB).

11. The Baron de Montesquieu, *The Spirit of Laws*, trans. Thomas Nugent (New York, 1900), 1:XX.i.316. For a thorough discussion of the issue, see Pagden, especially chapters six and seven.

12. For an extended account of the island's history under the Hospitallers, see Alison Hoppen, *The Fortification of Malta by the Order of St. John, 1530-1798* (Edinburgh, 1979). The history of the Hospitallers is discussed at length in Desmond Seward, *The Monks of War: The Military Religious Orders*, 1972, revised ed. (Harmondsworth, 1995).

13. Emily Bartels, "Malta, The Jew, and the Fictions of Difference: Colonialist Discourse in Marlowe's *The Jew of Malta*," *English Literary Renaissance* 20 (Winter 1990), 9.

14. Stephen Greenblatt, *Renaissance Self-Fashioning* (Chicago, 1980), 206, points out that Marlowe's heroes frequently engage in repetitive acts that signify their efforts constantly to reproduce themselves in a universe where theatricalized identity is as much identity as one ever possesses. Subsequent citations are given parenthetically.

15. G.K. Hunter, *Dramatic Identities and Cultural Tradition* (New York, 1978), 26. Regarding Marlowe's treatment of anti-Semitism, see Bartels; Stephen Greenblatt, "Marlowe, Marx, and Anti-Semitism," *Critical Inquiry* 5 (1978), 291-307; Thomas Cartelli, "Shakespeare's *Merchant*, Marlowe's *Jew*: The Problem of Cultural Difference," *Shakespeare Studies* 20 (1987), 255-260; and Marion D. Perret, "Shakespeare's Jew: Preconception and Performance," *Shakespeare Studies* 20 (1987), 261-268.

16. Raymond de Roover, *Business, Banking, and Economic Thought in Late Medieval and Early Modern Europe*, ed. Julius Kirshner (Chicago, 1974), 11:347; Geoffrey Parker, *The Military Revolution: Military Innovation and the Rise of the West, 1500-1800* (Cambridge, 1988), 62.

17. Marlowe creates a parallel to this insult in *2 Tamburlaine*. Tamburlaine recruits Theridimas to join his campaign to be "Monark of the East" by dangling the plum that together they shall make "Christian Merchants," whose ships "plow up huge furrowes in the Caspian sea," "vaile to us [lower their topsails], as Lords of all the Lake" (*2 Tamb* 1.2.185, 194-96).

18. Michael Drayton, *The Barrons Warres*, cited in *Edward the Second*, ed. W. Moelwyn Merchant, New Mermaids (London, 1987), xxi.

19. Erasmus, in *The Adages*, complains of priests such as Jacomo and Barnardine: "The Romanists of today have become market-stall holders. What is it they sell? It is male and female pudenda, goods most worthy of these merchants whose avarice and irreligion are worse than the most

sordid obscenity imaginable" (quoted from *Erasmus on his times*, ed. Margaret Mann Phillips [Cambridge, 1967], 74).

20. Simon Shepherd, *Marlowe and the Politics of Elizabethan Theatre* (Brighton, 1986), 172, sees it as evidence of Marlowe's critique of Barabas' imperial notion of paternity. I prefer his reading to Alan Friedman's in "The Shackling of Accidents in Marlowe's *Jew of Malta*," *Texas Studies in Language and Literature* 8:2 (Summer 1966), 159, who argues that in conjuring Agamemnon's sacrifice of Iphigenia, Barabas reveals a naïve grasp of the emotional impact of sacrificing Abigail.

21. Patricia Klindienst Joplin, "The Voice of the Shuttle is Ours," *Rape and Representation*, ed. Lynn A. Higgins and Brenda R. Silver (New York, 1991), 44.

22. Richard A. McCabe, *Incest, Drama and Nature's Law, 1550-1700* (Cambridge, 1993), 292.

23. Jean-Louis Flandrin, *Families in Former Times: Kinship, Household, and Sexuality*, trans. Richard Southern (Cambridge, 1979), 130: "It seems that the authority of parents and their powers of coercion of their children increased from the sixteenth century onwards" as a result of renewed faith in absolute monarchy, Roman law, and the ideas of antiquity.

24. Mary Douglas, *Purity and Danger: an Analysis of Concepts of Pollution and Taboo* (1966; New York, 1970), 126-27, 121.

25. For a fascinating analysis of the cultural assumptions behind bodily functions in early modern England, see Gail Kern Paster, *The Body Embarrassed: Drama and the Disciplines of Shame in Early Modern England* (Ithaca, 1993), to which my reading of the poisoning episode is indebted.

26. Augustine, *De Ordine* 2.4, *Patrologiae Cursus Completus Series Latina*, ed. J.P. Migne (Paris, 1845), 32:1000. Quoted by Aquinas in *Summa Theologica*, 2.2.10.11, in *Opera Omnia* (Rome, 1895), 8:93.

27. Jacques Rossiaud, *Medieval Prostitution*, trans. Lydia G. Cochrane (London, 1988), 42.

28. Rossiaud, 132, speculates that a courtesan was "held to be infinitely more dangerous than other women of easy virtue . . . because she demanded ever more money and fine clothing."

29. William Kerrigan and Gordon Braden, describing the Petrarchan lover in *The Idea of the Renaissance* (Baltimore, 1989), 160.

30. Philip J. Finkelpearl, *Court and Country Politics in the Plays of Beaumont and Fletcher* (Princeton, 1990), 92-93.

31. Francis Beaumont, *The Knight of the Burning Pestle*, ed. John Doebler. Regents Drama Series (Lincoln, 1967), 1:242-43, 4:70.

The Massacre at Paris: Marlowe's Messy Consensus Narrative

Rick Bowers

Christopher Marlowe's *The Massacre at Paris* is a fragmented play that dramatizes the events leading up to, during, and following the sectarian violence that occurred in Paris on August 24th, St. Bartholomew's Day, 1572. This date of political mass murder of French Protestants was seared in memorable infamy into the minds of English Protestants. If Marlowe gleaned his Latin at the King's School in Canterbury and on a Matthew Parker scholarship at Corpus Christi in Cambridge, he no doubt learned the terrible story of the massacre at Paris at home and in the streets. His native Canterbury had a thriving immigrant community, and religious refugees arrived there in large numbers from the Continent. Their accounts of persecution and atrocity were very much current to Protestant Englishmen in general, Canterbury citizens in particular, and, without a doubt, eight-year-old Christopher Marlowe.[1] Staged some twenty years later, Marlowe's play delineates and rehearses the French atrocity as performed by English actors for a distinctly English audience. By dramatizing what he called a "massacre" (the *OED* credits Marlowe with first use of the term as appellation for an historical atrocity), Marlowe presents terrorist violence and murder which, while officially criticized, also excites the very passions which it seeks to condemn.

The Massacre at Paris conveys sectarian hatred through scenes of violence that are brutal, abrupt, and noncausal:

> *Anj.* Who have you there?
> *Retes.* 'Tis Ramus, the King's professor of Logic.
> *Guise.* Stab him.
>
> (9.20-22)

> *Ser.* O let me pray unto my God!
> *Mount.* Then take this with you.

131

Stab him.

(8.13-14)

Guise.   Come, sirs,
I'll whip you to death with my poniard's point.
He kills the Schoolmasters.

(9.78-79)[2]

Scabrous cameos such as these animate the play with messily realistic language and action. Dialogue is effectively "cut off" at the same time as moral order is dispelled, but the play itself continues to "speak." The communication thus effected "tells" a first-person political story *of* and *to* an English audience in the terms of its military, political, and cultural enemy: Catholic France. Such telling, however, is reflexive. In what follows, I plan to argue that *The Massacre at Paris* dramatizes, with directness and subversive irony, the cultural idealizations of a consensus narrative.

A "consensus narrative" is a culturally determined story around which the truths, morals, and self-identifying features of a society revolve. Conceptually rooted in anthropology, the term "consensus narrative" itself is borrowed from communications critic David Thorburn.[3] The enabling conditions of a consensus narrative are all-inclusive and widespread, and try to represent as much of the culture as possible. The "story" operates at the very centre of cultural life, incorporating but also transcending features of popular entertainment, history, and morality in the interests of self-explanation. Such explanation, however, is notoriously unstable, serving also as a kind of cultural self-fashioning which, as noted by Stephen Greenblatt, always involves an encounter of self and other, a collision with "something perceived as alien, strange, or hostile."[4] And delineation of a chaotic Other always involves exposure (not always flattering) of an authoritative self. In *The Anthropology of Performance*, Victor Turner explains the relationship: "though, for most purposes, we humans may divide ourselves between Us and Them, or Ego and Alter, We and They share substance, and Ego and Alter mirror each other pretty well."[5] Take a look at the enemy: it is *us.*

By enacting the atrocity and instability of a neighbor state, *The Massacre at Paris* attempts to validate the political culture of England, recently excommunicated by prevailing religious authority but determined to elucidate and defend features of its own moral, political, and cultural ascendancy. Assuredly, moral and political commentators such as Leicester, Walsingham, Sidney, Spenser, and a host of Protestant preachers conveyed a similar partisan message. But Marlowe's drama works differently by conveying a consensus that is messy both in terms of its staged violence and in terms of its self-assured explanations. English Protestant "self" and French Catholic "other" are set up in a relationship of dialogical consciousness that complicates the monological rancor of moral pamphlets, allegories, or letters of complaint. This relationship involves a terrifying theater of dominance and submission and disclosure of power wherein overt initiative, momentum, and success resides almost totally with the enemy. In Marlowe's play, an English conception of order is assumed to represent harmony between the passions excited by political power and the moral ideals which political power was to serve. What the play actually represents, however, is the French "order," an order expressed as moral incoherence, as continuing conflict and violence, as political assertion and mastery. Such were the political facts of the period at home and abroad, facts against which cultural idealizations and providential best wishes were meaningless. Such violence and incoherence was by no means completely alien to English cultural experience. As Greenblatt puts it: "The power generated to attack the alien in the name of the authority is produced in excess and threatens the authority it sets out to defend."[6] Indeed, the excessive nature of *The Massacre at Paris* undermines its own radical English consensus.

English-French relations were notoriously unstable, and hard-line Protestant propaganda on the topic — whether promulgated by a zealot like John Stubbs or a courtier such as Sir Philip Sidney — was punished with some severity in the Elizabethan regime. As punishment for his unlicensed pamphlet entitled *The Discovery of a Gaping Gulf whereinto England is like to be swallowed by another French Marriage*, Stubbs, along with his publisher, was publicly dismembered in the marketplace at Westminster.[7] Sidney was rusticated to Wilton after receipt of his letter condemning Elizabeth's possible marriage to the French Duke of Alencon.[8] Marlowe's play, by contrast, was popular, well-attended, and approved for performance by the State censor. Indeed, although there is plenty of room for it, Marlowe deliberately omits anything having to do with Henry III's brother Francois, Duke of Alencon and his lengthy marriage negotiations with Elizabeth I. For Protestant propaganda, such a theme would be irresistible. Instead the play, concerned primarily with French political chaos, aims itself reflexively at English response, integration, and anxiety.

Whether or not Marlowe's play was new or performed at Newington Butts in January 1593 when Henslowe designated it "ne" in his *Diary*,[9] it certainly enjoyed remarkable success. The following summer of 1594, *The Massacre at Paris* seems to have enjoyed something of a theatrical "run," anticipating the topical success of Middleton's *A Game at Chess* early in the next century.[10] After all,

Henry IV (known popularly to the English as Henry the Great) was still on the French throne, although recently converted to the Catholicism which Marlowe's play condemns. Marlowe could not have known this crucial irony, but the play is enlivened with other ironies of retributive violence through language, action, and plot — ironies that pamphleteers and contemporary commentators such as Stubbs and Sidney rigorously avoid. Marlowe's play on the French atrocity on St. Bartholomew's Day 1572, however, circulated freely and messily as mass entertainment that asserts ironies even as it corroborates the cultural norms of English Protestantism.

The central figures of the play are — to contemporary Protestant Englishmen at least — completely treacherous European nobles: Charles IX of France is weak and uncertain even as he gives away his sister in marriage to the Protestant Henry of Navarre; Catherine, the Queen Mother is in fact Catherine de Medici (in Sidney's notorious letter "that Jezabel of our age" [Sidney 52]), daughter of Lorenzo and thus linked to that most problematic of political theorists, Machiavelli; the Duke of Anjou switches loyalties with disturbing aplomb, while the Duke of Guise represents fanatical Machiavellianism as a pan-European Catholic terrorist. An ostensible Protestant hero such as Navarre (later Henry IV) is only a windy, dramatic extra among such devious and violent figures. And the more Navarre appeals to moral abstractions such as "Truth" and "Righteousness," the more immoral the action of the play becomes.

But how can Navarre compete dramatically, when the real "hero" of the play is clearly one of the most despicable characters in it: the Guise. In scene 1, the worried members of the Protestant faction spend all their time speaking about him. Scene 2 is all his own. The audience witnesses his swift dispatching of assassins followed by a soliloquy of sustained dramatic and rhetorical power. His tone is retributive; his words are considered and venomous. The cumulative energy and rhythmic intensity of his first eight lines acts as index to the entire scene:

> If ever Hymen lour'd at marriage-rites
> And had his altars deck'd with dusky lights;
> If ever sun stain'd heaven with bloody clouds
> And made it look with terror on the world;
> If ever day were turn'd to ugly night,
> And night made semblance of the hue of hell;
> This day, this hour, this fatal night,
> Shall fully show the fury of them all.
>
> (2.1-8)

Demented, determined, and coldly self-assured — the enemy speaks.

He is not a cartoon to be descried and mocked from a safe distance. The audience vicariously experiences his procedures. No source exists for this scene, but the writing is reminiscent of Tamburlaine's vaunted ambition. Power, of course, is the Guise's main object. But the power that the Guise seeks is closer to self-assertion than to political influence. Judith Weil perceptively characterizes him as "a vengeful meddler of twisted pretensions,"[11] and his first-person monologue is extensive in presenting *him* rather than presenting anything resembling a legitimate political prerogative or vision. Unlike Shakespeare's *Richard III*, this is not a world to bustle in; it is a world in which to spread terrorism and engender fear in the service of an ideology.

And action quickly ensues after the Guise's bristling soliloquy. When next we see him, he is giving direct orders for the massacre. And, while the King momentarily withholds ratification, there is no doubt but that a "massacre" is what the Guise intends. The Queen Mother even uses the word directly in addressing the Guise, "What order will you set down for the massacre?" (4.27). Her unemotional usage links itself to Margaret's distressed use of the word in the previous scene in relation to her unblessed, religiously mixed married state: she claims her soul is "massacred" (3.26). The new bride, wed to a sectarian other, makes first use of this terrible term just as Marlowe's play introduces the term in its modern terrorist sense. A terminology of willful terror — slippery, relative, and unfixed — spreads throughout the play with ease.

The premeditated violence that ensues is, in the minds of the perpetrators at least, not the massacre of the abattoir, but rather the expunging of religious pollution. Those who perform this righteous task will wear a uniform of purity, according to the specifications of the Guise:

> They that shall be actors in this massacre
> Shall wear white crosses on their burgonets
> And tie white linen scarfs about their arms.
> (4.29-31)

Natalie Zemon Davis links this ceremoniousness directly to contemporary rites of violence in the St. Bartholomew Day massacre.[12] She argues an acting-out of clerical and magisterial roles in an attempt to rid society of heresy perceived as pollution. René Girard, too, in *Violence and the Sacred*, argues the unifying nature of ritual violence. Thus, it is a terrible irony that St Bartholomew's symbol in art is a knife and skin;[13] also that the period of St. Bartholomew's feast was an especially joyous festival time in Elizabethan London. Here, in Paris, the Guise costumes his cohorts in

ceremonial purity to effect a mental distance from the atrocity to
ensue, but also to intensify that same atrocity as meaningful and
unifying.

Volatile, momentary, and brutal, these short scenes of loathsome
purification through violence are punctuated purposely by scenes of
politics. They graphically illustrate the randomness, mindlessness,
and embittered confusion of violent ideological action. Against the
background tolling of a bell, disparate murder ensues. *"Tue, tue,
tue!* Let none escape" (6.1-2, 12.7) is the chilling and repeated
imperative of the Guise, an imperative that rings directly and
threateningly in the ears of an opposition audience. The drama
moves scene-by-scene from desecration of the corpse of the
Protestant Lord Admiral to the mass-drowning of his followers, from
the slaughter of a group of nameless Huguenots to the summary
execution of Loreine, a Protestant preacher. Then follows the
domestic terror of Seroune murdered remorselessly as his wife looks
on. These brief scenes allow for quick entry, execution, and exit.
Paradoxically, the random, desperate violence which they enact is
perceived as joyfully unifying on the part of the perpetrators. Their
actions are considered to be actions of unity and consensus. Just as
paradoxical, however, is the fact that Marlowe dramatizes these
actions for the purposes of opposite ideological consensus.

Scene 9 focuses at great length ("great length" in this play at
least) on the murder of renowned international scholar Peter Ramus.
Dignified, tolerant, and self-assured, the Protestant academic faces his
Guisian tormentors without fear. But he is summarily dispatched in a
violent cameo that presents in little the brutalized rationality upon
which the whole play is based.[14] Within the play, righteous violence
easily breaks containment and exceeds boundaries, as in the random
slaughter of the Protestants in the woods — the concluding atrocity
of the "massacre" proper. Violence within the play generally acts as
a signal, marking sectarian boundaries, declaring cultural differences,
stressing dramatic closure. Violent official power attempts
cumulatively to assert its "truth," a truth asserted by official acts of
punishment — public shamings, maimings, and executions — on
either side of the English Channel. The murderous fanaticism of
French policy is portrayed for the purposes of equally fanatical
reaction. But the Guise obliterates opposition with the same
efficiency as the Elizabethan regime.

In the Guise's demented understanding, this is the correct and
appropriate time for wiping out heresy. Those whom he murders are,
like Ramus, not people on whom to waste the intricacies of Catholic
dogma, but perverted heretics to be expunged without judicial
process. And yet the Guise receives similarly extreme treatment
within the play as hilarious lampoon. He is ridiculed as a cuckold by

the newly crowned Henry III who, in a telling stage direction, publicly *"makes horns at the Guise"* (17.11 s.d.). As a consequence, the Guise launches into an aria of enraged recrimination, culminating in French bluster: *"Par la mort dieu, il mourra!"* (17.28). The irony of the entire play is implicit in that line. In broader terms of cultural stereotype, the enraged Frenchman has always been a satirical butt for English humor; the enraged French cuckold would double the hilarity for an English audience. And the scene plays itself out after the departure of the Guise in a series of double entendres that further emphasize the derisive comic nature of his predicament as cuckolded Machiavel.

Despicable, but also powerful, the Guise must be liquidated in a scene of some significance. Thus, hired assassins are secreted by the French state itself and made ready for the Guise's assassination. Here, he displays his arrogance to the full, but also his significance. His Caesarean self-references emphasize his megalomania but also his real political power. And his murder is presented with some sympathy, a backhanded sympathy that favors the Guise dramatically at the same time as it denigrates French morality in general. The treachery of Henry III here can easily be linked to that of the previous monarch Charles IX, who visited the Protestant Lord Admiral in peace (4.50-70) just before the Guisians assassinated him. As Julia Briggs notes, Marlowe's strategy here is "to remind the audience of something they have seen before."[15] Such irony within the play effects the sense of a vicious cycle of violence that — to the audience — is unredressed, ongoing, typically French, double-crossing, and Catholic. Whether the audience would be as alive to the irony of the scene as they would be to the seemingly poetic justice of it is debatable. But destructive energies are portrayed as powerful and random. The Guise gets what he deserves, and he goes down every bit the detestable noble to the end. His ensuing, disconnected bluster reinforces the wickedness of his character at the same time as it intensifies the depth of his fanatical commitment.

Eliminating the Guise seems to exhilarate Henry III. He experiences an unprecedented sense of his own power, and immediately links this self-determination to Protestant sympathy. For the first time, *he* — not the Guise — is in control. Henry's first enlightened command, however, is to plow back into sectarian violence by ordering the death of the Cardinal of Lorraine, the Guise's brother. The scene of the Cardinal's torment and assassination is uneasily familiar. Catholic murderousness shades into Protestant murderousness. And the new murderers exhibit the same mindless violence and grotesque glee as the Guisians did in their killings of the homonymic clergyman Loreine,[16] the Protestant Lord Admiral, and the various, terrified Parisian Huguenots. Seeking retribution, the Guise's brother Dumaine dispatches an assassin in search of Henry III. This hands-on killer, however, is a cleric himself, a Jacobin friar. At last, an officer of religion murders in the name of religion. The murderous cleric with his poison-tipped dagger is a literalization of every sectarian atrocity that has previously occurred in the play.

Of course regicide in general is a topic most heinous to consider for a Protestant English monarchy. And, in fact, as soon as the taboo topic of regicide is broached, the play turns its attention to England. A dying Henry III intends to make an example of his captured assassin:

> All rebels under heaven
> Shall take example by his punishment
> How they bear arms against their sovereign.
> Go call the English agent hither straight.
> I'll send my sister England news of this,
> And give her warning of her treacherous foes.
>
> (24.46-51)

The mission of the English agent in France at the time was to "send thy mistress word / What this detested Jacobin hath done" (24.55-56), which will serve as the basis for wise English foreign policy for years to come.[17] And, in a sense, the "news" that is sent is a rehearsal of all that has transpired: the action of the play itself. This "news" is precisely not new, however, in the sense that political violence is presented throughout the play as the routine assertion of authority. And such assertion, open or clandestine, characterizes English authority too. The play carefully de-emphasizes anti-monarchical Protestant sentiment while stressing Protestant suffering. But Elizabeth of England knows without having to be told by Henry of France that "treacherous foes" lurk within.

The concluding scene gets personal, as Henry III, himself a victim of sectarian strife, finally sees things clearly and appeals to righteous English Protestantism. The play takes this "English" turn near the conclusion to reinforce a generalized sense of cultural bad example in French action and policy. Consequently, the audience itself acts as a collective and vicarious English Agent by directing the story inward. Like any explanation of sectarian assertion, the "story" is a long rehearsal of atrocity and counter atrocity that takes on the form of a consensus narrative. That which is good and worthy involves the native, familiar, and comfortable: *us*; that which is evil and treacherous involves the foreign, unfamiliar, and threatening: *them*. In familiar adage-phrasing terms (itself a consensus understanding): if the massacre at Paris in August 1572 had not actually occurred it would have to be invented.

But, as depicted, *us* and *them* are uneasily familiar. This inventive noninvented story is shared by French and English through dramatic representation of reflexive amity and enmity. The play reveals a deeply equivocal power; a power which, according to Clifford Geertz, speaks to "the consoling piety that we are all like to one another and to the worrying suspicion that we are not" (*Local Knowledge* 42). Each infects the other in mutual apprehension. A popular English audience may rest assured that such internal sectarian horror would never occur within a harmonious Protestant state. But the acts of violence perpetrated in *The Massacre at Paris* were perpetrated by Christian monarchs and nobles not unlike their own. Marlowe rehearses the French atrocity and then veers it towards England where authority too asserts itself over "treacherous foes" through official public displays of violence. Even-handed retribution within the play undermines a stable sense of moral or ideological righteousness.

Inventive storytelling is a large part of Marlowe's accomplishment in presenting *The Massacre at Paris* as a focus for and consideration of English cultural consensus. This ideological construction and rehearsal of experience is more than simply "slanted" history or crude propaganda derived through partisan tracts. The play represents a matrix of inherited cultural assumptions and values through which a society "tells" itself in terms of historical rivalry and suffering. For Protestant England, the rival is Catholic France, and the lengthy bloodthirsty manifesto with which Henry ends his life is really only the same hatred that inspired the massacre of the play's title. Each side gets messy with the blood of the other. Navarre's concluding sanctimony is puny and especially ironic in light of the fact that he himself converted to Catholicism in 1593.

Those well-attended performances of *The Massacre at Paris* in 1594 must have enjoyed additional point and irony in light of Navarre's recent conversion. Historically, Navarre chose a centrist religious option that ensured the crown on his head and peace within the realm of France. Doubtless, Elizabeth I of England understood this political maneuver. But the English public stage made money by providing popular, topical entertainment, by holding a critical mirror up to society. In presenting recent French history, Christopher Marlowe's *The Massacre at Paris* presents a mirror in which to stare with morbid fascination and a less-than-secure sense of English satisfaction. After all, the play puts its audience within the minds of the perpetrators, risking dangerously reflexive associations, conflicting possibilities, treasonous imaginings.

Admittedly, the play as it exists is a truncated text, but its power as a consensus narrative speaking to the cultural assumptions of a threatened English body politic might well be what has saved it for posterity. And two distinct audience reactions might be considered for this polemical drama: For the audience to identify with the victims is to elicit headshaking disdain for sick, ongoing violence. To identify with the oppressors — especially the Guise as villain-hero — is to maneuver the audience into an intolerable moral position. Yet within the play, the two options are presented as simultaneous and complementary. Crude propaganda does not permit such messy consideration of options. *The Massacre at Paris*, however, deliberately presents messy violent action and messy reflexivity of audience association. It works like a mirror, reflecting not only what one is and what one sees but, moreover, what one does as an Other. Even as the play confirms English assumptions on the rotten sectarianism of French civil chaos, it reflects mutually understood assertions of political and religious authority. And because the action of the play is so politically, culturally, and geographically close, it is also a mirror from which to turn away.

Notes

1. In this regard, see William Urry, *Christopher Marlowe and Canterbury*, ed. Andrew Butcher (London, 1988). See also A. G.. Dickens' historical essay, "The Elizabethans and St. Bartholomew," *The Massacre of St. Bartholomew: Reappraisals and Documents*, ed. Alfred Soman (The Hague, 1974), 52-70.
2. Throughout, I quote *The Massacre at Paris* from the Revels edition of H. J. Oliver (Cambridge, 1968).
3. See David Thorburn, "Television as an Aesthetic Medium," *Media, Myths, and Narratives*, ed. James W. Carey, Sage Annual Reviews of Communication Research 15 (Newbury Park, CA, 1988), 48-66. See also the widely suggestive anthropological work of Clifford Geertz, *The Interpretation of Cultures* (New York, 1973); and *Local Knowledge: Further Essays in Interpretive Anthropology* (New York, 1983).
4. Stephen Greenblatt, *Renaissance Self-Fashioning: From More to Shakespeare* (Chicago, 1980), 9. My consideration of self and other is also informed theoretically by the work of Mikhail Bakhtin, especially *The Dialogic Imagination*, ed. Michael Holquist; trans. Michael Holquist and Caryl Emerson (Austin, 1981). On *The Massacre at Paris* specifically, Emily Bartels makes intelligent passing mention in *Spectacles of Strangeness: Imperialism, Alienation, and Marlowe* (Philadelphia, 1993).
5. Victor Turner, *The Anthropology of Performance* (New York, 1986), 81.
6. *Renaissance Self-Fashioning*, 9. In this connection, see also Simon Shepherd, *Marlowe and the Politics of Elizabethan Theatre* (Brighton, 1986).

7. On text and circumstances, see Lloyd E. Berry ed., *John Stubbs's "Gaping Gulf" with Letters and other Relevant Documents* (Charlottesville, 1968).
8. See Sidney's letter titled "A Discourse of Syr Ph. S. To The Queenes Majesty Touching Hir Mariage With Monsieur" in *The Prose Works of Sir Philip Sidney*, ed. Albert Feuillerat (1912; Cambridge, 1962), 3: 51-60.
9. See *Henslowe's Diary*, ed. R. A. Foakes and R. T. Rickert (Cambridge, 1968), 20, 22-24. On Henslowe's "ne" designation, see Winifred Frazer's note, "Henslowe's 'ne,'" in *Notes and Queries* 236 (1991), 34-35.
10. On dates and figures concerning *The Massacre at Paris*, see Oliver's introduction, xlix.
11. Judith Weil, *Christopher Marlowe: Merlin's Prophet* (Cambridge, 1977), 86.
12. See Natalie Zemon Davis, "The Rites of Violence: Religious Riot in Sixteenth-Century France," *The Massacre of St. Bartholomew: Reappraisals and Documents*, ed. Alfred Soman (The Hague, 1974), 203-42. On the unifying nature of ritual violence see René Girard, *Violence and the Sacred* (Baltimore, 1977).
13. See John Coulson, *The Saints: A Concise Biographical Dictionary* (New York, 1958), 64.
14. On this particular episode, see John Ronald Glenn, "The Martyrdom of Ramus in Marlowe's *The Massacre at Paris*," *Pages on Language and Literature* 9 (1973), 365-79.
15. Julia Briggs, "Marlowe's *Massacre at Paris*: A Reconsideration," *Review of English Studies* 34 (1983), 267.
16. Revels editor H. J. Oliver draws attention to the sameness of pronunciation, explaining in his note to scene 7: "'Follow Loreine', as Ethel Seaton noted (*Review of English Studies* 9 [1933], 330) was the war-cry of the Guise (Lorraine) faction, so that 'Follow Loreine' may be a pun on the victim's name and in line with the other jesting associated with each of the murders" (114).
17. On direct historical circumstances concerning the assassination of Henry III and English anxiety about it, see John Archer, *Sovereignty and Intelligence: Spying and Court Culture in the English Renaissance* (Stanford, 1993), 91-93.

"Full Possession":
Service and Slavery in
Doctor Faustus

Judith Weil

When, in *The Jew of Malta*, Barabas visits a slave market and buys Ithamore, Marlowe dramatizes the institution of chattel slavery, flourishing around the borders of the Mediterranean and beginning its westward expansion into the New World.[1] The question I will raise in this essay is whether Marlowe and his audience would have criticized slavery, or accepted it as an extreme form of the subordination practiced in their own households. Because they commonly used the word "slave" as a metaphor for moral knavery, financial debt, or passionate obsession, we may be tempted to assume that they took the institution of slavery for granted. Before the development of a discourse of individual rights, Christian moralists, influenced by the renewed authority of classical and Old Testament family values, often explicitly justified slavery as part of the fallen order of life on earth.[2]

To find a criticism, indeed a condemnation of the slave's condition, I suggest that we look at a group of plays which synthesize the vocabularies of two traditional discourses — service and demonic possession. This group includes *The Old Wives Tale*, *The Comedy of Errors*, *Twelfth Night*, and *King Lear*, as well as *The Alchemist*, *The Devil is an Ass*, and *The Witch of Edmonton*. Influential in generating a remarkable succession of possessed servants and richly illuminated by it is Marlowe's *Doctor Faustus*, but its distinctive synthesis of service and possession will only emerge if we attend more carefully to the domestic, familial aspects of Marlowe's play.

Marlowe produces this synthesis by writing a tragedy of damnation. He brings into focus attitudes toward work and toward dependent relationships which are pathological in their contradictions and disastrous in their effects. His play offers evidence that particular ideas about service may generate enslavement. It does not, by any means, indicate that all servants are possessed or that domestic service, a dynamic set of customs and

143

practices, is co-extensive with slavery. Indeed, Marlowe's tragedy clarifies important differences between service and slavery which are erased by Jean Louis Flandrin, an historian of the early modern family, when he writes:

> The large family, with a sizeable domestic household, is not a creation of the period with which we are concerned, nor even of the Middle Ages: it is merely a continuation of the family based on slavery of the ancient world. . . . All that appears unfamiliar to us, in the status of the domestic servant, was already characteristic of that of the slave.[3]

Perhaps because of excitement with magic and metaphysics, one particularly significant emendation of the A-text has received little notice. The B-text reviser who decided that Faustus should bid "oeconomy" rather than "on kai me on" "farewell" might, W. W. Greg suggests, have been making a "learned or would-be learned" guess.[4] On the one hand, "on kai me on" seems indispensable: this expression of "being or non-being" sends readers diving into their notes, and must have been the sort of weighty classical quip which a pretentious Faustus could use to impress spectators who had ventured into the Rose without their Greek dictionaries. On the other hand, "oeconomy," even if an error, registers a response to a dimension of *Doctor Faustus* which disappears when we allow "on kai me on" to ravish us up to the heights or down to the depths of theological and psychological speculation. More awareness of "oeconomy," taken in its Renaissance meaning as the art of managing an entire household or family, is, I think, vital for an understanding of *Doctor Faustus*.

The B-text reveals a domestic sensibility in a number of other emendations and additions. For example, "The devill and illiberall" becomes "servile and illiberal" (1.66, 63), while "men in armour" becomes "men in harness" (1.612, 533).[5] B invents crowds of servants and followers; it emphasizes the servile status of Faustus himself by enhancing his role as entertainer in the expanded court scenes and by the snobbery of Benvolio. Another decidedly familial addition, and one to which I return below, is the provision of a will for Wagner, now firmly identified both as servant and as ultimately heir to Faustus. Such changes are scarcely as transgressive or exciting as the major shifts in style of audience provocation recently pointed out by Leah Marcus.[6] "Oeconomical" details in B simply make more explicit conditions which are already evident in A, rather than revising A in a new direction. In both texts, Faustus himself behaves at the papal banquet like a serving-man run amok, and is exorcised like a demon. In both texts, he must depend on "servile spirits" if he is to have the joys of magic in "full possession."

Although spirits have been studied at length and servants have begun to receive their due, few critics have examined the ways in which they may function together as dramatic roles.[7] Francis E. Dolan's *Dangerous Familiars* touches briefly on the terrors of being possessed by witches or reduced to an instrumental status but emphasizes the contradictory gender politics of witchcraft beliefs.[8] Moreover, by reading dramatic conflicts as products of social ideologies rather than as consequences of character relationships, Dolan sometimes treats drama as passive convention and simplifies her treatment of agency.[9] I think it improbable that Marlowe — a highly complex agent himself — was ever much at the mercy of literary formulas or contemporary ideologies. As a playwright, Roger Sales maintains, he "confronts spectators with their own demons."[10] Inevitably, Marlowe's representations of servants and spirits have formulaic and ideological elements. For wild confusions of on kai me on and oeconomy, metaphysics and domesticity, provide the stuff of popular entertainment from the *Mostellaria* or *Haunted House* of Plautus to the latest installment of the film, *Halloween*. As well, the language of service had been used to describe the relation of witches and demoniacs to the devil long before Protestant elites emphasized the mechanics of the demonic pact.[11] But by historicizing the effects of possession on work and by looking carefully at specific interactions of servants and spirits, we can see that the hows and whys of agency are central questions for Marlowe. They are also questions which should arouse more interest in the links between Faustus and those minor agents who make action possible at all.[12]

Doctor Faustus is a sufficiently sensational play without the episodes of pin-spitting, wild roaring and fierce tumbling which animate descriptions of demonic possession from the period.[13] It replaces bizarre symptoms with the energetic and articulate despair of its protagonists, while seeming to draw upon witchcraft beliefs only for the more incidental appeal of charms, tricks, and familiars.[14] I suggest that we may not have glimpsed the full significance of witchcraft for this play precisely because we expect all of its effects to be vividly terrific. In a more oeconomical humor, it may be observed that when the servants are possessed, productive work ceases. A connection between witchcraft and the failure to perform as a creative, useful agent was suggested by Keith Thomas when he indicated that witchcraft accusations may have been used by supposedly possessed children and servants to displace blame for their own mistakes and failures in carrying out appointed tasks. As examples of such disingenuous or self-deceived accusations, Thomas cites the case of the twenty Lancashire witches of 1634, whose troubles began when the boy Edmund Robinson invented a fantastic story, to save himself a whipping for playing truant instead of bringing home his father's cattle. When in 1582 a cow kicked over Alice Baxter's pail, thereby losing the morning's milking, she rushed back to her employer to explain that the animal had been petrified by an evil spirit. 'When a country wench cannot get her butter to come,' observed Selden, 'she says the witch is in her churn.[15]

Threatened with the dangers of masterlessness and beggary, it must have been tempting to blame a witch.[16]

Many such accusations could have been genuinely sincere, for how was the early modern worker to explain sudden headaches, a muscle spasm, or the stinging joints now known as tennis or housewife's elbow? The traditional, rural witchcraft studied by such scholars as Thomas and Emmanuel Le Roy Ladurie, was always regarded as particularly dangerous when directed against radical productivity, meaning childbirth and children, but also the strength to work. Ladurie's Gascon witches afflict cows and crops, to be sure, but their power is most maleficent through its effects on arms and tools. In one discussion of what he calls "the very familiar theme of the onslaught on the arm," Ladurie writes that the evil caused by witches especially "affects the whole arm from the hand to the shoulder, this upper limb being, as a rule, the source of wealth in agriculture and in the crafts carried on by the manual workers of the village."[17]

It is Mephistophilis who, immediately after promising to be "thy slave" in return for Faustus' soul, urges Faustus, "Stab thy arm courageously" (2.1.49). Thereupon, this arm begins to act on its own, staunching the flow of blood and flashing the inscription, "*Homo fuge*" (2.1.76-77). The moment is dramatically crucial, suggesting that Faustus is too foolish to recognize a real miracle, or that (in a reading both persuasive and fashionable) he denies the wisdom of his own body.[18] I don't wish to discredit these readings, but can't help wondering whether they reveal a sophisticated, modern indifference to manual labor and its creative potential. Part of the temptation with which Mephistophilis tricks Faustus here may be a seductive hint that, having a devil for his "slave," he won't really be needing his arm! To see this sequence in a different perspective, we might put ourselves in the shoes of the apprentices and servants who were playgoers, according to Andrew Gurr.[19] These young people may well have been reminded by the ideologists of the patriarchal household — preachers, the authors of manuals, and personal masters — that the servant's role was that of a hand or tool. The servant, writes Torquato Tasso in *The*

Housholder's Philosophie (translated, probably by Kyd, in 1588), is as the hand to the brain, or "a lively & several instrument of action" (sig. C1v). For working spectators, Faustus' arm might resemble a rebellious household attendant or apprentice, compelled by an abuse of authority to oppose reduction to mere instrumentality, forced to choose resistance or escape.

In a fine essay on the "faithful servant" who does resist Cornwall's plan to blind Gloucester in *King Lear*, Richard Strier scrutinizes the Renaissance contexts for virtuous disobedience. He regards the behavior of Cornwall's servant as the "most radical possible sociopolitical act."[20] Paradoxically, by rebelling, this virtuously disobedient servant refuses to support or participate in his master's madness, his rebellion against himself (Strier 110). I suspect that servant-spectators would readily understand that the virtuous arm resists, not service or subordination *per se*, but a madness in Faustus which will ultimately reduce him, or any servant for that matter, to a tool and a slave.

What this madness might be or why an instrumental role could seem peculiarly horrible are questions which we cannot answer if we sharply distinguish Faustus from servants like Wagner and Robin. Historians now recognize the interpenetration of high and low cultures in Renaissance witchcraft beliefs.[21] Similarly, the high and low, learned and popular cultures within Marlowe's play often coalesce. There can be little point in defending one dimension of the play against the other.[22] Consider, for a moment, the grotesquely powerful realism with which Marlowe represents Robin's career. When we first meet Robin, initially called "Clown," he is a masterless man and bearded "boy" being "pressed" by Wagner into a seven-year contract. Wagner's threat, "I'll turne all the lice about thee into familiars, and they shall tear thee in pieces" (1.4.25-26), caricatures both domestic order and popular magic by fusing the agencies of the personal parasite and the rebellious subordinate, acting upon, rather than within, the Clown's politic body. By the time he reappears (scene eight in A or 2.3. in B), the Clown has acquired a name, become a tavern ostler, and forged designs upon his mistress. No longer merely a host to his own lice, he is prepared to do some biting himself, by attempting to possess another dependent whose status in the domestic oeconomy is superior to his own. Such clown comedy is neither mere "comic entertainment" nor "relatively harmless."[23] It drops us into the yards, kitchens and doorways of Renaissance households, where future Iagos learn to serve themselves by preying on others. Robin's antics can no more be separated from the fortunes of Faustus than his arm can be separated from his body.

Like Robin, Faustus attaches himself to someone with greater power: "When Mephastophilis shall stand by me / What God can hurt me?" (2.1.24-25) Like Robin, Mephistophilis attaches himself to an employer in order to increase his own power; he will eventually "fetch or carry" Faustus to Hell (2.1.110), enlarging the kingdom of his master, Lucifer. Faustus and Mephistophilis play host and parasite at one and the same time. They make a binding agreement which entraps them both. Marlowe turns such mutual possession into farce when Mephistophilis punishes the "damned slaves" (Robin and the Vintner) who could summon him from Constantinople with a mere spell (3.2). More tragically, he suggests that the parasite can possess his host from the outside, as it were, because he needs only the power of the host, not his personal character, self, or soul. Hence, the trivialization, the emptying out of such qualities in *Doctor Faustus*. In the early modern world, where service provided vocation, education, and mutual support, the effects of parasitism would have been especially pernicious. Between them, Faustus and Mephistophilis utterly confound the responsibilities of masters and servants.

In *The Jew of Malta*, a slave market openly exemplifies the human price of a general mania for security. The parasitic oeconomy of *Doctor Faustus* presents us with a more insidious protection racket. However alien to English experience the ritual of a demonic pact might have been, Marlowe has recognized its appropriateness as a symbol for the destruction of ordinary creative agencies. The devil, wrote George Gifford (1587), poses as the servant but in fact rules the witch.[24] A practiced servant himself, he knows how to pick "fit instruments" (Gifford J1v). A major qualification for becoming the devil's slave and initiating a household run on principles of predatory dependency is an aversion to productive work. Studying law, says Faustus, is "servile and illiberal"(1.1.36) as befits a "mercenary drudge"(1.1.34). Valdes and Cornelius will be a greater help than "all my labors" (1.1.70). What labors?

When Faustus "tires" his brains to "get a deity" (1.1.64), enter Wagner, suggesting that this is all he will ever get or engender: Wagner and a host of servile spirits who enable him to have his joys in "full possession." For Faustus, "deity" means the ability to "make spirits fetch me what I please / Resolve me of all ambiguities / Perform what desperate enterprise I will?" (1.1.80-82). Faustus shares this desire to be waited on with Valdes and Cornelius; Valdes is so enchanted by the prospect of having "serviceable" spirits that he imaginatively transforms the common running footman to a whole troupe of "Lapland giants trotting by our sides" (1.1.127). Wagner, of course, wants to have his own personal servant, who will wait upon him in "beaten silk and stavesacre" (1.4.16).

Mephistophilis encourages Faustus to believe that he will be an all-purpose, super-capable attendant, whom Faustus can expect,

> To give me whatsoever I shall ask,
> To tell me whatsoever I demand,
> To slay mine enemies and aid my friends
> And always be obedient to my will.
>   (1.3.94-97)

Four out of five of the articles in the demonic pact signed by Faustus specify the servile duties of Mephistophilis, including the stipulation that he be invisible in house or chamber (2.1.102). The first article makes Faustus himself a "spirit," identifying him with beings described in scene one of the A-text as "subjects" (123). In *Doctor Faustus*, any distinction of spirit from "subject" would appear to be a distinction without a difference, as William Empson perhaps recognized.[25]

What makes *Doctor Faustus* highly effective as a dose of stavesacre or parasite control is Marlowe's grasp of a condition which captivates by simulating trust and reliability. Such a condition might be both attractive and gruesome for anyone in the Elizabethan population (estimates run as high as 60%) who had actually worked as a servant in a domestic oeconomy. Marlowe makes visible through his servile characters the nexus between servants as "things" created by masters (Prospero's "This thing of darkness I acknowledge mine") and spirits as "things" which are unclassifiable because monstrous or imperfectly alive (Horatio's "What, has this thing appeared again tonight?"). The creatures of Faustus are familiars, not a family. If Helen *were* a succuba, as Greg argues, she would fit right into his domestic establishment. The B-text makes this development more explicit by stressing, just before the final sequence, that Wagner has become heir to Faustus' fortunes. The revisers of B may have recalled that in *The Jew of Malta*, Barabas adopts his slave as his heir. Perhaps if, as Greg notes (370-71), Marlowe himself did not read the English *Faust Book,* with its suggestion that only Faustus was willing to "entertain" a "knave" like Wagner, the revisers did. Knowing full well that Faustus is about to die, Wagner promises "in all humble dutie, I do yeeld / My life and lasting service for your love" (B 1918-19). In any case, the will, another instrument or tool, confirms the way in which Faustus has turned himself into a living instrument — a slave who offers to sell himself yet again when threatened with "arrest" for disobedience to Lucifer.

I would like to end with two examples which may help to justify my lack of attention to "on kai me on" in this paper. The first is an anecdote which sheds new light on the character of Faustus himself. It concerns a very young girl, Judith Klatten, who took to her bed for five years, during which time she was never seen to eat or drink. Eventually she explained her miraculous fast by saying that "Little People" ran about every day under her bed and brought her food from whatever was being cooked at home or roasted elsewhere.[26] This young girl enacts a living death in obedience to her fantasy of total service and care. Unmoving and thing-like in her bed, kept alive by invisible servants, she may epitomize the way in which the de-humanized and instrumental functions and effects of service, as well as an "illiberal" dependence on invisible power, come together in Marlowe's play. Snow commented that one cannot "really imagine Faustus, in spite of his desire to 'have' his joys 'in full possession' (185), inhabiting any achievement, living and dying *in* any work" (Snow, 83-84). Precisely! *And*, I would add, what a thorough corruption of labor and laborers this kind of madness or "full possession" brings about.

The second example is provided by Ben Jonson, who like the B-revisers and William Shakespeare, often illuminates and untangles Marlovian contradictions. I am thinking particularly of how he satirizes the institution of service in *The Devil is an Ass* (1616). In this play, Pug, a real devil, proves to be no match for real servants (with the wonderfully "instrumental" names of Engine, Trains, and Ambler) when it comes to possessing masters — i.e., serving their own turns by implementing the wild desires of their employers. He fails as a servant *because* he fails as a parasite. Jonson emphasizes the destructiveness of such agents when he has his devil, Pug, borrow the body of a dead cut-purse and the clothes of a lecherous "usher." Like the actual slaves who, through violent conquest or capture, have exchanged freedom for life, these servants are in a important sense "socially dead."[27] But they thrive (as slaves do not) on processes which destroy creative growth in any human society.

Faustus, in contrast to his arm, does *not* resist "full possession." He signs with Lucifer a contract which promises that he will be an invisible "spirit" and enjoy the unlimited services of Mephistophilis. Invisible spirits, as playwrights recognized, might seem to make perfect servants. The anxious master might hide his reliance upon agents; the anxious servant might cover up his production of mayhem, as goblets fly and dishes crash. In practice, however, liveried Renaissance servants were often most visible. Whether we regard the master-servant relation in professional, educational, or strictly financial terms, servant visibility must have promoted mutual responsibility and have limited the mutual confounding of roles so evident in parasitic dependency. As a social contract based on service begins its long disappearance, playwrights use "possession" to characterize a slavery that can begin in chambers or libraries or innyards, as well as in battlefields, Mediterranean pirate ships or African villages. Long before the Enlightenment critique of slavery as a violation of individual rights, Renaissance dramatists like Marlowe were stigmatizing a condition widely accepted in their world.

Notes

1. Useful discussions of early modern slavery may be found in Fernand Braudel, *The Mediterranean and the Mediterranean World in the Age of Philip II*, 2 vols. (London, 1975); David Brion Davis, *The Problem of Slavery in Western Culture* (Ithaca, 1966); and Orlando Patterson, *Slavery and Social Death* (Cambridge, MA, 1982). On the presence and regular use of black slaves in England at this time, see Peter Fryer, *Staying Power: The History of Black People in Britain* (London, 1984) and James Walvin, *Black and White: The Negro and English Society, 1555-1945* (London, 1973).

2. On the widespread acceptance of slavery, see the valuable discussion by Carolyn Prager in "The Problem of Slavery in *The Custom of the Country*," *Studies in English Literature* 28 (1988), 301-17. An influential apologist for household order, William Perkins, could maintain that Christ purchased spiritual liberty alone; slavery, described in the Bible, was not against the law of a "corrupted nature." See [Christian] *Oeconomie: or Hous-hold Government: A Short Survey of the Right Manner of Erecting and Ordering a Family, According to the Scriptures*, in *Works* (London, 1631), 3: 697-98.

3. Jean Louis Flandrin, *Families in Former Times: Kinship, Household, and Sexuality* (Cambridge, 1979), 63.

4. W. W. Greg, ed., *Marlowe's Dr. Faustus 1604-1616* (Oxford, 1950), 64. This emendation interested Greg because "oeconomy" appeared in the 1609 or A2 text of *Doctor Faustus*, as well as in the B-text of 1616, and therefore indicated, Greg believed, the dependence of a composite B-text upon a particular edition of A. Roma Gill also believes that the printer of A2 was "uncomprehending," and adds that he was followed by the A3 text as well. See *The Complete Works of Christopher Marlowe*, vol. 2, *Dr. Faustus* (Oxford, 1990), 54.

5. Line references for these and later textual comparisons are to Greg's parallel text edition. Otherwise, in subsequent references I normally cite Michael Keefer, ed., *Christopher Marlowe's Doctor Faustus: A 1604-Version Edition* (Peterborough, 1991). Although "armour" has no household meanings, "harness" may refer not only to armor but also to tackle or gear generally or to household and personal equipment

specifically (OED).

6.   Leah Marcus, "Textual Indeterminacy and Ideological Difference: The Case of *Doctor Faustus*," *Renaissance Drama* 20 (1989), 1-29.

7.   Recent literary studies of service are particularly indebted to the following historical studies: Peter Laslett, *The World We Have Lost* (London, 1965); Ann Kussmaul, *Servants in Husbandry in Early Modern England* (Cambridge, 1981); Keith Wrightson, *English Society 1580-1680* (New Brunswick, 1982); Ralph A. Houlbrooke, *The English Family 1450-1700* (London, 1984); and Susan Dwyer Amussen, *An Ordered Society: Gender and Class in Early Modern England* (Oxford, 1988). See Thomas Moisan, "'Knock Me Here Soundly': Comic Misprision and Class Consciousness in Shakespeare," *Shakespeare Quarterly* 42 (1991), 276-90. For a brilliant and entertaining account of the servants in English fiction, see Bruce Robbins, *The Servant's Hand: English Fiction From Below* (New York, 1986).

8.   Francis E. Dolan, *Dangerous Familiars: Representations of Domestic Crime in England 1550-1700* (Ithaca, 1994), 180ff., stressing the permeability of bodies and subjects; 209, associating instrumental function with more skeptical views of witchcraft. For brief but suggestive ideas, linking ghosts and spirits with domestic obligations which are unfulfilled or disturbed, see Jonathan Arac, *Commissioned Spirits: The Shaping of Social Motion in Dickens, Carlyle, Melville, and Hawthorne* (New Brunswick, 1979) 10, 127. William Ringler, Jr. worked out the doubling of fairies and mechanicals in *A Midsummer Night's Dream* in "The Number of Actors in Shakespeare's Early Plays," *The Seventeenth Century Stage*, ed. G. E. Bentley (Chicago, 1968), 110-34.

9.   "While the drama sometimes presents witchcraft as trivial and amusing and at other times as deeply threatening, the dramatic options closely correspond to the previously identified positions in the controversy over witches' agency" (Dolan 211).

10. Roger Sales,*Christopher Marlowe* (London, 1991), 131.

11. Christina Larner, *Witchcraft and Religion: The Politics of Popular Belief*, ed. Alan MacFarlane (Oxford, 1984), 7. Historians of witchcraft agree that demonic pacts were less important in England. See Robert W. West, *Reginald Scot and Renaissance Writings on Witchcraft* (Boston, 1984), 55. Rossell Hope Robbins includes an alleged pact, guaranteeing total wish-fulfillment and protection, in *The Encyclopaedia of Witchcraft and Demonology* (New York, 1959), 374-75.

12. I follow Eric Segal, who has shown in his discussion of slavery in Roman comedy that the most seemingly conventional clowning routines may often reflect specific social conditions. See *Roman Laughter: The Comedy of Plautus* (Cambridge, MA, 1968). See Thomas Cartelli's stimulating comments on "anxiety about social agency" in *Macbeth* in *Marlowe, Shakespeare and the Economy of Theatrical Experience* (Philadelphia, 1991), 117.

13. Numerous examples may be found in the tracts collected and edited by Barbara Rosen, in *Witchcraft in England, 1558-1618* (Amherst, 1991).

14. Marlowe's characters show few symptoms of the melancholy which seems to have plagued actual servants and made them acutely susceptible to suggestion when family or communal outbreaks of possession occurred. Michael MacDonald's analysis of the records of Dr. Napier makes the psychological disorders of servants especially prominent. For example, in a table listing the occupations of disturbed patients, 50, MacDonald shows that servants formed by far the largest group. See *Mystical Bedlam: Madness, Anxiety, and Healing in Seventeenth Century England* (Cambridge, 1981).

15. Keith Thomas, *Religion and the Decline of Magic: Studies in Popular Beliefs in Sixteenth- and Seventeenth-Century England* (Harmondsworth, 1973), 645.

16. On the significance of these conditions for an understanding of the *Tamburlaine* plays, see Mark Thornton Burnett, "Tamburlaine: An Elizabethan Vagabond," *Studies in Philology* 84 (1987), 308-23.

17. Emmanuel Le Roy Ladurie, *Jasmin's Witch* (Aldershot, 1987), 64, 39. See David Warren Sabean's fascinating account of a thirteen-year old witch, a servant girl whose father could not carry on his craft as a mason because of a crippled arm. (*Power in the Blood: Popular Culture and Village Discourse in Early Modern Germany* [Cambridge, 1984], 95-96.) Alan MacFarlane cites George Gifford's point that when Scripture failed to protect the "bones" of the faithful from witches, they resorted to other remedies, in *Witchcraft in Tudor and Stuart England: A Regional and Comparative Study* (London, 1970), 106. Rosen's Intro. 43-49, speculates with great sensitivity about the diseases and accidents which made villagers feel helpless. These specific misfortunes are frequently glossed over by scholars more interested in village social dynamics or in the behavior attributed to witches themselves.

18. Edward A. Snow, "Marlowe's *Doctor Faustus* and the Ends of Desire," in *Two Renaissance Mythmakers: Christopher Marlowe and Ben Jonson. Selected Papers from the English Institute 1975-76,* Ed. Alvin Kernan and Margaret R. Higonnet (Baltimore, 1977), 93-94. I emphasized the folly of Faustus in *Christopher Marlowe: Merlin's Prophet* (Cambridge, 1977), 60-61.

19. For examples of their presence in audiences, see Andrew Gurr, *Playgoing in Shakespeare's London* (Cambridge, 1987), 119, 133, 155.

20. Richard Strier, "Faithful Servants: Shakespeare's Praise of Disobedience," *The Historical Renaissance: New Essays on Tudor and Stuart Literature and Culture*, ed. Heather Dubrow and Richard Strier (Chicago, 1988), 119.

21. Larner, 54-55. Dolan documents her argument for the intersection of popular and elite cultures in witchcraft discourses by pointing out that "some 'popular' pamphlets were written by legal personnel"(179).

22. Sales observes, concerning editor John D. Jump's condescension toward

the comic scenes, that "Renaissance societies allowed those who belonged to the culture of the university to participate as well in the culture of the market place" (136).

23. See Michael D. Bristol, *Carnival and Theater: Plebeian Culture and the Structure of Authority in Renaissance England* (London, 1985), 151, and Weil, 68. Bristol is generally more alert to "social experimentation" (52).

24. George Gifford, *A Discourse of the Subtill Practises of Devilles by Witches and Sorcerers* (London, 1587) sig. G1v.

25. He speculates that Marlowe's devils are in fact "middle spirits" who can escape comic drudgery if they manage to trick Faustus out of his soul by fooling him with the absurd mythology of hell and damnation. (William Empson, *Faustus and the Censor: The English Faust-book and Marlowe's 'Doctor Faustus.'* Recovered and ed. by John Henry Jones [Oxford, 1987].)

26. H. C. Erik Midelfort, "The Devil and the German People: Reflections on the Popularity of Demon Possession in Sixteenth-Century Germany," *Religion and Culture in the Renaissance and Reformation, Sixteenth Century Essays & Studies*, ed. Steven Ozment (London, 1989), 2: 99. I am indebted for this reference to Judith Owens.

27. This is Patterson's basic definition of slavery.

Writing in the Margins:
Theatrical Manuscripts and the
B-Text of *Doctor Faustus*

Eric Rasmussen

It has long been something of a bibliographical certainty that the printer's copy for the 1616 B1 quarto of *Doctor Faustus*, the B-text, was not a theatrical manuscript. W. W. Greg asserted with some confidence that the printer's copy for B1 was "definitely . . . not a promptbook," and Fredson Bowers concurred, "it was clearly not the promptbook."[1] There are so few certainties associated with the *Faustus* texts that it may seem almost ungrateful for an editor to question this one. However, the view of theatrical manuscripts that had informed textual criticism from McKerrow to Greg and Bowers has recently been challenged by Paul Werstine, William B. Long, and Marion Trousdale, who argue that conjectures about the type of manuscripts behind printed dramatic texts have too often been guided by an editor's idea of what a Renaissance playbook would or should have looked like, rather than by a careful examination of the dozen or so extant theatrical manuscripts from the period.[2] Consequently, many of the traditional assumptions about "promptbooks" and their characteristics do not square with the empirical evidence. Indeed, the terminology itself is at issue. *Promptbook* apparently did not enter the language until the early nineteenth century, and, when it did, it referred to a regularized and thoroughly annotated theatrical document very different from the book that was used by the prompter or bookkeeper in the Renaissance playhouse. Sixty years ago, Greg wrote that "considering their importance for textual criticism it is surprising that more attention has not been given to those prompt copies of early plays that have actually survived."[3] And yet, even Greg, when he assumes the role of textual critic, often seems to forget what he knew so well as a paleographer and theater historian; as Werstine wryly observes, Greg sometimes "misrepresents what he himself has taught us about theatrical manuscripts" (Werstine 233).

It is, in part, our newly augmented awareness of the Renaissance playbook that justifies a reconsideration of Bowers' claim that "the general characteristics" of B1 *Faustus* "do not suggest a promptbook."[4] I wish to focus here on a few specific details of the B1 quarto, as they appear in light of some Elizabethan and Jacobean playbooks. In a number of Renaissance playbooks, entry or exit directions in the text are repeated in the margin. In Massinger's manuscript of *Believe as You List* (1631), for instance, the bookkeeper for the King's Men, Edward Knight, repeated many of Massinger's faintly written entry directions in a bold, heavy Italian script in the margins, which, as Greg notes, "could not fail to catch the prompter's eye" (Greg, *Dramatic* 298). Sometimes Knight deleted the original direction; at other times he left it standing.

A stage direction in B1 *Faustus* exhibits what Greg calls a "curious duplication" in that the *Exeunt* appears twice:

> *Beate the Friers, and fling fier-workes among*
> *them, and so Exeunt.*
> A1 quarto (sig. D2v)

> *Beate the Friers, fling fire worke among them,*
> *and Exeunt.*   *Exeunt.*
> B1 quarto (sig. E1v)

For Greg, "the only reasonable explanation" is that Marlowe's manuscript simply had the direction *Exeunt*; the rest would have been written in by someone preparing the manuscript for the B1 printers, copying from an earlier printed text of the play, possibly the 1611 A3 quarto (Greg, *Parallel Texts* 75). But there is, I would suggest, another equally reasonable explanation. An author might be content to bury an *Exeunt* direction in the middle of a page; and since A1 was apparently printed from an authorial manuscript (as I have argued elsewhere),[5] it is not surprising to find such a direction in that text. A bookkeeper, however, might need to make the direction more obvious for purposes of prompting. Greg elsewhere suggests that if stage directions were "too long to be taken in at a glance . . . the prompter might yet make these serviceable . . . . [T]he simplest thing was to note their essence in bold script" in the opposite margin (Greg, *Dramatic* 213). Accordingly, the bookkeeper preparing a manuscript of *Faustus* for use as a playbook might have written another *Exeunt* in the right margin, perhaps without bothering to delete the original direction (as is frequently the case in the *Believe as You List* playbook). If such a playbook were then to be used as printer's copy, a compositor might well have set both *Exeunt*s. Greg himself held that "the repetition of stage directions" in printed texts "points to prompt copy."[6]

A second textual detail that, so far as I know, has not been previously noticed, deserves attention in any new attempt to determine the B-text's provenance. In the A1 quarto, mid-scene entrances are usually centered, but in B1 these same entrances are printed in the right margins with no break in the text: *Enter Wagner* (A3v26); *Enter Valdes / and Cornelius* (A3v27-28); *Enter Wag.* (A4v16); *Enter 2 deuils.* (B3r18); *Enter the scholers* (G4v35).[7] A few of the mid-scene entrances unique to the B-text also appear in the right margins of B1 with no break in the text: *Ent. Meph. & other Diuels.* (F2r19-20); *Enter Faustus and Wagner* (G4v30). This textual feature is of some significance because, as Greg pointed out, entrances within a scene in some manuscript playbooks "are often relegated to the right margin without any break in the text."[8] The reason for placing these directions in the margins seems fairly straightforward. For, although we need to be careful about inferring what Elizabethan "prompters" did and did not do, there is ample evidence that someone in the theater held the playbook and, at the very least, was responsible for getting the actors onstage. A character in *Every Woman in her Humour* "would swear like an elephant and stamp and stare . . . like a playhouse bookkeeper when the actors miss their entrance."[9] Entrance directions in the right margins of playbooks would be particularly well-suited to the needs of what Long has termed the "glancing bookkeeper," that is, someone who does not necessarily follow the play word-for-word, but only glances at the book when he needs to do so (Long 106). We know, moreover, that mid-scene entrance directions are sometimes found in the right margins in printed texts that were apparently set up from theatrical manuscripts.[10] In this respect, the texts of *Hamlet* offer an interesting analog to *Faustus*. Several mid-scene entrance directions that are centered in Q2 *Hamlet* (a text almost certainly printed from Shakespeare's foul papers) are printed in the right margins of the Folio (a text that derives, at least in part, from a playbook) with no break in the text of the play.[11]

The mid-scene entrances printed in the right margins of B1 *Faustus*, then, present a significant challenge to the assertion that "the general characteristics" of the B-text "do not suggest a promptbook." Such marginal entrance directions are, in fact, a characteristic feature not only of some extant manuscripts, but of some printed texts set in type from playbooks. In addition to these textual features, the impression that some sort of playbook may lie behind the B-text is further strengthened by the evident censorship of B1. For it is clear that the B-text represents a censored version of the play. The censorship may have been undertaken in an attempt to bring the play into conformity with the 1606 *Acte to Restraine Abuses of Players* which forbade the use of "the holy Name of God or of Christ Jesus, or of the Holy Ghoste or of the Trinitie" in stage plays (cited in Chambers, IV, 338-39). Two references to Christ are deleted but others remain;[12] Mephistopheles' advice to "abjure the Trinity" (A 1.3.54) becomes "abjure all godliness" (B 1.3.51); and several references to God are removed or altered to the less objectionable "heaven" (2.1.9, 2.1.25, 2.1.78, 5.2.150, 5.2.155, 5.2.157, 5.2.168, 5.2.188) but others survive in the text (e.g., 5.2.57-67).

Greg always contended that there existed in the Renaissance "a purely literary tradition of expurgation";[13] accordingly, it is not surprising that he should have argued that this B-text censorship was undertaken by the scribe who prepared the printer's copy in 1616 (*Parallel Texts* 85). It is perhaps worth remembering, however, that the 1606 Act applied only to stage performances, not to printed plays, and that John Wright had already published two texts of *Faustus* after the passage of the 1606 Act (A2 in 1609 and A3 in 1611), neither of which show any signs of censorship. Although a scribe preparing copy for a printed text would have had no obligation to remove profanity, T. H. Howard-Hill has shown that the scribe Ralph Crane, in an apparent attempt to make "literary" improvements, did in fact sometimes delete offensive language from the material he was copying.[14] Yet the systematic, albeit sporadic, way in which profanity was excised from *Faustus* — with apparently little attention paid to the effect on the sense of the line (the masculine pronoun survives in "if unto heaven, he'll throw me down to hell," 2.1.78) or to the effect on the meter (e.g., "And hide me from the heavy wrath of heaven," 5.2.157) — suggests a censor whose sole concern was to remove "the holy Name of God or of Christ Jesus" rather that a scribe with literary sensibilities. Gary Taylor has argued that the wholesale excision of profanity in a printed text is a clear sign of an underlying playbook altered for performance after 1606, such as the expurgated Folio texts of *The Merry Wives of Windsor* and *Othello*.[15]

But the matter is complicated by a number of B-text episodes that were evidently *not* censored. Specifically, the Benvolio scenes (4.1-3), which were added to the play in 1602 or perhaps even later,[16] teem with strong profanities, including "Zounds" (4.1.87, 132, 138, 150, 4.2.67, 4.3.13) and "'Sblood" (4.1.152, 164). How did these added scenes escape the rigorous censorship found elsewhere in the B-text? Again, the available manuscript evidence from the period offers a clue: Edmund Tilney's censorship markings appear on several pages of the original manuscript of *Sir Thomas More*, but are nowhere to be found on the pages containing the additions;[17] Sir George Buc left his mark on nearly every leaf of the prompt manuscript of Thomas Middleton's *The Second Maiden's Tragedy*

(1611), but no such marks appear on any of the five slips containing added passages;[18] and, as T. H. Howard-Hill observes, the three additional leaves in the playbook of John Fletcher and Philip Massinger's *Sir John van Olden Barnavelt* (1619) "are the only sheets in the play without signs of Buc's censorial vigilance."[19] Apparently, when passages were added to a playbook that had already been licensed for performance, the additions themselves may not have been subjected to censorship. So too, by analogy, the added Benvolio scenes may have been inserted into a pre-existing playbook that had already been systematically altered to bring the play into conformity with the 1606 Act.

I would suggest that manuscript behind the B1 quarto of *Faustus* may have resembled *The Book of Sir Thomas More*: an interleaved manuscript in a number of different hands, with various layers of addition, revision, playhouse annotation, and censorship. Some theater historians argue that *The Book of Sir Thomas More* could have served as an unwieldy but usable playbook in the Elizabethan theater.[20] Others contend that the extent of the revision in the *More* manuscript would have necessitated a completely new prompt copy.[21] If we agree that *More* represents a playbook, then we could legitimately argue that the manuscript behind B1 is a playbook as well. If, on the other hand, we believe that such a heavily revised script would necessarily have been replaced by a fair copy playbook, then the superseded manuscript presents itself as a likely candidate to be released to a printer. In either case, the features that the composite manuscript would have imparted to B1 would, of course, be the same. For our understanding of the *Faustus* texts, the issue of whether or not *The Book of Sir Thomas More* is a "finished" playbook and the related question of whether or not to call the manuscript behind B1 a "playbook" are ultimately less important than the empirical fact of the extant *More* manuscript, demonstrating as it does the type of hybrid dramatic manuscript that existed in the Renaissance and that might well have been available to the printers of the B1 quarto.

Notes

1. W. W. Greg, ed. *Marlowe's 'Doctor Faustus' 1604-1616: Parallel Texts* (Oxford, 1950), 80; Fredson Bowers, "Marlowe's *Doctor Faustus*: The 1602 Additions," *Studies in Bibliography* 26 (1973), 12n.
2. See Paul Werstine, "'Foul Papers' and 'Prompt-books': Printer's Copy for Shakespeare's *Comedy of Errors*," *Studies in Bibliography* 41 (1988), 232-46; Werstine, "McKerrow's 'Suggestion' and Twentieth-Century Textual Criticism," *Renaissance Drama* 19 (1988), 149-73; William B.

Long, "Stage-Directions: A Misinterpreted Factor in Determining Textual Provenance," *Text* 2 (1985), 121-37; Long, "'A Bed / for Woodstock': A Warning for the Unwary," *Medieval and Renaissance Drama in England* 2 (1985), 91-118; Marion Trousdale, "Diachronic and Synchronic: Critical Bibliography and the Acting of Plays," *Shakespeare: Text, Language, Criticism. Essays in Honor of Marvin Spevack*, ed. Bernhard Fabian and Kurt Tetzeli von Rosador (Zurich, 1987), 307-14, and "A Second Look at Critical Bibliography and the Acting of Plays," *Shakespeare Quarterly* 41 (1990), 87-96.

3. W. W. Greg, *Dramatic Documents from the Elizabethan Playhouses: Commentary* (Oxford, 1931), 189.

4. Fredson Bowers, ed., *The Complete Works of Christopher Marlowe*, 2 vols. (Cambridge, 1973), 2: 140.

5. See my "Rehabilitating the A-text of Marlowe's *Doctor Faustus*," *Studies in Bibliography* 46 (1993), 221-38.

6. W. W. Greg, ed., *The Shakespeare First Folio* (Oxford, 1955), 138.

7. Another example is *Enter Mephosto.* (B3v25); but, in this instance, the earlier quartos, A1-3, also set the direction at the end of the line following Faustus' conjuration: *Veni veni Mephastophile enter Meph:* (B4v5).

8. *Dramatic Documents: Commentary*, 207. See, for example, the *Charlemagne* promptbook fol. 119v, 120r, 121r, 121v, 122r, 122v, 123r, 124r, 124v, 125r, 125v, 126r, 126v, 127r, 127v, 128r, 128v, 129r, 129v, 130r, 131r, 131v, 132r, 132v, 133r, 133v, 134r, 134v, 135r.

9. Cited in E. K. Chambers, *The Elizabethan Stage*, 4 vols. (Oxford, 1923), 2: 540-41.

10. See, for example, Folio *Macbeth* sig. mm1v-mm2r.

11. Compare the Q2 *Hamlet* directions on B1v and K2r with their Folio counterparts on nn4v and pp2v.

12. "See, see where Christ's blood streams in the firmament!" (A 5.2.78) and "Yet for Christ's sake, whose blood hath ransomed me," (A 5.2.100) do not appear in the B-text; but "Ah / O, my Christ! / [Ah] Rend not my heart for naming of my Christ!" appears in both texts (A 5.2.79-80; B 5.2.151-52). Citations are from *Doctor Faustus: A- and B-texts (1604, 1616)*, ed. David Bevington and Eric Rasmussen, The Revels Plays (Manchester, 1993).

13. Greg, *The Shakespeare First Folio*, 152. For more recent treatments of Renaissance censorship, see Janet Clare, *"Art Made Tongue-tied by Authority": Elizabethan and Jacobean Dramatic Censorship* (Manchester, 1990); and Richard Dutton, *Mastering the Revels* (Iowa City, 1991).

14. T. H. Howard-Hill, "Shakespeare's Earliest Editor: Ralph Crane," *Shakespeare Survey* 44 (1992), 113-29.

15. Gary Taylor, "Zounds Revisited: Theatrical, Editorial, and Literary Expurgation," *Shakespeare Reshaped, 1606-1623* (Oxford, 1993).

16. A previously unrecognized echo from Shakespeare suggests a late date of composition for the Benvolio scenes. Benvolio's comment at B 4.2.27,

"But yet my heart's more ponderous than my head," has the appearance of being an echo of Cordelia's aside in the Folio version of *King Lear*: "And yet not so, since I am sure my love's / More ponderous than my tongue" (1.1.76-77; TLN 83-84). The Quarto *Lear* version of these lines is significantly different: "& yet not so, since I am sure / My loues more richer then my tongue" (sig. B2r). *King Lear* was first performed in 1606, but the revised version preserved in the Folio may not have been written until 1609-10. Shakespeare may, of course, be the debtor here. But if the phrase was original with Shakespeare, then this addition to *Faustus* could not have been written before 1606, and may be as late as 1609-10. This hypothesis of a late date of composition gains some small reinforcement from the fact that the *Damnable Life*, from which the Benvolio scenes draw heavily, was reprinted (perhaps for the first time since 1592) in 1608.

17. Tilney's notes and deletions appear on fol. 3r, 3v, 5r, 10r, and 17v. G. Harold Metz points to the absence of Tilney's hand in the additions and suggests that "the Booke was under review by Tilney and the revisions and additions were being made in the text simultaneously" ("The Master of the Revels and *The Booke of Sir Thomas More*," *Shakespeare Quarterly* 33 [1982], 494).

18. Buc's marks can be found on fol. 29r, 30r, 33r, 37r, 43r, 43v, 44v, 49r, 51r, 52r, 54v, 55v. See Greg's Malone Society edition (Oxford, 1910), xi; see also T. H. Howard-Hill, "The Censor and Four English Promptbooks," *Studies in Bibliography* 36 (1983), 175.

19. T. H. Howard-Hill, ed., *Sir John van Olden Barnavelt*. By John Fletcher and Philip Massinger (Oxford, 1980), x.

20. See Giorgio Melchiori, "*The Booke of Sir Thomas More*: A Chronology of Revision," *Shakespeare Quarterly* 37 (1986), 301.

21. See Peter Blayney, "*The Booke of Sir Thomas More* Re-Examined," *Studies in Philology* 69 (1972), 176.

The Subversion of Gender Hierarchies in *Dido, Queene of Carthage*

Sara Munson Deats

Dido, Queene of Carthage, frequently relegated to the status of Marlowe's juvenilia, is second only to *The Massacre at Paris* as the most neglected play in the Marlowe canon. Yet, even so, as with many of Marlowe's dramas, almost every aspect of the play has been debated — the authorship has been challenged, the date has been questioned, and the genre has been disputed. Questions come naturally to the reader or viewer of this oxymoronic drama, which balances contrarieties of genre (comedy, tragedy, epic, romance), tone (comic, farcical, solemn, tragic), and value (romantic, heroic, feminine, masculine) into an intriguing *concordia discors*.

Dido exemplifies a type of interrogative drama popular during the early modern period and discussed at length by Joel Altman in *Tudor Play of the Mind*. Like Castiglione's popular dialogue, *The Courtier*, these plays are constructed from a series of statements and counter statements, both of which are often equally valid. They frequently imitate the form of a sophistical debate, a kind of arguing on both sides of the subject, *in utramque partem*, in which thesis provokes antithesis yet without a resolving synthesis. These plays pose questions rather than make statements — questions, Altman posits, about love, justice, sovereignty, nature, imagination, and, I would add, about sex, gender, and desire.[1] This essay will explore the interrogative structure of Marlowe's *Dido*, particularly as this dramatic forensic problematizes questions of sex, gender, and sexuality, issues debated incessantly in both the formal controversy over the nature of woman, the *querelle des femmes*, and the drama of the period. Through this examination, I will attempt to rescue *Dido* from the status of juvenilia and establish it as a mature and sophisticated experiment in interrogative drama, Marlowe's dramatic *querelle des femmes*, in which, like so many of his predecessors in this mode, he argues on both sides of the question.

Although Plato, in one of his more radical gestures, insists that the only difference between the natures of man and woman is "that

163

the female bears and the male begets,"[2] the majority of the spectators flocking to the Swan or the Rose, or to the Royal Chapel or the Blackfriars, were probably conditioned to agree with Lord Julian, the fashioner of the ideal lady in Castiglione's *The Courtier*, that although "some qualities are common and necessarie as well for the woman as the man, yet are there some other more meete for the woman than for the man, and some again meete for the man, that she ought in no wise to meddle withall."[3] Nevertheless, the view that gender derives more from nurture than from nature, although doubtless not the dominant discourse of the early modern period, was certainly a discourse in circulation, and questions concerning the necessary equation of sex and gender were vigorously debated at this time. This issue is also interrogated in Marlowe's *Dido*.

On one hand, it can be argued — and, indeed, has been argued — that *Dido* reinscribes rather than questions gender stereotypes, positioning "feminine" passion in opposition to "masculine" reason in a manner legitimated by the patriarchy since the time of Pythagoras.[4] According to this reading, the Queen of Carthage exemplifies the stereotypical female ruled by passion, the woman for whom love is not a thing apart but the very essence of her being, whereas the Trojan Prince takes the Herculean role of the stalwart hero at the crossroads who appropriately chooses duty over pleasure. Thus, each protagonist performs according to expected stereotypes of gender identity and the play ultimately celebrates the "masculine" ethics of honor and duty over the "feminine" values of love and passion. However, closer scrutiny of the playtext discovers an oppositional discourse embedded within the play, a subversive perspective revealing itself through fissures in the deceptively smooth ideological surface of the narrative that Marlowe inherited from Virgil, a discourse disrupting sexual difference and challenging societal categories of sex, gender, and sexuality.[5]

The first rift in the drama's ideological facade appears in the opening scene of the playtext in the portrait of the archetypal patriarch, Jupiter — god, king, husband, and father. This opening scene presents the King of the Gods from a comic perspective. Like the mortals whose destinies he (at least partially) controls, Jupiter is depicted as a victim of passionate love, displaying the foolishness and excess conventionally associated with amorous seizures. Jupiter seems totally willing to abrogate his divine prerogatives to the "female wanton boy," to relinquish to the peevish Trojan youth the power "to control proud fate and cut the thread of time," to subject to his minion's caprices all the deities of heaven and earth. The tableau of Jupiter dandling Ganymede on his knees, besotted by his infatuation for the petulant boy, plucking feathers from the slumbering Mercury's wings as he alternately blusters, boasts, and bribes, offers a graphic stage emblem for the destructive passion that the playtext, at least from one perspective, vividly dramatizes. Significantly, therefore, the playtext's first exemplum of excessive passion ruling reason is not the smitten Queen of Carthage or even her enamored sister Anna, but that classical patriarchal icon, Jupiter, the King of the Gods. Moreover, in this scene, it is Venus, the Goddess of Love and Beauty and thus traditionally the most "feminine" of the Olympians, who paradoxically exhorts Jupiter to fulfill his "masculine" duty. Just as Jupiter's behavior fails to conform to gender expectations, so his sexual preference does not follow socially sanctioned sex/gender patterns as he lavishes his affection on a bonny youth rather than on a nubile maiden. The opening scene thus provides a proleptic prologue for the playtext as a whole, prefiguring the numerous violations of traditional patterns of gender and desire enacted in the drama.

The Jupiter-Ganymede interlude, like many of the transgressive relationships inscribed in the playtext, finds no analogue in Marlowe's primary source, Virgil's *Aeneid*, or even in his probable secondary source, Ovid's *Heroides*. However, two different passages in the *Aeneid* might have suggested this episode. The opening lines of Virgil's epic (I. 6, p. 3) refer to Juno's hatred of the Trojans, for which Trojan Ganymede — who replaced both Juno as Jupiter's bedfellow and her daughter Hebe as his cupbearer — traditionally receives blame.[6] A narration of Ganymede's abduction further appears in Book V of the *Aeneid*, in which the legend of the boy kidnapped by the eagle is embroidered on the mantle awarded to the victor at the funeral games for Anchises:

> the winner has a mantle,
> Woven with gold, and a double seam of crimson.
> With a story in the texture, Ganymede
> Hunting on Ida, breathless, tossing darts
> And racing after the deer, and caught and carried
> In the talons of Jove's eagle, soaring skyward,
> While the boy's old guardians reach their hands up,
>   vainly,
> And the hounds let out a cry.
>
> (121-22)

However, adept classical scholar that he was, Marlowe might have found his inspiration for this scene in a number of places besides the *Aeneid*. The rape of Ganymede is recounted briefly in one of Marlowe's most thoroughly mined classical lodes, Ovid's *Metamorphoses*, and is more fully reprised in another potential classical gold mine, Lucian's *Dialogues of the Gods*.[7] The effervescent and irreverent banter of the latter work, in particular, recalls the Olympian induction of Dido.[8]

The second fissure in the playtext's deceptively smooth ideological surface is produced by the actions of another Olympian, Venus. As noted above, at her debut Venus, Goddess of Love and Beauty, elevates duty (conventionally gendered "masculine") over passion (traditionally gendered "feminine"). However, throughout the play, she is ostensibly associated with the amorous rather than the martial impulse. Moreover, the structure of the play initially appears to reinforce this ethical stereotyping. The drama divides into two antithetical halves that mirror the play's polarized value systems. Venus presides over the first movement: as catalytic petitioner, she persuades Jupiter to rescue Aeneas; as supportive counselor, she advises Aeneas to seek aid from Dido; as wily machinator, she abducts Ascanius and conspires with Cupid to seduce Dido so that the Queen will succor and supply Aeneas. As appropriate to a scenario scripted by the Goddess of Love, all the kinetic forces in Venus' production converge to move the action centripetally toward sexual consummation. Conversely, Jupiter, through his messenger Hermes and incited by the petitioner Iarbus, assumes the role of patron deity in the playtext's second movement: Iarbus acts the part of catalytic petitioner, first exhorting Jupiter to banish Aeneas from Carthage and later providing the supplies necessary for the Trojan's departure; Hermes portrays both rebuking messenger, commanding Aeneas to leave Carthage and desert Dido, and rescuer of the kidnapped Ascanius, making possible Aeneas' escape. Significantly, in the drama's second movement, males assume control, cooperating to sever the lovers and exalt "masculine" honor over "feminine" passion, and the momentum of the play reverses, speeding the action centrifugally away from love's fulfillment. (Appropriately, Venus never appears in the play after the consummation of love in the cave, although her impish viceroy Cupid continues to strut and fret throughout the scenes initiating chaos.) The shift in authority from forces gendered "feminine" to those gendered "masculine" occurs after the consummation in the cave: a male plaintiff (Iarbus) petitions a male deity (Jupiter) who sends a male messenger (Hermes) to affirm "masculine" values. Gender principles thus appear to be naturally linked to sex as would be conventionally expected.

However, a more probing gaze reveals that — as so often in Marlowe's plays — things are not as simple as they first seem. The telos inspiring Venus' machinations is not romantic fulfillment but heroic quest, a stance established in the first scene of the play when the Goddess of Love ironically chides the King of the Gods for allowing passion to distract him from duty. Later Venus plots the romance of Dido and Aeneas as a way of assuring proper rest and recuperation for her son before he continues his voyage to Italy, and although she does briefly consider the possibility of Aeneas' remaining in Carthage, this plan assumes a low priority on her list of alternatives (2.1.223-31).[9] Because I do not credit a word that either Juno or Venus utters in their flattery contest over the slumbering Ascanius (3.2.36-100) while fully believing Aeneas' grudging admission that his mother wishes him to leave Carthage (4.3.5), I interpret Marlowe's Venus as atypically supporting heroic (gendered "masculine") values rather than amorous (gendered "feminine") principles. The Goddess of Love thereby colonizes "feminine" passion in the service of "masculine" honor.[10] Just as conventionally "masculine" ideals motivate Venus' petition to Jupiter, so conventionally "feminine" impulses incite Iarbus' sacrifice and suit to the same divinity, as the King of Getulia colonizes masculine duty in the service of feminine desire. The play thus deconstructs the traditional binary of "feminine" love and "masculine" honor and interrogates any intrinsic nexus between symbolic gender principles and the actions of females and males, either human or divine, within the universe of the play.

The third rupture in the play's ideological surface is provided by the relationship between Dido and Aeneas. Aeneas dominates Virgil's epic by both word and deed, whereas in Ovid's poem the entire tragic narration is filtered through the consciousness of the Queen of Carthage. Marlowe's playtext follows Ovid by placing Dido center stage, and this reorganizing of Virgil's sex/gender priorities is signaled not only by the change of eponymous hero to privilege the tragic Queen of Carthage over the Trojan epic hero but also by the transference of initiative from Aeneas to Dido. Dido's first meeting with Aeneas introduces a pattern of overture and response that is repeated at least three times in the playtext. In the series of interactions between the Queen of Carthage and the Trojan refugee, Dido reverses gender expectations to perform the role of the Courtly lover rather than the coy mistress: she initiates and directs the action, she praises Aeneas, and she gives him gifts. All of these aspects of Dido's behavior intensify as the action progresses. The gracious welcome of the initial encounter (2.1) rises to the impassioned wooing of the grotto interlude (3.4) and reaches its crescendo in Dido's desperate, fervid pleading after Aeneas' abortive escape (4.4). Aeneas' response follows a parallel although less intense progression, modulating from diffidence in the welcoming scene, to tentative acceptance during the exchange of vows in the cave, to a final ringing affirmation of love — his only moment of unalloyed passionate response in the playtext — as he (temporarily) agrees to remain with Dido. In all of their scenes together, however, Dido's passion remains the galvanizing force, with Aeneas' affection only a flickering reaction to her burning desire, a fiery passion perhaps inspired by the sensuous cadences of Ovid's Dido in the *Heroides*.

In act 2, scene 1, Dido ceremoniously greets Aeneas, offers him the garment formerly worn by her dead husband, and attempts to seat him on her throne, in "Dido's place" (79-85; 90-93). When a self-effacing Aeneas demurs, Dido insists, somewhat preemptively: "Ile have it so, Aeneas, be content" (95). The action and dialogue of this scene — Dido's gift of her husband's robe, the placing of Aeneas on her throne, Ascanius' childish declaration, "Madam, you shall be my mother," and Dido's ready acquiescence to this prospect (96-97) — coalesce to foreshadow the abortive betrothal in the grotto and the mock coronation of act 4. Clearly, Dido takes a fancy to "warlike Aeneas," as she ironically terms him, even before she is pricked by Cupid's puissant weapon.

Virgil treats the first meeting between the Carthage Queen and the Trojan refugee very differently. Virgil's Dido gives the Trojan no personal gifts and shows no attraction to him before her amorous wounding by Cupid, although Aeneas, observing the Queen from the seclusion of an obscuring cloud, admires her beauty and majesty even before their first meeting (21). Ovid's *Heroides*, which concentrates on Dido's farewell lament, makes no reference to the specifics of this initial encounter, although Dido does recall to Aeneas, "You were cast ashore by the waves and I received you to a self abiding-place; scarce knowing your name, I gave to you my throne" (91).[11] Finally, the humility of Marlowe's hero is totally un-Virgilian and un-Ovidian. In Marlowe's playtext, Aeneas' own followers fail to recognize their tattered leader, and the Queen herself gently rebukes the hero's self-effacement: "Remember who thou art, speake like thy selfe, / Humilitie belongs to common groomes" (100-01). Conversely, in Virgil's account, Aeneas, emerging from a cloud illumined like a god, is the cynosure, captivating all with his charisma (24, 25). Moreover, in the opening sequence, Virgil's Aeneas, not his Dido, becomes the symbol of royal largess, as the Trojan Prince in gratitude for her hospitality bestows on the Carthaginian Queen rich gifts saved from the sack of Troy (26). Marlowe's playtext thereby reverses the relationship of Virgil's two protagonists, rendering Dido more dynamic and dominant, and thus more conventionally "masculine," while portraying Aeneas as more reticent and passive, and thus more conventionally "feminine."

The premonitions of the welcoming scene are fulfilled in the rapturous love duet in the cave. Isolated with her lover in the forest, Dido continues to direct the action, struggling against her wild passion as she strives to maintain decorum. Earlier, Dido had graciously hosted Aeneas; now, she fervently woos him. Earlier she had dressed him in her husband's robe; now, she begs that he assume her husband's role — that "Sicheus, not Aeneas be thou calde" (3.4.59) — as she bestows upon him her wedding ring and other jewels (61-63). Earlier, she had seated Aeneas on the throne beside her; now, she places her "Crowne and Kingdome" (58) at his command. Throughout the interlude in the cave, as in the earlier sequence of arrival and greeting, Aeneas maintains his humble demeanor, displaying as well "either coyness or obtuseness in his slowness to catch Dido's drift."[12] Most importantly, Aeneas' coyness, balanced with Dido's boldness, highlights the gender role switching occurring in the scene. Although foregrounding the stormy consummation in the cave, neither Virgil's epic nor Ovid's poem makes reference to Dido's gift of wedding jewels to her lover.

The encounter between the torrid Queen and the tepid Prince is replayed with variations later in act 4, after Aeneas' abortive attempt to escape from Carthage. Discovering and preventing Aeneas' secret departure, Dido rejects all decorum. Earlier, she had seated Aeneas on her throne and vowed to place her crown and kingdom at his command; now, she puts the diadem on his head and the scepter in his hand. Earlier, she had dressed him in her husband's garment and given him her wedding ring; now, she sends him riding "as Dido's husband, through the Punic streets" (67). The stage action of Dido arraying Aeneas in emblems of wealth and rule combine with recurrent verbal patterns to link these three episodes of bribery and control, and remind us how often love, power, and wealth intersect in the plays of Marlowe. Moreover, in this scene, as in the earlier parallel sequences, even as she invests Aeneas with the symbols of suzerainty, Dido struggles to retain command, confiscating and destroying the naval equipment that she had earlier granted him even as she parades him through the streets as a monarch. Yet despite the parallelism of the three scenes of royal generosity, stage action and dialogue suggest that a subtle shift of power occurs in this final sequence. The stage picture of Dido entangled in the snarled nautical tacking confiscated from her lover literalizes the verbal imagery of webs and snares that pervades the playtext, recalling particularly Aeneas' apt (although tactless) allusion in the grotto scene to Mars and Venus caught *in flagrante delicto* in Vulcan's net (3.4.4-6). This tableau of entrapment further emphasizes that whereas Dido's power in the opening movement appears absolute, all her efforts in the final acts prove futile, as she becomes further tangled in the seine woven from her own passion and cast by the gods.[13]

In this third sequence, just as Dido reprises her characteristic enticement through language and gifts, so Aeneas reacts with a conditioned response. During their first meeting, Aeneas tentatively accepts Dido's proposals; in the amorous cave interlude, the labile Prince is momentarily fired by Dido's ardor; in act 4, scene 4, Aeneas, for once, actually matches Dido's soaring poetry with his own impassioned oratory (55-60). However, like the oaths in the cave, these vows will all too soon be violated. Yet despite Aeneas' imminent apostasy, we need not consider these hyperbolic pledges mere rhetorical pacifiers designed to placate Dido. Rather, like Dido and the Nurse in the comic whirligigs triggered by Cupid's arrows, Aeneas responds with a vacillating attraction and withdrawal to the total commitment demanded by Dido. Significantly, the entire episode of Aeneas' thwarted escape and return is original to Marlowe's playtext and finds no suggestion in any of the sources. In the *Aeneid*, after the appearance of Hermes, Virgil's Aeneas shows no hesitation; although he sorrows at Dido's suffering, he refuses to mollify her with vows of love (96, 98-101). Ovid's Dido also presents Aeneas as resolute, even as she pleads with him to become "changeable with the winds" (77) and to renege on his decision to depart (87). In both Virgil's epic and Ovid's poem, therefore, Aeneas remains the stern, resolute hero, a role traditionally gendered "masculine," whereas in Marlowe's playtext, the Trojan Prince assumes a pliant, changeable stance, a posture traditionally gendered "feminine."

The depiction of Dido in Marlowe's playtext is more problematic. Virgil's epic portrays Dido as totally victimized by the gods, whereas Ovid's poem avoids any reference to celestial constraint. Marlowe's drama, drawing on both Virgil and Ovid, limns Dido as both agent and patient, simultaneously the victim of divine manipulation, the captive of "feminine" passion, and the "masculine" instigator of the action.

Contemporary critical theory provides a convenient lens through which to view the reversal of roles dramatized in the encounters between Dido and Aeneas. In Jacques Lacan's model of subjectivity, only the "masculine" can occupy the position of speaking and desiring subject; the "feminine" is ineluctably situated as the object of desire. Although no early modern discourses, to my knowledge, discuss the positioning of "masculinity" and "femininity" in precisely these terms, the concept of woman as object of desire is certainly a salient feature of the gender economy of the period, reflected, for example, in the objectification of the sonnet mistress and the dismemberment of the female anatomy in the traditional blazon. The reversal whereby Dido becomes the desiring subject and Aeneas the fetishized object further destabilizes traditional gender roles. Not only does Dido entice Aeneas with gifts, but she also describes him with the reverent religious imagery of the Courtly lover (3.1.87-88) while also celebrating his charms in the traditional blazon of the sonneteer (3.1.85-93). Moreover, the playtext's pervasive imagery of sight associates Dido with the objectifying gaze (3.1.72-74; 3.4.16-18, 35-42; 4.3.25-30; 5.1.200-01, 251-52, 258-61), identified by Freud and his followers with the "masculine," and the dressing of Aeneas on stage, as well as his arraying in jewels, further locates him in the conventional feminine position of object of barter as well as of desire.[14]

Our judgment of Dido, however, depends crucially on our interpretation of her wounding by Cupid. The action of the Dido-Cupid encounter, if interpreted illusionistically, shows Dido's passion to be constrained, the result of Cupid's golden arrows, not Dido's rampaging libido. Yet the question of volition, like so many aspects of this puzzling play, remains ambiguous. This ambiguity may derive from the collision within the playtext of the emblematic and illusionist modes, identified by Catherine Belsey. As Belsey asserts: "The conjunction of the two [modes], or indeed the superimposition of one on the other, is capable of generating a radical uncertainty precisely by withholding from the spectator the single position from which a single and unified meaning is produced."[15] The spectator of *Dido* experiences just such a radical uncertainty in evaluating the Queen's passion for Aeneas. Even viewed solely from an illusionist position, the verdict remains problematic. Textual evidence implies that despite her protests to the contrary (3.1.82-83), Dido favors Aeneas before being pricked by Cupid, and the examples of Anna and Iarbus further illustrate that destructive passion can exist without divine interference. Yet the literal action of the play dramatizes Dido's manipulation by the gods. From an illusionist perspective, therefore, Dido lacks agency; she is reduced to a puppet, pathetic but not tragic. However, when viewed from an emblematic perspective, with Cupid and the supernatural personae generally functioning as allegorical correlatives for the human characters' psychological traits (Cupid = passion, Hermes = ambition), both Aeneas and Dido can be seen as either multifaceted characters, demonstrating the complexity and ambiguity traditionally associated with tragic figures, as the fragmented, discontinuous subjects of the medieval drama, or as rhetorical constructs in the gender debate in which the playtext engages.[16]

Whichever interpretation we adopt, if we grant the two protagonists some degree of volition, they both emerge as androgynous characters. Dido — assertive in her wooing of Aeneas yet pliant in her response to Cupid's darts, alternately imperious and acquiescent, a woman displaying "masculine" eloquence and "feminine" feeling, desiring both power and pleasure — trespasses traditional boundaries of "feminine" demeanor. Similarly, Aeneas — bold yet timid, pious yet passionate, ambitious yet sensuous — violates conventional patterns of "masculine" behavior. Thus in their continual gender role switching, the two protagonists smash stereotypes of sex and gender.

The fourth crack discovered in the play's ideological veneer (now demonstrated to be considerably crazed) is another non-traditional woman, this one clearly not manipulated by divine forces, who also woos and pursues the man of her choice and dies of unrequited love. The subplot of the play depicts the amorous frustrations of Iarbus and Anna, whose unreciprocated passions offer dual counterparts for Dido's unfulfilled desire. Although acting as catalyst to Mercury's monitory mission to Aeneas, Iarbus is otherwise a minor character in Virgil's epic. Anna, as Dido's confidante, plays a larger role. However, although both Virgil and Ovid feature Iarbus as one of Dido's unsuccessful suitors, the rejected love of Anna for Iarbus finds no suggestion in either the *Aeneid* or the *Heroides*. Marlowe's playtext enlarges the parts of both characters, partially to amplify the fatal triumph of desire over reason, partially to offer another example of gender role reversal and transgressive passion.[17] Anna's suit to Iarbus as he sacrifices to Jupiter (4.2) provides a salient analogue to Dido's many attempts to captivate Aeneas. In both instances a woman overturns all the venerated canons of courtship and woos her desired mate. Moreover, Anna's order, "Be rul'd by me" (4.2.35) comments on the tacit control that Dido exercises over Aeneas throughout much of the play. Anna's plea, "Iarbus stay, loving Iarbus stay" (52), further mimics Dido's numerous appeals to Aeneas "to stay" and relates both sisters to the abandoned women of Troy, who similarly plea with Aeneas not to desert them.

However, although the two sisters play similar roles, the objects of their desire respond very differently. Aeneas hesitates but is soon ensnared in the net of Dido's allure, whereas Iarbus unceremoniously casts aside Anna's overtures. Moreover, Aeneas ebbs and flows in his love for Dido, like the surging sea that he and the Queen appropriately evoke as a metaphor for their passion — whereas Iarbus remains constant in his devotion to the scornful Dido. Anna's indecorous wooing parallels Dido's gender violation; Iarbus' steadfastness and candor foil Aeneas' fluctuations; and the behavior of both of the leading characters is increasingly problematized, if not necessarily deflated by these associations.

A fifth exemplar of gender role reversal — and thus a fifth fissure in the much-fractured ideology of the play — burlesques the subversive behavior of both Dido and Anna. In act 3, scene 1, Cupid wounds Dido; in act 4, scene 5, the naughty god finds yet another target for his amorous arrows. The droll old Nurse, holding Cupid, pierced by his darts, succumbing to inappropriate lust, and resorting to enticement to achieve her desires, travesties the irrational passion similarly evoked in Dido. The ancient Nurse parallels the Queen on several levels, similarities accentuated by the repeated tableau of a woman cradling a young boy, an iconic parody of the madonna and child.

In fact, the tableau of an adult dandling a domineering youth appears three times in the play. In the opening scene, Jupiter dandles Ganymede on his knee, and in ensuing scenes Dido and the ancient Nurse both cuddle and are controlled by the little god of love. In all three instances, the child manipulates the adult (an appropriate stage icon for carnival inversion);[18] in all three instances, the spiteful or sportive juvenile incites a transgressive passion.

In the opening sequence, Jupiter rains jewels and feathers on Ganymede; in act 3, Dido cajoles Cupid with a (feathered?) fan, although her bribery of Aeneas later in this scene — her carrot of golden tackling and ivory oars — presents a much closer analogue to Jupiter's hyperbolic promises to Ganymede. (Later in the cave, the smitten Queen will precisely parallel Jupiter's irreverent gift to Ganymede by bestowing her wedding jewels upon her lover.) Dramaturgical clues suggest a similar staging for the two adult-child tableaux. In the final "recognition" scene (5.1), Aeneas refers to Dido's "dandling" Cupid in her arms (5.1.44-45), the exact term used in the stage directions to describe Jupiter's pose with Ganymede in the opening *mise en scene*. Moreover, the repeated invitations of monarch to child to "Sit on my knee" (1.1.28) or "in my lap" (3.1.25) clarify the similar postures. Verbal echoes — references to Helen (1.1.17; 3.1.28) and repetitions of the teasing epithet "wag" (1.2.24, 34; 3.1.31) — further link the two scenes of fond dalliance. The two cognate episodes thus present the similar tableaux of a throned ruler holding and fondling a youth and bribing a lover (simultaneously in the case of Jupiter, sequentially in that of Dido) while becoming consumed with irrational desire.

Dido's posture, dialogue, and actions are further mirrored in the grotesque carnival glass of the ancient Nurse in the third adult-child tableau. Both widows recall their lying with the mischievous Cupid (4.4.31-32; 5.1.212-14) and both women allow the impish god, metamorphosed into Ascanius, to wheedle himself into their laps while both caress the child and promise maternal nurturance (3.1.22-25; 4.5.14-16). Between playful embraces, Cupid pierces each victim with his potent darts inciting in each a comic *psychomachia*, a wavering between passion and prudence.

Although the parallel between the Nurse and Jupiter is much less exact than the analogies treated above, the rhetoric of seduction and the use of the affectionate term "wag" by all three doting adults combines with suggested stage posture, gesture, and action to associate the octogenarian Nurse with both of the enamored rulers. The incongruous desire of the superannuated Nurse also comments on the inappropriate liaisons of both Queen and God-King. All three amours incited by a capricious lad violate accepted norms of propriety and hierarchy. Jupiter's indecorous behavior toward Ganymede is adulterous, homoerotic, and irresponsible; Dido's infatuation for Aeneas leads to gender reversal and abdication of royal responsibility; the senescent Nurse's sexual desire for the juvenile god perverts a whole host of normative relationships — those between age and youth, male and female, god and human. The examples of the elderly Nurse controlled by the imperious child-god, the Queen ruled by her pampered surrogate son, and the God-King commanded by the cosseted Trojan youth provide indelible emblems for the carnival inversion that the play dramatizes. The triple repetition of this motif thus stresses the power of passion, which sweeps the spectrum of the Great Chain of Being from god to ruler to servant.

Eugene Waith links the sequences in which Jupiter tempts Ganymede with gifts and Venus lures Ascanius with treats and costly baubles to Dido's bribery first of Cupid and later of Aeneas. I would add to this list the episode in which the Nurse entices Cupid with sweets and pastoral pleasures and would agree with Waith that the parallelism between these scenes of bribery and persuasion link the epic hero Aeneas with the three other spoiled boys (Ganymede, Ascanius, and Cupid) coddled and bribed by fond women.[19]

Virgil's epic and Ovid's poem narrate only one tragic passion — Dido's obsessive love for Aeneas (with Iarbus' unrequited infatuation for Dido mentioned only in passing). Marlowe's playtext expands these unhappy amours to include five examples of unreciprocated (or at least unequal) desire — Jupiter lusting for Ganymede, Dido yearning for Aeneas, Iarbus chafing over Dido, Anna aching for Iarbus, and the Nurse panting after Cupid — some comic, some tragic, some constrained, some voluntary. Moreover, in the topsy-turvy world of the play, lovers rarely conform to conventional codes of behavior. Errant eros runs amok as men pursue boys, females woo males, and old crones seek to seduce pinkfaced lads. Of the five amours in the play, only one — Iarbus' rather drab suit to Dido — adheres to conventional rubrics. These multivalent romances invite dual perspectives. On the one hand, these destructive (or comic) loves can be interpreted as prudential warnings against the perils (or puerility) of uncontrolled desire. On the other hand, the polymorphically perverse array of sexualities and gender transgressions represented by these five passions can be seen as undermining, even burlesquing the inflexibility and limitation of traditional amorous systems in the early modern patriarchal society. Judith Butler argues that "the cultural matrix through which gender identity has been intelligible requires that certain kinds of 'identities' cannot 'exist' — that is, those in which gender does not follow from sex, and those in which the practices of desire do not follow from either sex or gender."[20] Just such discontinuances and incoherencies circulate throughout the sexual economy of *Dido*, perhaps suggesting that these regulatory codes are socially constructed, not biologically determined, and that in society, as on the stage, they are honored more in the breach than the observance. Here, as so often in this play, our evaluation depends on our position in viewing the action, reminding us of the poststructuralist dictum that "meaning is the effect of interpretation, not its origin."[21] Yet whatever reading we endorse — and there are, I am sure, still other viewing positions that I have not examined — the variety of gender violations circulating throughout the sexual economy of *Dido* serves to demystify both compulsory heteroeroticism and many of its standard features (active men/passive women, dominant men/submissive women, older men/younger women) and call into question traditional categories of sex, gender, and desire.

Notes

1. Joel Altman, *Tudor View of the Mind: Rhetorical Inquiry and the Development of Elizabethan Drama* (Berkeley, 1978). Other commentators praising the complexity and ambiguity of *Dido* include J. R. Mulryne and Stephen Fender ("Marlowe and the Comic Distance," *Christopher Marlowe*, ed. Brian Morris [New York, 1968]); Brian Gibbons ("Unstable Proteus: Marlowe's *The Tragedy of Dido, Queene of Carthage*," *Christopher Marlowe*, ed. Brian Morris); Judith Weil (*Christopher Marlowe: Merlin's Prophet* [Cambridge, 1977]); and Richard Martin ("Fate, Seneca, and Marlowe's Dido," *Renaissance Drama* 11 [1980]: 45-66). Altman further approaches Marlowe's plays generally as a species of explorative rather than demonstrative drama (322-23); Lawrence Danson casts Marlowe's dramas in an interrogative mood ("Christopher Marlowe: The Questioner," *English Literary Renaissance,* 12 [1982]: 3-29); and James Shapiro comments on the ambiguity derived from Marlowe's characteristic juxtaposition of heterodox behavior and moral

closure (*Rival Playwrights: Marlowe, Jonson, Shakespeare* [New York, 1991], 96). However, none of these commentators has focused on Marlowe's interrogation of conventional attitudes toward sex, gender, and sexuality. Also, despite a growing awareness of the contrariety in Marlowe's plays, a much greater emphasis has been placed on the plurality of Shakespeare's dramas than on those of Marlowe.

2. Plato, *The Republic*, trans. H. D. P. Lee (Baltimore, 1956), 5:208.

3. *The Courtier*, in *Three Renaissance Classics*, ed. Burton A. Milligan (New York, 1953), 242-618.

4. David Rogers supports this traditional interpretation, maintaining that Marlowe's playtext reduces rather than expands the complexity of the moral conflict in *Dido*: "Marlowe's simplification sets the male characters with their concern for honor, in dramatic opposition to the female characters with their concern for love" ("Love and Honor in Marlowe's *Dido: Queene of Carthage*," *Greyfriar* 6 [1963]: 3). Barbara Baines agrees, presenting the play as "a straightforward demonstration of masculine-feminine polarity and of the triumph of the masculine over the feminine" ("Sexual Polarity in the Plays of Christopher Marlowe," *Ball State University Forum* 23.3 [1982]: 4).

    Throughout this essay, I use the terms "feminine" and "masculine" with some trepidation, since the very use of these terms reinscribes the gender polarities that I am seeking to interrogate. However, these conventional polarities are so imprinted on our consciousness that it is difficult to examine historically specific gender roles without adopting this accepted terminology. Therefore, throughout this study, although I use the conventional terms "feminine" and "masculine" to discuss traditional gender stereotyping, I am implicitly placing these terms under erasure, and employing these arbitrary designations in an historically accepted although not necessarily linguistically valid sense. Gayatri Chakravorty Spivak explains Jacques Derrida's practice of placing a term "sous rature," or "under erasure" as follows: "This is to write a word, cross it out, and then print both word and deletion. (Since the word is inaccurate, it is crossed out. Since it is necessary [for communication], it remains legible.)" (Derrida, *On Grammatology*, trans. Spivak, [Baltimore, 1974], Preface xiv). I ask the reader to imagine that each time I employ the misleading but necessary terms in this essay, they are put under erasure in this fashion.

5. This provocative phrase is adapted from Catherine Belsey's article, "Disrupting Sexual Difference: Meaning and Gender in the Comedies," *Alternative Shakespeares*, ed. John Drakakis (New York, 1985).

6. All references to Virgil's *Aeneid* are from the prose translation by Rolfe Humphries (New York, 1951). Citations will be included within the text.

7. Ovid, *Metamorphoses* (1567), trans. Arthur Golding, ed. H. D. Rouse (Carbondale, 1961), 10: 155-61; Lucian, *Dialogue of the Gods*, trans. M. D. Macheod (Cambridge, MA, 1969), 7: 281-91.

8. Bruce Smith suggests Lucian's dialogue between Jupiter and Ganymede as an inspiration for the Jupiter/Ganymede sequence in *Dido* (*Homosexual Desire in Shakespeare's England: A Cultural Poetics* [Chicago, 1991], 206). I find many similarities in the two texts. Not only the bubbling, irreverent tone, but also the motif of bribery may have been suggested by Lucian's dialogue.

9. All quotations from *Dido* are taken from Roma Gill's 1987 edition of the play in vol. 1 of *The Complete Works of Christopher Marlowe* (Oxford). References to *Hero and Leander* are from the same volume. Citations to both works will be included within the text.

10. This appropriation is not without precedent. In her most familiar guise, Venus "tames and mitigates the contentiousness of Mars" (Edgar Wind, *Pagan Mysteries of the Renaissance*, 1958 [Boston, 1967], 91). However, among her many personae — *Venus Coelistis, Venus Genetrix, Venus Vulgaris* — the Goddess also includes the role of *Venus Virago*, a conflation of Venus and the huntress Diana (Wind, *Pagan Mysteries*, 75-77) — a guise that she employs in both Virgil's epic and Marlowe's play — and also *Venus Armarta*. In her latter incarnation, Venus, rather than putting Mars to sleep, confiscates his martial weapons for her own (Wind, *Pagan Mysteries*, 91). A learned classicist, Marlowe was probably familiar with these various avatars of Venus and employed them to interrogate the roles of the Goddess Venus in *Dido*.

11. All quotations from Ovid's *Heroides* are from the verse translation by Grant Showerman for the Loeb Classical Library (*Heroides and Amores* [Cambridge, MA, 1914).

12. Clifford Leech, "Marlowe's Humor," *Essays on Shakespeare and Elizabethan Drama in Honor of Hardin Craig*, ed. Richard Hosley (Columbia, MO, 1982), 73.

13. Mary Smith discusses the staging of this sequence in terms similar to those used here ("Staging Marlowe's *Dido, Queene of Carthage*," *Studies in English Literature 1500-1900* 17 [1977]: 188). However, although Smith suggests that Dido's physical entanglement presents an ironic visual corollary for her desire to ensnare and constrain Aeneas, Smith does not relate this tableau to Dido's own entrapment — either by the gods or by her own passions — or to the play's recurrent imagery of restraining "nets and bands."

14. Simon Shepherd observes that the bedecking of Aeneas on stage places him in the "feminine" position (*Marlowe and the Politics of Elizabethan Theatre* [New York, 1986], 193-94, 201). Moreover, Freud invests "the gaze" with a kind of phallic power, associating the fear of losing one's sight with castration anxiety. In Freudian terms, therefore, Dido, in co-opting the male gaze, also appropriates the phallic position ("The Uncanny," *Psychological Works of Sigmund Freud*, ed. James Starchey [London, 1953-74], 17: 219-52; cited by Luce Irigaray, *Speculum of the Other Woman*, trans. Gillian C. Gill [Ithaca, 1985], 47). For a parodic

treatment of Freud's theory of the phallic gaze, see Irigaray, *Speculum*, 47-48; 145.

15. Catherine Belsey, *The Subject of Tragedy: Identity and Difference in Renaissance Drama* (London, 1985), 29.

16. See Belsey's description of the fragmented, discontinuous medieval subject, *Subject of Tragedy*, 13-54). Scholars advocating an emblematic interpretation of the deities include Charles Masinton (*Christopher Marlowe's Tragic Vision: A Study in Damnation* [Athens, OH, 1972], 7); William Godshalk (*The Marlovian World Picture* [The Hague, 1974], 56); and Weil, (*Merlin's Prophet*, 5-6). In developing her defense of an emblematic reading, Weil cites another character in Elizabethan drama, Sappho in *Sappho and Phao* — who fondles Cupid without the deleterious effects suffered by Dido (184-85, n.39), suggesting that the ironic "mother and child" tableau of a young woman holding the naughty Cupid was familiar to audiences of the period and that the allegorical implications of the stage picture might have been immediately recognized by the majority of the spectators. Despite the hazards involved in postulating a homogeneous audience or predicting the response of any audience to any theatrical production at any time, the allegorical heritage from the medieval morality play can certainly be adduced to give credence to this emblematic reading. Commentators interpreting the deities from an illusionist perspective and thus seeing the free-will of Dido as severely limited include Leech ("Marlowe's Humor," 71) and Martin ("Fate, Seneca, and Dido," 50).

17. Mary Smith argues convincingly that in his expansion of the role of Iarbus, Marlowe was probably influenced (directly or indirectly) by three earlier Italian Dido dramas — Alessandro Pazzi's *Dido in Carthagine* (circa 1524), Giovambattista Giraldi-Cinthio's *Didone* (1543), and Ludovico Dolce's *Didone* (1547), all of which amplify Iarbus' role as jealous rival of Aeneas and all of which establish Dido, not Aeneas, as eponymous hero ("Marlowe and the Italian Dido Drama," *Italica* 53 [1976]: 223-35). However, none of these dramas includes the frustrated romance of Iarbus and Anna. Moreover although Dolce anticipates Marlowe by having Anna, as well as Dido, commit suicide, Dolce's Anna dies not from unrequited love but from sisterly sorrow, and her suicide, occurring later than Dido's, in no way detracts from the Queen's tragic catastrophe.

18. For the definitive work on the tradition of carnival inversion, see Mikhail Bakhtin, *Rabelais and His World*, trans. Helene Iswolsky (Cambridge, 1968).

19. Eugene Waith, "Marlowe and the Jades of Asia," *Studies in English Literature 1500-1900* 5 (1965), 234.

20. Judith Butler, *Gender Trouble: Feminism and the Subversion of Identity* (New York, 1990), 17.

21. Catherine Belsey, *Milton, Language, Gender, Power* (Oxford, 1988), 7.

"Won with thy words and conquered with thy looks": Sadism, Masochism, and the Masochistic Gaze in *1 Tamburlaine*[1]

Lisa S. Starks

In her analysis of the Marquis de Sade's cruel heroine of *Juliette*, Angela Carter remarks that "Juliette's life is like the reign of Tamburlaine the Great, an arithmetical progression of atrocities."[2] Constant, perpetual motion and violent act following upon violent act characterize both Sade's novels and Marlowe's *1 Tamburlaine*. Tamburlaine's obsession with conquest, his desire to be a superhuman despot who enslaves the world (1.2.21-32) until "Emperors and kings lie breathless at . . .[his] feet" (5.1.469), leads him to successive acts of brutality which prefigure the Sadeian vision of violence and tyranny, in which "Only motion is real; creatures are nothing but motion's changing phases" (Carter 79). In *1 Tamburlaine*, Marlowe exploits this economy of desire, along with that of masochism, through the creation of Tamburlaine as a god-like tyrant who dominates the play as spectacle and object of the masochistic gaze.

In his essay "Coldness and Cruelty," Gilles Deleuze distinguishes sadism from masochism and refigures both in terms of literary narrative and desire. According to Deleuze, literary representations of sadism and masochism indicate that the two libidinal economies consist of disparate logics and fantasies, which have derived from antithetical literary and philosophical traditions. Analytical and mathematic, sadism is characterized by cold detachment and a desire to destroy and mutilate the foundation of religious sentiment and culture, the virgin/mother.[3] Similar to Marlowe's play, Sade's novels are episodic, his hedonists moving quickly from one event to the next, deriving pleasure from engagement in ceaseless activity.[4] The libertines of Sade's universe transgress laws they view as arbitrary, artificially imposed on a "Nature" that follows its own laws of evil (a satire of Rousseau and Rabelais), forming communities or institutions through which they

179

exert the force of their tyranny on unwilling victims (Deleuze 70). Conversely, the heroes of Leopold von Sacher-Masoch's novels validate laws and, in fact, create them through contractual arrangements with their torturesses (Deleuze 20-21, 77, 83, 87-88). Contrary to the sadist,[5] the male masochist — an idealist — prefers the world of the imagination, one of fetishes and fantasies, in which he creates an image of the woman as a pagan goddess whom he adores and to whom he submits himself.[6] As Deleuze has observed, Sacher-Masoch's novels reveal that the masochist derives pleasure not from frenetic activity, but from aesthetic contemplation and suspended scenes (Deleuze 33, 69).

In dealing with circulations of desire in an early modern play like *1 Tamburlaine*, can one speak of sadism and masochism? The nomenclature is anachronistic; it did not appear until the nineteenth century, when the terms "sadism" and "masochism" emerged in psychological discourses as sexual "perversions" or symptoms of neuroses.[7] Nevertheless, circulations of desire that resemble what was later referred to as "sadism" and "masochism" (and "sadomasochism") existed in variant literary forms before they became constructed as sexual aberrations or preferences in modern subjects.[8] In the sixteenth and seventeenth centuries, literary fantasies of dominance and submission, cruelty and eroticism were eventually transformed into the traditions of later eighteenth-, nineteenth-, and twentieth-century "sadomasochism"(Siegel 9-17). Both Sade at the end of the eighteenth century and Sacher-Masoch at the close of the nineteenth drew from extant philosophical and literary texts to create their erotic novels: Sade from those of Voltaire, Rousseau, Rabelais, and Montaigne; Sacher-Masoch from Goethe, Cervantes, Shakespeare, Petrarch, Medieval romance, and Classical mythology. In this sense, one can trace representations of sadism and masochism in early modern texts as projections of cultural fantasies and anxieties later transformed and manifested in those of Sade and Sacher-Masoch. Therefore, these novels, which eventually became the foundation of modern "sadomasochism," materialized from past cultural narratives, myths, and icons, including that of Marlowe's despot, Tamburlaine.

Tamburlaine's sadism, often discussed by critics, is obvious in his aggressive desire to break laws, torture victims, kill virgins, and so forth.[9] In many respects, Tamburlaine resembles Sade's later heroes and heroines. Although often referred to as "atheistic," Tamburlaine believes in a kind of "moral" structure in the universe, an inversion of traditional moral order in promoting evil in its purest form. The conqueror repeatedly refers to his cosmic fate, calling himself "the scourge and wrath of God" (3.3.44),[10] affirming his destiny as a destructive force in a universe that, far from being indifferent to humankind, actively produces evil within its Nature in a quasi-religious devotion to savage brutality. Similarly, Pierre Klossowski emphasizes that the Sadeian hero is devoted to evil for evil's sake, much like that inherited in St. Augustine's *Confessions*, his "conscience . . .always activated by remorse; indeed, the remorse seems to provide the energy for his crimes. The debauched libertine does not seek to commit actions which have been rendered indifferent by perpetual motion, as the atheist philosophers claim."[11]

Sade's libertines believe in a Nature characterized as a satire of Rabelais' "lawless" abbey of Thelemes, Rousseau's affirmation of "man's innate goodness," and the eighteenth-century conception of Nature as "the new incarnation of Supreme Good" shared by Christians and atheists alike.[12] Simone de Beauvoir notes that like Hobbes, whom he cited, Sade overturns the "religion of optimism" to assert that "the state of Nature is one of war." Sade inverts the belief that "Nature is good," but he retains the notion that one should follow Nature rather than impose exterior laws on "her" (Beauvoir 43-44). This legislation imposed on Nature becomes that which the Sadeian hero must transgress. Like Tamburlaine, the self-proclaimed scourge of God who blatantly breaks the laws of Mahomet (4.4.51) and violates military "codes of honor," the Sadeian hero revels in committing crimes against legitimate religion and the state, breaching the decrees of society and validating those of savage Nature.

In Marlowe's play, sadism extends beyond its hero; it pervades the play and its characters. Although those vulnerable to Tamburlaine (Agydas, The Soldan of Egypt, Bajazeth) criticize the conqueror's brutality, other characters praise it and still others mirror it. In a blatantly sadistic scene, when Zenocrate harasses Zabina and then allows her servant, Anippe, to chastise her new slave, Marlowe exposes the hierarchy or chain of oppression and tyranny common in sadistic narratives. In her role as the despot, Anippe emulates Tamburlaine's sadism and "silences" the caged Zabina by exclaiming,

> Let these be warnings for you then, my slave,
> How you abuse the person of the King;
> Or else I swear to have you whipp'd stark nak'd.
> (4.2.72-74)

Only Tamburlaine, however, transgresses the limits of "decency" to an extreme Sadeian degree. He conquers all disgust and abhorrence that characterize such "decent" behavior. In one of the most sadistic scenes in the play, Tamburlaine, decked in a scarlet, blood-red robe, eats his banquet while simultaneously torturing the starving Bajazeth and Zabina (4.4). He torments his famished captives, spouting words like "blood," "bowls," and "heart." In this scene, Tamburlaine repeatedly refers to cannibalism in mocking his prisoners' starvation, asking Bajazeth, "Are you so daintily brought up, you cannot eat your own flesh?" (4.4.36-37). The sadist taunts his victims, offering them tidbits of food, stamped under his foot — at the point of his sword. When Bajazeth refuses the morsels, Tamburlaine refers to flesh-eating again and prods him to "Take it up, villain, and eat it, or I will make thee slice the brawns of thy arms into carbonadoes and eat them" (43-44). Under the suggestion of Usumcasane, Tamburlaine then advises Bajazeth to devour his wife before she wastes away. He goads Bajazeth to "Dispatch her while she is fat, for if she live but a while longer she will fall into a consumption with fretting, and then she will not be worth eating" (48-50).

Similar to Rabelais and Sade, Marlowe does not shirk from exploiting the open flesh, the body as product — as meat — in *Tamburlaine*.[13] As Carter points out, this obsession of the flesh as meat and products of the flesh as "delicacies" exposes Sade's "Puritanical" anti-sensuality (Carter 138). To Carter, Sade's libertines conquer disgust of the body by eating its products in order to achieve a "superhuman" status, the mutual goal of Sade's heroes and Marlowe's conqueror. As she puts it, "For Sade, mankind doesn't roll in shit because mankind is disgusting, but because mankind has overweening aspirations to be superhuman" (Carter 34). Even while engaging in coprophagy, the sadist is removed, detached. Refusing to acknowledge the subjectivity of others, the sadist inflicts pain on the Other to reify his or her own existence (Carter 142).

Marlowe's *1 Tamburlaine* even provides the sadist's choice victims for the debauched libertine's pleasure: submissive virgins (*2 Tamburlaine* includes an analogous scene with concubines). Tamburlaine's killing of the virgins enacts a sadistic desire to rape and mutilate the virgin/mother, as both John B. Steane and Constance Brown Kuriyama have noted (Steane 86; Kuriyama 31). According to Carter, the sadist relishes the murder of a virgin, for like Sade's character Justine, the virgin is

> Always the object of punishment, [for] she has committed only one crime and that was an involuntary one; she was born a woman, and, for that, she is ceaselessly punished. The innocent girl pays a high price for the original if imaginary crime of Eve, just as Saint Paul said she should, and . . . an exemplary Calvary makes her a female Christ whom a stern and patriarchal god has by no means forsaken

but at this spectacle is not unrelated to the uncomfortable truths it contains. (Carter 39)

Even though Tamburlaine ostensibly kills the virgins to intimidate the people of Damascus not to satisfy erotic desire, the scene's details — the laments of the virgins, Tamburlaine's sadistic "teasing" with them about "death" and his "sword" — do in fact contain the makings of a sadistic fantasy. Thomas Cartelli contends that this scene exceeds a play on the audience's pity for the victims, "guarantee[ing] far more pleasure to the audience" in its "imaginative engagement with a seemingly omnipotent human aggressor, capable of making his will his act."[14]

Despite Tamburlaine's sadistic treatment of the virgins and others, in his "lover's discourse" with Zenocrate he employs the Petrarchan figures of male masochistic fantasy: she becomes the "icy" goddess, the embodiment of the pre-Christian, pagan Venus.[15] In *Venus in Furs* and his other writings, Sacher-Masoch draws from this poetic tradition, creating an image of the woman as a "Venus" worthy of divine worship and adoration, a goddess characterized by a frozen, marble exterior, usually wrapped in fetish furs.[16] Similarly, Tamburlaine refers to Zenocrate as a divine object of worship, "goddess" of a cold, icy climate, clothed in silks rather than furs. Praising Zenocrate's beauty, Tamburlaine promises her that

> Thy garments shall be made of Median silk,
> Enchas'd with precious jewels of mine own,
> More rich and valurous than Zenocrate's.
> With milk-white harts upon an ivory sled
> Thou shalt be drawn amidst the frozen pools
> And scale the icy mountains' lofty tops,
> Which with thy beauty will be soon resolv'd.
>   (1.2.95-101)

In this passage, Tamburlaine draws a portrait of Zenocrate — what she will wear, what background will frame her. The description is of a suspended scene, like a painting, a crucial element in *Venus in Furs* and in the male masochist's imagination.[17] Throughout *1 Tamburlaine*, the conqueror refers to his lady as "divine Zenocrate" (4.4.28; 5.1.135), and, employing the rhetoric of the Petrarchan poet or courtier and his lady as outlined in Castiglione's *The Courtier*, Tamburlaine meditates and fetishizes Zenocrate as a neoplatonic object of beauty.[18] Like a Petrarchan sonneteer, Tamburlaine employs oxymorons in his poetic effusions of love for Zenocrate, as in "Fair is too foul an epithet" (5.1.136); and he focuses on the eyes, flowing with tears, as objects of meditation. Zenocrate, Tamburlaine's "inspiration," is thus immortalized by the poet's pen, like Petrarch's Laura, for "Beauty, mother to the Muses, sits / And comments volumes with her ivory pen" (5.1.144-45).

As long as Zenocrate exists as his concubine, Tamburlaine is able to fetishize her beauty and chastity while keeping his masochism at bay.[19] The warrior continually checks these masochistic tendencies, for fear that they lead to effeminacy, lack of manly valor in war; nevertheless, he employs the rhetoric of masochism to mitigate his harshest sadistic deeds when necessary. Immediately after the virgins are taken away to be killed, Tamburlaine rejects the virgin/mother/goddess, claiming that he "will not spare these proud Egyptians," nor change his martial policy "for the love of Venus" (5.1.121-22; 124). Tamburlaine's appropriate shift from the virgins to "Ah, fair Zenocrate, divine Zenocrate! / Fair is too foul an epithet for thee" (5.1.135-36) highlights his fetishization of Zenocrate in the service of the virgins' desecration (see Shepherd 182-83). Moreover, the scene helps to explain *why* there exists such a prominent sadistic logic in a play that is steeped in the aesthetics and idealism of masochism: the mitigation of male fear and anxiety at the possibility of becoming truly masochistic — in this case, totally vulnerable and submissive to a woman.[20]

At the close of his "beauty" speech, Tamburlaine reveals his fear that such adoration of a woman could cause him to veer from his manly course, for

> how unseemly is it for my sex,
> My discipline of arms and chivalry,
> My nature, and the terror of my name,
> To harbor thoughts effeminate and faint!
>   (5.1.174-77)

Tamburlaine eases this anxiety by noting that the discourse of chivalry is built upon this idolization of woman. As long as the woman remains an object of worship benefiting the man in *his* meditation of her beauty, then she cannot challenge his performance as a warrior. At the close of the play, Tamburlaine remarks on Zenocrate's role as the "mirror" of his victories, the lady for whom he has gained "triumphs" and won "trophies." Like Zenocrate, the lady of Chivalric fantasy, as Cervantes most profoundly dramatizes in *Don Quixote*, exists only as a silent image created in and controlled by the knight's imagination. This logic is also at work in Sacher-Masoch, for the masochistic male creates and loves an ideal figure or idol of his own fancy, and like a poet he composes scenes of his erotic fantasy, in which he vows total obedience to his mistress or master.

At the close of *1 Tamburlaine*, the marriage of Zenocrate and Tamburlaine coincides with Tamburlaine's law-making: he divides territory and delegates responsibilities for founding and enacting legislation. Having conquered his enemies, Tamburlaine may now establish law, the very thing he has prided himself in transgressing. Tamburlaine instructs his followers to "cast off your armor, put on scarlet robes / . . . And there make laws to rule your provinces" (5.1.24, 27). Tamburlaine follows his own decree by marrying his concubine, the first step toward her ultimate demise. In *2 Tamburlaine*, Zenocrate transforms from the chaste goddess and object of desire into the mother (soon to become the dead mother), the figure most abhorred in the sadistic imagination and most revered in the masochistic. Although sadism is not vanquished in *2 Tamburlaine*[21] (especially with the concubines), the emphasis shifts at the close of Part One, for at this moment Tamburlaine moves from the transgressive desecration of the virgin/goddess/mother to the contained reverence of the chaste wife and mother. No more of use as the manifestation of beauty, Zenocrate will provide a functional vessel through which Tamburlaine will produce his sons, and then she will cease to exist.

Zenocrate is disposable in both *1* and *2 Tamburlaine* because, even though she functions as Tamburlaine's object of desire, and she does not become the primary fetish of Marlowe's play. For the play's characters and spectators, it is Tamburlaine, in all his horrifying glory, who maintains the central position as visual spectacle, as the predominate object of the gaze.[22] In the seventies, Laura Mulvey identified three aspects of the gaze in classical Hollywood cinema: that of the camera, the characters within the film, and its spectators (Mulvey, 17-18). On stage, the gaze of the camera is substituted by other effects to direct the viewers' focus. In the case of early modern theatrical performance, with no artificial lighting and other technical means of directing the look of the spectators, the gaze would have been constructed primarily by the words, gestures, and positions of the actors on stage, indicated primarily by the language of the text.[23] Therefore, this paper focuses on only two of the three aspects of Mulvey's gaze: the characters within the play and its spectators.

The dynamics of looking in *Tamburlaine* include both the female and male masochistic gaze of the Sadeian hero as spectacle.[24] Female masochistic desire of Tamburlaine is foregrounded in *1 Tamburlaine* through the character of Zenocrate, who exceeds her role as objectified other in speaking as a desiring subject, one who longs to be subjected to the cruel tyrant. In her scene with Agydas, Zenocrate expresses her devotion to Tamburlaine in the language of masochism, which may channel the spectator's desire towards Tamburlaine and also promote spectator identification with the tyrant who has inspired her complete devotion.[25] Zenocrate offers her life and soul to Tamburlaine, vowing to live and die with him (3.2.21-24). Understandably, Agydas expects her to feel violated, for she *has* been violated, whether or not the "rape" to which he refers signifies seizure or forced sexual intercourse. Agydas fails to comprehend that Zenocrate has internalized the violation and transformed it into a female masochistic fantasy. In direct contrast to the males in *1 Tamburlaine* who idolize our Sadeian hero, Agydas cannot fathom her love for "a man so vile and barbarous" (3.2.26), one who "looks so fierce" (40). Zenocrate attempts to relate her view of the tyrant to Agydas, idealizing and fetishizing the figure of Tamburlaine, as he has her own, but with a difference. In her imagination, the image of Tamburlaine becomes one of significant potency and god-like presence:

> As looks the sun through Nilus' flowing stream,
> Or when the morning holds him in her arms,
> So looks my lordly love, fair Tamburlaine:
> His talk much sweeter than the Muses' song
> They sung for honor 'gainst Pierides,
> Or when Minerva did with Neptune strive;
> And higher would I rear my estimate
> Than Juno, sister to the highest god,
> If I were match'd with mighty Tamburlaine.
>
> (3.2.47-55)

In response to Agydas' remark that Tamburlaine is but a lowly shepherd, Zenocrate concludes that it is not he but she who should feel unworthy in their relationship, for "Thence rise the tears that so distain my cheeks, / Fearing his love through my unworthiness" (3.2.64-65).[26]

The male characters' adulation and awe of the Sadeian hero extend the effect of Zenocrate's desiring looks even further. Their male masochistic gaze focuses on Tamburlaine and his conquests, ensuring the tyrant's position as central figure, producing Tamburlaine as an awe-inspiring conqueror. This look compares to Zenocrate's in its worship of the despot's image. As early as scene two of the play, Techelles describes Tamburlaine in his armor as "princely lions when they rouse themselves, / Stretching their paws and thret'ning herds of beasts." Techelles pictures Tamburlaine as the central figure in a vivid tableau, with

> kings kneeling at his feet,
> And he with frowning brows and fiery looks
> Spurning their crowns from off their captive heads.
>   (1.2.52-57)

Furthermore, after Usumcasane has directed the spectator's look to the spectacle of the conqueror, Theridamas (in language much like that of Zenocrate) tells Tamburlaine that he has been "Won with thy words and conquered with thy looks," so much that he wishes to "yield myself, my men and horse to thee" (1.2.228-29). In Act II, Theridimas, in awe of Tamburlaine's ability to "command and be obeyed," claims that "power attractive shines in prince's eyes" (2.5.62-64).

The most visual descriptions come from 2.2, when Menaphon describes Tamburlaine to Cosroe, indicating a masochistic delight in suspended action, in aesthetic adoration. Menaphon's speech both reifies and glorifies Tamburlaine as a god-like warrior who is "Of stature tall, and straightly fashioned, / Like his desire, lift upwards and divine," and also "large of limbs," with "Such breadth of shoulders as might mainly bear / Old atlas' burden" (2.1.7-11). Menaphon's description continues, painting a portrait of Tamburlaine as an Achilles, one with "lofty brows" and "amber hair," with

> arms and fingers long and sinewy,
> Betokening valor and excess of strength —
> In every part proportioned like the man
> Should make the world subdued to Tamburlaine.
>   (2.1.27-30)

This male gaze, like Zenocrate's, resembles the masochist's obsession with the male despot in Sacher-Masoch's *Venus in Furs.* Unlike the female objectified by the voyeuristic male gaze, however, Tamburlaine aggressively returns the look, relegating both the other characters in the play and its spectators to a masochistic position of fetishistic viewing.[27]

As film theorists have recently claimed, spectatorship involves various kinds of pleasures involved with "looking," even those derived from the desire to feel humiliated, horrified, or traumatized.[28] In its submissiveness, aestheticism, love of suspended action, fantasy, and especially fetishism, masochism is closely linked to spectatorship, both male and female.[29] As John Ellis contends, masochistic fetishism suggests a much different relationship of spectator-image than sadistic voyeurism — one in which the viewer desires the look to be returned:

> Fetishistic looking implies the direct acknowledgement and
> participation of the object viewed . . .With the fetishistic attitudes,
> the look of the character towards the viewer is the central feature . . .
> . The voyeuristic look is curious, inquiring, demanding to know. The
> fetishistic gaze is captivated by what it sees, does not wish to inquire
> further, to see more, to find out . . . The fetishistic look has much to
> do with display and the spectacular.[30]

The masochistic pleasure involved in this fetishistic look would
produce desire for and worship of Tamburlaine without impeding
spectator identification with Tamburlaine himself, for the play
weaves both strands of masochism and sadism in its fabric of visual
fantasy. As a sadistic narrative, *1 Tamburlaine* is, in Cartelli's words,
"expressly designed to allow the audience to fulfill vicariously its
own fantasies of omnipotence" (Cartelli 36). Yet this identification
only occurs simultaneously with the idolization of Marlowe's tyrant,
who figures as the play's central object of desire even as he
objectifies all who surround him.

Evidence of Marlowe's success in creating this superhuman
conqueror through exploitation of the masochistic gaze can be
found in surviving textual allusions to Tamburlaine that point to the
circulation of the character's image in early modern popular
culture.[31] Richard Levin, in his examination of various recorded
mentions of Tamburlaine,[32] observes that the responses — all from
educated, well-born men — give a similar impression, one that bears
out the role of Tamburlaine as Sadeian hero and object of the
masochistic gaze. Several references to Tamburlaine link him
obviously to sadistic and masochistic fantasies as in *Greene's Tu
Quoque* (1611), when the character (Gertrude) is described as "the
terrible tyrannizing *Tamburlaine*," dominating "ouer him [her
suitor]," who has "turne[d] Turke, from a most absolute compleate
Gentleman, to a most absurd ridiculous and fond lover" (qtd. in
Levin 59); or in another allusion in Philip Massinger's *The Maid of
Honor* (ca. 1621), in which

> the Page, preparing to "take a leape" to kiss Clarinda, commands
> Sylli to "hold my cloake, / . . .Or having first tripp'd up thy heeles,
> I'll make / Thy backe my footstoole"; and Sylli exclaims,
> "*Tamburlaine* in little! / Am I turn'd Turke! what an office am I put
> to!" (qtd. in Levin 59)

Levin notes additional references that indicate admiration and awe
of Tamburlaine's might and prowess. In interpreting these

responses, Levin concludes that "the overwhelming impression created by all these allusions is that Tamburlaine was perceived as a triumphant figure who possessed and wielded tremendous power"; indeed, Tamburlaine "evoke[d] the audience's wonder . . .and admiration" (Levin 56, 50).

John Davies, fetishizing and glamorizing the figure of Tamburlaine in a sonnet from *Wit's Pilgrimage* (1605), describes the grandeur he sees when he "behold[s] / . . .great Tamburlaine," appearing like "Phaeton drawne, encoacht in burnisht Gold" (qtd. in Levin 61). In one account from a satirical poem written in 1597, the poet observes that Tamburlaine is an object who returns the gaze, one who "ravishes the gazing 'scaffolders.'"[33] In another written in 1628, Tamburlaine is said "to strike his hearers dead with admiration."[34]

The appeal of Tamburlaine to "baser" pleasures did not go unnoticed. Ben Jonson, appalled at the spectacle of *Tamburlaine* and its sensational appeal, censures the play's "*scenicall* strutting, and furious vociferation, to warrant them to the ignorant gapers."[35] Does *1 Tamburlaine* appeal to the "worst" in its audience? Does the sensationalism Jonson condemns indicate much deeper involvement of the "ignorant gapers" than he acknowledges? Interestingly, despite the immense appeal of Tamburlaine in sixteenth- and seventeenth-century culture, *Tamburlaine's* popularity did not outlive the early modern era. Marlowe's play does not appear to have been performed after its successful Elizabethan run until the twentieth century, and even then the play was dramatically altered for performance. As George Geckle explains, early twentieth-century directors drastically cut the script, usually omitting much of the sadism, including the death of the virgins.[36] Later productions from the sixties on, however, have emphasized the extreme brutality of Marlowe's play. Why such ambivalence to *Tamburlaine*? What is so frightening about the violence in Marlowe's play? Perhaps it is *not* the sadism that audiences find disconcerting — after all, any revenge tragedy offers sadistic titillation — but the extreme masochistic desire produced by the play that has made the violent visual pleasures of *1 Tamburlaine* both threatening and troubling to post-seventeenth-century audiences.

Notes

1.   I am grateful to Peter Rudnytsky, David Leverenz, David Willbern, and especially Paul Whitfield White for their very helpful comments and

suggestions.

2. Angela Carter, *The Sadeian Woman and the Ideology of Pornography* (New York, 1978), 80.

3. Gilles Deleuze, "Coldness and Cruelty," *Masochism*, 1971, trans. Jean McNeil (New York, 1989), 29, 51-53.

4. In 1885 Richard von Krafft-Ebing coined the term "masochism" after the writer Leopold von Sacher-Masoch in *Psychopathia Sexualis: A Medico-Forensic Study*, 1885, trans. Harry E. Wedeck (New York, 1965), 82-83; 159-244.

5. Please note that the term "sadist" as employed in this paper does *not* correspond to its current use in contemporary sadomasochistic counter-culture practices, in which it refers to the role of the torturer in a contractual arrangement between consenting adults. This contemporary "sadist" differs tremendously from the literary tyrants of Sade's novels or Marlowe's *Tamburlaine* as described in this paper. For excellent articles on contemporary sadomasochistic culture, see Thomas Weinberg and G. W. Levi Kamel, eds., *S and M: Studies in Sadomasochism* (Buffalo, 1983).

6. In his literary analysis, Deleuze deals with primarily heterosexual male masochism (see esp. 20-21, 47, 51, 55, 62, 73). Nevertheless, other types of masochism that extend beyond the scope of this paper, including homoerotic female and male masochism, figure prominently in literary texts as well.

7. Because at the present time there are not more accurate words to signify "sadism" and "masochism" in early modern drama as described in this paper, I am employing the terms anachronistically. Nevertheless, I do not wish to imply that "sadism" and "masochism" are essential, unchanging categories, but rather narratives of desire that have undergone radical transformation in literary and cultural constructions throughout history. Except in reference to contemporary culture, I will use the terms "sadism" and "masochism" rather than "sadomasochism" because the latter implies a modern conflation of the two as complementary aspects of one another.

8. Carol Siegel argues that Renaissance poetry of domination and submission constitutes an early form of the modern narrative of male masochism in *Male Masochism: Modern Revisions of the Story of Love* (Bloomington, 1995), 8-9.

9. For a traditional analysis of sadism in *Tamburlaine*, see J. B. Steane, *Marlowe: A Critical Study* (Cambridge, 1975), 85-87; for a traditional psychoanalytic reading, see Constance Kuriyama, *Hammer or Anvil: Psychological Patterns in Christopher Marlowe's Plays* (New Brunswick, 1980), 1-52.

10. All Marlowe quotations are from *Tamburlaine the Great, Parts I and II*, ed. John D. Jump (Lincoln, 1967).

11. Pierre Klossowski, "Nature as Destructive Principle" in the Marquis de Sade, *The 120 Days of Sodom and Other Writings*, trans. and ed. Austryn

Wainhouse and Richard Seaver (New York, 1966), 66.

12. Simone de Beauvoir, "Must We Burn Sade?" in Sade, *120 Days of Sodom and Other Writings*, 42.

13. For an analysis of Marlowe's *Tamburlaine* and how it relates to Mikhail Bahktin's theory of the "Body Grotesque," see Mark Thornton Burnett, "*Tamburlaine* and the Body," *Criticism* 33 (1991), 31-47. According to Burnett, Tamburlaine transforms from the open Renaissance body to the closed Classical body in his rise to legitimated power.

14. Thomas Cartelli, *Marlowe, Shakespeare, and the Economy of the Theatrical Experience* (Philadelphia, 1991), 36.

15. Krafft-Ebing was the first to note the connection between the courtly love tradition of Medieval chivalry and the sexual inclination he labelled "masochism": "It is probable that the courtly chivalry of the Middle Ages arose in this way. In its reverence for women as 'mistresses' in society and in individual love-relations; its transference of the relations of feudalism and vassalage to the feminine whims; its love-tests and vows; its duty of obedience to every command of the lady — in all this, chivalry appears as a systematic, poetical development of the 'bondage' of love" (Krafft-Ebing 233, n. 1).

16. Leopold von Sacher-Masoch, *Venus in Furs* in Deleuze, *Masochism*, 142-293, esp. 143, 149, 153, 164, 171, 173.

17. For more on masochism and suspense, see Theodore Reik, *Masochism in Modern Man*, trans. Margaret H. Beigel and Gertrud M. Kurth (New York, 1941), 59-71 and 320-96.

18. See Kimberly Bentson, "Beauty's Just Applause: Dramatic Form and the Tamburlainian Sublime," in *Christopher Marlowe*, ed. Harold Bloom (New York, 1986), 207-27.

19. See Simon Shepherd, *Marlowe and the Politics of Elizabethan Theatre* (New York, 1986), 187.

20. See Kuriyama, 16, 31. In reading this scene, Kuriyama suggests that Tamburlaine must pay for the virgins' deaths by praising Zenocrate even more after he, in effect, murders a part of her symbolized by the virgins.

21. On *2 Tamburlaine* and the "perverse fascination" of audiences to the play's "punishing fantasies," see Cartelli, 90-91.

22. See Laura Mulvey, "Visual Pleasure and Narrative Cinema," *Screen* 16 [1975], 6-18. In this influential article, Mulvey employs Lacanian psychoanalysis to argue that Classical Hollywood cinema perpetuates the "male gaze," which incorporates both fetishistic scopophilia (worshipping the female image) and voyeurism (punishing or saving the female character) to assuage the threat of sexual difference (castration) for the male viewer. According to Mulvey, the male spectator is then led to identify with the male star of the film. Since Mulvey's ground-breaking article, film theorists have revised notions of the gaze and spectatorship to include variations on the female spectator, the homoerotic gaze, and the spectator as a historical/cultural construct. For an overview of

contemporary theories of film spectatorship, see Linda Williams, ed. *Viewing Positions: Ways of Seeing Film* (New Brunswick, 1994).

23. For more on the gaze and Renaissance theatre, see Barbara Freedman, *Staging the Gaze: Postmodernism, Psychoanalysis, and Shakespearean Comedy* (Ithaca, 1991), esp. 47-77.

24. For a discussion of Tamburlaine as manipulator of visual effects in the play, see David Thurn, "Sights of Power in *Tamburlaine*," *English Literary Renaissance* 19 (1989), 3-21.

25. It would be possible for both male and female spectators to experience cross-gendered desire and identification offered by the characters. Consequently, female spectators could identify with Tamburlaine and desire Zenocrate *or* male viewers could identify with Zenocrate and desire Tamburlaine. With a boy playing Zenocrate on the early modern stage, male identification with her may have been emphasized even more strongly.

26. The woman willing to give herself masochistically, a familiar theme in sexual mythologies, also figures in Sacher-Masoch's novel, *Venus in Furs*, in which even the torturess Wanda succumbs to female masochistic desire of a dominant male (Sacher-Masoch 253). Female masochism is, of course, also strongly implicated in ideological constructions of gender and patriarchy, issues which extend beyond the limits of this discussion.

27. Both Phyllis Rackin and Harry Berger, Jr. have analyzed the spectator's "submissive" relationship to the play and its implications. See Phyllis Rackin, "Engendering the Tragic Audience: The Case of *Richard III*," *Shakespeare and Gender: A History*, ed. Deborah E. Barker and Ivo Kamps (London, 1995); and Harry Berger, Jr., "Text Against Performance in Shakespeare: The Example of *Macbeth*," *Genre* 15.2-3 (1982), 49-79. Jonas Barish reviews Berger in "Shakespeare in the Study; Shakespeare on the Stage," *Theatre Journal* 40 (1988), 33-47; and Berger reformulates his ideas in *Imaginary Audition: Shakespeare on Stage and Page* (Berkeley, 1989).

28. These descriptions of masochism and spectatorship also correspond to Reik's discussion of masochistic fantasies, in which the subject derives pleasure from identifying with the victims rather than (or in addition to) the aggressors viewing scenes of punishment. See Reik, esp. 147-65.

29. On masochism and spectatorship in film theory, see Kaja Silverman, *Male Subjectivity at the Margins* (New York, 1992), esp. 185-213; and Gaylyn Studlar, *In the Realm of Pleasure: Von Sternberg, Dietrich, and the Masochistic Aesthetic* (Urbana, 1988).

30. John Ellis, *Visible Fictions* (New York, 1982), 47; qtd. in Cartelli, 25.

31. For an analysis of Tamburlaine's popularity and its relationship to spectatorship and class identification, see Cartelli, 67-93.

32. Richard Levin, "The Contemporary Perception of Marlowe's *Tamburlaine*," *Medieval and Renaissance Drama in England* 1 (1984): 51-70. Levin gathered most of the responses from C. F. Tucker Brooke, "The

Reputation of Christopher Marlowe," *Transactions of the Connecticut Academy of Arts and Sciences* 25 (1922), 366-72.

33. Joseph Hall, Book One of *Virgidemiarum* in *The Collected Poems of Joseph Hall, Bishop of Exeter and Norwich*, ed. Arnold Davenport (1597; Liverpool, 1949), 15; qtd. in Levin, 53.

34. George Wither, *Britain's Remembrancer* (1628); qtd. in Levin, 54.

35. *Ben Jonson*, eds. C. H. Herford and Percy and Evelyn Simpson, vol. 8 (Oxford, 1947), 587; qtd. in Levin, 54. The characterization of the audience as "ravished" by the actors is also prominent in anti-theatrical tracts, which has often been noted by Renaissance scholars. See Catherine Eisaman Maus, "Horns of Dilemma: Jealousy, Gender, and Spectatorship in English Renaissance Drama," *English Literary History* 54 (1987), 561-83; esp. 568.

36. George Geckle, *Text and Performance: "Tamburlaine" and "Edward II"* (Atlantic Highlands, NJ, 1988).

Marlowe, Queer Studies, and Renaissance Homoeroticism

Mario DiGangi

In 1982, Alan Bray's groundbreaking book *Homosexuality in Renaissance England* introduced a provocative thesis that has remained the focus of scholarly and political contention. Despite the title of the book, Bray in effect argued that "homosexuality" did not exist in Renaissance England, at least not in a way that could be explained by recourse to modern notions of sexual orientation and identity. While some literary critics and historians have presented nuanced qualifications and detailed elaborations of Bray's historical findings, others have responded with more anxiety to the political implications of the idea that there were "no homosexuals" in the Renaissance. As a contribution to this debate, I want to provide an account of Renaissance homoeroticism that denies the importance neither of historical difference nor of using the historical past to intervene in the political present. I approach this project in three stages. First, I want to argue that a historical understanding of pre-modern sexuality requires us to recognize that homoerotic relations in Renaissance England could be socially orderly as well as socially disorderly or sodomitical. Second, I hope to show that the dominance of sodomy as a critical paradigm in Renaissance studies depends upon certain problematic, and anachronistic, assumptions about homosexuality. Finally, I will put these theoretical and political arguments into practice through a reading of Marlowe, with particular reference to the depiction of favoritism in *Edward II*.

I

Like Bray, I start from the premise that we cannot speak of a homosexual identity or minority in the early modern period. The homophobic ideology that would eventually proscribe the eroticization of all male bonds had not yet developed in sixteenth- and early seventeenth-century England.[1] Before the modern definition of homosexuality as an identifiable behavior or condition that deviated from "normal" gender identities, object choices, or sexual roles, homoerotic practices were "normal" aspects of even the most socially conventional relationships.[2] The "homosocial" and the "homoerotic" overlapped to a greater extent, and with less attendant anxiety, in the early modern period than would be possible under a modern regime of sexuality. As David Halperin writes:

> Before the scientific construction of "sexuality" as a supposedly positive, distinct, and constitutive feature of individual human beings — an autonomous system with the physiological and psychological economy of the human organism — certain kinds of sexual acts could be individually evaluated and categorized, and so could certain sexual tastes or inclinations, but there was no conceptual apparatus available for identifying a person's fixed and determinate sexual orientation, much less for assessing and classifying it.[3]

We can maintain a sense of the different organization of sexuality in early modern England by reserving the terms "homosexuality" and "homosexual" for the specific concepts of sexual orientation and subjectivity that developed in the medical, psychological, and sexological discourses of nineteenth-century Europe.

To make these claims, it is not necessary to reject the possibility that sexual desires are in part biologically or genetically determined. Nevertheless, it's undeniable that the representational strategies of biological or genetic discourses limit and shape what can be understood about anatomical sex or sexuality at any particular historical moment, including our own. Thomas Laqueur has argued that eighteenth-century epistemological and political developments are responsible for producing "sex" — the idea that there are "two stable, incommensurable, opposite sexes" that differentiate (and dictate) the "political, economic, and cultural lives of men and women."[4] Far from providing an objective, purely scientific account of sexual difference based on new empirical data, the very language of biology was already laden with cultural and political assumptions about gender. As Judith Butler cogently argues, while the "materiality" of the body is not reducible to discursive constructions (the body is not totally "constructed" or determined by language), the body is nevertheless intelligible only through signifying practices, which are in themselves material practices (historically contingent and produced, hence politically charged).[5] Hence whatever claims modern science might make for homosexuality as a "materiality" pertaining to the body will still tell us nothing about the materiality of sexual practices and discourses — how bodies were used and understood — in early modern England.

What can tell us something about how bodies were used and understood in early modern England is the language through which homoerotic relations were defined and described. Whatever patterns we might detect among them, Renaissance homoerotic relations were not subsumed under a term like "homosexual" or "gay" that prioritized same-sex object choice. Nor is the Renaissance term "sodomite" equivalent to "homosexual": when it referred to male-male sex, "sodomite" meant more than "a man who has sex with another man." The label also meant that this particular man was treasonous, monstrous, heretical, and so on, and that he shared these defining traits with other deviants who may or may not have participated in same-sex relations. In the Renaissance, as Jonathan Goldberg shows in *Sodometries*, the category of "sodomy" could be deployed to stigmatize anyone who was perceived to threaten dominant conceptions not only of sexuality, but of gender, class, religion, or race. "Sodomy" is not a politically neutral term: it always signifies social disorder of a frightening magnitude, and as such occupies one end on a spectrum of practices signified by the politically neutral term "homoeroticism." At the other end of this spectrum are homoerotic practices that were perceived to be consonant with social hegemony. It is therefore impossible to discuss Renaissance homoerotic relations meaningfully outside of the precise social contexts that gave them shape and language.

Establishing these contexts is by no means easy. Even the most astute historicist readers of Renaissance culture are prone to definitional confusion. Perhaps the most striking instance of such a lapse appears in Alan Bray's important essay, "Homosexuality and the Signs of Male Friendship in Elizabethan England," which explores the difficulty Elizabethans sometimes had in distinguishing between friendship and sodomy, categories that were supposed to remain ideologically distinct. Although Bray initially appears to define male friendship as a potentially homoerotic relation, he goes on to claim that "homosexuality" was "regarded with a readily expressed horror" in Renaissance England, and therefore the intimacy between "masculine friends" was "in stark contrast to the forbidden intimacy of homosexuality."[6] Yet Bray's own book argues that whereas the metaphysical idea of sodomy was regarded with horror in Renaissance England, same-sex intimacies were not generally forbidden or stigmatized.[7] In this later essay, however, Bray conflates "homosexuality" with "sodomy," identifies both terms with the commission of transgressive sexual acts, and then cordons off these proscribed acts from the kind of chaste intimacy deemed appropriate for "friends." According to this logic, only the presence or absence of a sexual act will determine whether a given male relationship promotes social disorder (sodomy) or social order (friendship). While granting that "[h]omosexual relationships did indeed occur within social contexts which an Elizabethan would have called friendship," Bray does not consider that the languages and practices of male friendship in early modern England might have been openly and normatively homoerotic.[8]

To illustrate what I mean by this claim, I want to consider an early seventeenth-century pastoral poem that represents an explicitly homoerotic relationship through the language of friendship. In this virtually unknown poem from 1607, Lewes Machin describes how the sun-god Apollo "dote[d] upon" the "lovely youth" Hyacinth:[9]

> But *Phebus* heart did pant and leape with joy,
> When he beheld that sweete delicious boy.
> His eyes did sparkle, love his heart flamde fire,
> To see this sweete boy smile, is his desire.
> Then with an ardent gripe his hand he crusht,
> and then he kist him, and the boy then blusht,
> That blushing coulour, so became his face
> That *Phebus* kist againe, and thought it grace
> To touch his lips, such pleasure *Phebus* felt,
> That in an amarous deaw his heart did melt.
>
> (E5v-E6r)

It is not entirely clear what, exactly, Apollo and Hyacinth do together, because the poem goes on to describe their physical intimacy somewhat obliquely as dalliance, "toying," "play," "sport," embracing, and hours spent "in delight." Nevertheless, the nature of their relationship is identified on two occasions, when Hyacinth declares that the "parting of true friends all paines excell" (E6r), and when Apollo is said to prefer his "male paramore" to women (E6v). The poem defines a homoerotic relationship through the languages of male friendship and of heteroerotic romance. It therefore suggests that the Renaissance ideology of male friendship accommodated not only the expression of erotic desire but the performance of sexual acts. The tragic outcome of this particular relationship, I would argue, should not be taken as a sweeping condemnation of sex between male friends. For by interpreting Apollo's grief at Hyacinth's death as an etiologic myth of the sun's withdrawal during the winter months, Machin gives their homoerotic friendship an enduring cosmic significance.

The mere existence of a homoerotic discourse of friendship reveals nothing conclusive about *actual* male sexual activity in early modern England. Nevertheless, considering that only certain kinds of socially transgressive behaviors were labeled as sodomitical, it is impossible to be sure that sexual acts did *not* take place between friends who shared beds or other intimacies. Furthermore, as Machin's poem indicates, we cannot be entirely confident that we know which bodily acts count as "sexual." When is kissing an expression of sexual desire, of affection, or of a social bond? Under what circumstances might the ability even to distinguish these realms be frustrated? In a patriarchal culture, is intercourse always more "sexual" than kissing? Is it more *erotic*? Might non-penetrative eroticism, such as kissing between women or "sport" between men, subvert patriarchal sexuality? These questions cannot be answered outside of particular contexts, and even then with reservations. In any case, the indeterminacy of the "sexual" should make us skeptical of approaches that deem homosexual "acts" more subjectively and socially meaningful than homoerotic desires or discourses, and that require "evidence" of homosexual acts — what would this entail for non-procreative sex? — before granting the existence of homoerotic desires.

At the same time, it is important neither to totalize nor to homogenize same-sex desires and practices. The actual form any social or sexual relationship takes is overdetermined by competing discourses, ideologies, and institutions, as well as by the various subjective positions taken in relation to them. Early modern representations of male intimacy reveal a multiplicity of possible social configurations, erotic investments, and sexual acts: this multiplicity cannot be reduced to a uniform system of behavior, to "homosexuality." Moreover, we need to resist idealizing Renaissance homoeroticism by way of nostalgic disidentification — as a once universally available freedom we have since lost   or by way of activist identification — as the subversive practice of an oppressed minority. Such claims fail to do justice to the particular complexities of historically distinct social formations, be they early modern or postmodern.

II

If, as I have been arguing, orderly male relations were normative and unexceptional in early modern England, then why has the concept of sodomy exerted such a powerful explanatory force in recent assessments of Renaissance homoeroticism? Whereas many critics have analyzed sodomy in the Renaissance, the few detailed accounts of orderly homoerotic relations have been mostly limited to Shakespeare's *Sonnets* and a few of his plays.[10] This might have the unfortunate consequence of establishing Shakespeare's depictions of homoeroticism as culturally "representative," even though such a claim must remain speculative, if not presumptuous, in the absence of equally thorough studies of his predecessors, contemporaries, and successors. On the other hand, such attention may render Shakespeare exceptional in the realm of homoerotic love, as in so much else. Bruce Smith, for instance, argues that Shakespeare's articulation of a "private" or subjective homosexual desire in the *Sonnets* represents a radical divergence from cultural norms. Although Smith describes early modern English society as ideologically located somewhere between "homophobia" and "homophilia," he tends to dilute the force of this contradiction by attributing homophobia to legal and religious writings and homophilia to poetic writings, Shakespeare's *Sonnets* foremost among them.[11]

As a result of this bifurcation, I think, Smith's crucial attempt to establish the presence of orderly homoerotic relations in Renaissance England does not forcefully enough displace the critical dominance of "sodomy." Consider, for example, the skewed perspective on homoeroticism provided by Leah Marcus in her recent overview of Renaissance scholarship. While she acknowledges that sexuality was organized differently in the Renaissance, Marcus nevertheless articulates a characteristically modern notion of homosexuality as the always-already deviant. Even as she cites the work of Bruce Smith and Stephen Orgel on *homoeroticism*, not sodomy, Marcus writes that "the early modern era had vastly different, usually less rigid, ways of defining sexual deviance than our society does."[12] This formulation reproduces an assumption that Smith himself disputes: in the Renaissance, homoerotic practices were not always considered sexually deviant, but rather could inform the most "straight" social relations.[13]

The tendency to collapse male homoeroticism into deviance may be a consequence of a similar operation in American sexual ideology. Militant conservatives are not alone in promoting deliberately pathologizing, judgmental, or fear-inducing representations of gay men as leather-clad freaks, bizarre crossdressers, child molesters, or psychopathic serial murderers.[14] In American culture, monstrous images of gay men are as memorable as they are pervasive. Alan Sinfield has observed that even the most celebratory representations of queer sexuality have been appropriated for homophobic agendas: "the prevailing order is hostile to same-sex passion, and will dirty up any image that we produce."[15] Homophobic appropriations of queer imagery operate under the premise that "we all know" what sodomy looks like — and it isn't pretty. Similarly, the Renaissance category of sodomy derived its stigmatizing power from threateningly exotic significations. The sodomite could be a devil, heretic, papist, Italian — the categories overlap — cannibal, Turk, or African; or, as the satirists portrayed him, the victim of beastly lust for whores, boys, and goats. The specificity, strangeness, and variety of sodomitical images doubtless contributes to our continued fascination with them.

Nevertheless, I want to argue the importance of dislodging the hegemonic status of sodomy as an explanatory theory and imaginary referent for early modern homoeroticism. We might attribute the slip in Marcus's text to an unconscious tendency to read early modern homoeroticism through modern categories of "gay" deviance or subversion. Yet a more overt political agenda motivates certain accounts of early modern homoeroticism as sodomitical. For some gay critics, these accounts can provide a history of the Western persecution of "homosexuals." Louis Crompton's 1978 article on gay history cites the 1533 English buggery law (which, he misleadingly claims, made "gay love a felony") as one moment in a larger history of "gay genocide" from Leviticus to Hitler.[16] Crompton concludes this grim survey by citing the transhistorical "dilemma of the homosexual," evidenced by the fact that many homosexual survivors of Hitler's genocidal policies have remained as silent as "the men of the sixth or eighteenth centuries" who suffered under the murderous regimes of "religion" and "morality."[17]

Crompton's promotion of a transhistorical narrative of homosexual oppression cannot be attributed merely to an early, "essentialist" moment in gay historical scholarship that has long since passed. In an article published in 1993, Joseph Cady insists that a homosexual minority did exist in Shakespeare's England, and that this minority was persecuted by the heterosexual majority.[18] Cady considers it politically expedient to stress the repression of homosexuality in the Renaissance. If we can prove that homosexuals have always been unjustly oppressed, he argues, then we can present a more compelling case that the government should grant us the same civil rights and protections enjoyed by everyone else. Cady worries that scholars who deny the existence of homosexuals in the Renaissance are erasing gay history; worse, they might "undermine gay people's relatively recent gains in positive self-understanding, openness of expression, and social freedom."[19]

While Cady's concern may be understandable, the insistence on a history of victimization may also have a negative impact on contemporary gay causes. The image of homosexuals as a universally repressed minority may result from a problematic association between homosexuality and the abject, whether in the guise of criminality, sin, shame, death, or disease. In this regard, it is disturbing that many critics consider Marlowe's *Edward II* the *locus classicus* of homosexuality in Renaissance drama, since regardless of the sympathy an audience might feel for Edward, his demise seems to confirm a modern ideology of doomed homosexual desire. E. M. Forster explains that the happy ending of his 1914 novel *Maurice* "made the book more difficult to publish . . . . If it ended unhappily, with a lad dangling from a noose or with a suicide pact, all would be well."[20] Representations of homosexual desire may be more acceptable when the participants end up dead, a point powerfully made by Vito Russo's classic study of homosexuality in Hollywood cinema, *The Celluloid Closet*. In an appendix called "Necrologies," Russo lists forty-three films, mostly from the 1960s and 1970s, in which "overt, active or predatory gays . . .were killed off," whereas the "repressed, tormented types usually committed suicide."[21] For all the theoretical and historical knowledge critics bring to bear on *Edward II*, they may still find in Marlowe's king the stereotypical "overt homosexual" who must be killed off. To straight and gay readers alike, especially in the age of AIDS, Edward's tragedy may appear "realistic" or "natural," a confirmation of the modern idea that homosexual desire is doomed to failure and death.

As a manifestation of unexamined assumptions about homosexuality, then, the belief that same-sex relations were deviant or repressed or persecuted in early modern England can inadvertently serve to reinforce homophobia. A decade ago, the Supreme Court put a supposed "history" of homosexual repression to just such a homophobic use. In their ruling on the *Bowers v. Hardwick* case, the majority justices upheld the constitutionality of Georgia's sodomy laws, which criminalize private consensual sex between men. They justified their decision on the grounds that "homosexuality" has always been legally forbidden in western societies, as witnessed by the passing of a law against sodomy in sixteenth-century England.[22] The fact that the Renaissance category of "sodomy" meant something very different from the modern category of "homosexuality" did not prevent the Supreme Court from upholding the criminalization of gay male sex through the authority of history. Clearly, the claim that homosexuals have been transhistorically oppressed does not necessarily combat homophobia. In *Bowers v. Hardwick*, it justified it.

III

As a way to put into practice the various methodological, theoretical, and political positions sketched above, I want now to offer a reading of Marlowe's *Edward II* that will resist reading Edward, and by extension King James I of England, as a sodomite. The assumption that sodomy plays an equally defining role in the lives of Marlowe's Edward II and of the historical James I has led to the frequent linkage of these monarchs by Renaissance scholars. There is a precedent for this linkage: James' contemporaries did in fact compare him to the historical Edward II, and when Marlowe's play was republished in 1612 and 1622, its depiction of Edward's court may well have reminded readers of their own king's patronage of favorites like Somerset and Buckingham.[23] However, neither early modern nor modern readers need the personal example of James to make political sense of the male homoerotic relations depicted in *Edward II* (or, for that matter, in Shakespeare's *Richard II* or Jonson's *Sejanus*), which in any case were all written *before* James took the English throne in 1603. Drawing largely from English, Roman, and French history, Renaissance playwrights turned to the relation between male monarch and male favorite as a means of dramatizing various matters of contemporary political relevance: the limits of sovereign power and of resistance to it; the means by which political authority is established, maintained, and transferred; the dangers of flattery, misgovernment, and civil war; the interdependence among sovereign, peers, courtiers, subjects, and foreign powers; the conflict between sovereign will and sovereign duty.

Certainly, the circulation of erotic desire in the court was in itself a political matter worthy of a dramatist's attention. New historicist and feminist scholars have explored how Petrarchan conventions shaped relations between Elizabeth and her courtiers.[24] More recent literary and historical scholarship has revealed the significant presence of male homoerotic relations between courtier and courtier, patron and client, in the courts of Elizabeth and James.[25] So even if certain plays that were written, performed, or published during James' reign have particular topical application to his notorious promotion of male favorites, they did not simply materialize as direct "responses" to his homoerotic behavior. Rather, such texts constitute interventions in a sustained cultural discourse about political power and desire — a discourse that was also available to, and just as compelling for, Elizabethan playwrights and audiences.[26]

As for James' promotion of favorites, it was not the homoerotic nature of the king's attachments to these men so much as the threatening power his seemingly disorderly desire bestowed on them that provoked criticism. Censures of James' sexual behavior, like accusations of sodomy generally in this period, were motivated by fears of socially disorderly kinds of male intimacy. Since a favorite could acquire tremendous power through his access to the royal body, the monarch's relations with male intimates were the focus of intense scrutiny, interpretation, and debate. Satirical accounts of James found evidence of the king's *political* weakness manifested in his *personal* frailties: his bodily debilitation from disease and old age, his undignified doting on handsome, much younger men, his inability to manage ambitious favorites. The analogy between ungoverned body and ungoverned state explains why Anthony Weldon's caricature of James as a weak old man leaning on his favorites would be used as anti-royalist propaganda during the Civil Wars.[27]

In *Edward II*, Marlowe's staging of a destructive conflict over the legitimacy of a king's homoerotic desires may induce us to regard those desires as sodomitical. Despite the social upheaval that ensues from Edward's patronage of Gaveston, however, the king's actions are not as unequivocally sodomitical as the peers, and certain critics of the play, would claim. To understand Marlowe's contribution to a cultural preoccupation with favoritism, we need to acknowledge that male homoerotic relations can be socially orderly as well as disorderly, and that "sodomy" names not a form of homoerotic desire but a political transgression often associated with inappropriate forms of intimacy between men.

From the start, Marlowe's play challenges us to distinguish orderly from disorderly forms of male homoeroticism. Gaveston speaks the first words of the play — more accurately, Gaveston speaks Edward's written words: "'My father is deceased; come, Gaveston, / And share the kingdom with thy dearest friend.'"[28] Gaveston's voice collaborates with Edward's text to articulate a bond of favoritism, itself a collaborative relationship of ambiguous status in early modern England. Edward regards favoritism as a species of friendship. So does Francis Bacon in his essay "Of Friendship," but with the caveat that favorites often violate the great trust placed in them:

> It is a strange thing to observe how high a rate great kings and monarchs do set upon this fruit of friendship whereof we speak; so great, as they purchase it many times at the hazard of their own safety and greatness. For princes, in regard of the distance of their fortune from that of their subjects and servants, cannot gather this fruit, except (to make themselves capable thereof) they raise some persons to be as it were companions and almost equals to themselves, which

many times sorteth to inconvenience. The modern languages give
unto such persons the name of favourites, or privadoes, as if it were a
matter of grace or conversation. But the Roman name attaineth the
true use and cause thereof, naming them *participes curarum*, for it is
that which tieth the knot.[29]

Although Bacon does not explain how the monarch's elevation of a
social inferior might become a "hazard" or "inconvenience," the
Roman name he attaches to favorites is telling.[30] *Participes curarum*
was the name Tiberius gave to Sejanus, who not only participated in
the rule of Rome, but began to usurp it. The prince hazards his
safety by depending on the favorite's intimate involvement not only
in household matters "of grace or conversation" — a private
function signified by the label *privadoes* — but in the public
management of the state.

Despite the suggestion that a powerful favorite might subvert the
state, however, Bacon's essay is titled "Of Friendship," not "Of
Sodomy." If the legitimate favorite is expected to serve as a
companion and counselor, then at what point, and according to
whose authority, does the favorite's intimacy with the king become
perceptible as something other than friendship — as sodomy? When
do participants in care become rivals for power? In Marlowe's play,
Edward's request that Gaveston "share the kingdom" with him
establishes from the outset the classical model of the favorite as
friend. This model is familiar and authorized: "the mightiest kings
have had their minions" (1.4.393). In order to delegitimize their
king's minions, then, the peers must perform the ideological work
of representing them, in Bacon's terms, as "hazards." The peers do
this by describing the favorites as parasites. Yet the discourses of
parasitism and sodomy are not equivalent; and this discrepancy
suggests that we might locate sodomy elsewhere than in the
homoerotic intimacy between monarch and minion.

Our first perspective on that intimacy comes from Gaveston,
whose opening monologue reveals an apparent concern for the
king's welfare. Gaveston loves London because "it harbours him I
hold so dear, — / The king, upon whose bosom let me die" (1.1.13-
14). Gaveston wishes to experience the sexual consummation or
"death" that will secure and announce his position as the king's
favorite; but this position requires absolute loyalty, a willingness to
perish on the bosom of his patron as if in the act of shielding him
from harm. These are not the sentiments of a man motivated
entirely by cynical self-interest. Despite Gaveston's intention to
manipulate Edward — to "draw the pliant king which way I please"
(1.1.53) — the strong alliteration of this statement suggests the

harmony between the king's pliancy and the favorite's *pleasure*. Howsoever Edward is being "drawn," it is not against his will.

Significantly, Marlowe does not directly represent the wasteful actions for which the peers repeatedly attack Gaveston. We hear reports of but do not actually see Gaveston flattering the king or manipulating him with "lascivious shows" (2.2.157), mocking the peers' attire, or squandering the realm's treasure on extravagant ornaments and masques for Edward's entertainment. In the aggregate, these accusations of Edward's mismanagement of his household and realm do gain credibility, and they corroborate what we actually see of Edward's extravagant and irresponsible behavior. Nevertheless, the truth of the accusations is never conclusively demonstrated. As Emily Bartels has rightly observed, "the sexual/social transgression is the crucial framing source and subject of obfuscation" in the play.[31] Mortimer's frequent efforts to delineate this transgression highlight his own obsession with Edward's "wanton humor," despite his assertion that his complaints lie elsewhere (1.4.404-20).[32] An interested party in Gaveston's demise, Mortimer does not provide an unbiased, authoritative, account of Edward's disorderly rule.

Whatever the legitimacy of their grievances, Mortimer and the peers attempt to delegitimize both Gaveston and Spenser by representing them as parasites on the royal body. Lancaster protests that "arm in arm, the king and he [Gaveston] doth march" as if they were of equal status (1.2.20). Lancaster's image of parasitically intertwined limbs is elaborated by Mortimer, who scorns Gaveston as "a night-grown mushrump" and fashions for his own chivalric emblem a "lofty cedar tree" besieged by a "canker" grown equally high (2.2.16-18). Like "the Greekish strumpet" Helen, Gaveston is reduced to a promiscuously erring body; Spenser is condemned as "a putrifying branch / That deads the royal vine" (2.5.16, 3.2.165-66). Such images of parasitical mobility and malignancy obscure the fact that in Renaissance emblem books, intertwined limbs and branches have more positive significations. The vine embracing the elm is a common emblem of mutual love within marriage or male friendship.[33] To promote their own interests, the peers translate an archetypal image of loving support into a sign of the favorites' destructive ambition.

Against this construction of favoritism, the play opposes an elevated discourse borrowed from Ovidian erotic narratives and conventional love lyric. Like Leander, Gaveston would swim across the ocean merely to receive a "smile" and hug from the king (1.1.9). Edward sentimentally exchanges pictures with Gaveston and fondly remembers him as the "sweet favorite" to whom his "soul was knit" (3.3.43-44). Even according to their antagonists, the physical intimacy between Gaveston and Edward occurs in the upper bodily regions: Lancaster notes their passage "arm in arm" (1.2.20); Warwick discovers Gaveston "leaning on the shoulder of the king" (1.2.23); Isabella complains that her husband "claps his cheeks, and hangs about his neck, / Smiles in his face, and whispers in his ears" (1.2.52). In the mouths of other speakers, these accounts might sound like neutral observations or even approbations of male intimacy. Imagine Isabella's lines spoken by Spenser Sr., proud of his son's advancement: "[The King] claps his cheeks, and hangs about his neck, / Smiles in his face, and whispers in his ears."

A satirical language focused on the lower body and on the private pursuit of illicit sexual acts — in other words, the language of Jonson's *Sejanus* — would have conveyed a much stronger sense of sodomitical disorder in Edward's court. Instead, Edward and Gaveston are described, or imagined, as walking arm in arm, embracing, laughing out from a window, and frolicking together in a distant corner of the realm. Such representations of household intimacy evoke not the physical performance of "sodomy" (as a non-reproductive sexual act) but a physical closeness in which it becomes impossible to tell if king and favorite are whispering amorous phrases or state secrets as they pass conspicuously through chambers and halls. Edward, then, does not resemble the King James described by an unsympathetic commentator as always "fidling about his cod-piece" in public.[34] Neither does the dominant language of the play suggest Edward's preoccupation with "those parts which men delight to see" (1.1.64); rather, it somewhat nebulously alludes to his erotic disposition as a love-sickness (1.4.87), dotage (1.2.50), wanton humor (1.4.201), vain toy (1.4.403), and, simply, love (1.4.76).

To find a specification of sodomitical discourse and sodomitical transgression in the play, we have to turn to Mortimer. Although the peers vividly represent the favorites as parasites, Gaveston and Spenser do not violate Edward's body; Mortimer and his agents do.[35] Under Mortimer's command, Matrevis and Gurney shave off Edward's beard in filthy puddle-water, a ritual which not only emasculates the king but christens him anew as a mere subject. They later imprison Edward in "the sink / Wherein the filth of all the castle falls" (5.5.58-59). These tortures are scatological: they take place in, and allude to, the grotesque lower regions of the castle and the body. Mortimer's manipulation of Edward's body evokes the anal imagery common to Renaissance discourses of sodomy.

Most significantly, by authorizing Lightborn to murder Edward, Mortimer commits a regicidal and sodomitical act. Regarding the unpointed letter Mortimer uses to command Edward's death, John

Archer has observed that regicide as much as sodomy becomes a crime not to be named in Marlowe's play. While Archer refers to Mortimer's *regicide* and Edward's *sodomy*, Mortimer also commits the crime of sodomy.[36] He leads a rebellion against and engineers the death of his king, scatologically violating the royal body. Whether or not the poker actually appeared in the Renaissance staging of Marlowe's murder scene is debatable; yet the notorious legend of Edward's death from an act of anal penetration implicates neither Edward nor Gaveston in "sodomy," but those responsible for that regicidal act.[37] Denouncing Gaveston's privileges and Edward's patronage, Mortimer acquires an even more dangerous access to the monarch's body and power.

That Mortimer's scatological and sodomitical tortures of the king's body occur at one remove, through various agents, does not imply his absolute difference from Gaveston, the favorite who has direct access to the king's body. Rather, it shows that "sodomy" is a category dependent as much upon a social relationship as upon a bodily relationship. Sodomy is a matter of *degree*, in both senses of the term. Bodily access to the king is secured, for Gaveston, by his status as favorite, and for Mortimer, by his status as peer. As if playing Gaveston in a sadistic register, Mortimer aspires to rule by achieving exclusive access to Edward's pliant body, which he will manipulate as he pleases: "[N]one but we shall know where he lieth" (5.2.42). Tellingly, Mortimer's knowledge and power finally converge to murder Edward just "where he lieth" — in bed. From the perspective of royal authority, the sodomite is not Gaveston but Mortimer. Young Edward III's ritual display of the regicide's head reveals the lesson he has already learned from the symbolic and material practices of court favorites, parasites, and sodomites: that power is established through access to and manipulation of the bodies of the powerful.

Favoritism is just one of the political issues relevant to the Elizabethan regime under which Marlowe's play was originally performed and published. As I mentioned earlier, however, *Edward II* was also performed and published during the reign of James. A quarto appeared in 1612, the year in which James appointed Robert Carr, Viscount Rochester, to the Privy Council. In 1613 Carr (now Earl of Somerset) married Lady Frances Howard, whose divorce from the Earl of Essex the King had successfully engineered. By 1615 Somerset, implicated in the scandalous murder of Sir Thomas Overbury, had fallen from royal favor, and James' greatest favorite began his ascent. During this period, Marlowe's play was performed at the Red Bull; by 1622, the date of its publication in yet another quarto, the notorious Buckingham had acquired tremendous financial and political influence with James. A variety of seventeenth-century sources attest that James' favorites, especially Buckingham, were easy targets for censure aimed at the monarch's personally and politically offensive behavior.

Yet a Jacobean reader or playgoer might not have interpreted *Edward II* as a transparent critique of the homoerotic intimacies of James' court. Such an application was certainly possible, but by no means inevitable. For while the play may represent the *homoerotic* relations between the king and his favorites as disorderly, scandalous, improvident, or parasitical, it locates the political crime of sodomy in a rebellious peer's transgressive access to the royal body. Marlowe's Edward II and the historical James I might still be linked through sodomy, then, not as sodomitical monarchs, but as homoerotically inclined monarchs who had to define and defend themselves against sodomitical subjects.[38]

Notes

1. Eve Kosofsky Sedgwick, *Between Men: English Literature and Male Homosocial Desire* (New York, 1985), 1-5, 83-89.
2. On the normativity of male homoerotic relations in the earlier Renaissance, see Jonathan Goldberg, *Sodometries: Renaissance Texts, Modern Sexualities* (Stanford, 1992), esp. 18-19, 162-63. According to Alan Bray, a homosexual subculture and social identity (the "molly") first emerged in the late seventeenth century (*Homosexuality in Renaissance England* [London, 1982], 92, 103-04). The emergence of homophobia in the eighteenth century and its relation to the theater is the topic of Kristina Straub, *Sexual Suspects: Eighteenth-Century Players and Sexual Ideology* (Princeton, 1992).
3. David M. Halperin, "One Hundred Years of Homosexuality," *One Hundred Years of Homosexuality and Other Essays on Greek Love* (New York, 1990), 26.
4. Thomas Laqueur, *Making Sex: Body and Gender from the Greeks to Freud* (Cambridge, MA, 1990), 6.
5. Judith Butler, *Bodies That Matter: On the Discursive Limits of "Sex"* (New York, 1993), 65-69.
6. Alan Bray, "Homosexuality and the Signs of Male Friendship in Elizabethan England," in *Queering the Renaissance*, ed. Jonathan Goldberg (Durham, 1994), 40, 42.
7. On Bray's occasional reification and anachronistic use of "homosexual" and "homosexuality," see Sedgwick, *Between Men*, 84-87; Goldberg, *Sodometries*, 68-71; and Elizabeth Pittenger, "'To Serve the Queere': Nicholas Udall, Master of Revels," in *Queering the Renaissance*, 166-69.
8. Bray, "Homosexuality," 54.

9. Lewes Machin, *Three Eglogs* . . . (London, 1607), E5v. Subsequent citations to the poem appear in the text.

10. A few exceptions to this focus on Shakespeare appear in *Queering the Renaissance*, notably Elizabeth Pittenger's essay on Nicholas Udall and Forest Tyler Stevens's essay on Erasmus. Nevertheless, these essays still focus on well-known individual figures.

11. Bruce R. Smith, *Homosexual Desire in Shakespeare's England: A Cultural Poetics* (Chicago, 1991), 73.

12. Leah S. Marcus, "Renaissance/Early Modern Studies," in *Redrawing the Boundaries: The Transformation of English and American Literary Studies*, ed. Stephen Greenblatt and Giles Gunn (New York, 1992), 47.

13. Otherwise historically minded critics may display a blindspot with regard to homoeroticism. In his introduction to *As You Like It* (New York, 1988), editor David Bevington assures us that no "deviate sexual practice" is to be feared in Orlando's romantic courtship of Ganymede (xxii-xxiii). This formulation leaves only two options for Renaissance homoerotic desire: no sex (platonic friendship) or sex (sodomy).

14. It's important to clarify that while I deplore the use of sensationalistic media tactics for anti-gay agendas, I do not subscribe to the idea that men who engage in sadomasochism, leather fetishism, or cross-dressing are providing "negative images."

15. Alan Sinfield, *The Wilde Century: Effeminacy, Oscar Wilde and the Queer Moment* (New York, 1994), 202.

16. Louis Crompton, "Gay Genocide: From Leviticus to Hitler," in *The Gay Academic*, ed. Louie Crew (Palm Springs, CA, 1978), 70.

17. Crompton, "Gay Genocide," 82.

18. Joseph Cady, "Renaissance Awareness and Language for Heterosexuality: 'Love' and 'Feminine Love,'" in *Renaissance Discourses of Desire*, ed. Claude J. Summers and Ted-Larry Pebworth (Columbia, MO, 1993), 143-58.

19. Joseph Cady, "'Masculine Love,' Renaissance Writing, and the 'New Invention' of Homosexuality," in *Homosexuality in Renaissance and Enlightenment England: Literary Representations in Historical Context*, ed. Claude J. Summers (New York, 1992), 32.

20. E. M. Forster, *Maurice* (New York, 1971), 250.

21. Vito Russo, *The Celluloid Closet: Homosexuality in the Movies*, rev. ed. (New York, 1987), 156.

22. Cf. Janet E. Halley, "*Bowers v. Hardwick* in the Renaissance," in *Queering the Renaissance*, 15-39.

23. Stephen Orgel, "Nobody's Perfect: Or Why Did the English Stage Take Boys for Women?" in *South Atlantic Quarterly* 88 (1989): 7-29.

24. See the influential account of Louis A. Montrose, "*A Midsummer Night's Dream* and the Shaping Fantasies of Elizabethan Culture: Gender, Power, Form," in *Rewriting the Renaissance: The Discourses of Sexual*

Difference in Early Modern Europe, ed. Margaret W. Ferguson, Maureen Quilligan, and Nancy J. Vickers (Chicago, 1986), 65-87.

25. See Bray, "Homosexuality," 46-56; Goldberg, *Sodometries*, 29-61; Smith, *Homosexual Desire*, 176-79; Simon Shepherd, "What's So Funny About Ladies' Tailors? A Survey of Some Male (Homo)sexual Types in the Renaissance," *Textual Practice* 6 (1992), 23-25; John Michael Archer, *Sovereignty and Intelligence: Spying and Court Culture in the English Renaissance* (Stanford, 1993), 76-78.

26. Cf. Shepherd, "What's So Funny," 24; and Daryl W. Palmer, "Edward IV's Secret Familiarities and the Politics of Proximity in Elizabethan History Plays," *ELH* 61 (1994), 279-316.

27. Caroline Bingham, *James I of England* (London, 1981), 165-66. Cf. Bray, "Homosexuality," 53-56, and Bray, *Homosexuality*, 12-32.

28. *Edward II, Christopher Marlowe: The Complete Plays*, ed. J. B. Steane (Harmondsworth, 1986), 1.1.2. Subsequent citations to the play will refer to this edition.

29. Francis Bacon, *The Essayes or Counsels, Civill and Morall*, 1625, in *Francis Bacon: A Selection of His Works*, ed. Sidney Warhaft (New York, 1985), 113-14.

30. Compare the weighty significance of "inconvenience" in the title of George Eglisham's *The Fore-Runner of Revenge, Being two Petitions . . . Wherein is expressed divers actions of the late Earle of Buckingham; especially concerning the death of King James, and the Marquess Hamilton, supposed by poyson. Also may be observed the inconveniences befalling a State where the Noble disposition of the Prince is mis-led by a Favourite* (London, 1642).

31. Emily C. Bartels, *Spectacles of Strangeness: Imperialism, Alienation, and Marlowe* (Philadelphia, 1993), 163. Bartels' assessment of the play resembles my own, in as much as it concludes that Marlowe "legitimates" Edward's homoerotic desire and delegitimates the peers' accusations (171) However, Bartels sometimes speaks of anal sex and homoerotic desire as "sodomy," which she considers a private matter distinct from "the political" (159). While male-male sex might not always have political implications, I consider "sodomy" a political category in the sense that it names forms of physical intimacy socially defined as disorderly. In other words, "sodomy" is not a neutral description of a sexual act such as anal intercourse.

32. Whereas most critics accept Mortimer at his word, Archer rightly perceives Mortimer's discomfort at Gaveston's erotic comportment (*Sovereignty*, 81). On Mortimer's obsession with the bodily intimacy between Edward and his favorites see also Gregory W. Bredbeck, *Sodomy and Interpretation: Marlowe to Milton* (Ithaca, 1991), 71-77. Viviana Comensoli notes Mortimer's obsession with the "pathologized body" of Gaveston and discusses his engineering of scatological torments for Edward much as I do below. However, she anachronistically attributes

Mortimer's behavior to a homophobia generated by his own "repressed homosexuality" and "anal-erotic impulses." This approach has an unfortunate and ironic result: while creating sympathy for Edward and Gaveston as victims of a brutal homophobia, it locates the source of this homophobia in Mortimer's pathological homosexuality ("Homophobia and the Regulation of Desire: A Psychoanalytic Reading of Marlowe's *Edward II*," *Journal of the History of Sexuality* 4 [1993], 196-97).

33. Peggy Munoz Simonds, "The Marriage Topos in *Cymbeline*: Shakespeare's Variations on a Classical Theme," *ELR* 19 (1989), 94-117.

34. Anthony Weldon, *The Court and Character of King James* (1651; London, 1817), qtd. in Jonathan Goldberg, *James I and the Politics of Literature: Jonson, Shakespeare, Donne, and Their Contemporaries* (Stanford, 1989), 55.

35. Thomas Cartelli finds Marlowe's peerage "unsympathetic," "treacherous," and "sadistic" (*Marlowe, Shakespeare, and the Economy of Theatrical Experience* [Philadelphia, 1991], 131).

36. Archer, *Sovereignty*, 85.

37. Gregory Woods provides a detailed consideration of Lightborn's role in the sodomitical and scatological murder of Edward. While his intentions are anti-homophobic, Woods problematically considers Lightborn "the last lover to penetrate the king," who "clearly wants him to be an angel, lover, and liberator" and "is expected to consent to his own death as if to the loving intercourse he craves." How does Woods know that Edward's lovers "penetrate" him, or that Edward "craves" such intercourse? More disturbingly, to whom is Woods attributing the expectation that Edward would consent to such a horrific death? ("Body, Costume, and Desire in Christopher Marlowe," in *Homosexuality in Renaissance and Enlightenment England*, (New York, 1992), 74, 79).

38. I would like to thank Cambridge University Press for permission to include material in this essay from my book, *The Homoerotics of Early Modern Drama* (1997).

Queer Edward II: Postmodern Sexualities and the Early Modern Subject

Thomas Cartelli

Queer Edward II is the title of the book that Derek Jarman published as a companion piece to his recent film, *Edward II* (1991), in order to itemize and emphasize points that he wanted to make in excess of those he felt able to make in the film.[1] I have put the book's title to work in the heading of this essay because it highlights, in a direct and aggressive manner, the film's affinities with contemporary queer theory which it is at least part of my purpose to examine here. According to Michael Warner, the "preference for 'queer'" in contemporary gay discourse "represents, among other things, an aggressive impulse of generalization; it rejects a minoritizing logic of toleration or simple political interest-representation in favor of a more thorough resistance to regimes of the normal."[2] Jarman's affiliation with queer theory is evinced less by his film's predictably sympathetic representation of the relationship of Edward and Gaveston than by his vigorous integration into the film of militant gay liberation positions, including actions of resistance undertaken in their behalf by actual members of OutRage, described as "*the* Gay Activist Group" in the book's introductory matter. The book's debt to positions associated with the contemporary queer movement is even more pronounced and is paraded in the aggressive slogans that frame Jarman's generally more anecdotal commentary on the successive sequences of the film, the film's development, and his own, now concluded, struggle with AIDS.

These slogans operate in a wry but conscientiously polarizing manner and aim to privilege both homosexual and homosexist positions at the expense of the insistently demystified protocols of heterosexuality. Most of the slogans — "YOUR CLOSET *IS* YOUR COFFIN"[3]; "gender is apartheid" (36); "DEVIATE or *die*" (88); "LAWS MAKE NATURE" (150); "HETEROPHOBIA *liberates* HOMOSEXISM *empowers*" (168) — plainly reject accommodation to the residual biases of the resisting heterosexual reader. In their

213

insistence on a thoroughgoing transformation of the "regimes of the normal," the slogans also underwrite the similarly unaccommodating construction of the heteronormative in Jarman's film.

But what, Jarman provokes one to ask, does all this have to do with Marlowe's *Edward II*, the presumptive occasion around which both book and film are assembled? In *Queer Edward II* Jarman offers competing answers to the same question. On his dedication page, Jarman rather archly writes: "How to make a film of a gay love affair and get it commissioned. Find a dusty old play and violate it." Marlowe's play becomes, in this formulation, merely an enabling medium or ruse that affords Jarman the means/financial backing to stage something else entirely: "a film of a gay love affair." A few lines down, however, Jarman adds, "Marlowe outs the past — why don't we out the present?," thereby appearing to enlist Marlowe as a kindred spirit or collaborator who has done for the past what Jarman hopes to do for the present. Throughout both book and film, Jarman maintains this same casual ambivalence about his actual debt to Marlowe. One gets the sense that should Jarman attribute too much to Marlowe as a violator of his age's presumed heterosexual consensus, Jarman will have less to claim for his own violations or interventions. There is, on this account, quite a bit of strategic self-congratulation on Jarman's part, premised on a recognizably postmodern embarrassment at having to deal at all with "a dusty old play" that may have helped get his film funded but lacks the panache of the "pop songs" which, as he says elsewhere, only "the best lines in Marlowe sound like."

Although Jarman would undoubtedly prefer to sustain both the mystery and erotic charge carried by the word *violation*, he provides a more accurate — and modest — explanation of his aims in the running-head printed across each of the facing pages of *Queer Edward II*, which reads "EDWARD II *improved by* DEREK JARMAN." In the sections of *Queer Edward II* that refer directly to Marlowe's play, Jarman promotes his film as an improvement of *Edward II* in two primary respects: (1) It unqualifiedly displays and celebrates, in the best postmodern manner, homoerotic behaviors that Marlowe allegedly presents in a more qualified, constrained way; (2) it replaces Marlowe's allegedly neutral perspective on the play's "action" with a militantly partisan point of view that champions homosexuality and demonizes heterosexism, if not heterosexuality itself. Having measured Jarman's claims against my own understanding of Marlowe's play, I would suggest that by selectively foregrounding issues that the play's critics — as opposed to Marlowe himself — have chosen either to marginalize or to treat from a moralized perspective, Jarman has done more to hasten the demise of an already unraveling critical consensus on *Edward II* than he has to improve a play that, in many respects, invites the treatment Jarman has given it.[4]

This is not to suggest that Jarman brings nothing new to *Edward II*'s realization. Jarman makes a series of political interventions that do, indeed, "improve" on Marlowe by substituting a clearly positioned emphasis on gay victimization and empowerment in place of Marlowe's generally unpositioned fascination with power and the powerful. Although Marlowe initially situates his audience in sympathetic relation to Edward and Gaveston's carnivalesque reign of misrule, playgoers are ultimately directed to accommodate themselves to the drama's often shifting fields of force and the dramatic agents who command them. As I have argued elsewhere, gravitation to power, not to sexual orientation, is the play's prevailing medium of receptive engagement.[5] Jarman, however, appears to assume that the homosexual subject — even in the guise of a king — is always the victimized object of an established heterosexist power structure. He consequently positions the filmgoer in sympathetic relation to whatever forces of resistance he can enlist to recuperate the play's potential to promote the cause of dissident sexualities. Superimposing a militantly homoerotic point of view on the play's reconstruction, Jarman energizes its dramatically foreclosed capacity to stage resistance to heterosexist aggression.

That Marlowe's play succumbs to an identification with power is at least in part owing to the historical untenability of exactly the kind of oppositional sexual politics Jarman's film provides.[6] By the same token, Marlowe's capacity to generate, most notably through his characterization of Gaveston, a staging-ground for the operation and development of homosexual agency provides Jarman with a fertile site on which to structure his improvements.[7] While scholars like Alan Bray consider it "anachronistic and ruinously misleading" to identify "an individual in [the early modern] period as being or not being 'a homosexual'" (16-17), and while neither Edward nor Gaveston confines himself to same-sex encounters, it nonetheless seems clear, as Bruce Smith has argued, that in his constructions of both characters, "Marlowe introduces us to the possibility of a homosexual subjectivity."[8] Moreover, he does so in a manner that stands in much the same relation to other early modern constructions of Edward and Gaveston as Jarman stands in relationship to Marlowe.

As in other histories of Edward's reign, Marlowe casts Gaveston as the more profoundly sexualized figure, unmoored from the normative attachments of family, social, and political obligation.[9] Unlike them, he does not seek to explain, clarify, or judge Gaveston's sexual or social exceptionalism. It is, on this account and others, worth comparing Marlowe's conception with Michael Drayton's construction of Gaveston in a poem datable to 1593-94 whose dedication suggestively states that Gaveston's name "hath been obscured so many yeeres, and over-past by the Tragedians of these latter times."[10] Gaveston notably speaks in his own voice throughout this sustained dramatic monologue and is given a good deal of sympathetic access to his readers in shaping his versions of events. Implicitly countering the conventional charge of unnaturalness leveled against his relationship with Edward, Gaveston speaks of a "naturall attracting Sympathie" (164), adding

> O depth of nature, who can looke into thee?
> O who is he that hath thy doome controuled?
> Or hath the key of reason to undoe thee:
> Thy workes divine which powers alone doe knowe,
>   Our shallow wittes too short for things belowe.
>
> (164)

The naturalness of Edward and Gaveston's love appears to extend to its physical realization as Gaveston states,

> And like two Lambes we sport in every place,
> Where neither joy nor love could well be hid
> That might be seal'd with any sweet embrace.
>
> (182)

But Drayton's Gaveston is elsewhere made to proclaim "What act so vile, that we attempted not?" (167) and to moralize regretfully on sexual practices that are now graphically presented as unnatural acts:

> My soule now in the heavens eternall glory,
> Beholds the scarrs and botches of her sin,
> How filthy, uglie, and deformed shee was,
> The lothsome dunghill that shee wallowed in.
>
> (202)

A similar ambivalence attends the representation of Gaveston and his relationship to Edward in the history of Edward II authored by one E. F. in 1627, but now generally attributed to Elizabeth Cary. Cary mines what we will recognize as a stereotypical vein of homosexual inscription in stating of Gaveston that "the most curious eye could not discover any manifest errour, unles it were in his Sex alone since he had too much for a man, and Perfection enough to haue equal'd the fairest Female splendour that breath'd within the confines of this Kingdom."[11] But Cary puts this overendowed sexuality into play in relation to Edward in a manner that romantically idealizes their attachment: "A short passage of time had so cemented their hearts, that they seem'd to beat with one and the self-same motion; so that the one seem'd without the other, like a Body without a Soul, or a Shadow without a Substance" (4-5). She later adds that "their Affections, nay their very Intentions seem'd to go hand in hand" (20), thereby appearing to naturalize what she had initially presented as a kind of excess of, or deformity in, nature itself. Cary's initial difficulty in accepting as natural these indisputable signs of reciprocal attachment is, however, recuperated in a still later formulation where she writes that "Such a masculine Affection and rapture was in those times without president, where Love went in the natural strain, fully as firm, yet far less violent" (28). *Excess* seems, finally, the distinguishing marker employed by Cary to designate where the natural ends and the unnatural begins. As such, it serves to map that space of difference a later age will come to identify — in other words, through other signs — as homosexuality.

Excess and the unnatural operate as the privileged spaces of homosexual activity in Francis Hubert's unqualifiedly negative appraisal of Gaveston in his 1629 *History of Edward II*, which, like Drayton's "Peirs Gaveston," is also structured as a verse monologue but this time spoken by Edward himself. In Hubert we discover the fully demonized face of the professed sodomite, appraised by Edward as "This highest Scholler in the School of Sinne, / This Centaure, halfe a man, and halfe a Beast," who "acted all" as "*Plantaganet* was turn'd to *Gaveston*."[12] Seductive as the serpent in the garden, Hubert's Gaveston pleads the case of pleasure as alluring bait "to tye [Edward] still in streighter bands" (13), reducing civil laws to "servile observations / Of this, or that, what pleas'd the Makers mind" (14) and making "the golden law of Nature, / Sweet Nature, (sweetest Mother of us all)" (15) the sole arbiter of approved behavior.

These competing representations of Gaveston and "masculine" love demonstrate how simultaneously settled and unsettled the categories for representing homosexuality were in the early modern period. For his part, Marlowe, in *Edward II*, effectively obviates the dispute regarding the natural and unnatural by representing homosexual behavior as one among many material practices that are motivated by irregular blends of affection, compulsion, and opportunism and that operate beyond the reach of moral or idealist categories. Where Drayton and Cary inscribe Edward and Gaveston as both sexually other and romantically the same, as at once perfectly and imperfectly natural, Marlowe approaches difference itself from the point of view of indifference, thereby implicitly normalizing the avowedly exceptional acts of the homosexual subject. And it is, I would submit, precisely in this refusal to impose normative binaries on homosexual practices that Marlowe's violation of his age's heterosexual bias becomes most apparent.[13]

The materialist basis of Marlowe's position may, in fact, be said to constitute another salient early modern marker of homosexual agency, as Hubert's conflation of Gaveston's Machiavellian discourse and sodomitical behavior indicates. The argument Hubert delegates to Gaveston regarding the social construction of laws — which he terms "scar Crowes [invented] to keepe [men] in some awe" (14) — falls squarely in the range of damnable opinions that were characteristically delegated to atheists and sodomites alike in the period, and that were specifically attributed to Marlowe in the wake of his violent death.[14] Indeed, the argument is remarkably consistent with statements regarding the social construction of religion attributed to Marlowe in the Baines Note ("That the first beginning of religion was only to keep men in awe") which appear alongside even more provocative celebrations of homosexual practices. The Baines Note itself may either be construed as a particularly rich repository of early modern queer theory — if we accept Marlowe's authorship of its notorious opinions — or of early modern theory about queers — if we assume, instead, that it was deliberately constructed to implicate Marlowe. I assume that it is both and that its travesties of normative beliefs and behaviors in claims like "St John the Evangelist was bedfellow to Christ and leaned alwaies in his bosom, [and] used him as the sinners of Sodoma" need not have been exactly rendered by Marlowe to be considered Marlovian.[15] Should we, nonetheless, choose to accept Marlowe's authority for such pronouncements, we will have established an early modern precedent for Jarman's postmodern sloganeering, one that makes Marlowe a more outspoken advocate of transgressive knowledge and practices than Jarman would appear to allow.

The role played by travesty in marking the space of transgression is, of course, equally prominent in Marlowe's *Edward II*, where it is less their lovemaking than the practice of Edward and Gaveston to "flout our train, and jest at our attire"[16] that Mortimer finds objectionable. Compelled by the peers to stand outside the socially constituted realm of the natural, Edward and Gaveston play at, and against, orders of behavior that are established and dictated by the heteronormative consensus. Sexual difference thus becomes the enabling site for the production of both emulative and alternative discourses and behaviors. This is made even more abundantly clear in Jarman's film in scenes which feature Edward and Gaveston's exuberantly abandoned dancing to the music of a string quartet, their respective entertainment of a sensuous snake-charmer and a poet's suggestive re-signifying of Dante's "I came to myself in a dark wood where the straight way was lost," and in their wholesale reconfiguration of court life as a privileged preserve of play and fantasy. In such scenes, the "straight way" is travestied in the very act of being superseded by a "crookedness" that has developed aesthetic and moral parameters of its own.

It is particularly through his elaboration of alternative subject positions for Edward and Gaveston to inhabit that Jarman is able to extend and move beyond the circuit of Marlowe's comparatively more emulative travesties of the heterosexual consensus. Whereas Marlowe's Gaveston is, for the most part, a reactive character, miming and mocking the sober behaviors of the peers, Jarman's Gaveston is a decidedly more unpredictable figure, who draws on passions and resources that are conspicuously different from those of Mortimer and his supporters. As played by Andrew Tiernan, Jarman's Gaveston operates both within and against contemporary stereotypes of homosexual behaviors. In the first place, he betrays a good deal more passion and commitment for Edward than Gaveston does even in Marlowe's play, transforming the early modern space of sexual excess and Machiavellian opportunism into a site of erotic preference and romantic solidarity. In keeping with Jarman's desire to insist on differences to which Marlowe was indifferent, Tiernan's Gaveston generally keeps the space of lovemaking free of the impulse to travesty that characterizes his other appearances. For example, in the farewell scene that features Annie Lennox singing a Cole Porter lovesong and that would consequently appear ripe for parody, Tiernan chooses to play Gaveston romantically "straight," unsettling even further the stereotypes within which he would otherwise be confined.

In other appearances, Tiernan variously plays Gaveston as loutish, vicious, and demonic. For example, in taunting Mortimer by performing naked acrobatics on Edward's throne (sequence 15), Tiernan, as Jarman writes, "pulled out all the stops, turning himself into a frightful clucking demon" (30). In another sequence (#22) in which he thuggishly supervises the merciless beating of the archbishop, Tiernan "looked as if he'd stepped from 'The Krays'" (44), a recent film that conflates homosexual practices and homicidal pathologies. Tiernan is so adept at sexually arousing, and subsequently taunting, Isabella in the next sequence that he provokes Jarman to remark, rather defensively, that "Not all gay men are attractive. I am not going to make this an easy ride. Marlowe didn't" (46).

In refusing to ennoble Gaveston, Jarman reminds us that homosexual subjectivity does not consist of one or more enduring attributes, but issues from the conditioned force of homosexual agency which has historically been compelled to operate in — and as — resistance to enforced constraints.[17] Jarman does not allow these constraints to rationalize Gaveston's behavior. But in exaggerating their strength in scenes like the one in which an exiled Gaveston is first made to pass through a gauntlet of cursing and spitting priests, Jarman makes palpable the fierce repressiveness that church, state, and "civil" society can muster in the face of resistance and also indicates why resistance may come to resemble what it opposes. As the closing sections of the film make plain, Gaveston's enjoyment of the license to brutalize is, in any event, summarily revoked when this heterosexist consensus re-establishes its control over king and court. Aware of the raised stakes of this moment, Jarman chooses to transpose several of these scenes to the present and to stage Edward's final contention with Mortimer in the form of militant gay resistance to police repression. His decision to delegate Edward's actual execution to the province of nightmare is, however, altogether more problematic.

While consistent with his transformation of Edward's long-lost struggle against members of his own ruling class into a more hopeful contemporary battle between opposed sexualities, Jarman's ending magically elides the very relation between past and present oppressions that he otherwise seeks to document. (History, in this respect, becomes a nightmare from which we all too easily awaken.) Jarman seems specifically unwilling to allow a too powerful imaging of the material oppression of homosexuals to carry over into the present without simultaneously providing a way out. His decision to have Lightborne cast his hot-poker away, and to embrace Edward as a lover, has the added effect of making fantasy seem the preferred medium of resistance in the battle for homosexual rights. This particular "improvement" of *Edward II* arguably constitutes the most indisputable violation of Marlowe's play in Jarman's film.[18]

It is, moreover, decidedly less effective than Jarman's inspired imaging of the future in the cross-sexed person of Edward III who, at the end of Jarman's film, orchestrates the demise of the caged Mortimer and Isabella to the tune of "The Sugar Plum Fairy." Although just as fantastical as the elision of Edward's murder, this is a victory that the film may claim to have earned. I say this in light of Jarman's similarly inspired treatment of the young Edward throughout the film, whose questions, perceptions, and experiments in gender displacement speak eloquently on behalf of subjects and sexualities still in the process of formation.

Jarman's construction of Isabella is, however, considerably more problematic and symptomatic of his indifference to contemporary efforts to reconcile queer and feminist political agendas. Jonathan

Goldberg, for example, argues that in embracing adultery, Marlowe's Isabella "refuses the boundaries of the licit" and operates in much the same transgressive space as Edward. According to Goldberg, "what Marlowe intimates, insofar as it is possible to think of Isabella as a sodomite, is that the possibility for 'strong' female behavior lies outside of marriage and its regularization of gender" (123). He pointedly concludes that "her 'strength' as a woman lies in refusing the limits of marriage" (126).

Although Jarman brings similar conceptions of Isabella to bear in the course of his film, in the end he resists Goldberg's reconciliation of feminist and queer agendas by transforming the Queen into a bloodsucking vampire in evening dress, bent on exacting the cruelest revenge on Edward and his supporters. Moreover, he does so while extending, in a predictably extreme manner, the conventional appraisal of the lovesick queen into the representation of a scorned woman who, however illicit her adulterous arrangements, remains firmly committed to the established regimes of the normative, if not the normal.[19] Dressed to kill any suggestion of normality, Jarman's Isabella is nonetheless presented as well-practiced in the protocols of self-regarding mastery and royal control, and repeatedly placed in the company of the most banal representatives of social conformity. Heterosexual adultery in no way qualifies the Queen to operate in the space of sodomy Goldberg explores which, as far as Jarman is concerned, has "men only" inscribed on the door, as the slogan that closes the book on *Queer Edward II* indicates. While the slogan — HETEROPHOBIA *liberates*, HOMOSEXISM *empowers* — is no doubt meant to function in the same wryly overstated manner as are the others scattered through the book, it also suggests that as far as women are concerned, it is every man for himself.

Notes

1. In his repeated attacks on the vicissitudes of dissident filmmaking in Britain, Jarman indicates that he was unable to be as forthright in *Edward II* as he was in *Queer Edward II*. Indeed, although the film starts with two of the play's "poor men" making unabashed love as Gaveston reads Edward's letter, the film is generally a good deal more inhibited in its representation of homosexual practices than Jarman indicates in his book.
2. Michael Warner, "Fear of a Queer Planet." *Social Text* 29 (1991), 3-17; 16.
3. Derek Jarman, *Queer Edward II* (London, 1991), 8. All subsequent references to Jarman's text will be to this edition and placed in

parentheses.
4. The already unraveling critical consensus on *Edward II* was considerably intensified by three books published by avowedly gay literary scholars in the same period (1991-92) in which Jarman's book and film were distributed. See the sections devoted to the play in Gregory Bredbeck, *Sodomy and Interpretation: Marlowe to Milton* (Ithaca, 1991); Jonathan Goldberg, *Sodometries: Renaissance Texts, Modern Sexualities.* (Stanford, 1992); and Bruce Smith, *Homosexual Desire in Shakespeare's England* (Chicago, 1991).
5. See the chapter devoted to *Edward II* in Thomas Cartelli, *Marlowe, Shakespeare, and the Economy of Theatrical Experience* (Philadelphia, 1991).
6. According to Alan Bray, "What determined the skewed and recurring features of homosexual relationships [in the early modern period] was the prevailing distribution of power, economic power and social power, not the fact of homosexuality itself." See Alan Bray, *Homosexuality in Renaissance England* (London, 1982), 56.
7. As Jonathan Goldberg observes, "it is possible, imperative, to recognize in Marlowe a site of political resistance" (141).
8. Bruce Smith, 223. It is, according to Smith, worthy of note that "In Edward and Gaveston we have, not a man and a boy, but two men" (213-14).
9. Bredbeck notes that "a number of anecdotal summaries of the king's life, all written between 1590 and 1650, were widely reprinted," and offers illuminating accounts of several of them in *Sodomy and Interpretation* (48-50; 53-56).
10. Michael Drayton, "Peirs Gaveston" (orig. 1593-94); in *The Works of Michael Drayton.* 5 vols., ed. J. William Hebel (Oxford, 1931), 1: 158.
11. Elizabeth Cary, *The History of the Life, Reign and Death of Edward II, King of England, and Lord of Ireland. With the Rise & Fall of his great favourites, Gaveston & the Spencers. Written by E. F. in the year 1627. And Printed verbatim from the Original* (London, 1680), 4. All subsequent references are to this edition.
12. Francis Hubert. *The History of Edward II* (London, 1629), 13. All subsequent references are to this edition.
13. See Goldberg: "On the basis of the illicit, a defoundational site that cannot be read through or merely as a reflection of the licit, Marlowe's play negotiates difference — in gender and in sexuality — differently. Modern heterosexist presumptions are not in place" (125).
14. The full text of Gaveston's argument reads as follows:
    For what are Lawes, but servile observations
    Of this, or that, what pleas'd the Makers mind?
    The selfe-conceited sowers Imaginations
    Of working braines, which did in freedom find
    Our humaine state, wch they forsooth would bind

> To what they lik't, what lik't not, was forbidden
> So Horse and Mule, with bitt are ridden. (14)

15. See Bray: "Baines' depositions should . . . be taken as documents which have been carefully constructed but which are none the less based on Marlowe's actual opinions" (63).
16. Christopher Marlowe, *Edward II*. ed. Irving Ribner (New York, 1970), 1.4.417.
17. I am attempting to work here with Paul Smith's distinction between the human *agent*, on the one hand, and the human *subject*, on the other. According to Smith, the *agent* may be seen as "the place from which resistance to the ideological is produced or played out, and thus as not equivalent to either the 'subject' or the 'individual.'" See Paul Smith, *Discerning the Subject* (Minneapolis, 1988), xxxv. The *subject* may be understood "to describe what is actually the series or the conglomeration of *positions*, subject-positions, provisional and not necessarily indefeasible, into which a person is called momentarily by the discourses and the world that he/she inhabits" (xxxv).
18. As Goldberg writes, "Marlowe affirms *as proper* what his society sees as warranting death; his unflinching representation of the death of Edward is one sign of this, a making manifest of sodomy as the ungrounded truth of the play" (129).
19. Kathleen Anderson has recently made a strong case for abandoning the commonplace appraisal of Marlowe's Isabella as "an inconsistent, lovesick" character, "motivated mainly by her need to have a man love her" (31), in favor of a more expressly Marlovian conception of "a powerful political figure who uses her sexuality, her son, her position, and all of the gender stereotypes available to her to get and hold on to power" (39). See Kathleen Anderson, "'Stab as Occasion Serves': The Real Isabella in Marlowe's *Edward II*," *Renaissance Papers* (1992), 29-39.

BIBLIOGRAPHY

Adams, Robert P. *The Better Part of Valor: More, Erasmus, Colet, and Vives, on Humanism, War, and Peace, 1496-1535*. Seattle, 1962.

Agnew, Jean-Christophe. *Worlds Apart: The Market and the Theater in Anglo-American Thought, 1550-1750*. Cambridge, 1986.

Alexander, Nigel, ed. *Elizabethan Narrative Verse*. The Stratford-Upon-Avon Library 3. Cambridge, MA, 1968.

Allen, Don Cameron. *Doubt's Boundless Sea*. Baltimore, 1964.

Allen, Michael J. B. "Tamburlaine and Plato: A Colon, A Crux." *Research Opportunities in Renaissance Drama* 23 (1980): 21-31.

Allen, Walter. "The Non-existent Classical Epyllion." *Studies in Philology* 55 (1958): 515-18.

Altman, Joel. *The Tudor Play of the Mind: Rhetorical Inquiry and the Development of Elizabethan Drama*. Berkeley, 1978.

Amussen, Susan Dwyer. *An Ordered Society: Gender and Class in Early Modern England*. Oxford, 1988.

Anderson, Kathleen. "'Stab as Occasion Serves': The Real Isabella in Marlowe's *Edward II*," *Renaissance Papers* (1992): 29-39.

Aquinas, Thomas. *Opera Omnia*. Rome, 1895.

Arac, Jonathan. *Commissioned Spirits: The Shaping of Social Motion in Dickens, Carlyle, Melville, and Hawthorne*. New Brunswick, 1979.

Arber, Edward, ed. *A Transcript of the Registers of the Company of Stationers of London*. 5 vols. London, 1875-77.

Archer, John Michael. *Sovereignty and Intelligence: Spying and Court Culture in the English Renaissance*. Stanford, 1993.

Ascham, Roger. *The Schoolmaster*. London, 1570. STC 832.

―――. *The Schoolmaster*. 1570. Ed. Lawrence V. Ryan. Ithaca, 1968.

Axton, Marie. *The Queen's Two Bodies: Drama and the Elizabethan Succession*. London, 1977.

Aylmer, G. E. "Unbelief in the Seventeenth Century." *Puritans and Revolutionaries*. Ed. Donald Pennington and Keith Thomas. Oxford, 1978. 22-46.

Babington, Gervase. *A Very Fruitful Exposition of the Commandments by Questions and Answers*. 1583. London, 1590.

Bacon, Francis. *The Essayes or Counsels, Civill and Morall*. Ed. Michael Kiernan. Oxford, 1985.

―――. *Francis Bacon: A Selection of His Works*. Ed. Sidney Warhaft. New York, 1985.

―――. *The Works of Francis Bacon*. Ed. James Spedding, Robert Ellis, and Douglas Heath. 7 vols. London, 1857-59.

225

Baines, Barbara. "Sexual Polarity in the Plays of Christopher Marlowe." *Ball State University Forum* 23.3 (1982): 3-17.

Bakeless, John. *The Tragicall History of Christopher Marlowe*. 2 vols. 1942. Hamden, CT, 1964.

Bakhtin, Mikhail. *The Dialogic Imagination*. Trans. Michael Holquist and Caryl Emerson. Ed. Michael Holquist. Austin, 1981.

————. *Rabelais and his World*. Trans. Helene Iswolsky. Cambridge, 1968.

Baldwin, T. W. "The Genesis of Some Passages Which Spenser Borrowed from Marlowe." *English Literary History* 9 (1942): 157-87.

————. *William Shakspere's Petty School*. Urbana, 1943.

Barish, Jonas. "Shakespeare in the Study; Shakespeare on the Stage." *Theatre Journal* 40 (1988): 33-47.

Barrow, Henry. *The Writings of Henry Barrow*. Ed. Leland Carlson. London, 1962.

Bartels, Emily. *Critical Essays on Christopher Marlowe*. Ed. Emily C. Bartels. New York, 1997.

————. "Malta, The Jew, and the Fictions of Difference: Colonialist Discourse in Marlowe's *The Jew of Malta*." *English Literary Renaissance* 20 (1990): 1-16.

————. *Spectacles of Strangeness: Imperialism, Alienation, and Marlowe*. Philadephia, 1993.

Basille, Theodore. *The Golden Boke of Christen Matrimonye*. London, 1542. STC 4047.

Bate, John. *The Portraiture of Hypocrisy*. London, 1589.

Battenhouse, Roy. *Marlowe's Tamburlaine: A Study in Renaissance Moral Philosophy*. 2nd ed. Nashville, 1964.

Beard, Thomas. *The Theatre of God's Judgements*. London, 1597.

Beaumont, Francis. *The Knight of the Burning Pestle*. Ed. John Doebler. Regents Drama Series. Lincoln, 1967.

Bellamy, Elizabeth J. *Translations of Power: Narcissus and the Unconscious in Epic History*. Ithaca, 1992.

Belsey, Catherine. "Disrupting Sexual Difference: Meaning and Gender in the Comedies." *Alternative Shakespeares*. Ed. John Drakakis. New York, 1985. 166-90.

————. *Milton, Language, Gender, Power*. Oxford, 1988.

————. *The Subject of Tragedy: Identity and Difference in Renaissance Drama*. London, 1985.

Belt, Debra. "Anti-Theatricalism and Rhetoric in Marlowe's *Edward II*." *English Literary Renaissance* 21 (1991): 134-60.

Benston, Kimberly. "Beauty's Just Applause: Dramatic Form and the Tamburlanian Sublime." *Christopher Marlowe*. Ed. Harold Bloom. New York, 1986. 207-27.

Berdan, John M. "Marlowe's *Edward II*." *Philological Quarterly* 3 (1924): 197-207.

Berek, Peter. "*Tamburlaine*'s Weak Sons: Imitation as Interpretation Before 1593." *Renaissance Drama* 13 (1982): 55-82.

Berger, Harry, Jr. *Imaginary Audition: Shakespeare on Stage and Page.* Berkeley, 1989.

———. *Revisionary Play: Studies in the Spenserian Dynamics.* Berkeley, 1988.

———. "Text Against Performance in Shakespeare: The Example of *Macbeth.*" *Genre* 15.2-3 (1982): 49-79.

Berry, Lloyd E., ed. *Stubbs's "Gaping Gulf" with Letters and Other Relevant Documents.* Charlottesville, 1968.

Berry, Philippa. *Of Chastity and Power: Elizabethan Literature and the Unmarried Queen.* London, 1989.

Beza, Theodore. *The Psalms of David Truly Opened and Explained.* London, 1580.

Bingham, Caroline. *James I of England.* London, 1981.

Birringer, Johannes H. "Marlowe's Violent Stage: 'Mirrors' of Honor in *Tamburlaine.*" *English Literary History* 51 (1984): 219-39.

Blandy, William. *The Castle, or picture of pollicy shewing forth . . . the duety, quality, profession of a perfect and absolute souldiar, the martiall feates, encounters, and skirmishes lately done by our English nation.* 1581. New York, 1972.

Blayney, Peter. "*The Booke of Sir Thomas More* Re-Examined." *Studies in Philology* 69 (1972): 167-91.

Boas, F. S. *Christopher Marlowe: A Biographical and Critical Study.* Oxford, 1940.

Boose, Lynda. "The 1599 Bishop's Ban, Elizabethan Pornography, and the Sexualization of the Jacobean Stage." *Enclosure Acts: Sexuality, Property, and Culture in Early Modern England.* Ed. Richard Burt and John Michael Archer. Ithaca, 1994. 185-200.

Bowers, Fredson. "The Early Editions of Marlowe's *Ovid's Elegies*" *Studies in Bibliography* 25 (1972): 149-72.

———. "Marlowe's *Doctor Faustus*: The 1602 Additions." *Studies in Bibliography* 26 (1973): 1-18.

Bradbrook, M.C. "Beasts and Gods: Greene's *Groats-Worth of Witte* and the Social Purpose of *Venus and Adonis.*" *Shakespeare Survey* 15 (1962): 62-72.

Braden, Gordon. *The Classics and English Renaissance Poetry: Three Case Studies.* New Haven, 1978.

Braudel, Fernand. *The Mediterranean and the Mediterranean World in the Age of Philip II.* 2 vols. London, 1975.

Bray, Alan. *Homosexuality in Renaissance England.* London, 1982.

———. "Homosexuality and the Signs of Male Friendship in Elizabethan England." *Queering the Renaissance.* Ed. Jonathan Goldberg. Durham, 1994.

Bredbeck, Gregory W. *Sodomy and Interpretation: Marlowe to Milton.* Ithaca, 1991.
Breight, Curt. "Realpolitik and Elizabethan Ceremony: The Earl of Hertford's Entertainment of Elizabeth at Elvetham, 1591." *Renaissance Quarterly* 45 (1992): 20-48.
Brenner, Robert. *Merchants and Revolution: Commercial Change, Political Conflict, and London's Overseas Traders, 1550-1653.* Princeton, 1993.
Briggs, Julia. "Marlowe's *Massacre at Paris*: A Reconsideration." *The Review of English Studies* 34 (1983): 257-78.
Bristol, Michael D. *Carnival and Theater: Plebeian Culture and the Structure of Authority in Renaissance England.* London, 1985.
Brooke, C. F. Tucker. *The Life of Marlowe.* London, 1930.
———. "The Reputation of Christopher Marlowe." *Transactions of the Connecticut Academy of Arts and Sciences* 25 (1922): 366-72.
Bruster, Douglas. *Drama and the Market in the Age of Shakespeare.* Cambridge, 1992.
Buckley, George. *Atheism in the English Renaissance.* Chicago, 1932.
Bullinger, Heinrich. *The Christian State of Matrimonye.* Trans. Miles Coverdale. Antwerp, 1541. STC 4045.
———. *Fifty Godly and Learned Sermons. Divided into Five Decades.* London, 1577.
Burgess, Anthony. *A Dead Man in Deptford.* 1987. London, 1993.
Burnett, Mark Thornton. "Giving and Receiving: *Love's Labour's Lost* and the Politics of Exchange." *English Literary Renaissance* 23 (1993): 287-313.
———. "*Tamburlaine* and the Body." *Criticism* 33 (1991): 31-47.
———. "*Tamburlaine* and the Renaissance Concept of Honour." *Studia Neophilologica* 59 (1987): 201-06.
———. "*Tamburlaine*: An Elizabethan Vagabond." *Studies in Philology* 84 (1987): 308-23.
Bush, Douglas. "Marlowe and Spenser." *Times Literary Supplement* 1 January 1938: 12.
Butler, Judith. *Bodies That Matter: On the Discursive Limits of "Sex."* New York, 1993.
———. *Gender Trouble: Feminism and the Subversion of Identity.* New York, 1990.
Cady, Joseph. "'Masculine Love,' Renaissance Writing, and the 'New Invention' of Homosexuality." *Homosexuality in Renaissance and Enlightenment England: Literary Representations in Historical Context.* Ed. Claude J. Summers. New York, 1992. 9-40.
———. "Renaissance Awareness and Language for Heterosexuality: 'Love' and 'Feminine Love.'" *Renaissance Discourses of Desire.* Ed. Claude J. Summers and Ted-Larry Pebworth. Columbia, MI, 1993. 143-58.
Cain, Thomas H. "Spenser and the Renaissance Orpheus." *University of Toronto Quarterly* 41 (1971): 24-47.

Calvin, John. *Institutes of the Christian Religion.* Trans. John Allen. 2 vols. Philadelphia, 1936.

Camden, William. *The History of the Most Renowned and Victorious Princess Elizabeth Late Queen of England.* Ed. Wallace T. MacCaffrey. Chicago, 1970.

Cardwell, Edward, ed. *The Reformation of Ecclesiastical Laws as Attempted in the Reigns of King Henry VIII, King Edward VI and Queen Elizabeth.* Oxford, 1850.

Cartelli, Thomas. *Marlowe, Shakespeare, and the Economy of Theatrical Experience.* Philadelphia, 1991.

———— "Shakespeare's *Merchant,* Marlowe's *Jew*: The Problem of Cultural Difference." *Shakespeare Studies* 20 (1987): 255-60.

Carter, Angela. *The Sadeian Woman and the Ideology of Pornography.* New York, 1978.

Cary, Elizabeth. *The History of the Life, Reign and Death of Edward II, King of England, and Lord of Ireland. With the Rise and Fall of his great favourites, Gaveston and the Spencers. Written by E.F. in the year 1627. And Printed verbatim from the Original.* London, 1680.

Cave, Terence. *Recognitions: A Study in Poetics.* Oxford, 1988.

Chamberlain, John. *The Letters of John Chamberlain.* Ed. Norman Egbert McClure. 2 vols. Philadelphia, 1939.

Chambers, E. K. *The Elizabethan Stage.* 4 vols. Oxford, 1923.

Chapman, George. *Hero and Leander.* London, 1598.

Chapman, Roger. *Christopferus or Tom Kyd's Revenge.* London, 1993.

Charney, Maurice. "Jessica's Turquoise Ring and Abigail's Poisoned Porridge: Shakespeare and Marlowe as Rivals and Imitators." *Renaissance Drama* 10 (1979): 33-44.

Chaudhiri, Sakunta. "Marlowe, Madrigals and a New Elizabethan Poet." *Review of English Studies* 39 (1989): 199-216.

Cheney, Patrick. "Love and Magic in *Doctor Faustus*: Marlowe's Indictment of Spenserian Idealism." *Mosaic* 17.4 (1984): 93-109.

————. *Marlowe's Counterfeit Profession: Elizabethan Career Rivalry and the Writing of Counter-Nationhood.* forthcoming.

————. *Spenser's Famous Flight: A Renaissance Idea of a Literary Career.* Toronto, 1993.

Cicero. *An Epistle or Letter of Exhortation.* Trans. G. Gylby. London, 1561.

Clare, Janet. *"Art Made Tongue-tied by Authority": Elizabethan and Jacobean Dramatic Censorship.* Manchester, 1990.

Cleaver, Robert, and John Dod. *A Godlie Form of Householde Government.* London, 1610. STC 5382.

Coe, David Wright. "Arthur and Tamburlaine's Cosmological Dispute: A Clash of Realities in the Works of Spenser and Marlowe." Diss. U of Texas at Austin, 1980.

Cole, Douglas. *Suffering and Evil in the Plays of Christopher Marlowe.* Princeton, 1962.

Colie, Rosalie. *The Resources of Kind: Genre-Theory in the Renaissance*. Ed. Barbara K. Lewalski. Berkeley, 1973.

Collinson, Patrick. *The Religion of Protestants*. Oxford, 1982.

Comensoli, Viviana. "Homophobia and the Regulation of Desire: A Psychoanalytic Reading of Marlowe's *Edward II*." *Journal of the History of Sexuality* 4 (1993): 175-200.

Cook, Judith. *The Slicing Edge of Death*. London, 1993.

Cooper, Thomas. *An Admonition to the People of England*. London, 1589.

Coulson, John. *The Saints: A Concise Biographical Dictionary*. New York, 1958.

Cowell, Stephanie. *Nicholas Cooke: Actor, Soldier, Physician, Priest*. New York, 1993.

Cox, John D. *Shakespeare and the Dramaturgy of Power*. Princeton, 1989.

Crawford, Charles. "Edmund Spenser, 'Locrine,' and 'Selimus.'" *Notes and Queries* 7 (1901).

Cressy, David. *Literacy and the Social Order*. Cambridge, 1980.

Crewe, Jonathan. "The Theater of the Idols: Marlowe, Rankins, and Theatrical Images." *Theater Journal* 36 (1984): 321-33.

Crompton, Louis. "Gay Genocide: From Leviticus to Hitler." *The Gay Academic*. Ed. Louie Crew. Palm Springs, CA, 1978. 67-91.

Cuddy, Neil. "The Revival of the Entourage: the Bedchamber of James I, 1603-1625." *The English Court: From the Wars of the Roses to the Civil War*. By David Starkey, et al. New York, 1987. 173-225.

Cutts, John P. *The Left Hand of God: A Critical Interpretation of the Plays of Christopher Marlowe*. Haddonfield, NJ, 1973.

Dabbs, Thomas. *Reforming Marlowe*. Lewisburg, PA, 1991.

Daiches, David. "Language and Action in Marlowe's *Tamburlaine*." *Christopher Marlowe*. Ed. Harold Bloom.

Danson, Lawrence. "Christopher Marlowe: The Questioner." *English Literary Renaissance* 12 (1982): 3-29.

Darmon, Pierre. *Trial by Impotence: Virility and Marriage in Pre-Revolutionary France*. Trans. Paul Keegan. London, 1985.

Davies, John. *The Scourge of Folly*. London, 1611. STC 6341.

Davis, David Brion. *The Problem of Slavery in Western Culture*. Ithaca, 1966.

Davis, Natalie Zemon. "Boundaries and the Sense of Self in Sixteenth-Century France." *Reconstructing Individualism: Autonomy, Individuality, and the Self in Western Thought*. Ed. Thomas C. Heller, Morton Sosna, and David E. Wellbery. Stanford, 1986. 53-63.

———. "The Rites of Violence: Religious Riot in Sixteenth-Century France." *The Massacre of St. Bartholomew: Reappraisals and Documents*. Ed. Alfred Soman. The Hague, 1974. 203-42.

Deats, Sara M. "Biblical Parody in Malrowe's *Jew of Malta*: A Re-examination." *Christianity and Literature* 37 (1988): 27-48.

Deleuze, Gilles. *Masochism*. 1971. Trans. Jean McNeil. New York, 1989.

Derrida, Jacques. *On Grammatology.* Trans. Gayatri Chakravorty Spivak. Baltimore, 1974.

Dickens, A.G. "The Elizabethans and St. Bartholomew." *The Massacre of St. Bartholomew: Reappraisals and Documents.* Ed. Alfred Soman. The Hague, 1974. 52-70.

Dolan, Francis E. *Dangerous Familiars: Representations of Domestic Crime in England 1550-1700.* Ithaca, 1994.

Dollimore, Jonathan. *Radical Tragedy.* Chicago, 1984.

Donno, Elizabeth Story, ed. *Elizabethan Minor Epics.* London, 1963.

————. "The Epyllion." *English Poetry and Prose 1540-1674.* Ed. Christopher Ricks. London, 1970. 82-98.

Douglas, Mary. *Purity and Danger: An Analysis of Concepts of Pollution and Taboo.* 1966. New York, 1970.

Drayton, Michael. *Epistles of Poets and Poetry.* London, 1635.

————. *The Works of Michael Drayton.* Ed. J. William Hebel. 5 vols. Oxford, 1931.

Dubrow, Heather. *A Happier Eden: The Politics of Marriage in the Stuart Epithalamium.* Ithaca, 1990.

Dutton, Richard. *Mastering the Revels.* Iowa City, 1991.

Eccles, Mark. *Christopher Marlowe in London.* Cambridge, MA, 1934.

————. "Marlowe in Kentish Tradition." *Notes and Queries* 13, 20, and 27 July 1935. 20-23, 39-41, 58-61.

Edwards, Thomas. *Narcissus.* London, 1595.

Eglisham, George. *The Fore-Runner of Revenge . . . .* London, 1642.

Elias, Norbert. *The Civilizing Process.* 1978, 1982. Trans. Edmund Jephcott. Cambridge MA, 1994.

Eliot, T. S. *The Sacred Wood.* London, 1920.

Elizabeth I. *Proclamations. A Declaration of the Causes Mooving the Queene of England to give aide to the Defence of the People afflicted and oppressed in the lowe Countries.* London, 1585. STC 9189.

Ellis, John. *Visible Fictions.* New York, 1982.

Ellrodt, Robert. *Neoplatonism in the Poetry of Spenser.* Geneva, 1960.

Elton, William. *King Lear and the Gods.* San Marino, 1966.

Empson, William. *Faustus and the Censor: The English Faust-book and Marlowe's 'Doctor Faustus.'* Ed. John Henry Jones. Oxford, 1987.

————. "Two Proper Crimes." *The Nation* 163 (1946): 444-45.

Erasmus. *Erasmus on his Times.* Ed. Margaret Mann Phillips. Cambridge, 1967.

Feasy, Lynette and Eveline. "Marlowe and the Homilies." *Notes and Queries* 195 (1950): 7-10.

————. "Nashe's *The Unfortunate Traveller.* Some Marlovian Echoes." *English* 7 (1948): 125-29.

Field, John. *A Godly Exhortation by Occasion of the Late Judgement of God, Shewed at Paris Garden.* London, 1583.

Fineman, Joel. *Shakespeare's Perjured Eye: The Invention of Poetic Subjectivity in the Sonnets.* Berkeley, 1986.

Finkelpearl, Philip J. *Court and Country Politics in the Plays of Beaumont and Fletcher.* Princeton, 1990.

Flandrin, Jean-Louis. *Families in Former Times: Kinship, Household, and Sexuality.* Trans. Richard Southern. Cambridge, 1979.

Fletcher, John and Philip Massinger. *Sir John van Olden Barnavelt.* Ed. T. H. Howard-Hill. Oxford, 1980.

Forker, Charles R. "Sexuality and Eroticism on the Renaissance Stage." *South Central Review* 7.4 (1990): 2, 18-19.

Forster, E. M. *Maurice.* New York, 1971.

Foucault, Michel. *Power/Knowledge: Selected Interviews and Other Writings 1972-1977.* Ed. Colin Gordon. Hassocks, 1980.

Fraser, Russell. *The War Against Poetry.* Princeton, 1970.

Frazer, Winifred. "Henslowe's 'ne.'" *Notes and Queries* 236 (1991): 34-35.

Freedman, Barbara. *Staging the Gaze: Postmodernism, Psycho-analysis, and Shakespearean Comedy.* Ithaca, 1991.

Freeman, Arthur. "Marlowe, Kyd, and the Dutch Church Libel." *English Literary Renaissance* 3 (1973): 44-52.

Friedenreich, Kenneth, Roma Gill and Constance Kuriyama, eds."*A Poet and a Filthy Play-maker*": New Essays on Christopher Marlowe. New York, 1988.

―――. *Thomas Kyd: Facts and Problems.* Oxford, 1967.

Friedman, Alan. "The Shackling of Accidents in Marlowe's *Jew of Malta.*" *Texas Studies in Language and Literature* 8.2 (1966): 155-67.

Frye, Susan. "The Myth of Elizabeth at Tilbury." *Sixteenth Century Journal* 23 (1992): 95-114.

Fryer, Peter. *Staying Power: The History of Black People in Britain.* London, 1984.

Garber, Marjorie. "'Here's Nothing Writ': Scribe, Script, and Circumspection in Marlowe's Plays." *Theatre Journal* 36 (1984): 301-20.

―――. "Marlovian Vision/Shakespearean Revision." *Research Opportunities in Renaissance Drama* 22 (1979): 3-9.

Gascoigne, George. *A Larum for London.* 1602. London, 1872.

Gates, Geofferey. *The Defence of Militarie Profession.* London, 1579. STC 11683.

Geckle, George. *Text and Performance: "Tamburlaine" and "Edward II."* Atlantic Highlands, NJ, 1988.

Geertz, Clifford. *The Interpretation of Cultures.* New York, 1973.

―――. *Local Knowledge: Further Essays in Interpretive Anthropology.* New York, 1983.

Gibbons, Brian. "Unstable Proteus: Marlowe's *The Tragedy of Dido, Queene of Carthage.*" *Christopher Marlowe.* Ed. Brian Morris. New York, 1968.

Gibbons, John, and John Fenn, eds. *Concertatio Ecclesiae Catholicae in Anglia adversus Calvinopapistus et Puritanos.* Trier, 1588.

Gifford, George. *A Discourse of the Subtill Practises of Devilles by Witches and Sorcerers*. London, 1587.

Girard, René. *Violence and the Sacred*. Baltimore, 1977.

Glenn, John Ronald. "The Martyrdom of Ramus in Marlowe's *The Massacre at Paris*." *Pages on Language and Literature* 9 (1973): 365-79.

Godshalk, W. L. *The Marlovian World Picture*. The Hague, 1974.

Goldberg, Jonathan. *James I and the Politics of Literature: Jonson, Shakespeare, Donne, and Their Contemporaries*. Stanford, 1989.

————. *Sodometries: Renaissance Texts, Modern Sexualities*. Stanford, 1992.

————. "Sodomy and Society: The Case of Christopher Marlowe." *Staging the Renaissance: Reinterpretations of Elizabethan and Jacobean Drama*. Ed. David Scott Kastan and Peter Stallybrass. London, 1991. 75-82.

————. "Sodomy and Society: the Case of Christopher Marlowe." *Southwest Review* 69 (1984): 371-78.

————. *Writing Matter*. Stanford, 1990.

Goldstein, Lisa. *Strange Devices of the Sun and Moon*. New York, 1993.

Gores, Joe. "A Sad and Bloody Hour." *The Mammoth Book of Historical Whodunnits*. Ed. Mike Ashley. London, 1993.

Gosson, Stephen. *The Schoole of Abuse*. London, 1579. STC 12097.

————. *The Schoole of Abuse 1579: and A Short Apologie of The Schoole of Abuse 1579*. Ed. Edward Arber. English Reprints 3. London, 1868.

Grafton, Anthony, and Lisa Jardine. *From Humanism to the Humanities: Education and the Liberal Arts in Fifteenth- and Sixteenth- Century Europe*. Cambridge, MA, 1986.

Grantley, Darryll, and Peter Roberts, eds. *Christopher Marlowe and English Renaissance Culture*. Aldershot, England, 1996.

Greenblatt, Stephen. "Invisible Bullets." *Shakespeare's "Rough Magic."* Ed. Peter Erickson and Coppélia Kahn. Newark, DE, 1985. 276-302.

————. "Marlowe, Marx, and Anti-Semitism." *Critical Inquiry* 5 (1978): 291-307.

————. *Renaissance Self-Fashioning: From More to Shakespeare*. Chicago, 1980.

Greg, W. W. *Dramatic Documents from the Elizabethan Playhouses: Commentary*. Oxford, 1931.

————, ed. *The Shakespeare First Folio*. Oxford, 1955.

Gurr, Andrew. *Playgoing in Shakespeare's London*. Cambridge, 1987.

Haigh, Christopher. *Elizabeth I*. London, 1988.

Hale, J.R. *War and Society in Renaissance Europe, 1450-1620*. New York, 1985.

Halley, Janet E. "*Bowers v. Hardwick* in the Renaissance." ed. *Queering the Renaissance*. Ed. Jonathan Goldberg. Durham, 1994: 15-39.

Halperin, David M. *One Hundred Years of Homosexuality and Other Essays on Greek Love*. New York, 1990.

Harrison, Robert and Robert Browne. *The Writings of Robert Harrison and Robert Browne*. Ed. Leland Carlson and Albert Peel. London, 1953.

Harvey, Gabriel. *Pierces Supererogation*. London, 1593. STC 12903.

———. *The Scourge of Folly*. London, 1611. STC 6341.

Havran, Martin. *The Catholics in Caroline England*. Stanford, 1962.

Hayward, Sir John. *An answer to the first part of a certaine conference*. London, 1603. STC 12988.

Healy, Thomas. *Christopher Marlowe*. Plymouth, England, 1994.

Helgerson, Richard. *The Elizabethan Prodigals*. Berkeley, 1976.

———. *Self-Crowned Laureates: Spenser, Jonson, Milton and the Literary System*. Berkeley, 1983.

Heller, Agnes. *Renaissance Man*. Trans. Richard E. Allen. London, 1978.

Henslowe, Philip. *Henslowe's Diary*. Ed. R. A. Foakes and R. T. Rickert. Cambridge, 1968.

Hill, Christopher. *The World Turned Upside Down*. New York, 1972.

Hirschman, Albert. *The Passions and the Interests*. Princeton, 1977.

Hooker, Richard. *Laws of Ecclesiastical Polity*. Ed. George Edelen. Cambridge, MA, 1977.

Hope, A. D. "*Tamburlaine*: The Argument of Arms." *Christopher Marlowe*. Ed. Harold Bloom.

Hoppen, Alison. *The Fortification of Malta by the Order of St. John, 1530-1798*. Edinburgh, 1979.

Houlbrooke, Ralph A. *The English Family 1450-1700*. London, 1984.

Howard-Hill, T. H. "The Censor and Four English Promptbooks." *Studies in Bibliography* 36 (1983): 168-77.

———. "Shakespeare's Earliest Editor: Ralph Crane." *Shakespeare Survey* 44 (1992): 113-29.

Hubert, Francis. *The History of Edward II*. London, 1629.

Hulse, Clark. *Metamorphic Verse: The Elizabethan Minor Epic*. Princeton, 1981.

Hunter, G. K. "The Beginnings of Elizabethan Drama." *Renaissance Drama* 17 (1986): 29-52.

———. *Dramatic Identities and Cultural Tradition: Studies in Shakespeare and his* Contemporaries. New York, 1978.

Hunter, Michael. "The Problem of 'Atheism' in Early Modern England." Royal Historical Society. *Transactions* 35 (1985): 135-57.

———, and David Wooten, eds. *Atheism from the Reformation to the Enlightenment*. New York, 1992.

Ingram, John. *Christopher Marlowe and his Associates*. London, 1904.

Irigaray, Luce. *Speculum of the Other Woman*. Trans. Gillian C. Gill. Ithaca, 1985.

James, Mervyn. *Society, Politics and Culture: Studies in Early Modern England*. Cambridge, 1986.

Jardine, Lisa. *Still Harping on Daughters: Women and Drama in the Age of Shakespeare*. Totowa, NJ, 1983.

Jarman, Derek. *Queer Edward II*. London, 1991.

Joplin, Patricia Klindienst. "The Voice of the Shuttle is Ours." *Rape and Representation*. Ed. Lynn A. Higgins and Brenda R. Silver. New York, 1991.

Jump, John D. "Spenser and Marlowe." *Notes and Queries* 209 (1964): 261-62.

Karras, Ruth Mazzo. "The Regulation of Brothels in Later Medieval England." *Signs* 14 (1989): 399-433.

Keach, William. *Elizabethan Erotic Narratives*. Hassocks, 1977.

Keefer, Michael. "History and the Canon: The Case of *Dr. Faustus*." *University of Toronto Quarterly* 56 (1987): 498-522.

Keen, Maurice. *Chivalry*. New Haven, 1984.

Kendall, Roy. "The Baines Note in the Light of Further Evidence of Richard Baines' Activities in Rheims." *English Literary Renaissance*. forthcoming.

———. "Richard Baines and Christopher Marlowe's Milieu." *English Literary Renaissance* 24 (1994): 507-52.

Kerrigan, William, and Gordon Braden. *The Idea of the Renaissance*. Baltimore, 1989.

Kinney, Arthur F. *Humanist Poetics: Thought, Rhetoric, and Fiction in Sixteenth-Century England*. Amherst, 1986.

———. *Markets of Bawdrie: The Dramatic Criticism of Stephen Gosson*. Salzburg, 1974.

Knapp, Jeffrey. *An Empire Nowhere: England, America, and Literature from Utopia to The Tempest*. The New Historicism: Studies in Cultural Poetics 16. Berkeley, 1992.

Kocher, Paul. *Christopher Marlowe: A Study of his Thought, Learning, and Character*. Chapel Hill, 1946.

———. "English Legal History in Marlowe's *Jew of Malta*." *Huntington Library Quarterly* 26 (1963): 155-63.

Krafft-Ebing, Richard von. *Psychopathia Sexualis: A Medico-Forensic Study*. 1885. Trans. Harry E. Wedeck. New York, 1965.

Kuriyama, Constance B. *Hammer or Anvil: Psychological Patterns in Christopher Marlowe's Plays*. New Brunswick, 1980.

———. "Marlowe, Shakespeare, and the Nature of Biographical Evidence." *University of Hartford Studies in Literature* 20 (1988): 1-12.

Kussmaul, Ann. *Servants in Husbandry in Early Modern England*. Cambridge, 1981.

Ladurie, Emmanuel Le Roy. *Jasmin's Witch*. Aldershot, 1987.

Lake, Peter. *Anglicans and Puritans?* London, 1988.

Lambert, Sheila. "State Control of the Press in Theory and Practice: The Role of the Stationers' Company before 1640." *Censorship and the Control of Print in England and France 1600-1910*. Ed. Robin Myers and Michael Harris. Winchester, 1992. 1-32.

Laqueur, Thomas. *Making Sex: Body and Gender from the Greeks to Freud.* Cambridge, MA, 1990.

Larner, Christina. *Witchcraft and Religion: The Politics of Popular Belief.* Ed. Alan MacFarlane. Oxford, 1984.

Laslett, Peter. *The World We Have Lost.* London, 1965.

Lee, Maurice, Jr. *John Maitland of Thirlestane and the Foundations of the Stewart Despotism in Scotland.* Princeton, 1959.

Leech, Clifford. *Christopher Marlowe: Poet for the Stage.* Ed. Anne Lancashire. New York, 1986.

———. "Marlowe's Humor." *Essays on Shakespeare and Elizabethan Drama in Honor of Hardin Craig.* Ed. Richard Hosley. Columbia, MO, 1982. 69-81.

Leinwand, Theodore. "Negotiation and New Historicism." *PLMA* 105 (1990): 477-90.

Leishman, J.B., ed. *The Three Parnassus Plays.* London, 1949.

Lemnius, Levinus. *The Touchstone of Complexions.* Trans. Thomas Newton. London, 1581.

Levin, Harry. *The Overreacher: A Study of Christopher Marlowe.* Cambridge, MA, 1952.

Levin, Richard. "Another Possible Clue to the Identity of the Rival Poet." *Shakespeare Quarterly* 36 (1985): 213-14.

———. "The Contemporary Perception of Marlowe's *Tamburlaine.*" *Medieval and Renaissance Drama in England* 1 (1984): 51-70.

Levine, Laura. *Men in Women's Clothing: Anti-theatricality and Effeminization from 1579-1642.* Cambridge, 1994.

Levy, Leonard W. *Treason Against God: A History of the Offence of Blasphemy.* New York, 1981.

Lindley, David. *The Trials of Frances Howard: Fact and Fiction at the Court of King James.* London, 1993.

Loades, D. M. *Politics and the Nation 1540-1660: Obedience, Resistance and Public Order.* London, 1974.

Lodge, Thomas. *The Complete Works of Thomas Lodge.* 1883. 4 vols. New York, 1963.

Loewenstein, Joseph. "Echo's Ring: Orpheus and Spenser's Career." *English Literary Renaissance* 16 (1986): 287-302.

Long, William B. "'A Bed / for Woodstock': A Warning for the Unwary." *Medieval and Renaissance Drama in England* 2 (1985): 91-118.

———. "Stage-Directions: A Misinterpreted Factor in Determining Textual Provenance." *Text* 2 (1985): 121-37.

Lucian. *Dialogue of the Gods.* Trans. M. D. Macheod. Cambridge, MA, 1969.

MacCaffrey, Wallace. *Elizabeth I*. London, 1993.

———. "Place and Patronage in Elizabethan Politics." *Elizabethan Government and Society: Essays Presented to Sir John Neale.* Ed. S. T. Bindoff, J. Hurstfield, and C. H. Williams. London, 1961.

MacCary, W. Thomas. *Friends and Lovers: The Phenomenology of Desire in Shakespearean Comedy.* New York, 1985.

MacDonald, Michael. *Mystical Bedlam: Madness, Anxiety, and Healing in Seventeenth Century England.* Cambridge, 1981.

MacFarlane, Alan. *Witchcraft in Tudor and Stuart England: A Regional and Comparative Study.* London, 1970.

Machin, Lewes. *Three Eglogs. The first is of Menalcas and Daphnis: The other two is of Apollo and Hiacinth.* London, 1607.

Maclean, Ian. *The Renaissance Notion of Woman: A Study in the Fortunes of Scholasticism and Medical Science in European Intellectual Life.* Cambridge, 1980.

MacLure, Millar. *Marlowe: The Critical Heritage 1588-1896.* London, 1979.

Maguire, Liam. *Icarus Flying: The Tragical Story of Christopher Marlowe.* Morden, Surrey, 1993.

Mallin, Eric S. "Emulous Factions and the Collapse of Chivalry: *Troilus and Cressida.*" *Representations* 29 (1990): 145-79.

Marcus, Leah S. "Renaissance/Early Modern Studies." *Redrawing the Boundaries: The Transformation of English and American Literary Studies.* Ed. Stephen Greenblatt and Giles Gunn. New York, 1992: 41-63.

⸻. "Textual Indeterminacy and Ideological Difference: The Case of *Dr. Faustus.*" *Renaissance Drama* 20 (1989): 1-29.

Marlowe, Christopher. *The Complete Plays.* 1969. Ed. J. B. Steane. Harmondsworth, 1988.

⸻. *The Complete Poems and Translations.* 1971. Ed. Stephen Orgel. Harmondsworth, 1979.

⸻. *The Complete Works of Christopher Marlowe.* Ed. Fredson Bowers. 2 vols. Cambridge, 1973.

⸻. *The Complete Works of Christopher Marlowe.* Ed. Fredson Bowers. 2 vols. 2nd ed. Cambridge, 1987.

⸻. *The Complete Works of Christopher Marlowe.* Ed. Roma Gill. 2 vols. Oxford, 1987.

⸻. *Dr. Faustus: A 1604-Version Edition.* Ed. Michael Keefer. Peterborough, 1991.

⸻. *Doctor Faustus: A- and B-texts (1604, 1616).* Ed. David Bevington and Eric Rasmussen. The Revels Plays. Manchester, 1993.

⸻. *Edward II.* Ed. Irving Ribner. New York, 1970.

⸻. *Edward II.* Ed. Charles R. Forker. Manchester and New York, 1994.

⸻. *Edward the Second.* Ed. W. Moelwyn Merchant. New Mermaids. London, 1987.

⸻. *Hero and Leander By Christopher Marlowe: A Facsimile of the First Edition, London 1598.* Ed. Louis L. Martz. The Folger Facsimiles. New York, 1972.

⸻. *Marlowe's 'Doctor Faustus' 1604-1616: Parallel Texts.* Ed. W. W. Greg. Oxford, 1950.

————. *The Massacre at Paris*. Ed. H. J. Oliver. Cambridge, 1968.

————. *The Plays of Christopher Marlowe*. Ed. Roma Gill. London, 1971.

————. *Tamburlaine the Great*. Ed. J. S. Cunningham. Manchester, 1981.

————. *Tamburlaine the Great, Parts I and II*. Ed. John D. Jump. Lincoln, 1967.

————. *The Works of Christopher Marlowe*. Ed. A. H. Bullen. New York, 1885.

Marotti, Arthur. *Manuscript, Print, and the English Renaissance Lyric*. Ithaca, 1995.

Martin, Richard. "Fate, Seneca, and Marlowe's Dido." *Renaissance Drama* 11 (1980): 45-66.

————. "Marlowe's *Tamburlaine* and the Language of Romance." *PMLA* 93 (1978): 248-64.

Marx, Steven. "Shakespeare's Pacifism." *Renaissance Quarterly* 45 (1992): 49-95.

Masinton, Charles G. *Christopher Marlowe's Tragic Vision: A Study in Damnation*. Athens, OH, 1972.

Matar. N. I. "English Renaissance Soldiers in the Armies of Islam." *Explorations in Renaissance Culture* 21 (1995).

Maus, Katherine Eisaman. "Horns of Dilemma: Jealousy, Gender, and Spectatorship in English Renaissance Drama." *English Literary History* 54 (1987): 561-83.

McAdam, Ian. "Carnal Identity in *The Jew of Malta*." *English Literary Renaissance* 26 (1996): 47-74.

————. "*Edward II* and the Illusion of Integrity." *Studies in Philology* 92 (1995): 203-230.

McAlindon, Thomas. *Doctor Faustus: Divine in Show*. New York, 1994.

McCabe, Richard A. *Incest, Drama and Nature's Law, 1550-1700*. Cambridge, 1993.

McIntosh, Mary. "Who Needs Prostitutes? The Ideology of Male Sexual Needs." *Women, Sexuality and Social Control*. Ed. Carol and Barry Smart. London, 1978.

Mead, Stephen X. "Marlowe's *Tamburlaine* and the Idea of Empire." *Works and Days* 7 (1989): 91-103.

Melchiori, Giorgio. "*The Booke of Sir Thomas More*: A Chronology of Revision." *Shakespeare Quarterly* 37(1986): 291-308.

Metz. G. Harold. "The Master of the Revels and *The Booke of Sir Thomas More*." *Shakespeare Quarterly* 33 (1982): 493-95.

Midelfort, H.C. Erik. "The Devil and the German People: Reflections on the Popularity of Demon Possession in Sixteenth-Century Germany." *Religion and Culture in the Renaissance and Reformation, Sixteenth Century Essays and Studies*. Ed. Steven Ozment. London, 1989.

Miller, David L. "Spenser's Vocation, Spenser's Career." *English Literary History* 50 (1983): 197-231.

Milligan, Burton A., ed. *Three Renaissance Classics*. New York, 1953.

Moisan, Thomas. "'Knock Me Here Soundly': Comic Misprision and Class Consciousness in Shakespeare." *Shakespeare Quarterly* 42 (1991): 276-90.

Mol, Hans. *Identity and the Sacred: A Sketch for a New Social-Scientific Theory of Religion.* Oxford, 1976.

Montesquieu, Charles Louis de Secondat, Baron de. *The Spirit of Laws.* Trans. Thomas Nugent. New York, 1900.

Montrose, Louis. "*A Midsummer Night's Dream* and the Shaping Fantasies of Elizabethan Culture: Gender, Power, Form." *Rewriting the Renaissance: The Discourse of Sexual Difference in Early Modern Europe.* Ed. Margaret Ferguson, et al. Chicago, 1986. 65-87.

Moore, Hale. "Gabriel Harvey's References to Marlowe." *Studies in Philology* 23 (1926): 337-57.

Mulryne, J. R. and Stephen Fender. "Marlowe and the Comic Distance." *Christopher Marlowe.* Ed. Brian Morris. New York, 1968.

Mulvey, Laura. "Visual Pleasure and Narrative Cinema." *Screen* 16 (1975): 6-18.

Nashe, Thomas. *Christ's Tears.* 2nd Ed. London, 1594.

———. *Lenten Stuff.* London, 1599.

———. *The Works of Thomas Nashe.* Ed. R. B. McKerrow and F. P. Wilson. 5 vols. Oxford, 1958.

Nauert, Charles, Jr. *The Age of Renaissance and Reformation.* 1977. Lanham, MD, 1981.

Naunton, Sir Robert. *Fragmenta Regalia.* 1641. Ed. Henry Morley. London, 1889.

Neale, J. E. *Elizabeth I and her Parliaments.* 2 vols. London, 1969.

———. *Queen Elizabeth I.* Harmondsworth, 1967.

Nicholl, Charles. *A Cup of News: The Life of Thomas Nashe.* London, 1984.

———. *The Reckoning: The Murder of Christopher Marlowe.* London, 1992.

O'Day, Rosemary. *The English Clergy.* Leicester, 1979.

Orgel, Stephen. *Impersonations: The Performance of Gender in Shakespeare's England.* Cambridge, 1996.

———. "Nobody's Perfect: Or, Why Did the English Stage Take Boys for Men?" *South Atlantic Quarterly* 88 (1989): 7-29.

———. "What is a Text?" *Staging the Renaissance: Reinterpretations of Elizabethan and Jacobean Drama.* Ed. David Scott Kastan and Peter Stallybrass. New York, 1991. 83-87.

Ovid. *Heroides and Amores.* Trans. Grant Showerman. Cambridge, MA, 1914.

———. *Metamorphoses.* Trans. Arthur Golding. Ed. H. D. Rouse. Carbondale, 1961.

Pagden, Anthony. *Lords of All the World: Ideologies of Empire in Spain, Britain and France, c. 1500-1800.* New Haven, 1995.

Palmer, Daryl W. "Edward IV's Secret Familiarities and the Politics of Proximity in Elizabethan History Plays." *ELH* 61 (1994): 279-316.

Parker, Geoffrey. *The Military Revolution: Military Innovation and the Rise of the West, 1500-1800.* Cambridge, 1988.

Parker, Patricia. "Gender Ideology, Gender Change: The Case of Marie Germain." *Critical Inquiry* 19 (1993): 337-64.

Parsons, Robert. *A conference about the next succession to the crowne of Ingland.* London, 1594. STC 1939.

Paster, Gail Kern. *The Body Embarrassed: Drama and the Disciplines of Shame in Early Modern England.* Ithaca, 1993.

Patterson, Orlando. *Slavery and Social Death.* Cambridge, MA, 1982.

Peele, George. *The Honour of the Garter.* London, 1593.

Perkins, William. *A Treatise of Man's Imaginations.* London, 1607.

Perret, Marion D. "Shakespeare's Jew: Preconception and Performance." *Shakespeare Studies* 20 (1987): 261-68.

Persons, Father Robert. *Letters and Memorials of Father Robert Persons.* Ed. Leo Hicks. Catholic Record Society, 1942.

Pittenger, Elizabeth. "'To Serve the Queere': Nicholas Udall, Master of Revels.'" *Queering the Renaissance.* Ed. Jonathan Goldberg. Durham, 1994: 162-89.

Plato. *The Republic.* Trans. H. D. P. Lee. Baltimore, 1956.

Prager, Carolyn. "The Problem of Slavery in *The Custom of the Country.*" *Studies in English Literature* 28 (1988): 301-17.

Proser, Matthew. *Gift of Fire: Aggression and the Plays of Christopher Marlowe.* New York, 1995.

———. "*Tamburlaine* and the Art of Destruction." *University of Hartford Studies in Literature* 20 (1988): 37-51.

The Psalms of David and Others with J. Calvin's Commentaries. Trans. Arthur Golding. London, 1571.

Purdon, Noel. "Quod me Nutrit." *Cambridge Review* (1967).

Quint, David. "Epic and Empire." *Comparative Literature* 41 (1989): 4-8.

Rackin, Phyllis. "Engendering the Tragic Audience: The Case of *Richard III.*" *Shakespeare and Gender: A History.* Ed. Deborah E. Barker and Ivo Kamps. London, 1995.

———. *Stages of History: Shakespeare's English Chronicles.* Ithaca, 1990.

Raman, Shankar. "Desire and Violence in Renaissance England: Christopher Marlowe's *Edward II.*" *Deutsche Vierteljahrsschrift,* forthcoming.

Rambuss, Richard. *Spenser's Secret Career.* Cambridge, 1993.

Rankins, William. *A Mirror of Monsters.* London, 1587.

Rasmussen, Eric. "Rehabilitating the A-text of Marlowe's *Doctor Faustus.*" *Studies in Bibliography* 46 (1993): 221-38.

———. *A Textual Companion to 'Doctor Faustus'.* Manchester, 1994.

Read, Conyers. *Mr. Secretary Walsingham and the Policy of Queen Elizabeth.* 3 vols. Oxford,1925.

Reik, Theodore. *Masochism in Modern Man.* Trans. Margaret H. Beigel and Gertrud M. Kurth. New York, 1941.

Rev. of *Christopher Marlowe*, by Paul Kocher. *Times Literary Supplement* 19 July 1947, 364.

Rich, Barnabe. *Roome for a Gentleman*. London, 1609. STC 20985.

Ringler, William, Jr. "The Number of Actors in Shakespeare's Early Plays." *The Seventeenth Century Stage*. Ed. G. E. Bentley. Chicago, 1968. 110-34.

Robbins, Bruce. *The Servant's Hand: English Fiction From Below*. New York, 1986.

Robbins, Rossell Hope. *The Encyclopaedia of Witchcraft and Demonology*. New York, 1959.

Rogers, David. "Love and Honor in Marlowe's *Dido: Queene of Carthage*." *Greyfriar* 6 (1963): 3-7.

Roover, Raymond de. *Business, Banking, and Economic Thought in Late Medieval and Early Modern Europe*. Ed. Julius Kirshner. Chicago, 1974.

Rosen, Barbara. *Witchcraft in England, 1558-1618*. Amherst, 1991.

Rossiaud, Jacques. *Medieval Prostitution*. Trans. Lydia G. Cochrane. London, 1988.

Russo, Vito. *The Celluloid Closet: Homosexuality in the Movies*. Revised ed. New York, 1987.

Sabean, David Warren. *Power in the Blood: Popular Culture and Village Discourse in Early Modern Germany*. Cambridge, 1984.

Sade, Marquis de. *The 120 Days of Sodom and Other Writings*. Trans. and ed. Austryn Wainhouse and Richard Seaver. New York, 1996.

Sales, Roger. *Christopher Marlowe*. New York, 1991.

Schoeneich, Georg. *Der Litterarische Einfluss Spensers auf Marlowe*. Halle, 1907.

Schulenburg, Jane Tibbetts. "The Heroics of Virginity: Brides of Christ and Sacrificial Mutilation." *Women in the Middle Ages and the Renaissance: Literary and Historical Perspectives*. Ed. Mary Beth Rose. Syracuse, 1986. 29-72.

Scoloker, Anthony. *Diaphantus*. London, 1604. STC 21853.

Secret History of the Court of James I. 2 vols. Edinburgh, 1811.

Sedgwick, Eve Kosofsky. *Between Men: English Literature and Male Homosocial Desire*. New York, 1985.

Segal, Eric. *Roman Laughter: The Comedy of Plautus*. Cambridge, MA, 1968.

Seward, Desmond. *The Monks of War: The Military Religious Orders*. 1972. Rev. ed. Harmondsworth, 1995.

Shakespeare, William. *The Riverside Shakespeare*. Ed. G. Blakemore Evans, et al. Boston, 1974.

Shapiro, James. *Rival Playwrights: Marlowe, Jonson, Shakespeare*. New York, 1991.

———. "'Tragedies naturally performed': Kyd's Representation of Violence. *The Spanish Tragedy* (c. 1587)." *Staging the Renaissance:*

Reinterpretations of Elizabethan and Jacobean Drama. Eds. David Scott Kasten and Peter Stalybrass. New York, 1991. 99-113.

Shell, Marc. *Money, Language, and Thought: Literary and Philosophical Economies from the Medieval to the Modern Era*. Berkeley, 1982.

Shepard, Alan. "Endless Sacks: Soldiers' Desire in *Tamburlaine*." *Renaissance Quarterly* 46 (1993): 734-53.

Shepherd, Simon. *Marlowe and the Politics of Elizabethan Theatre*. New York and Brighton, 1986.

————. "What's So Funny About Ladies' Tailors? A Survey of Some Male (Homo)sexual Types in the Renaissance." *Textual Practice* 6 (1992): 17-30.

Sidney, Sir Phillip. "A Discourse of Syr Ph. S. To The Queenes Majesty Touching Hir Mariage With Monsieur." *The Prose Works of Sir Philip Sidney*. 4 vols. Ed. Albert Feuillerat. 1912. Cambridge, 1962. 3: 51-60.

Siegel, Carol. *Male Masochism: Modern Revisions of the Story of Love*. Bloomington, 1995.

Silverman, Kaja. *Male Subjectivity at the Margins*. New York, 1992.

Simonds, Peggy Munoz. "The Marriage Topos in *Cymbeline*: Shakespeare's Variations on a Classical Theme." *English Literary Renaissance* 19 (1989): 94-117.

Sinfield, Alan. *Faultlines: Cultural Materialism and the Politics of Dissident Reading*. Berkeley, 1992.

————. *Literature in Protestant England 1560-1660*. London, 1983.

————. "Power and Ideology: An Outline Theory and Sidney's *Arcadia*." *English Literary History* 52 (1985): 259-79.

————. *The Wilde Century: Effeminacy, Oscar Wilde and the Queer Moment*. New York, 1994.

Smith, Adam. *The Wealth of Nations*. Ed. Edwin Cannan. New York, 1937.

Smith, Bruce. *Homosexual Desire in Shakespeare's England: A Cultural Poetics*. Chicago, 1991.

Smith, G. Gregory, ed. *Elizabethan Critical Essays*. 1904. 2 vols. Oxford, 1950.

Smith, Mary. "Marlowe and the Italian Dido Drama." *Italica* 53 (1976): 223-35.

————. "Staging Marlowe's *Dido, Queene of Carthage*." *Studies in English Literature 1500-1900* 17 (1977): 177-90.

Smith, Paul. *Discerning the Subject*. Minneapolis, 1988.

Snare, Gerald. "Chapman's Ovid." *Studies in Philology* 75 (1978): 430-50.

Snow, Edward A. "Marlowe's *Doctor Faustus* and the Ends of Desire." *Two Renaissance Mythmakers: Christopher Marlowe and Ben Jonson. Selected Papers from the English Institute 1975-6*. Ed. Alvin Kernan and Margaret R. Higonnet. Baltimore, 1977. 70-110.

Spenser, Edmund. *Edmund Spenser's Poetry*. Ed. Hugh Maclean and Anne Lake Prescott. 3rd ed. New York, 1993.

————. *The Fairie Queene*. Ed. A. C. Hamilton. London, 1977.

————. *The Poetical Works of Edmund Spenser*. Ed. J. C. Smith and Ernest de Selincourt. 3 vols. Oxford, 1909-10.

————. *The Works of Edmund Spenser: A Variorum Edition*. Ed. Edwin Greenlaw, et al. 11 vols. Baltimore, 1932-57.

————. *The Yale Edition of the Shorter Poems of Edmund Spenser*. Ed. William A. Oram, et al. New Haven, 1989.

Sprott, S. E. "Drury and Marlowe." *Times Literary Supplement* 2 August 1974: 840.

Stallybrass, Peter. "Patriarchal Territories: The Body Enclosed." *Rewriting the Renaissance: The Discourse of Sexual Difference in Early Modern Europe*. Ed. Margaret W. Ferguson, et al. Chicago, 1986. 123-42.

Steane, J. B. *Marlowe: A Critical Study*. Cambridge, 1975.

Stone, Lawrence. *The Family, Sex and Marriage in England 1500-1800*. 1977. Abridged ed. New York, 1979.

Strabo. *Geography*. Trans. and ed. H. L. Jones. London, 1917.

Straub, Kristina. *Sexual Suspects: Eighteenth-Century Players and Sexual Ideology*. Princeton, 1992.

Strier, Richard. "Faithful Servants: Shakespeare's Praise of Disobedience." *The Historical Renaissance: New Essays on Tudor and Stuart Literature and Culture*. Ed. Heather Dubrow and Richard Strier. Chicago, 1988. 104-33.

Strype, John. *Annals of the Reformation*. Oxford, 1824.

————. *The Life of the Learned Sir John Cheke*. London, 1705.

Stubbes, Philip. *The Anatomy of Abuses*. London, 1583. STC 23376.

Stubbs, John. *The discouerie of a gaping gulf*. London, 1579. STC 23400.

Studlar, Gaylyn. *In the Realm of Pleasure: Von Sternberg, Dietrich, and the Masochistic Aesthetic*. Urbana, 1988.

Styward, Thomas. *The Pathwaie to Martiall Discipline*. London, 1581. STC 23413.

Suzuki, Mihoko. *Metamorphoses of Helen: Authority, Difference and the Epic*. Ithaca, 1989.

Tasso, Torquato. *The Housholder's Philosophie*. London, 1588.

Taunton, E.L. *History of the Jesuits in England*. London, 1925.

Taylor, Anthony Brian. "Britomart and the Mermaids: A Note on Marlowe and Spenser." *Notes and Queries* 216 (1971): 224-25.

————. "Notes on Marlowe and Golding." *Notes and Queries* 34 (1987): 2, 191-93.

————. "Tamburlaine's Doctrine of Strife and John Calvin." *English Language Notes* 27 (1989): 30-31.

Taylor, Gary. *Shakespeare Reshaped, 1606-1623*. Oxford, 1993.

Tenenti, Alberto. "The Merchant and the Banker." *Renaissance Characters*. Trans. Lydia G. Cochrane. Ed. Eugenio Garin. Chicago, 1991. 154-79.

Thomas, Keith. *Religion and the Decline of Magic: Studies in Popular Beliefs in Sixteenth- and Seventeenth-Century England*. Harmondsworth, 1973.

Thomas,Vivien and William Tydeman. *Christopher Marlowe: The Major Sources*. New York, 1994.

Thorburn, David. "Television as an Aesthetic Medium." *Media, Myths, and Narratives*. Ed. James W. Carey. Sage Annual Reviews of Communication Research 15. Newbury Park, CA, 1988. 48-66.

Thurn, David H. "Sights of Power in *Tamburlaine*." *English Literary Renaissance* 19 (1989): 3-21.

———. "Sovereignty, Disorder, and Fetishism in Marlowe's *Edward II*." *Renaissance Drama* 21 (1990): 115-41.

Traub, Valerie. *Desire and Anxiety: Circulations of Sexuality in Shakespearean Drama*. New York, 1992.

Trousdale, Marion. "Diachronic and Synchronic: Critical Biblio-graphy and the Acting of Plays." *Shakespeare: Text, Language, Criticism. Essays in Honor of Marvin Spevack*. Ed. Bernhard Fabian and Kurt Tetzeli von Rosador. Zurich, 1987. 304-14.

———. "A Second Look at Critical Bibliography and the Acting of Plays." *Shakespeare Quarterly* 41 (1990): 87-96.

Turner, Victor. *The Anthropology of Performance*. New York, 1986.

Udall, John. *The State of the Church in England*. London, 1588.

Urry, William. *Christopher Marlowe and Canterbury*. Ed. Andrew Butcher. London, 1988.

Venn, John and J.A.Venn. *Alumni Cantabrigienses*. 6 vols. Cambridge, 1922-27.

Virgil. *Aeneid*. Ed. Rolfe Humphries. New York, 1951.

Waith, Eugene M. "Marlowe and the Jades of Asia." *Studies in English Literature 1500-1900* 5 (1965): 229-45.

Wall, Wendy. *The Imprint of Gender: Authorship and Publication in the English Renaissance*. Ithaca, 1993.

Walvin, James. *Black and White: The Negro and English Society, 1555-1945*. London, 1973.

Warner, Michael. "Fear of a Queer Planet." *Social Text* 29 (1991): 3-17.

Warren, John. *Elizabeth I: Religion and Foreign Affairs*. London, 1993.

Watkins, W. B. C. "The Plagiarist: Spenser or Marlowe?" *English Literary History* 11 (1944): 249-65.

Webb, William Stanford. "Vergil in Spenser's Epic Theory." *Critical Essays on Spenser from "ELH."* Baltimore, 1970. 62-84.

Weil, Judith. *Christopher Marlowe: Merlin's Prophet*. Cambridge, 1977.

Weinberg, Thomas, and G. W. Levi Kamel, eds. *S and M: Studies in Sadomasochism*. Buffalo, 1983.

Weldon, Anthony. *The Court and Character of King James*. 1651. London, 1817.

Wentworth, Peter. *A pithie exhortation to her majestie for establishing her successor*. London, 1598. STC 25245.

Wernham, R. B. "Christopher Marlowe at Flushing in 1592." *English Historical Review* 91 (1976): 344-45.

Werstine, Paul. "'Foul Papers' and 'Prompt-books': Printer's Copy for Shakespeare's *Comedy of Errors.*" *Studies in Bibliography* 41 (1988): 232-46.

———. "McKerrow's 'Suggestion' and Twentieth-Century Shake-speare Textual Criticism." *Renaissance Drama* 19 (1988): 149-73.

West, Robert W. *Reginald Scot and Renaissance Writings on Witchcraft.* Boston, 1984.

Whelan, Peter. *The School of Night.* London, 1992.

White, Paul Whitfield. *Theatre and Reformation: Protestantism, Patronage, and Playing in Tudor England.* New York, 1992.

Whitgift, John. *The Works of John Whitgift.* Ed. J. Ayre. Cambridge, 1851-53.

Wiener, Carol Z. "The Beleaguered Isle: A Study of Elizabethan and Early Jacobean Anti-Catholicism." *Past and Present* 51 (1971): 27-62.

Williams, George. *Radical Reformation.* Philadelphia, 1962.

Williams, Linda, ed. *Viewing Positions: Ways of Seeing Film.* New Brunswick, 1994.

Willson, David Harris. *King James VI and I.* London, 1966.

Wind, Edgar. *Pagan Mysteries of the Renaissance.* 1958. Boston, 1967.

Woodbridge, Linda. *Women and the English Renaissance: Literature and the Nature of Womankind, 1540-1620.* Urbana-Champaign, 1984.

Woods, Gregory. "Body, Costume, and Desire in Christopher Marlowe." *Homosexuality in Renaissance and Enlightenment England: Literary Representations in Historical Context.* Ed. Claude J. Summers. New York, 1992: 69-84.

Woolton, John. *A Treatise of the Immortality of the Soul.* London, 1576.

Wooton, David. "The Fear of God in Early Modern Political Theory." Canadian Historical Association. *Historical Papers* 18 (1983): 56-79.

Wraight, A. D. *Christopher Marlowe and Edward Alleyn.* Chichester, 1993.

———. *In Search of Christopher Marlowe.* London, 1965.

Wrightson, Keith. *English Society 1580-1680.* New Brunswick, 1982.

Yates, Frances. *Astrea: The Imperial Theme in the Sixteenth Century.* London, 1975.

Zunder, William. *Elizabethan Marlowe.* Hull, 1994.

INDEX

247

AMS Studies in the Renaissance, No. 35
ISSN: 0195-8011

26. John Hazel Smith. *Shakespeare's "Othello": A Bibliography*
27. Alan R. Young, ed. *His Majestys Royal Ship: A Critical Edition of Thomas Heywood's "A True Description of His Majesties Royall Ship" (1637)*
28. M. J. B. Allen, Dominic Baker-Smith, and Arthur F. Kinney, eds. *Sir Philip Sidney's Achievements*
30. Paul Bertram and Bernice W. Kliman, eds. *The Three-text "Hamlet": Parallel Texts of the First and Second Quartos and First Folio*
31. Sara Jayne Steen. *Ambrosia in an Earthern Vessel: Three Centuries of Audience and Reader Response to the Works of Thomas Middleton*
32. Graham C. Adams. *The Ottoneum Theater: An English Survivor from Seventeenth-Century Germany*
33. Ingrid Brainard. *The Art of Courtly Dancing in the Early Renaissance*
35. Paul Whitfield White, ed. *Marlowe, History, and Sexuality: New Critical Essays on Christopher Marlowe*
36. Anthony Mortimer. *Variable Passions: A Reading of Shakespeare's "Venus and Adonis"*